Mastering Splunk 8

Become an expert at implementing the advanced features and capabilities of Splunk 8

James D. Miller

BIRMINGHAM—MUMBAI

Mastering Splunk 8

Copyright © 2020 Packt Publishing

All rights reserved. No part of this book may be reproduced, stored in a retrieval system, or transmitted in any form or by any means, without the prior written permission of the publisher, except in the case of brief quotations embedded in critical articles or reviews.

Every effort has been made in the preparation of this book to ensure the accuracy of the information presented. However, the information contained in this book is sold without warranty, either express or implied. Neither the author, nor Packt Publishing or its dealers and distributors, will be held liable for any damages caused or alleged to have been caused directly or indirectly by this book.

Packt Publishing has endeavored to provide trademark information about all of the companies and products mentioned in this book by the appropriate use of capitals. However, Packt Publishing cannot guarantee the accuracy of this information.

Commissioning Editor: Sunith Shetty
Acquisition Editor: Devika Battike
Senior Editor: Roshan Kumar
Content Development Editor: Athikho Sapuni Rishana
Technical Editor: Sonam Pandey
Copy Editor: Safis Editing
Project Coordinator: Aishwarya Mohan
Proofreader: Safis Editing
Indexer: Priyanka Dhadke
Production Designer: Roshan Kawale

First published: December 2020

Production reference: 1031220

Published by Packt Publishing Ltd.
Livery Place
35 Livery Street
Birmingham
B3 2PB, UK.

ISBN 978-1-83898-748-0

www.packt.com

Packt.com

Subscribe to our online digital library for full access to over 7,000 books and videos, as well as industry leading tools to help you plan your personal development and advance your career. For more information, please visit our website.

Why subscribe?

- Spend less time learning and more time coding with practical eBooks and Videos from over 4,000 industry professionals
- Improve your learning with Skill Plans built especially for you
- Get a free eBook or video every month
- Fully searchable for easy access to vital information
- Copy and paste, print, and bookmark content

Did you know that Packt offers eBook versions of every book published, with PDF and ePub files available? You can upgrade to the eBook version at packt.com and as a print book customer, you are entitled to a discount on the eBook copy. Get in touch with us at customercare@packtpub.com for more details.

At www.packt.com, you can also read a collection of free technical articles, sign up for a range of free newsletters, and receive exclusive discounts and offers on Packt books and eBooks.

Contributors

About the author

James D. Miller is an IBM Certified Expert, Master Consultant, and application/system architect with over 35 years of applications and system design/development experience across multiple platforms, technologies, and data formats, including big data. His experience includes IBM Planning Analytics, BI, web architecture/design, systems analysis, GUI design/testing, data modeling, and OLAP design/development. He has also worked on client/server, web, and mainframe applications. He has authored numerous books, including *Implementing Splunk, Second Edition*; *Mastering Splunk*, *Hands-On Machine Learning with IBM Watson*, *Watson Projects*, *Statistics for Data Science*, and *Mastering Predictive Analytics with R, Second Edition*.

About the reviewers

Laks Ganesan is a Splunk Certified Architect and Consultant with hands-on experience in Splunk Core, Enterprise Security, and User Behavior Analytics. He is an active member of the Splunk community and has been recognized by Splunk as a SplunkTrust member for his contributions. He holds a master's degree in electrical engineering from the Indian Institute of Technology, Madras, India, and has worked across the USA, Europe, the Middle East, and Australia for a number of global customers in various consulting roles.

Tom Kopchak is the director of technical operations and a Splunk implementation engineer at Hurricane Labs. A 2020 inductee to the SplunkTrust and a Splunk Certified Architect and Consultant, he has extensive experience designing and managing Splunk deployments as well as developing Splunk training materials. His speaking experience includes talks at Splunk .conf, DEFCON, and other conferences around the United States. He holds a master's degree in computing security from the Rochester Institute of Technology, and he volunteers as a competition director for the National **Collegiate Penetration Testing Competition** (**CPTC**). When he is not working, he enjoys composing, music improvisation, and playing both the piano and organ.

Packt is searching for authors like you

If you're interested in becoming an author for Packt, please visit `authors.packtpub.com` and apply today. We have worked with thousands of developers and tech professionals, just like you, to help them share their insight with the global tech community. You can make a general application, apply for a specific hot topic that we are recruiting an author for, or submit your own idea.

Table of Contents

Preface

Section 1: Fundamentals of Splunk 8

1
Overview of Splunk

Exploring Splunk and its key features	3	Splunk dashboards (public beta)	9
		Some other quick thoughts	9
Horizontal technologies	4	**Implementing Python 3.7**	**9**
Understanding the seven key features	5	Python 3 Readiness	11
Exploring Splunk 8.0's features	**6**	**An example use case**	**11**
Moving to Python 3.7	7	Adding data	11
Enhanced workload management	7	Searching the data source	17
Analytics Workspace	7	Saving your search	24
Alert grouping	7	Adding an alert	26
Histogram metric datatype support	8	Reviewing and editing	30
HEC timestamp extraction	8		
Monitoring and operability enrichments	8	**Summary**	**34**
Other optimizations of importance	8		

Section 2: Splunk Administration

2
Splunk Administration – Workload Management

About resource allocation	38	Virtual machines	38
Critical resources	38	The Monitoring Console	39

Resource usage dashboards	39	Health alerts	46
Dashboard interpretation	40	**Why workload management?**	**47**
Resource usage – deployment	40	Workload management advantages	47
CPU usage	41	Splunk Workload Management feature	47
Physical memory	41	The basics of Workload Management	48
Resource usage – machine/instance	42	The rules-based framework	49
Dashboard review hints	**42**	**Scheduling workloads –**	
Workload monitoring techniques	**42**	**schedule-based rules**	**51**
The Monitoring Console and workload management	43	Getting going	51
		In closing	52
The health report	**43**	**Summary**	**52**
Splunk feature settings	44		

3
Performance, Statistics, and Alerting in Splunk

Exploring data in Splunk	**54**	Searching metrics	64
The data pipeline	54	**Logs2Metrics**	**69**
Splunk components	56	**Alerting**	**72**
Understanding storage	**57**	Scheduled alert illustration	72
Storage metrics	**58**	**Summary**	**75**
Creating a metrics index	59		

4
Splunk Administration—Security

Security and security		**Role management**	**87**
enhancements	**78**	Permission granularity and customized roles	87
Roles	78		
Users	79	**Authentication**	**97**
Tokens	79	Authentication methods	97
Password management	83		
Granular access controls	**84**	**Summary**	**98**

5
Advanced Indexing

Splunk deployment basics	99	Single-site index clusters	113
Understanding index clustering and replication	100	Multi-site index clusters	113
		Disaster recovery sites	113
More copies of data means higher storage requirements	103	Backing up the master node	114
		Practicing recovery	114
Enabling clustering	104	Special multi-site configurations – the site replication factor	114
Editing and configuring the master node	108		
Configuring bundle actions	108	Converting the multi-site index cluster	115
Data rebalancing	110	Converting the single-site index cluster	116
Performing an index cluster rolling restart	111	Summary	116
Disabling clustering	112		

6
Splunk Integration with Azure and AWS

Splunk integration strategy	118	Integration	134
Using an app	119	Configuration	135
Finding an app	120	Setting up the input	138
Integrating Azure	121	Getting ready to search AWS logs	140
Connecting to the Azure app account	124	Summary	145
Integrating with AWS	134		

Section 3: Advanced Reporting and Dashboards

7
Advanced Reporting – Analytics Workspace

Workspace review	150	Using the analytics workspace	151
Workspace layout	151	Loading the data	152

Analyzing with the workspace	157	Stacking time series	166
Using Split By	158	**Adding reference lines**	**167**
Categorical charts	**159**	**Streaming alerts**	**169**
Multiple metrics	160	Management of alerts	171
Running analytical operations	**162**	**Expanding the time range picker**	**173**
Aggregation	162		
Comparing time range	164	Zooming to a time range	174
Filtering data	166	**Summary**	**175**

8
Advanced Reporting – Histogram Metric Data Types

Understanding Splunk metrics data types	**178**	Validation	185
		Histogram metrics before and after indexing	187
Histograms	179	Prometheus	190
Histogram metrics	**179**	Searching histogram metrics	192
Example of histogram metric use cases	181	**Summary**	**195**
Ingesting histogram metrics	181		

9
Search Performance Considerations

Gauging performance	**198**	Using multiple indexers to improve performance	215
Some typical causes	198		
Addressing search performance through architecture	210	Single search head	216
		Additional search heads	**218**
Adding indexers	**211**	Adding an additional search head	219
Scaling up	211	**Search head clustering**	**220**
Configuring the indexer	212	**Summary**	**221**

10
Advanced Reporting Using Macros

Understanding macros and SPL	**223**	Macro previewing	224

Macros and generating commands	226	Macro definitions	232
Search macro arguments	228	Creating a macro	232
Argument example	229	Summary	239

11
Dashboards – Advanced Data Analytics

Fundamentals of analytics frameworks	242	Establishing relevancy	243
		Performing EDA with Splunk	243
Analytics projects	242	Transaction and transactional analysis	269
Exploratory data analysis—exploring data	243	An example of transactional analysis	270
Determining the data details	243	Summary	272

12
Dashboards – Correlating Events

Understanding catalytic events and correlations	274	Ways to use event correlation in dashboards	280
Understanding event correlation	275	Identifying an overall goal/objective	281
		Identifying the specific KPIs or catalytic events	281
Transaction-based correlations	275	Developing individual SPL queries/correlation searches	282
Time/geolocation-based correlations	276		
Subsearch-based correlations	277		
Lookup-based correlations	279	Creating the panels and constructing the dashboard	283
Join-based correlations	280		
Event correlation dashboards	280	Summary	291

13
Dashboards – Workflow Actions

Understanding knowledge objects	293	Mastering workflows	296
		Creating a workflow action using Splunk web	297
Tags	294		
Knowledge object managers	296	Another workflow action example	304

Secondary search workflow action example	307	Summary	311

14
Dashboards – Monitoring and Operability

Monitoring without searching	314	instrumentation	319
Simple search example	314	Exploring the Splunk Monitoring Console	321
Using the Splunk Add-on for Windows	315	Accessing the Monitoring Console	322
Monitoring disk activity	317	Performing trigger-based diagnostics	325
Creating single-page trending metrics	318	Summary	329
Exploring Splunk platform			

15
Dashboards – Custom Visualizations

Understanding dashboards and their look and feel	332	Adding images and icons	344
		Exploring the Beta app	346
Splunk dashboards	332	Converting an existing dashboard	348
		Resizing the canvas	349
Building a new Splunk dashboard	334	Setting a custom background	350
		The dashboard editing bar	352
Accessing the editor	335	Editing the visualization source code	352
Starting with a search	336	Comparing the old and new editor	353
Saving a panel	338	Adding a visualization	353
Changing the theme	342	Summary	357
Adding a heat map overlay	343		

Section 4: What Next?

16
Machine Learning Overview

Machine learning with Splunk	362	Overview of the Splunk MLTK	362

What is the MLTK?	362

Implementing an MLTK use case 365

What questions can the MLTK help with?	366
Uploading the data	367
Populating model fields	367
Selecting the algorithm	369
Fitting the model	370
Looking at the results	371
Other algorithm options	373
Naming the model	374
Answering questions	376
Exploring the Experiments menu	378
Refining the model	383
Summary	**384**

17
Splunk Next

What is Splunk Next?	386
Splunk Business Flow	388
Splunk Data Fabric Search	389
Splunk Data Stream Processor	389
Splunk Cloud Gateway	390
Splunk Augmented Reality	391
Setting up AR with workspaces	392
Splunk Natural Language (beta)	392
Giving back	394
Splunk Insights for web and mobile	394
Mobile apps	395
Splunk TV	395
Summary	**397**

18
Dashboards – SplunkJS

Understanding SplunkJS	400
Getting started with SplunkJS	401
SplunkJS and Splunk apps	402
Creating a Splunk app	402
Creating a dashboard in SimpleXML using the dashboard editor	407
Modifying the dashboard by adding a SimpleXML extension to it	408
Modifying the dashboard by converting it to HTML	410
Dashboard conversion example	411
Getting back to our app	413
Style sheets and custom tables	415
Adding SplunkJS to a web app	419
Summary	**420**

Other Books You May Enjoy
Index

Preface

Splunk is the most widely used engine for working with machine-generated data. This expert-level guide will help you to leverage advanced use cases to drive business growth using operational intelligence and business analytics features.

You'll start with an introduction to the new features in Splunk 8, and cover step-by-step exercises that will help you to understand each feature in depth. Next, you'll explore key tasks such as workload management, performance and alerting, using Splunk Enterprise Security, and advanced indexing. You'll also learn how to create categorical charts and run analytical operations on metrics within the Splunk Analytics Workspace, before understanding how to deliver insights across your organization, even when faced with limited or complex data, using advanced data analytics. This book will also show you how to monitor and maintain Splunk environments using advanced dashboards. Later, you'll create custom data visualization and update dashboards using drag and drop and the UI-based dashboard editor. Finally, you'll add SplunkJS to a web app and use the Splunk **Machine Learning Toolkit** (**MLTK**) as an extension to the core Splunk platform using real-world use cases.

By the end of this book, you'll have learned how to use various Splunk features to extend intelligence capabilities and perform machine learning to explore data effectively.

Who this book is for

This Splunk book is for data professionals, data analysts, and Splunk users looking to leverage the advanced features of the Splunk Enterprise platform to derive valuable business insights from machine data. The book is also a useful expert-level guide for individuals from all facets of IT, business, and security. Prior knowledge of Splunk and its features is mandatory to get the most out of this book.

What this book covers

Chapter 1, *Overview of Splunk 8*, starts by describing the exciting merits of Splunk version 8.0 in contrast to previous versions of the software. Each new feature of this version is listed and reviewed, followed by a brief mention of deprecated and removed items and various recommendations and tips for migrating to the new release. Finally, it ends with a simple working use case example designed to illustrate some basic functionalities of Splunk, setting you up for performing the exercises throughout the book.

Chapter 2, *Splunk Administration – Workload Management*, identifies the resources critical to Splunk operation, and then we perform tasks illustrating how to best understand and align resource allocations with specific priorities using the various features available in Splunk, including the Monitoring Console, the Splunk health report, and the Splunk workload management feature.

Chapter 3, *Performance Statistics and Alerting in Splunk*, explains how to optimize data storage for cost savings as well as the intent and use of advanced alerting.

Chapter 4, *Splunk Security*, starts with a review of how Splunk security works, and then points out the security enhancements in Splunk version 8.0, such as a look at granular access and within-index controls concepts, and the latest interface for roles management. The chapter also touches briefly on authentication and authentication tokens (the REST API and CLI with SAML).

Chapter 5, *Advanced Indexing*, concentrates the discussion on developing an understanding of Splunk index clustering for **High Availability** (**HA**) as well as **Disaster Recovery** (**DR**) for Splunk instances and indexed data. Topics include single-site/multi-site index clusters, DR, and some multi-site configurations.

Chapter 6, *Splunk Integration with Azure and AWS*, looks at how Splunk can be easily integrated with other platforms and technologies, such as the AWS and Azure cloud platforms. In this chapter, we will cover this by providing Azure and AWS working integration examples.

Chapter 7, *Working with the Analytics Workspace*, teaches you how to create categorical charts (such as line, column, area, and time-column) and run analytical operations on metrics and accelerated datasets using reference lines-to-metrics data for comparison and analysis using the very latest features within the Splunk Analytics Workspace.

Chapter 8, *Advanced Reporting – Histogram Metric Data Types*, focuses on exploring the newly supported histogram metric data type, which enables you to bucket this more complex metric data into a time series of histograms.

Chapter 9, *Search Performance Considerations*, focuses on approaching searches and reporting from a performance perspective, starting with some general advice on identifying, avoiding, and addressing items that can cause diminished performance.

Chapter 10, *Advanced Reporting Using Macros*, discusses the whys and the hows of using Splunk macros to create effective and efficient searching solutions.

Chapter 11, *Dashboards – Advanced Data Analytics*, covers using advanced data analytics techniques to enhance productivity and gain advantages from data. The chapter starts with the fundamentals of an "analytics framework," then offers various tips (with examples) aimed at exploring data using Splunk datasets, the table editor, and pivot tool, and finally, touches on transactional analysis.

Chapter 12, *Dashboards – Correlating Events*, covers the difference between types of events to better understand event correlation. Techniques for correlating events and creating a working event correlation dashboard will also be covered.

Chapter 13, *Dashboards – Workflow Actions*, focuses on explaining the value and practical use of Splunk workflow actions, including definitions for workflows and knowledge objects, and includes creating a working workflow.

Chapter 14, *Dashboards – Monitoring and Operability*, illustrates various methods and approaches for monitoring and maintaining Splunk environments using advanced dashboards such as the Splunk Monitoring Console, the Instrumentation app, and some miscellaneous resource search approaches.

Chapter 15, *Dashboards – Custom Visualizations*, focuses on creating custom visualizations and updating dashboards using features such as "drag and drop" and the Splunk UI-based dashboard editor.

Chapter 16, *Machine Learning Overview*, focuses on providing an overview of approaching the topic of machine learning with Splunk, introducing the Splunk MLTK, and providing instructions on accessing and installing, as well as the basic use of, the kit.

Chapter 17, *Splunk Next*, focuses on providing an overview of the topic of Splunk Next, as well as a brief summary of each of its offerings.

Chapter 18, *Dashboards – SplunkJS*, shows you how adding the SplunkJS Stack libraries to a website can enable the use of numerous web framework components, which can assist in interacting with and viewing Splunk data.

To get the most out of this book

Both beginners as well as seasoned Splunk experts will find this book useful. However, to get the most value out of this book, you will need access to a Splunk 8.0 environment. If you do not have access, feel free to download the free trial version of Splunk version 8.0 and install it as a local instance. Even on most Windows laptops, all of the examples used throughout the chapters will still work.

If you are using the digital version of this book, we advise you to type the code yourself or access the code via the GitHub repository (link available in the next section). Doing so will help you avoid any potential errors related to the copying and pasting of code.

Download the example code files

You can download the example code files for this book from GitHub at `https://github.com/PacktPublishing/Mastering-Splunk-8`. In case there's an update to the code, it will be updated on the existing GitHub repository.

We also have other code bundles from our rich catalog of books and videos available at `https://github.com/PacktPublishing/`. Check them out!

Download the color images

We also provide a PDF file that has color images of the screenshots/diagrams used in this book. You can download it here: `https://static.packt-cdn.com/downloads/9781838987480_ColorImages.pdf`.

Conventions used

There are a number of text conventions used throughout this book.

- `Code in text`: Indicates code words in text, database table names, folder names, filenames, file extensions, pathnames, dummy URLs, user input, and Twitter handles. Here is an example: "Using the `splunkd` health report."

Any command-line input or output is written as follows:

```
mcatalog values(metric_name) WHERE index=jimssindex
```

Bold: Indicates a new term, an important word, or words that you see onscreen. For example, words in menus or dialog boxes appear in the text like this. Here is an example: "Click on **Settings** and then **Health report manager**."

> Tips or important notes
> The historical data in the Splunk Monitoring Console dashboards comes from `resource_usage.log` in the `_introspection` index.

Get in touch

Feedback from our readers is always welcome.

General feedback: If you have questions about any aspect of this book, mention the book title in the subject of your message and email us at `customercare@packtpub.com`.

Errata: Although we have taken every care to ensure the accuracy of our content, mistakes do happen. If you have found a mistake in this book, we would be grateful if you would report this to us. Please visit `www.packtpub.com/support/errata`, selecting your book, clicking on the Errata Submission Form link, and entering the details.

Piracy: If you come across any illegal copies of our works in any form on the Internet, we would be grateful if you would provide us with the location address or website name. Please contact us at `copyright@packt.com` with a link to the material.

If you are interested in becoming an author: If there is a topic that you have expertise in and you are interested in either writing or contributing to a book, please visit `authors.packtpub.com`.

Reviews

Please leave a review. Once you have read and used this book, why not leave a review on the site that you purchased it from? Potential readers can then see and use your unbiased opinion to make purchase decisions, we at Packt can understand what you think about our products, and our authors can see your feedback on their book. Thank you!

For more information about Packt, please visit `packt.com`.

Section 1: Fundamentals of Splunk 8

In this section, we will provide a brief narrative on the merits of upgrading to Splunk 8 – a high-level description or primer on each of the new features in this version.

This section comprises the following chapter:

- *Chapter 1, Overview of Splunk 8*

1
Overview of Splunk

In the opening chapter of this book, we will start our journey by describing the exciting merits of Splunk version 8.0 in contrast to previous versions of the software. Each new feature of this version will then be listed and reviewed, followed by briefly mentioning deprecated and removed items, as well as various recommendations and tips for migrating to the new release. This chapter will end with a simple working use case example designed to illustrate some basic functionalities of Splunk, all of which will set you up for completing the exercises in section two of this book.

We'll break down this chapter into the following sections:

- Exploring Splunk and its key features
- Exploring Splunk 8.0's features
- Implementing Python 3.7
- An example use case

Exploring Splunk and its key features

Before Splunk version 8 there were, of course, earlier versions of the Splunk platform. For those of you who are unfamiliar with the tool, here is a little background on what Splunk is.

Splunk is a **Software-as-a-Service** (**SaaS**) platform—not a single tool or app—that is excellent at searching, monitoring, and analyzing machine-generated big data through a web-style interface.

Splunk maintains its headquarters on the west coast of the United States in San Francisco, California. It is estimated that Splunk generates an average of 497 thousand dollars in revenue per employee and has raised a total of 269 million dollars in funding. One of its most recent acquisitions was Omnition for an undisclosed amount on Sep 2019. Splunk has more than 8,330 followers on Owler.

Although Splunk is a piece of software primarily used for searching, monitoring, and examining *machine-generated big data*, Splunk has also proved astute for combing almost any kind of data quickly and easily, identifying particular anomalies and patterns within the data that would otherwise be almost impossible to find or see.

Splunk can be configured to continually capture, index, and correlate real-time data within a *searchable container* (or repository) and, using that data, automatically produce updated graphs, reports, alerts, dashboards, and visualizations.

Splunk's architecture is such that, through the use of parallel processing (via MapReduce methodologies), it can take a search request and break it up into lesser parts in order to get answers faster.

Splunk is a great tool for data analysis and log monitoring since it can quickly ingest a very high amount of raw and unformatted data with ease and make it searchable by using a very simple-to-understand yet very powerful query language.

Horizontal technologies

A horizontal application is typically defined as *any software application that targets a large number of users; each most likely exhibiting different knowledge and skill sets*. Because an application of this type can encompass all kinds of markets and be used in a large range of industries, they typically do not offer what are called **market-specific** features. Splunk is, by definition, a horizontal technology platform that can be used for application management, security, and compliance, as well as all kinds of business and web analytics.

Splunk *turns data into action*, undertaking the toughest IT, IoT, security, and data challenges through searching, monitoring, and analyzing machine-generated big data. It can even create events based upon stored data that it can then monitor. It can also read different types of log files and alert us to occurrences of that type of event.

Thankfully, Splunk is powerful but also very well documented, so getting yourself going and up to speed is easy. This allows you to be productive almost immediately but also helps in quickly adding Splunk experience to your domain of expertise.

Another exciting trait of Splunk is that it allows you to visualize data characteristics though various forms of graphical dashboards. Somewhere online, I read that Splunk's aim is to convert and communicate between data and individuals or other applications, such as different open source platforms, to identify patterns, analyze metrics, diagnose problems, and provide actionable insights. Splunk most often communicates these insights in the form of dashboards.

Another key point to know about Splunk is that it does not use any kind of database. Splunk extensively makes use of indexes to store data—almost any kind of data—from websites, applications, sensors, devices, and so on. That is, after you've defined a data source, Splunk indexes the data stream (that is, all the incoming data) and parses it into a series of individual events that can be viewed and searched quickly. Splunk uniquely refers to this concept as a *schema on the fly*.

Lastly, many users use a web browser to connect to Splunk, and use Splunk Web to administer, manage, and create knowledge objects, run searches, create pivots and reports, and so on. However, you can also use Splunk's command-line interface to perform most administration work. In addition, Splunk allows the use of apps to *extend its functionalities* so that it can meet any requirement you may know of or can come across.

Understanding the seven key features

Given the preceding background information, the following section highlights the seven most fundamental features that make Splunk so great: **Indexing**, **Searching**, **Alerting**, **Dashboarding**, **Picoting**, **Reporting**, and **Data Modeling**.

Indexing

As I've already mentioned, Splunk uses indexes (rather than a database) to access data sourced from almost anywhere, including data from websites, applications, servers, databases, operating systems, and more. There is literally no limit to the number of indexes you can have, though the type of Splunk license being used, as well as available disk space, will need to be considered.

Searching

In Splunk, it's all about searching indexed data. Using Splunk's **Search Processing Language**, known as **SPL**, you can ask any sort of question about any of your indexed data. The search you create can then be saved as a report or as part of a dashboard.

Alerting

Splunk allows us to monitor both events and event patterns in real time by creating alerts with per-result triggering or rolling-time-window triggering based on saved searches. Alerts can then automatically send alert information in emails, post alert information to an RSS feed, and run custom scripts, such as one that posts an alert event to syslog.

Dashboarding

Splunk dashboards can be created to visualize various saved search results or even to show the outputs from searches running in the background in real time. Dashboards can be simple static reports or super complex and can contain multiple panels of modules that use search boxes, fields, charts, and so on – almost anything.

Pivoting

In Splunk, you can use the **Pivot Editor** to map attributes that are defined in a Splunk data model to tables, charts, or other visualizations so that you do not have to write additional searches to generate them. The outputs from the Pivot Editor you create can then be saved as a report or as part of a dashboard.

Reporting

Reports in Splunk are saved searches and pivots. Created reports can then be included in dashboards and be run on demand or scheduled to run at a regular interval. Reports can even be set up to generate alerts when a search result meets particular conditions.

Data modeling

In Splunk, data models can be created around specialized domain knowledge about one or more sets of data that have been indexed. Data models are typically used to standardize certain information and, of course, ease the effort of creating reports and dashboards around certain data.

Exploring Splunk 8.0's features

So, if you have already worked with Splunk, you've most likely skipped through the previous sections to reach this section of this chapter, where we'll go into the exciting new features that can be found in Splunk version 8.0 (first released on October 22, 2019). If you are new to Splunk, then hopefully you have garnered some feeling of comfort as to what the platform can do and are now ready to go over this version's latest features and improvements. So, let's move on and get started.

> **Note**
> If you are new to Splunk, you can read and learn more about it at: `https://docs.splunk.com/Documentation/Splunk/8.0.1/Overview/AboutSplunkEnterprise`.

Moving to Python 3.7

Python is a general-purpose and high-level programming language that is used today in many markets and industries, such as insurance, banking, finance, and healthcare, just to name a few. It is also frequently used to develop and extend existing technology platforms, including Splunk. Although Python is an integrally supported language in earlier versions of Splunk, Splunk version 8.0 introduces support for Python version 3.7. It allows you to choose to migrate any existing Python scripts used in Splunk applications to Python 3.7 individually or force Python 3.7 usage across an instance, all at once. More on this topic will be discussed in later chapters.

Enhanced workload management

The Splunk **Workload Management Model** allows us to manage Splunk resources so that they fit into a specific objective. In other words, with **workload management** (**WLM**), you use a set of rules to automatically place searches in different pools, and also provide granular access controls to certain Splunk users so that they can choose their own workload pools. WLM is not new to version 8.0, but in this version, there is increased flexibility for managing workloads during peak/off-peak hours through schedule-based rules.

Analytics Workspace

The Splunk **Analytics Workspace** provides a user interface, thus enabling you to monitor and analyze metrics, accelerated datasets, and other time series data without having to use Splunk's SPL to create complicated searches. Enhancements that have been made to the workspace feature in version 8.0 include the expanded time-range picker to provide better control over the data to be analyzed.

Alert grouping

In Splunk version 8.0, there is continued support for alert aggregation – in other words, grouping alerts to improve performance.

Histogram metric datatype support

In Splunk version 8.0, there is now support for what is called the **histogram metric** datatype, which enables you to **bucket** metric data into a time series of histograms.

HEC timestamp extraction

This new feature allows for the easy extraction of timestamps when ingesting event data from Apache Kafka or AWS Kinesis, without the need to use custom parsers.

Monitoring and operability enrichments

Splunk version 8.0 includes a good number of improvements in the areas of monitoring and operability. These include the following:

- **Single pane** monitoring of deployment-wide health stats without running searches.
- The ability to receive alerts from the **Pagerduty** app, via an email, as well as Splunk Mobile.
- Same page/real-time access to anomalies, deployment metrics, and component health stats, as well as topology.
- New health checks are now possible via the **Health Assistant Add-on**, which is accessible through the Splunk **Monitoring Console**.
- Trigger-based and simplified processes for collecting diagnostics information for performance-based monitoring.

Other optimizations of importance

In this release of Splunk, a good number of other improvements have been implemented, intended to improve performance, usability, manage costs, and other objectives. These include the following:

- **Distributed Search**: Improved speed with faster bundle replication.
- **Telemetry**: Enhanced telemetry collection to aid optimize deployments.
- **Security**: Granular access controls; within-index controls. New user interface for **Roles** management. Support for specific authentication tokens.
- **Metrics and Searching**: Cost savings through enhanced metrics data storage. Added wildcard functionality for logs2metrics. Better stats and commands. Improved memory usage and performance of lookups. Miscellaneous search evaluator performance improvements.

- **Data Model Acceleration Health Stats**: Additional information added for **Data Models** management.
- **Shared Data Model Acceleration Summaries**: Now, Splunk can share data model acceleration summaries between search heads in a cluster.

Splunk dashboards (public beta)

Also available in this release is an exciting UI-based **Splunk Dashboard Editor** app. This app looks to provide **pixel-level** layout control, making it super easy to achieve the look and feel you want in a Splunk dashboard. The editor allows you to use standard Microsoft Windows drag-and-drop functionality (as well as other usability features) to quickly and easily move, layer, and resize elements in a Splunk dashboard.

Some other quick thoughts

Before moving on, it's worth mentioning a few things here. That is, if you intend to upgrade an existing environment to Splunk version 8.0 (rather than a new, fresh installation), before proceeding, you should take some time to do the following:

- Review the *Known issues* for this release, which can be found online at https://docs.splunk.com/Documentation/Splunk/8.0.1/ReleaseNotes/Knownissues.
- Check out some migration best practices, which can be found online at https://docs.splunk.com/Documentation/Splunk/8.0.1/Installation/HowtoupgradeSplunk.
- Read through some reported *Tips and Tricks* and *READ THIS FIRST* suggestions, also found online at https://docs.splunk.com/Documentation/Splunk/8.0.1/Installation/AboutupgradingREADTHISFIRST.
- Review the *deprecated and removed features* for the new version (8.0). Again, this can be found online at https://docs.splunk.com/Documentation/Splunk/8.0.1/ReleaseNotes/Deprecatedfeatures.

Implementing Python 3.7

Splunk offers various ways for us to both use and extend the functionalities of what is referred to as its **algorithmic engine** (that is, the **Splunk engine**). One way is through integration with Python. With the Splunk Python **software development kit** or **SDK** (the Splunk Enterprise SDK for Python), you can develop applications that leverage the Splunk engine directly in Python.

10   Overview of Splunk

The Splunk Enterprise SDK for Python is built to wrap the REST API so that it is much quicker and easier to develop apps and functionalities that perform searching, run saved searches, update Splunk configurations, present customized sophisticated user interfaces, and so on.

It is not our intention to spend time walking through a Splunk upgrade or migration process in detail, but it is worth mentioning a few things relevant to Splunk version 8.0 and Python support.

Mostly, it's important to know that Splunk allows you to upgrade all of your existing Python scripts at once or individual scripts as needed.

If you are upgrading an existing Splunk environment, the **as needed** approach is recommended (in most scenarios), as long as you realize that older versions of Python are reaching their end of life, as shown in the following Splunk installation panel:

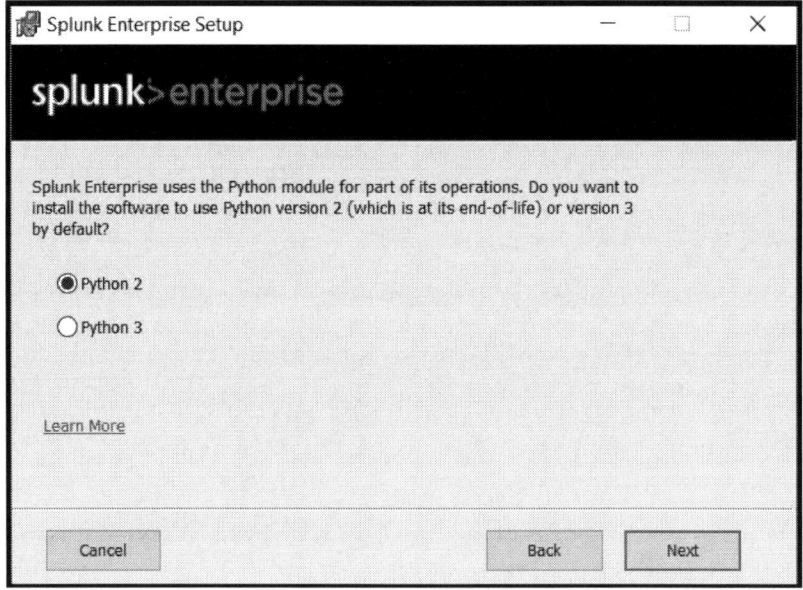

Figure 1.1 – Splunk installation panel

> **Note**
> The dialog shown in the preceding screenshot is a Microsoft Windows installation event and is not displayed during a Linux install.

Since Splunk might remove the Python 2.7 runtime altogether in a future release, it is wise to select the **Python 3** option shown in the preceding screenshot before clicking **Next**.

Python 3 Readiness

One last, concluding note on upgrading Splunk (with respect to its Python support) is that Splunk offers a really cool tool called the **Splunk Platform Upgrade Readiness** app. This tool helps you check a version (7.1, 7.2, 7.3, or 8.0) of a Splunk platform instance for removed features and potential required Python migration tasks before you upgrade. Having a look at and using this tool can be a real timesaver.

> **Note**
> You can find the Splunk Platform Upgrade Readiness App online at: https://docs.splunk.com/Documentation/UpgradeReadiness/2.0.0/Use/About.

An example use case

Most of you will agree that a hands-on approach to learning is better than just reading about a subject. Developers tend to be more hands-on learners who prefer to build and create while following along, working through realistic exercises or projects that test-drive the features and functionalities of a software platform.

Due to this, in this section, we will perform a simple working exercise designed to allow you to touch on some of the fundamental features of Splunk.

In this exercise, you will perform the following steps:

1. Log in and set up a data source for Splunk to continuously monitor.
2. Perform some simple but illustrative searches.
3. Visualize the results generated by a search command.
4. Save a search as a dashboard panel.
5. Use a search to create an alert.

Adding data

Well, first things first: you need to use a mainstream (Chrome and Firefox are the best choices) web browser to access Splunk. The official login URL will consist of the server ID where Splunk was installed, followed by `/app/launcher/home`, but simply `http://localhost:8000/` will work.

12   Overview of Splunk

The following is a simple example showing a localhost install:

```
http://localhost:8000/en-US/app/launcher/home
```

The following screenshot is a typical main login page:

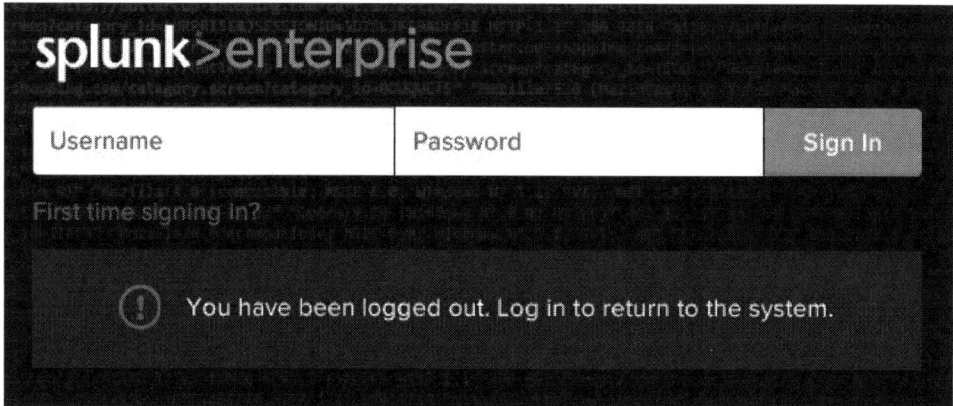

Figure 1.2 – Login page of Splunk Enterprise

During installation, you will be asked to provide a **Username** and **Password** for the **ADMINISTRATOR** account of the instance. If you're working with an existing Splunk server, it is likely that you have already been supplied with an ID to use. Once you have logged in, the default page is displayed (later on, you can set a new page as your default).

In this exercise, we will assume you have a fresh, new, first-time Splunk install and that you have logged in for the first time. The steps are as follows:

1. Open your Splunk Enterprise page by entering your credentials. The following screenshot shows you a panel with Splunk Explore icons on your Enterprise page. Click on the **Add Data** icon:

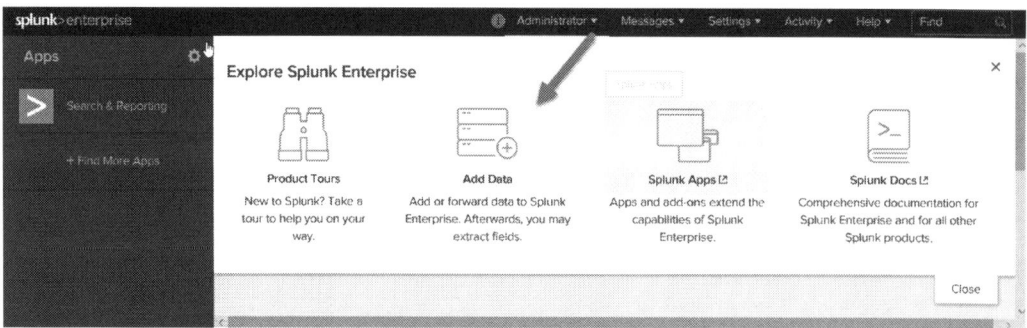

Figure 1.3 – Panel containing the Splunk Explore icons

> **Note**
> Depending on your role and Splunk environment, the preceding screen may not be visible. If not, you can click on **Settings** and then **Add Data**.

2. On the next page (shown in the following screenshot), you will see that Splunk has outlined the **Add Data** icon and that, to the right, various other options are listed. Click on **Add Data**:

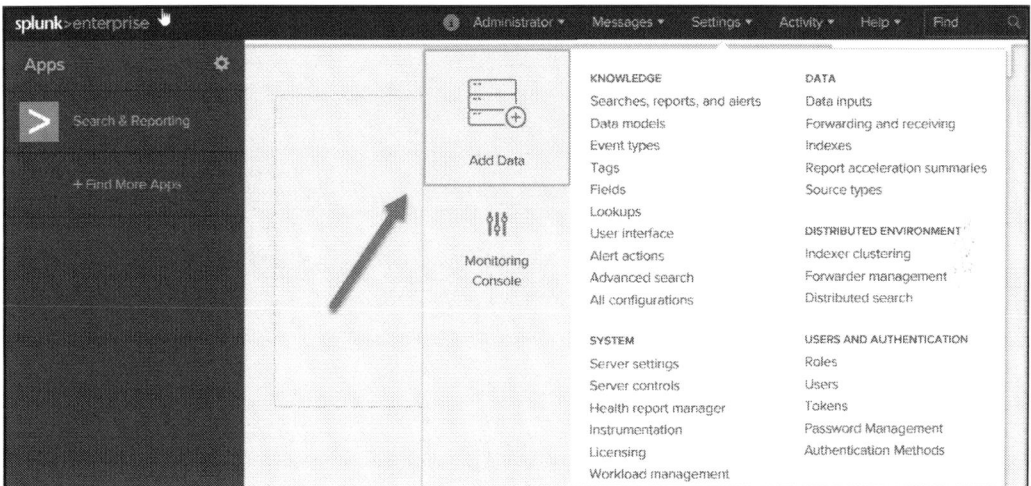

Figure 1.4 – Add Data option

3. Next, Splunk will ask you if you want to send data to Splunk using a popular data source or get data into Splunk using one of three methods—**Upload**, **Monitor**, and **Forward**. For this exercise, we want to set up a location where data is being accumulated and have our Splunk server monitor the data as a data source we can use. So, simply scroll down and locate and click on **Monitor**:

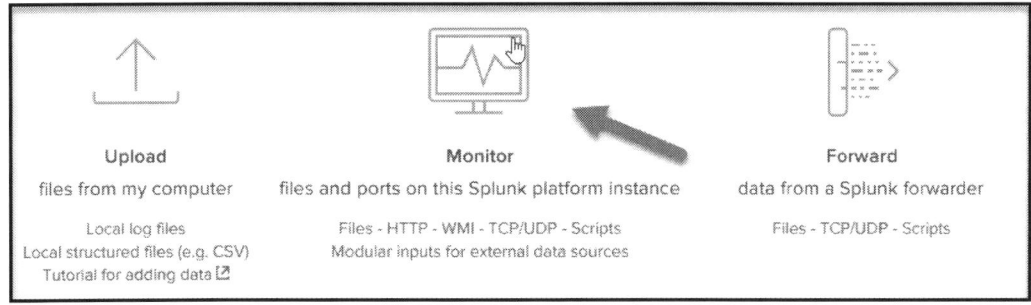

Figure 1.5 – List of three methods you can use to get data into Splunk

14   Overview of Splunk

4. In this practice exercise, we have a folder containing logging files where an application (**IBM Planning Analytics**) is constantly writing message logging information in real time. We want to search both the latest and historic data in this folder, so on the following page, click on **Files & Directories**:

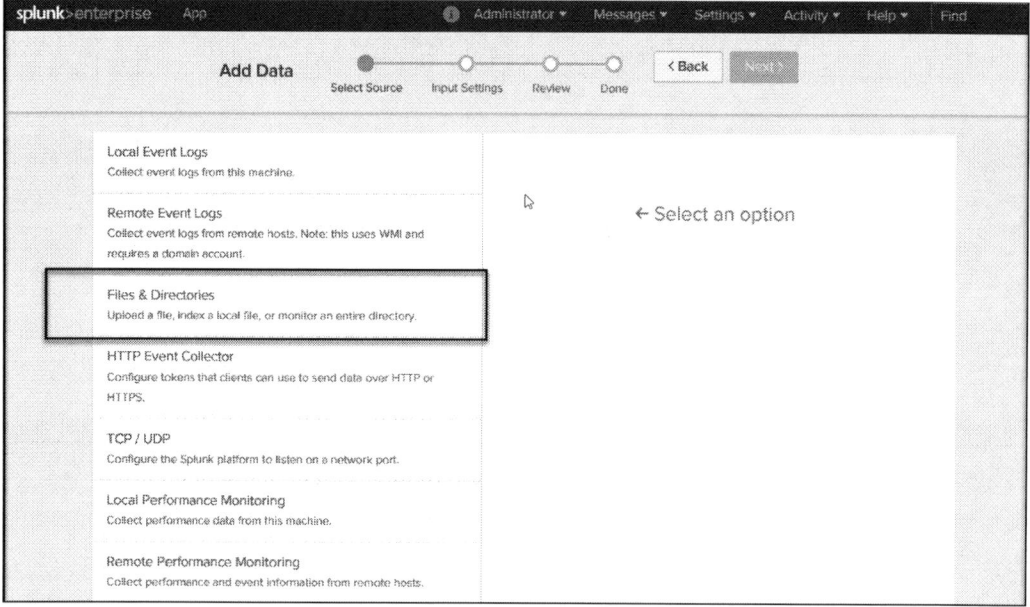

Figure 1.6 – Files & Directories

5. The next step is to configure the Splunk instance so that it continually monitors all the files and sub-directories for data in a selected directory. Across the top of the Splunk page, notice the **Add Data** progress workstream:

Figure 1.7 – Add Data

6. In the following screenshot, you can see the **Add Data** configuration panel. You can simply use the **Browse** button to navigate to a location where the log files exist. In my example, I am using a folder local to the Splunk server (`C:\MyTM1\24Retail\logs`), but you can use any reachable location. Using this configuration will cause Splunk to monitor any and all files that are in this folder now or in the future. For this exercise, that's okay, but in a more real-world scenario, that may or may not be advisable. You can also create **Whitelist** and **Blacklist** rules if you like (we will cover these in later chapters). For example, you could enter `\.log` as a whitelist rule to tell Splunk to only monitor files in the folder with a `.log` file extension/type, but for now, let's just leave these blank and click **Next**:

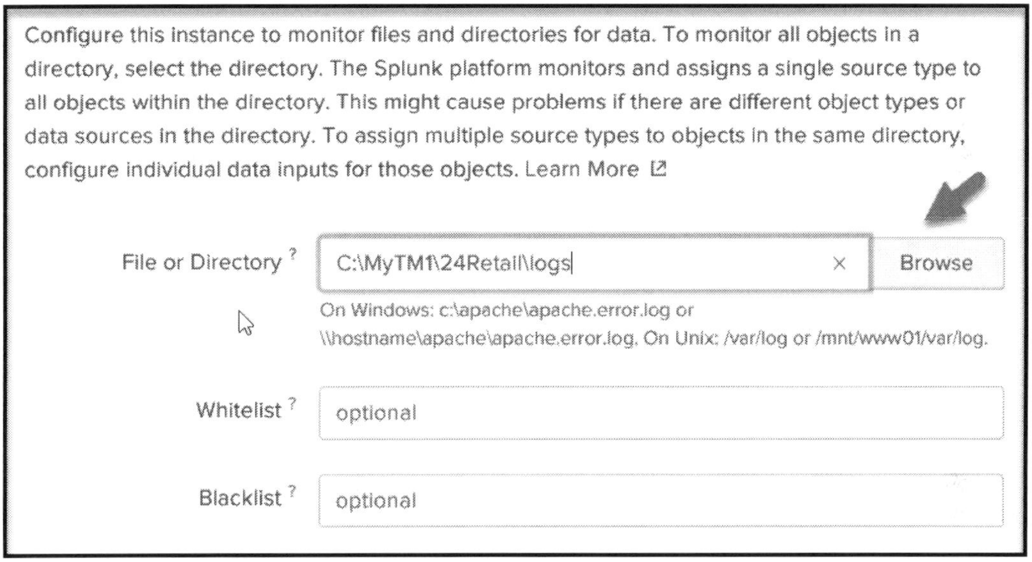

Figure 1.8 – The Browse button for navigating to the location of the log files

7. Now, Splunk will walk you through reviewing and updating **Source Type**, **App Context**, and **Host/Index Information**, and then provide us with a **Review** of these details.

   For now, you can leave all the default values shown. Again, this is just an exercise; in practice, taking the defaults is not necessarily recommended. For example, using automatic sourcetyping will likely result in many unusable—too small—sourcetypes.

16   Overview of Splunk

8. The following screenshot is of the **Review** page (notice again the **Add Data** progress workstream at the top of the page; we are now at **Review**). Go ahead and click **Submit**:

Figure 1.9 – Submitting the file

9. The **Add Data** workstream should now go to **Done**. Verify that you see the message **File Input has been created successfully** and then click **Start Searching**, as shown in the following screenshot:

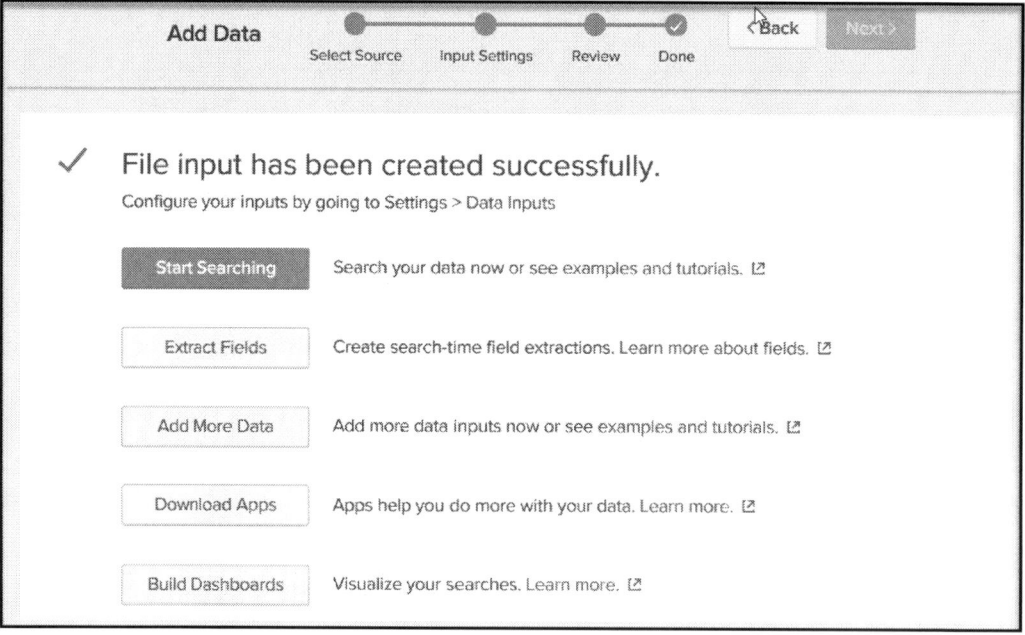

Figure 1.10 – File input created successfully

At this point, we have successfully added a data source to our Splunk instance, and it is ready to be searched!

Searching the data source

Splunk's robust search functionality enables you to search the entire data source that is indexed (with the same search command). The Splunk Search feature can be accessed through a Splunk app called **Search & Reporting**. This can be seen in the left-hand side bar, after logging into the web interface (in this exercise, we've accessed **Search & Reporting** from the **Add Data** page).

We just set up a data source that tells Splunk to monitor a folder where an application is writing messages and transaction log files to. If we take a quick look in the folder, we will see many, many .log files, as shown in the following screenshot:

Figure 1.11 – .log files in folder

In this circumstance, the application writing the logs manages the in-memory data of the users of the software update and changes it. The data is organized and stored in multidimensional cube structures and, as users access the cubes and change data, transactions and messages are recorded in the log files.

Since Splunk is now monitoring this folder, each newly written and/or updated message log file can be immediately searched for through the Splunk **Search & Reporting** app.

18   Overview of Splunk

The following screenshot shows the Splunk **Search** page:

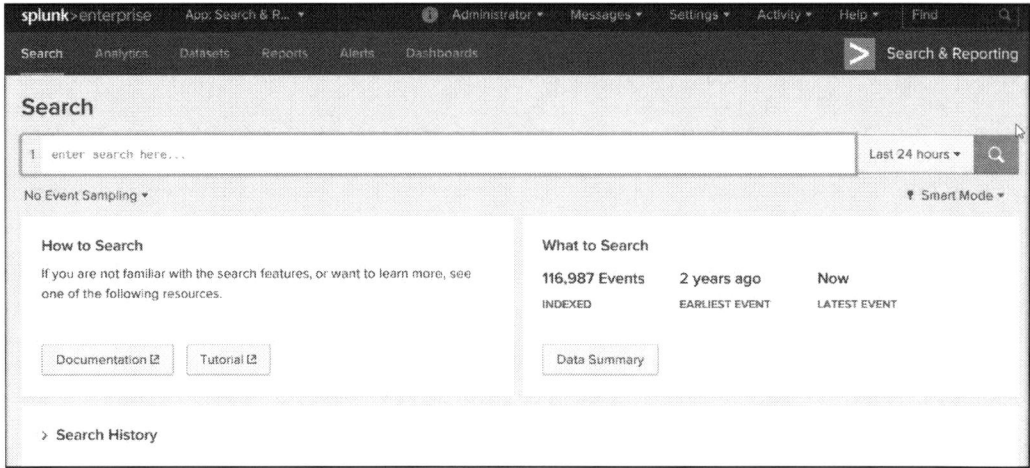

Figure 1.12 – Splunk search page

Let's assume there is a cube structure in the application called `Asset Life` that tracks the period of time that business assets will be considered to be in service and used for earning revenues. Now, what if we had to constantly monitor how often this cube is accessed and updated by any and all users?

Just as a point of reference, the following screenshot is a view of the `Asset Life` cube structure showing six asset types and their assigned `Asset Life` (in months):

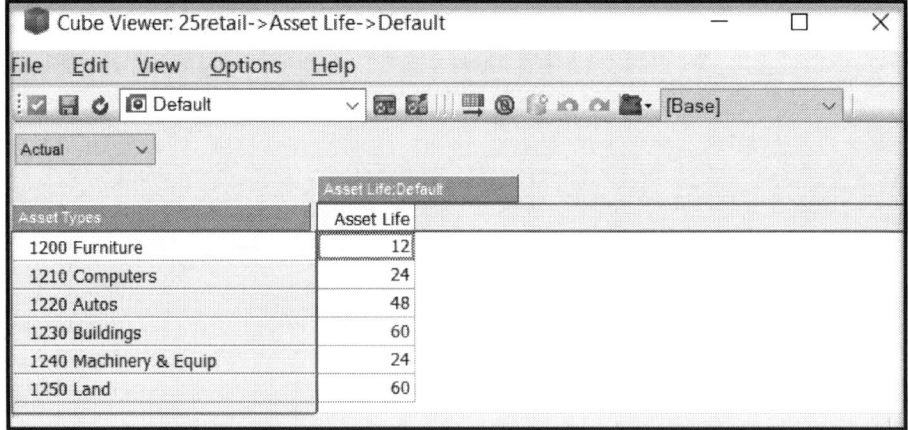

Figure 1.13 – View of the Asset Life cube structure

We can use the Splunk **Search & Reporting** app to easily view and then monitor this information. The **Search** app, which is the short name for the **Search & Reporting** app, is the way you navigate data in Splunk.

The Splunk **Search** app consists of a web-based interface (that is, Splunk Web), a **command-line interface** (**CLI**), as well as the Splunk SPL (we will go through examples of each later in this book).

Before you run a search, the **Search** summary view will show the following:

- The **App** bar
- The **Search** bar
- The time range picker
- The **How to Search** panel
- The **What to Search** panel
- The **Search History**

To get started with our example exercise, you can simply type asset life into the **Search** bar (as shown in the following screenshot):

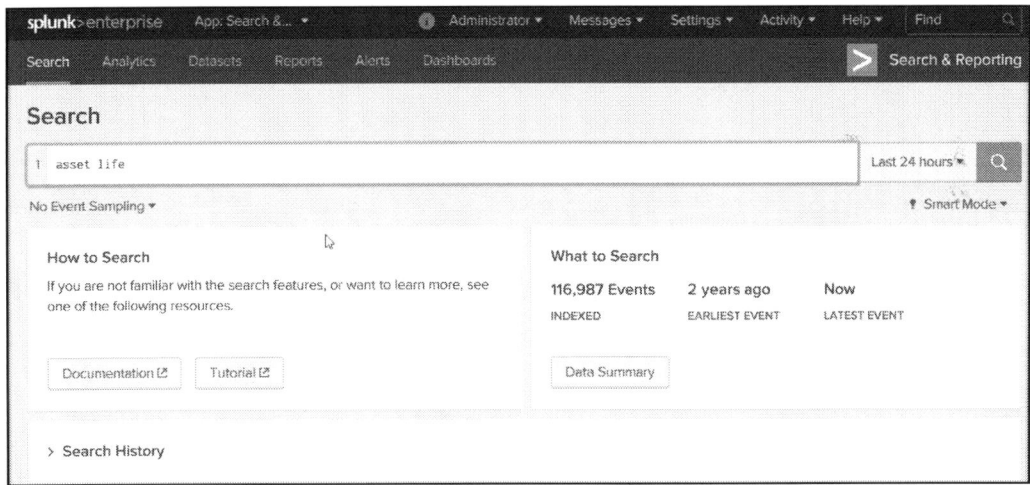

Figure 1.14 – Searching for asset life

What we are asking Splunk to do is search through all the data for the Asset and Life string literals. What Splunk is actually doing is searching Asset AND Life, whereas placing these strings in quotes ("Asset Life") would search for the Asset Life string. Understanding the implicit AND between terms is important and a key differentiator between other products, such as Elasticsearch.

Next, click on the down arrow to the right of **Last 24 hours** (the time range picker), as shown in the following screenshot. Notice that Splunk gives you various options for setting a timeline or time range, so for now, from **Presets**, change the value to **All Time**:

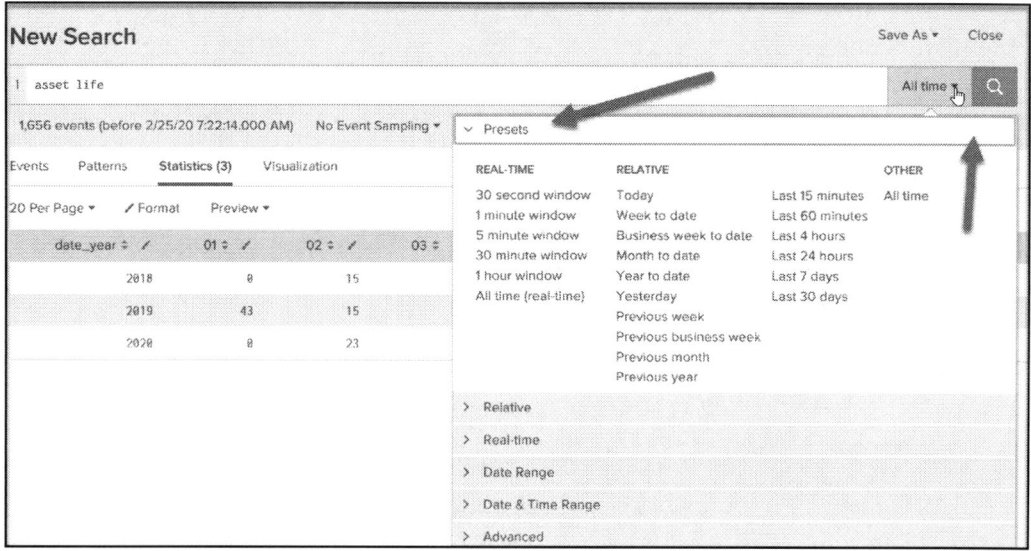

Figure 1.15 – Asset file

Next, go ahead and click the green search icon. The results of the search will be shown below the search bar:

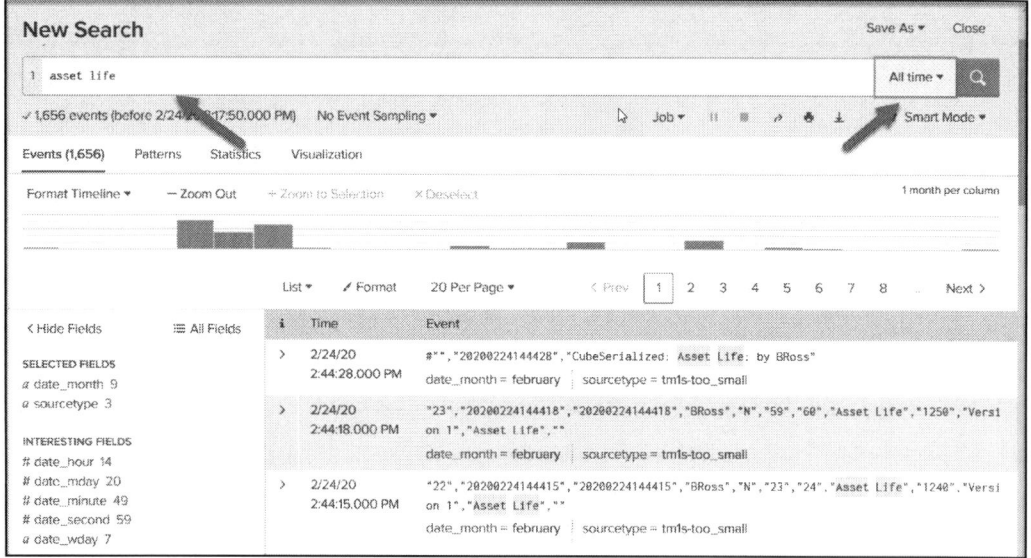

Figure 1.16 – Example search results

You will notice that, by default, the **Events** tab is selected (highlighted and underlined in the preceding screenshot) and that the search results show the raw data that was found in the log files that met our search criteria (in fact, the **Asset Life** literal is highlighted for visibility). We have just used Splunk's SPL to interact with the Splunk engine!

> Note
> The preceding screenshot shows that various fields have been selected. Depending on your installation of Splunk, not all of those fields may be displayed initially.

Now, to make our results a bit more interesting, go ahead and click on the **Visualization** tab (as shown in the following screenshot):

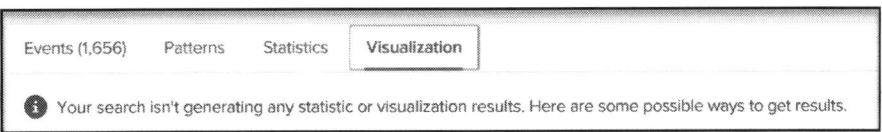

Figure 1.17 – Visualization tab

Unfortunately, Splunk will now give you a text message indicating that **Your search isn't generating any statistic or visualization results**, meaning that the current raw search results cannot be presented in any meaningful graphic.

In Splunk, a column chart represents one or more data series. To make sure that a Splunk search generates one or more series, check the **Statistics** tab. The table shown should have at least two columns; if not, know that **Search** results cannot generate a column chart.

To remedy this situation, you can change the search command line in the search bar to the following:

```
asset life | chart count BY date_year, date_month
| sort by date_year, date_month
```

22   Overview of Splunk

Then, click the green search icon again (as shown in the following screenshot):

Figure 1.18 – New Search

This time, the search results provide enough statistical data that if you click on the **Visualization** tab again, Splunk presents your search results in a **Column Chart**, as shown in the following screenshot:

Figure 1.19 – Revised New Search results

Splunk uses column charts to easily show comparisons of field values across a dataset. Our new search results aren't too bad, but if you look closer, you'll see that the results are not displaying the months in calendar order, within each year.

Before we break down the search command, let's address this by changing the search command again to the following:

```
asset life | eval month=strftime(_time,"%m") | chart count BY date_year, month
```

Now, we should get a better result (as shown in the following screenshot):

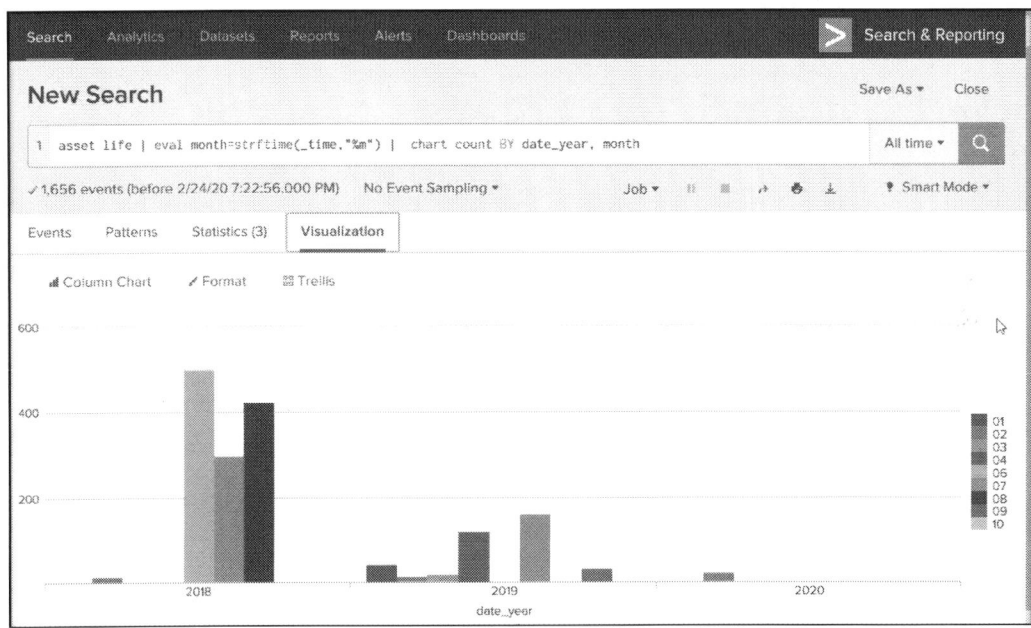

Figure 1.20 – New Search results

So, now, we can see that over the past 2 years, the Asset Life cube within the application has been accessed and/or updated during the various months, as displayed within our **Column Chart**.

Before moving on, let's break down the search command a bit. The search command we used is known as a **search expression** and has a required syntax, as shown in the following code:

```
<literal-expression> | <comparison-expression> | <time-expression> | <index-expression>
```

Each Splunk search expression can be a word or phrase, a field-value comparison, a list of values, or a group of search expressions. You can also use logical expressions by using IN, AND, OR, or NOT comparisons in your search. Also, note that each expression is separated by using the pipe or | character. There is plenty to know and understand about how to write useful and effective searches. We are using a simple example here for this exercise. It would be worth spending some time investigating the product documentation on this topic, available at https://docs.splunk.com/Documentation/Splunk/8.0.4/SearchReference/WhatsInThisManual.

Saving your search

At some point, you might be happy with your search and want to save it so that you and others can use it later on. The search can then be used when creating an **Alert** or **Dashboard**.

Again, for the sake of this first exercise, we are going to save this simplistic search as part of a Splunk dashboard. To accomplish this, do the following:

1. Click on the **Save As** icon.
2. Select **Dashboard Panel**, as shown in the following screenshot:

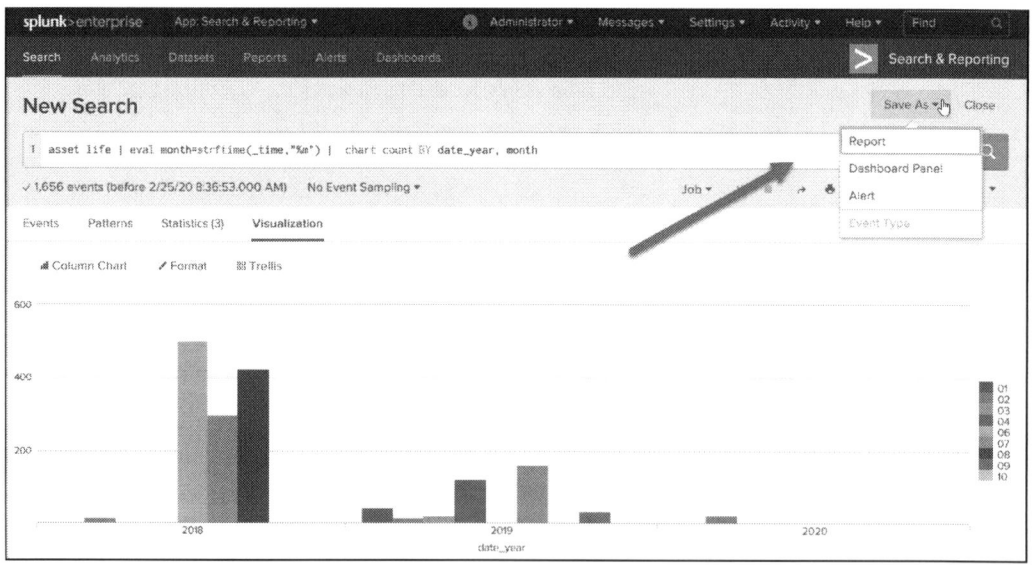

Figure 1.21 – Selecting the Dashboard Panel

A Splunk dashboard panel will frequently be made up of numerous saved searches that will drive or generate the data that is displayed within the panel.

The data being searched can be from multiple sources, such as an inline search that you create and edit using the Splunk **Panel Editor**, or user inputs that can modify the search results.

Once you have selected **Dashboard Panel**, the **Save As Dashboard Panel** dialog will be displayed. From here, you can set some configurations for your new panel.

For now, let's just enter the information that you see in the callout that follows.

> Note
> Just leave **Permissions** as its default of **Private** and **Panel Content** set to **Column Chart**.

When you are done entering the information, click on **Save**.

If you entered all the **Dashboard Panel** configurations correctly, you should see the following confirmation:

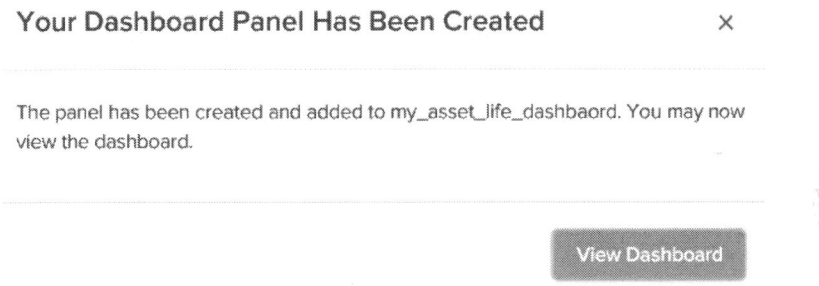

Figure 1.22 – Your Dashboard Panel Has Been Created confirmation message

26   Overview of Splunk

Splunk has now successfully created your **Dashboard Panel**! Next, you can click on the **View Dashboard** button to see our first (although pretty simplistic) Splunk dashboard panel:

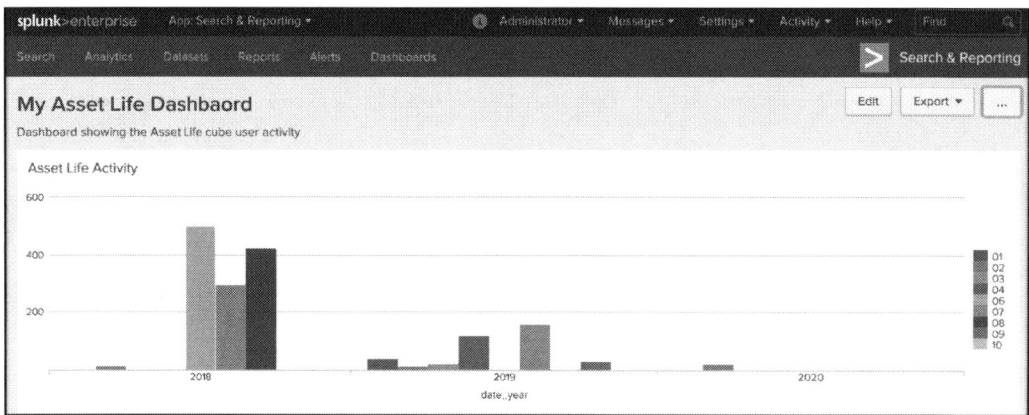

Figure 1.23 – Asset Life Dashboard

Adding an alert

Splunk alerts use a saved search to look for events in real time or on a schedule. Alerts will trigger when the results of a search meet specific conditions that you have set up. Alert actions can be used for responding when the interested alerts are triggered.

In our example exercise, let's assume that we want an event to be triggered when the previously mentioned **Asset Cube** has any activity related to it. So, let's go back to the Splunk **Search & Reporting** app and reenter (in the **Search** bar) the same **Search** command we used to create the dashboard panel in the previous section:

```
asset life | eval month=strftime(_time,"%m") | chart count BY date_year, month
```

Next, click on **Save As**. This time, select **Alert** (as shown in the following screenshot):

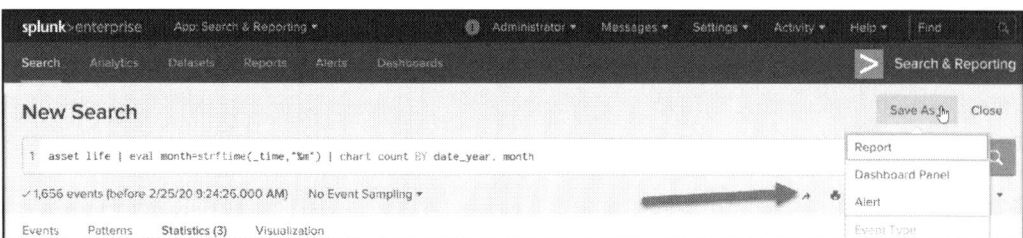

Figure 1.24 – Adding an alert

Splunk will now display the **Save As Alert** dialog (similar to the **Dashboard Panel** dialog we used earlier). Here, again, you can simply fill in the information shown in the following screenshot (don't worry – you can select and edit the **Alert** at any time!):

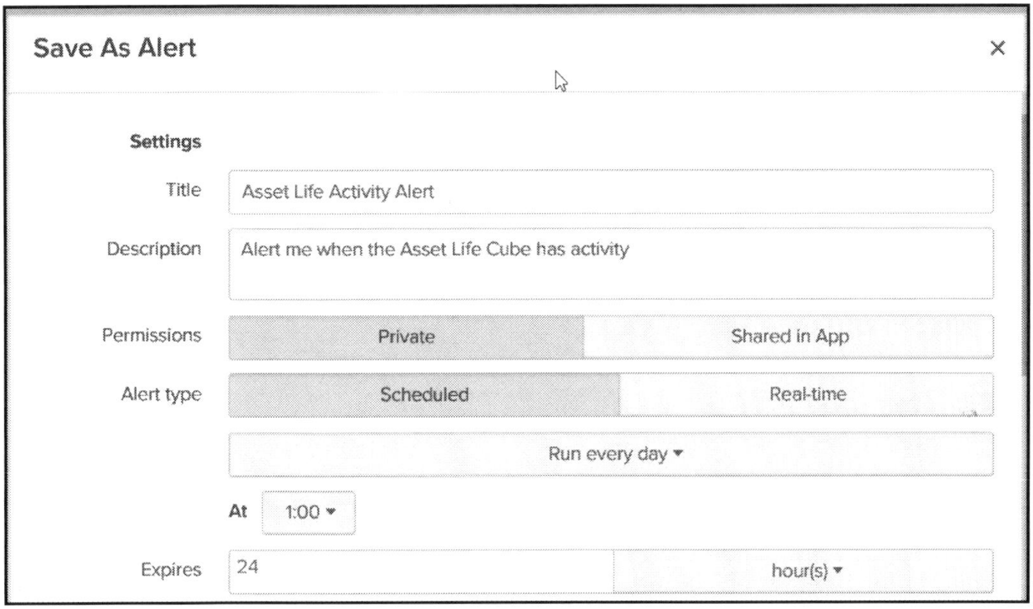

Save As Alert	
Settings	
Title	Asset Life Activity Alert
Description	Alert me when the Asset Life Cube has activity
Permissions	Private | Shared in App
Alert type	Scheduled | Real-time
	Run every day ▼
	At 1:00 ▼
Expires	24 hour(s) ▼

Figure 1.25 – Save As Alert

Title and **Description** are simply used to identify the alert and its objective. For now, set **Permissions** to **Private** and select **Scheduled** as the **Alert type**.

An **Alert** can be either **Scheduled** or **Real-time**. Fundamentally, scheduled alerts perform searches according to a schedule you set, while real-time alerts perform searches continuously. Our alerting scenario isn't critical (and it's our first alert), so let's leave it as a **Scheduled** alert and also leave the other options as you see them.

28　Overview of Splunk

The rest of the **Alert** dialog asks us to define the **Trigger Conditions** and **Trigger Actions** alerts (as shown in the following screenshot):

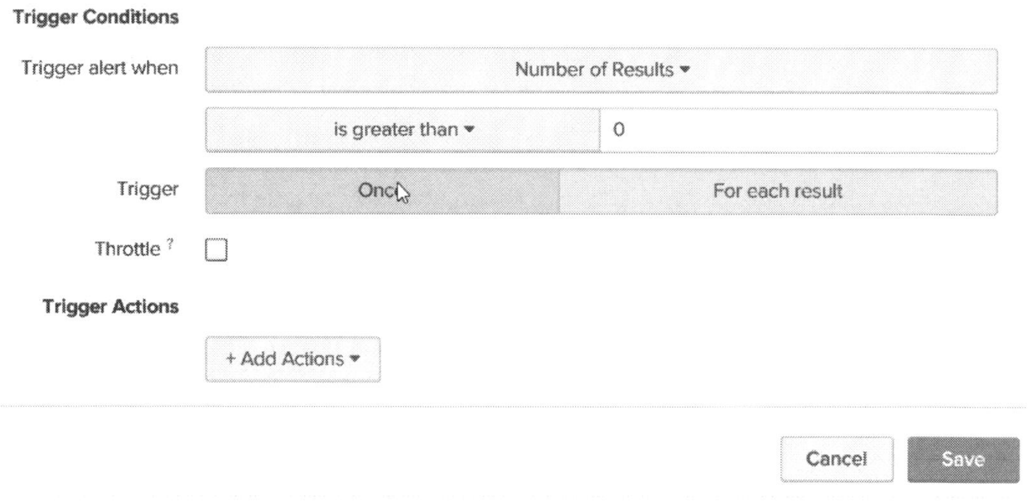

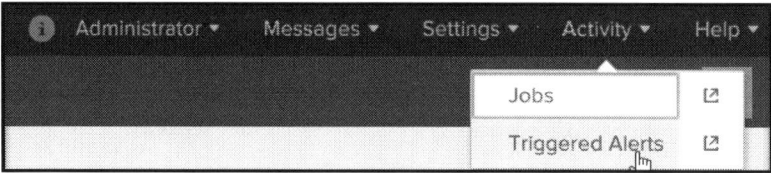

Figure 1.26 – Trigger Conditions

You can enter the information shown in the preceding screenshot to tell Splunk to trigger the alert when the number of results (from the search we created the alert on) is greater than 0 and trigger it once or for each result. Leave the **Throttle** checkbox unchecked (blank) and then click on **+ Add Actions** (at least one trigger action is always required for any alert).

Clicking on the **+ Add Actions** button will give you a list of actions to choose from.

Now, go ahead and select the first option displayed in the list, which is **Add to Triggered Alerts**.

This will allow you to easily view the activity of your Alerts. To do this, go to the main Splunk page and select **Triggered Alerts** from the upper-right, under **Activity**:

Figure 1.27 – Triggered Alerts

An example use case   29

You can see the **+ Add Actions** selection list in the following screenshot:

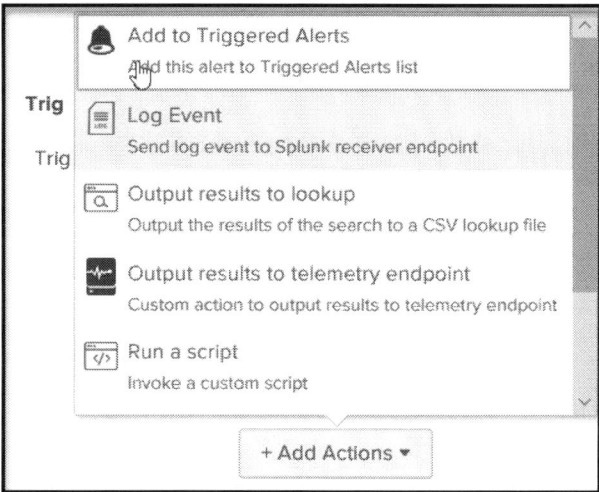

Figure 1.28 – Navigating to the Add to Triggered Alerts option

Once you have selected the action in the **Trigger Action** section, the **Save As Alert** dialog will show the selected **When triggered** action and allow you to set the **Severity** level of the alert (let's choose **Low**). Next, click the **Save** button:

Figure 1.29 – Add to Triggered Alerts

30   Overview of Splunk

Splunk will then confirm this with a message stating **Alert has been saved**:

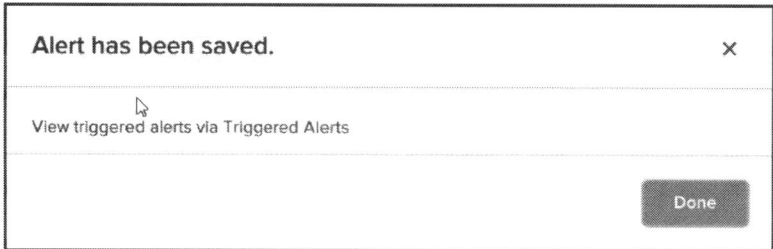

Figure 1.30 – Alert being saved

After the alert has been saved and you've clicked the **Done** button, Splunk will display the details of the alert, as shown in the following screenshot:

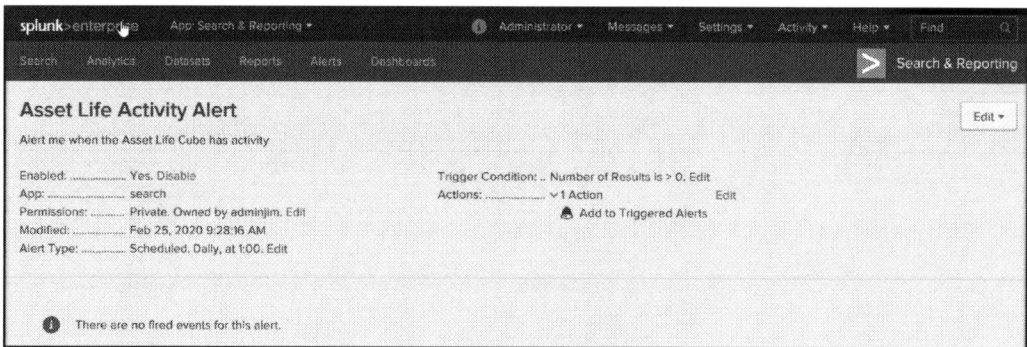

Figure 1.31 – Asset Life Activity Alert

Reviewing and editing

Now that we have created and saved a dashboard and an alert, we can review and edit them if we wish. Go back to the **Search** page and click on either **Alerts** or **Dashboards**, as shown in the following screenshot:

Figure 1.32 – Search page

Let's click on **Dashboards**. Splunk will display a list of all the dashboards that you have access to. You should be able to locate our **My Asset Life Dashboard** in the list, as shown in the following screenshot:

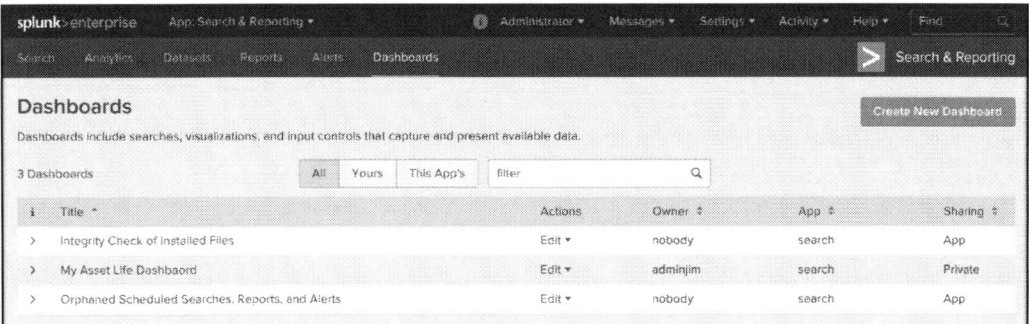

Figure 1.33 – Dashboards

In the list, go ahead and click on the name of our dashboard (**My Asset Life Dashboard**). Splunk will then run and display our saved dashboard for us. Should we want to edit the dashboard, we can click on the **Edit** button:

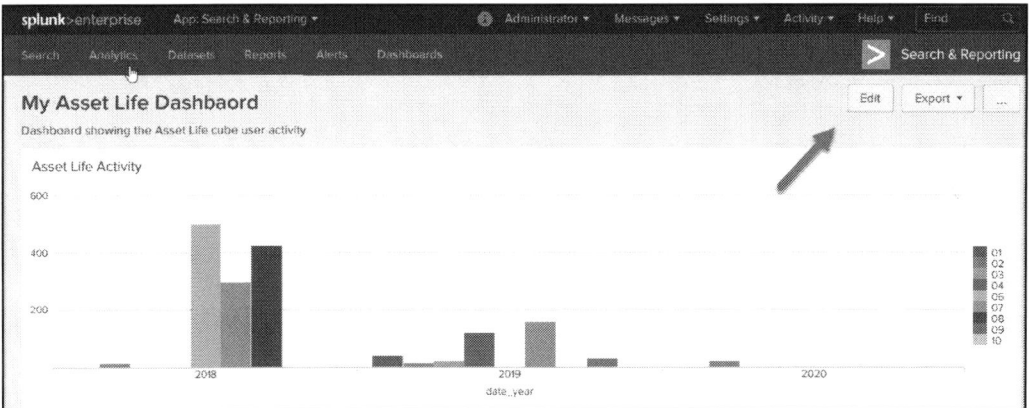

Figure 1.34 – Navigating to Edit for the Asset Life Dashboard

32   Overview of Splunk

For now, let's click on the **Edit** button. Splunk will send you to the **Edit Dashboard** page (shown in the following screenshot). From there, you can do some pretty useful things, such as view the **Raw UI** source, add additional panels and inputs to the dashboard, and change the **Theme**. One particularly nice feature is that you can use this dashboard as a starting point for a new dashboard by clicking on the **Save as…** button and creating a copy of it (under a new name):

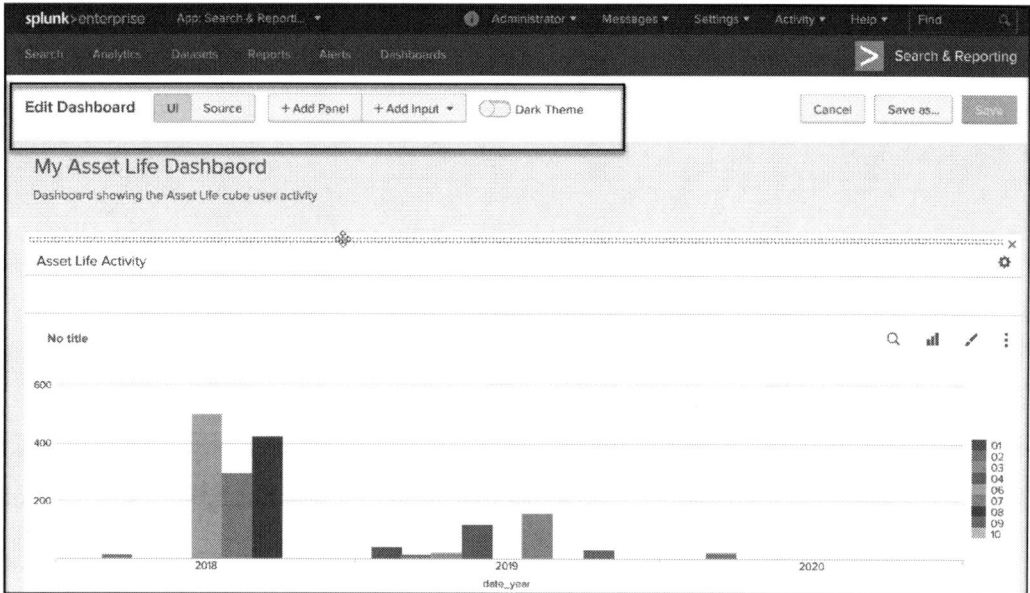

Figure 1.35 – Edit Dashboard

For now, let's just click the **Cancel** button, since we will explore more of these features later on in this book.

Going back to the **Search** page, this time, let's click on **Alerts**. Splunk will then show you all the Alerts you have access to:

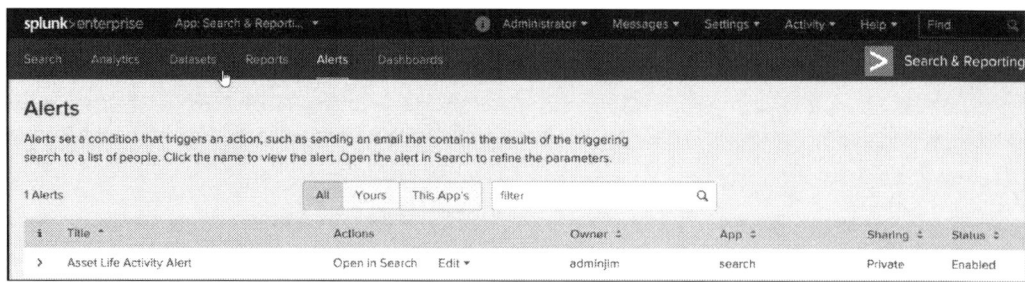

Figure 1. 36 – Alerts

Similar to the dashboard list, the alerts list provides us with multiple ways to access each alert. You can either click on **Open in Search** or **Edit**. The **Edit** option allows you to quickly edit the configurations set on the alert, change user access to the alert, turn it off (disable it), make a copy of it (**Clone**), or delete the alert. Through **Clone**, you can use the alert as the starting point for a new one (just like we saw with the **Dashboard** panel):

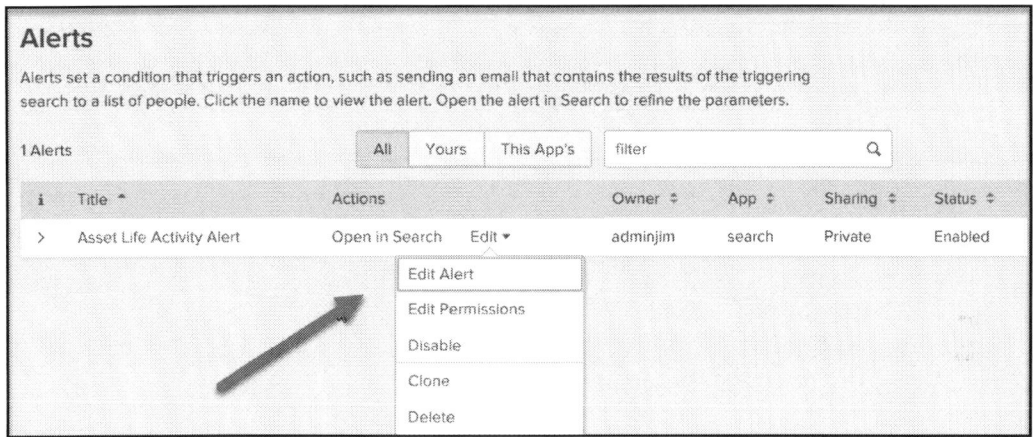

Figure 1.37 – Edit Alert

If you choose the **Open in Search** option, Splunk opens the selected alert within the **Search** page, ready to be reviewed, run, and/or edited:

Figure 1.38 – Asset Life Activity Alert

There is so much more to explore and try out, but for now, we will close this exercise and move on.

Summary

In this chapter, we introduced some of the basic fundamental features of the Splunk platform, called out the newest features in Splunk version 8.0, and then performed a simple exercise to illustrate how to create a new search, save it as a dashboard, and use it to create an alert.

In the next chapter, we will complete some tasks that illustrate how to best align Splunk resource allocations with particular priorities using the enhanced Splunk rules framework. This now includes search types, such as scheduled and ad hoc, and various search modes (real-time and historical).

Section 2: Splunk Administration

In this section, you will follow step-by-step exercises designed to both provide a thorough understanding of each of the new features in version 8 of Splunk as well as to build working code for each exercise.

This section comprises the following chapters:

- *Chapter 2, Splunk Administration – Workload Management*
- *Chapter 3, Performance Statistics and Alerting in Splunk*
- *Chapter 4, Splunk Administration – Security*
- *Chapter 5, Advanced Indexing*
- *Chapter 6, Splunk Integration with Azure and AWS*

2
Splunk Administration – Workload Management

In this chapter, we will identify the resources critical to Splunk operation and then perform tasks illustrating how to best understand and align resource allocations with specific priorities using the various features available in Splunk, including the Monitoring Console, Splunk health reports, and the Splunk Workload Management feature.

We'll break down this chapter into the following sections:

- About resource allocation
- Critical resources
- The Monitoring Console
- The health report
- Workload management techniques

- The rules-based framework
- Scheduling workloads

About resource allocation

Every discussion on resource allocation should start with establishing what are to be considered the critical resources for an application and/or system and what resources are required to be allocated (and why), and prior to that, of course, perhaps understanding what capacity planning is so as to establish the recommendations for minimum and maximum levels of those resources.

This chapter isn't intended to cover and teach capacity planning or offer recommendations for the minimum required specific resources (related to Splunk), but it is relevant to mention the key resources used and required for successfully running Splunk.

> **Note**
> The resources required by Splunk are directly proportionate to whether Splunk is a single or distributed installation, as well as the anticipated use and/or workload patterns. Splunk offers a great reference covering this topic online that can be found at `https://docs.splunk.com/Documentation/Splunk/8.0.4/Capacity/IntroductiontocapacityplanningforSplunkEnterprise`.

Critical resources

When we talk resource allocations in Splunk, we focus mainly on the following:

- The number of available cores/CPUs
- The amount of memory
- Available disk space

Virtual machines

Per the Splunk documentation, if you run Splunk Enterprise within a **virtual machine** (**VM**) on any platform, performance is expected to decrease. This is a result of how virtualization works: by providing hardware abstraction on a machine using what are referred to as **pools** of available resources.

The VMs defined on the system then draw from these resource pools.

The big challenge is that Splunk Enterprise needs sustained access to a number of resources, particularly disk **input/output** (**I/O**), for indexing operations. If you run Splunk Enterprise in a VM or alongside other VMs, indexing and search performance can deteriorate to unacceptable levels.

The Monitoring Console

The Splunk Monitoring Console is an *out-of-the-box* tool that can be used to view valuable information, including usage statuses on those resources critical to Splunk performance.

The Monitoring Console dashboards that are available provide visibility into the various areas of a Splunk deployment or instance and the resource usage dashboard options are indeed very *handy* for keeping track of the aforementioned resources.

> **Note**
> These Monitoring Console dashboards use data from Splunk Enterprise's internal log files such as the `metrics.log` file, as well as the data available from the Splunk Enterprise platform instrumentation.

Resource usage dashboards

There are several resource usage dashboard options, which you access in Splunk Web by clicking on **Settings**, then the **Monitoring Console** icon, then the **Resource Usage** menu:

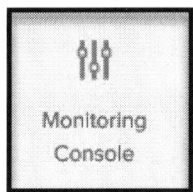

Figure 2.1 – The Monitoring Console icon

The deployment dashboard provides deployment-wide resource information on the three most critical resources to Splunk:

- CPU usage
- Physical memory usage
- Disk usage

The information provided on the three dashboard panels can be useful for capacity planning as well as allocating the proper levels of resources.

The other dashboards (**Resource Usage | Machine and Resource Usage | Instance**) provide usage information by instance and machine.

The next section of this chapter provides a little guidance on understanding the information provided within the dashboards.

Dashboard interpretation

As helpful as the Monitoring Console is, (as Splunk documentation warns) some of the information may be somewhat misleading.

As an example, some operating systems may loosely bind some resources (such as physical memory) so that they can reallocate those resources later for higher-priority processes as they see fit.

What this means is that resources shown as **available** to Splunk in the Monitoring Console may not actually be available, should events change, since the operating system may perform its own reallocation of those resources by itself.

Unfortunately, the reporting functionality in the Splunk Monitoring Console has no way of determining to what extent certain resources are loosely locked up in this way.

> **Note**
> The historical data in the Splunk Monitoring Console dashboards comes from `resource_usage.log` in the `_introspection` index.

Resource usage – deployment

It is possible to configure a Splunk indexer to use multiple partitions on the basis of multiple indexes and bucket types (configured from `indexes.conf`).

Splunk indicates that a common (proven) practice is to use a single high-performance filesystem to hold index data.

If you do use multiple partitions, the typical approach for arranging index data is to keep hot/warm buckets on the local machine and to put cold buckets on a separate array of disks suitable for longer-term storage. You'll want to store your hot/warm buckets on a machine with fast read/write partitions because most searching will happen there.

The **Deployment-Wide Median Disk Usage** panel within the Monitoring Console conveniently includes all partitions in use by each Splunk Enterprise instance, making it a bit easier to keep up to date on Splunk's consumption of disk resources.

What about CPU usage?

CPU usage

The **Median CPU Usage by Process Class** dashboard panel shows the levels of CPU resources for each Splunk process class. Remember that Splunk sorts all processes into specific process classes.

The Splunk process classes are as follows:

- The `splunkd` server
- `search`
- Splunk Web
- The `index` service
- Scripted input
- KVStore and others

Information on this panel can be employed to recognize upticks in CPU usage by a particular process, which typically foretells an underlying issue that needs to be addressed before it begins impacting Splunk's performance.

Physical memory

The **Median Physical Memory Usage by Process Class** dashboard panel shows the levels of physical memory resources for each Splunk process class and can be used in a similar way as the previously discussed CPU usage panel.

Additionally, these data points should not only be periodically checked, but should also be reviewed as an *overtime insight* to establish usage and/or growth patterns so as to avoid outages. This trending information of course is also a valuable input to most capacity planning exercises.

Usage/growth patterns help to distinguish between leaks and high usage.

> **Note**
> Helpful information on monitoring and troubleshooting memory usage patterns can be found online at `https://docs.splunk.com/Documentation/Splunk/8.0.5/Troubleshooting/Troubleshootmemoryusage`.

Resource usage – machine/instance

In addition to the **Resource Usage** dashboards that focus on the entire Splunk deployment, there are also versions of those dashboards that focus on each of the specific instances and even machines that are running within a Splunk deployment.

These dashboards can be used to drill deeper into the deployment, down to the **instance** and/or **machine** levels.

Dashboard review hints

You will find that all of the corresponding Splunk product documentation recommends taking note of and considering the following when reviewing each of the Splunk monitoring dashboards:

- Identify any outliers – any data point(s) that differ significantly from the other data points in that class or type.
- Find patterns appearing over time. For example, in the **Instance** and **Machine** dashboards, look for memory usage increasing over time (without recovering).
- In the **Instance** dashboard, if a process class that is using a lot of resources turns out to be a search process, investigate further by going to the **Search activity: Instance** dashboard.

Workload monitoring techniques

There are two ways to monitor workload management in Splunk Enterprise:

- Using the Monitoring Console (as we just covered in the prior sections of this chapter)
- Using the `splunkd` health report

The Monitoring Console and workload management

Within the Monitoring Console, under **Resource Usage**, you will find the following two options:

- **Workload Management Overview**
- **Workload Management Activity Instance**

The following is screenshot shows these options:

Figure 2.2 – Resource usage options

Workload Management Overview

This page includes a number of multi-panel dashboards, including the **Workload Management Status** and **Workload Pool Configuration** dashboard and the **CPU and Memory Usage** dashboard.

These dashboards provide details about the Splunk deployment, including whether Workload Management is supported and enabled on individual Linux instances. They also display error messages and workload pool configuration details.

Workload Management Activity Instance

These are also multi-panel dashboards designed to monitor workload management activity on a per-instance basis. You can use the dashboards' *snapshot* view to monitor current resource usage across all workload pools.

We will get back to the topic of workload management later in this chapter, but for now, let's have a look at the Splunk health report.

The health report

The Splunk (or `splunkd`) health report lets you view the current status of specific features enabled within the `splunkd` health status tree. In the health status tree, you can then view information about a feature's current status.

44 Splunk Administration – Workload Management

You can find the Splunk health report icon on the main page in Splunk Web as shown in the following screenshot:

Figure 2.3 – Splunk health icon

Features that are shown in the red or yellow state can be clicked on to see *root cause* information and up to the last 50 messages are listed to help identify the cause of a feature's status:

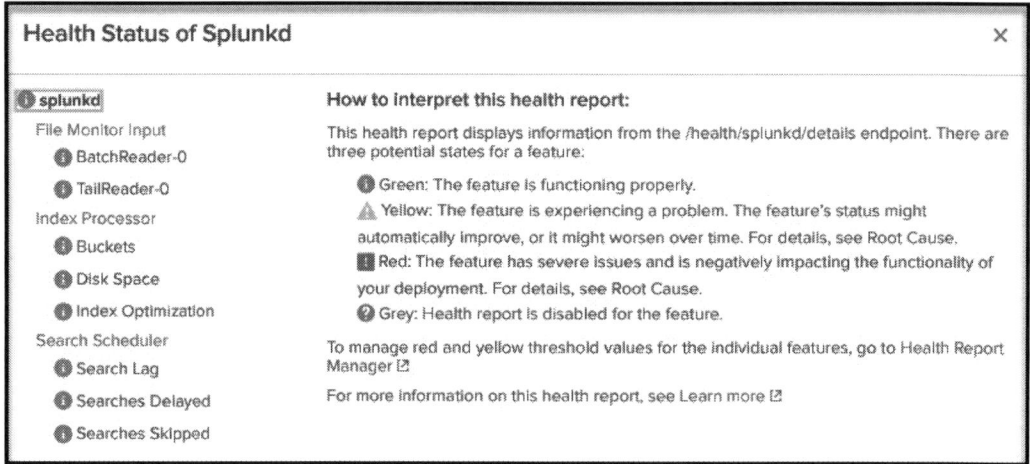

Figure 2.4 – Health Status of Splunkd

You can use the Splunk health report to identify problems within the Splunk deployment by feature and then investigate the cause of those problems.

Splunk feature settings

The Splunk health report initially displays the status of a default set of Splunk Enterprise features, but you have the ability to customize or modify the feature settings and thresholds. You can even disable and/or reenable a feature as required.

You can do this through Splunk Web. To make changes to the Splunk health report, from the main page in Splunk Web, click on **Settings** and then **Health report manager**:

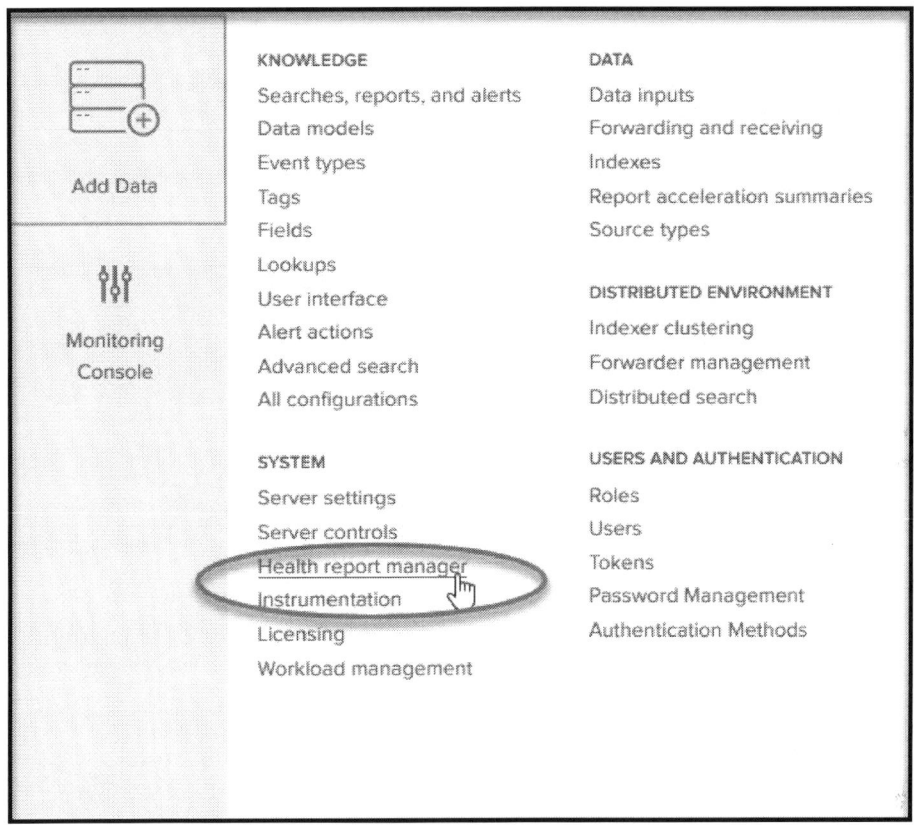

Figure 2.5 – Health report manager

On the **Features** page (shown in the following screenshot), you can edit feature settings or disable/enable a feature:

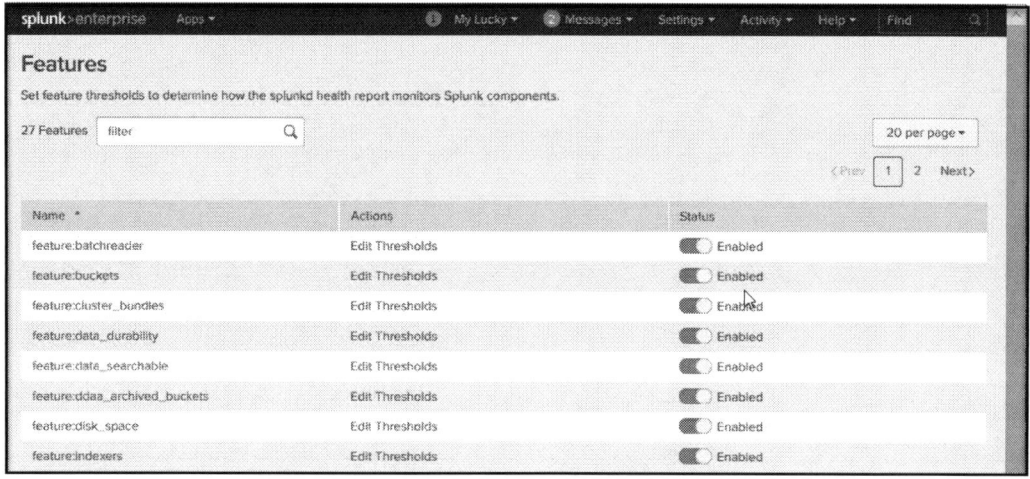

Figure 2.6 – Features page

Health alerts

The default behavior for the health report is to generate alerts for all features in the health status tree. This means that whenever any feature indicator meets the set threshold condition, the feature's health status changes and an alert fires.

Splunk health status alerts are very powerful in that they can be set to fire at the global, feature, or indicator levels, and do not require you to be logged in to Splunk Web to receive the feedback.

> **Note**
> You can configure health report alerts through Splunk Web or by directly editing the `health.conf` file or querying the server/health-config endpoint.

As you can see, there are many built-in approaches to monitoring the health of a Splunk deployment, as well as many recommended or proven practice techniques for troubleshooting difficulties caused by current resource consumption and/or preparing for future resource usage requirements.

In the next sections of this chapter, rather than monitoring Splunk resources, the focus will be on managing Splunk workloads to better address critical (and limited) system resource needs – in other words, workload management.

Why workload management?

A general description or definition of the idea of workload management might be thought of as managing a budget; that is, you spend or allocate a finite number of resources over time, based upon the actual, presumed, or anticipated number of work requests to be completed or processed.

This concept can be broken down into technical or practical terms.

For example, if suddenly there is a large number of searches submitted to run concurrently across the Splunk deployment, inefficient system resources may result and can impact search execution, and cause latency, skipped searches, and other performance issues.

Workload management means having the ability to perform things such as prioritizing searches into system-critical and trivial categories, and then setting limitations on the number of resources that Splunk is allowed to use (for example) for running trivial search queries. This will prevent the possibility of system-critical work encountering inadequate system resources, while trivial work enjoys too much.

Workload management addresses these issues and helps optimize resource usage by letting you set and manage the amount of system resources allocated to searches and other processes in Splunk Enterprise.

Workload management advantages

Workload management supports the following objectives:

- Prioritization of resources to be used to run critical search work
- Avoidance of data-ingestion latency due to heavy search loads
- Limitation of resource allocation to low-priority/trivial search work (such as real-time searches)
- The ability to monitor searches and apply automated remediation (such as aborting a search or throttling resources)

Splunk Workload Management feature

The Splunk Workload Management feature is a powerful Splunk Enterprise feature that provides Splunk administrators the ability to allocate (assign) system resources to Splunk workloads based upon specific priorities.

Splunk Workload Management is a rule-based framework that lets you allocate computation and memory resources to optimize search, indexing, and other processes in Splunk.

It allows you to limit resource allocations to low-priority search workloads (such as real-time searches).

> **Stop!**
> Unfortunately, this exciting feature – Splunk Workload Management – is only available on Linux operating systems, additionally, Splunk Workload Management requires Splunk Enterprise version 7.2.0 or later.

The basics of Workload Management

The Splunk Workload Management feature is designed to give you the ability to set aside certain amounts of CPU and memory resources (into **pools**) and then assign them for specific searches and other processes in Splunk.

The resource pools are referred to as **workload pools** and are specified amounts of CPU and memory resources that are a subset of the total amount of CPU and memory available in the workload category of which the resource pools is a member.

Typically, you would create multiple workload pools of different sizes (amounts of resources) to make it easier to assign or allocate different pools (levels of resources) to different workload categories, users, or groups, based upon need.

> **Note**
> You can create and edit workload pools using Splunk Web, the CLI, or the REST API. Workload pool configurations are stored in `workload_pools.conf`.

It is required that you create, at a minimum, the following two workload pools:

- **Default search category pool**: Searches that are not explicitly mapped to any workload rule are assigned to this pool by default.
- **Default ingest category pool**: Indexing and other non-search processes are assigned to this pool by default.

When you create a workload pool, you must assign it to a workload category.

There are currently three Splunk workload categories:

- **Search**: All kinds of searches, including accelerated data models
- **Ingest**: Includes indexing and other `splunkd` processes, such as the process runner, KV store, app server, and introspection
- **Miscellaneous**: Scripted inputs and modular inputs only

In the Splunk Workload Management feature, you create workload rules that specify which searches will have access to which workload pools. These rules are sometimes referred to as **policies**.

You use workload rules to design and build strategies to guarantee that high-priority work will have the resources it requires to successfully process and complete, while less important work is restricted as appropriate in the number of resources it can consume.

Rules are used to automatically assign individual searches to designated workload pools, although you can always assign searches to pools manually.

The rules-based framework

In an earlier version of Splunk Enterprise (+7), the ability to create workload management rules using attributes such as index, role, user, and app was implemented via a **rules framework**. In the latest version of Splunk, the rules framework was extended to include search types, search modes, and search time ranges. In addition, you can also use `index=*` as part of a workload rule.

Objectives of workload rules

To remind us, workload management rules can be used to provide **guardrails** for the processing that occurs within Splunk. For example, a rule can be defined to monitor a certain type of search at runtime and, if the condition(s) of the rule are met, take a predefined remediation action. This *identification* (of a potentially negative event) and *responding to it* would be nearly impossible to perform manually. Additionally, workload management rules are continually *active*, unless disabled by an administrator. This is referred to as Splunk's **automatic monitoring and remediation capability**.

Workload management rules are evaluated every 10 seconds and if a rule is triggered by a process, the corresponding action is taken.

Each Splunk workload management rule requires a predicate condition that a search must meet before a defined action is taken, such as placing the search in a specified workload pool or moving the search to an alternate pool.

There are two types of workload rules:

- Search placement
- Monitoring and actions

Search placement rules

These are workload management rules that define the workload pool in which a search is placed when a search starts. Using search placement rules, you can ensure that the appropriate level of resources is available to those Splunk searches that the enterprise deems to be high priority or critical.

Monitoring rules

These are workload management rules that automatically trigger actions on running search processes (based on the rule predicate and the status of the search). When you create a monitoring rule, you must specify a runtime value in the predicate. If a search exceeds the runtime value, Splunk Workload Management performs the specified action. Supported actions are **Abort search**, **Display in Messages**, and **Move search to alternate Pool**. You use monitoring rules to manage heavy search loads and prevent rogue processes from monopolizing pool resources.

Rule – the order of operation

The **order of operation** dictates the order to solve steps in expressions with more than one operation. The Splunk workload management rules' order of operations indicates that Splunk workload rules are evaluated in the order in which they appear in the rules list in the UI, from top to bottom.

As the rules execute, if a search meets the conditions of a rule, the action specified in that rule is taken, and any rules *below* that rule are *skipped* (not evaluated/executed).

You can re-order workload rules to ensure the desired behavior. Workload rules are evaluated for every search and reevaluated every few seconds. If an executing search does not meet the conditions of any rule, the search is automatically placed in the (previously mentioned) default search pool category.

Splunk workload management rules must contain the following attributes:

- A **name**
- A **predicate**
- A **schedule**
- An **action**
- A **workload pool**

> **Note**
> Predicates (or **conditions**) can be set for an app, role, user, index, `search_type`, `search_mode`, or `search_time_range` to control search placement.

Scheduling workloads – schedule-based rules

Finally, you can have Splunk workload management rules apply only during business hours or times designated as your organization's *peak processing hours*. Using the aforementioned (and optional) schedule value, you have the ability to enable workload rules based on a time schedule. This time schedule is used to determine the time period during which the rule is valid to be evaluated.

Using this approach, you can create a set of Splunk workload management rules for an organization's peak hours and then another set of rules for off-peak hours.

For example, you can create a rule to allow random searches from designated users to run using a high priority pool during only certain hours.

Getting going

Splunk recommends that it is a good idea that if you are just getting started with workload management rules, start with just one simple use case, prove its correctness, and then add another.

Typical *first-case* workload management options might be to divide searches into high- and low-priority groups or to create workload groups based upon various user groups.

A piece of bottom-line advice: keep workload management rules as simple and straightforward as possible and add them one by one, checking after each new rule is added to ensure that your expectations for the rule are met before you proceed to implement any additional rules.

In closing

The Splunk Workload Management feature provides a *policy-based* tool to reserve system resources (such as CPU and memory) for ingestion and search workloads that can be aligned with an organization's priorities.

With Splunk Workload Management, administrators can sort workloads into different workload groups and reserve portions of system resources per workload group regardless of the load on the system.

Monitoring workload pool resource consumption can help you provision resources efficiently and help you avoid assigning too many searches to a pool, which can degrade search performance.

Summary

In this chapter, we defined the concept of resource allocation, identified what resources are most critical to Splunk, reviewed the Monitoring Console and the health report, and then introduced the Splunk (Linux-based) Workload Management module.

In the next chapter on performance, statistics, and alerting, we will emphasize the understanding and optimization of data storage for cost savings, as well as the intent and uses of advanced alerting.

3
Performance, Statistics, and Alerting in Splunk

In the previous chapter, we reviewed Splunk's fundamental features and called out the newest features in Splunk version 8.0. In this chapter, the emphasis will be on understanding and optimizing data storage for cost savings, as well as the intent and use of advanced alerting.

In this chapter, we will cover the following topics:

- Exploring data in Splunk
- Understanding storage
- Storage metrics
- Logs2Metrics
- Alerting

Let's get started!

Exploring data in Splunk

Understanding (data) storage in Splunk starts with an understanding of how Splunk stores data and what kinds of data it can store. Actually, when you hear about Splunk storing data, what it really means is *collecting and indexing* logging and machine-generated data (which it can then combine with data sourced from relational databases, data warehouses, and Hadoop and NoSQL data stores). This collecting and indexing procedure is just one step of the Splunk data pipeline. We will touch on this in the next section of this chapter.

This data that's being collected and indexed (also sometimes called **ingesting data**) by Splunk is considered to be raw data at this point and is compressed down to approximately half its original size. The speed and efficiency in which Splunk collects, organizes, and compresses the data is measured as its indexing rate.

When Splunk indexes data, it breaks out the data into events based on timestamps. It should be noted that the term **indexing** is used in Splunk to refer to the entirety of event processing, which encompasses both parsing the data (into events) and indexing it.

As Splunk parses or transforms the raw incoming data into events, it stores them as indexes. These Splunk indexes are the repositories for all Splunk data. There is a bit more to indexes and storing data, such as how indexes are then broken out into what is called **buckets**, but we'll get to that later in this chapter.

The data pipeline

The Splunk data pipeline defines the workflow or the path that all data takes through Splunk, starting with raw data input or collection, then parsing the data (into events), and then finally indexing it (and of course, ultimately, searching it).

This pipeline illustrates that there is a continuous flow of raw data that provides information or insight to process the data.

The data pipeline includes four segments. You can assign each of these segments to a different Splunk instance or installation:

- **Input** (collection of raw data)
- **Parsing** (into searchable events)
- **Indexing** (compressing and storing)
- **Search** (using the Splunk **search processing language** or **SPL**)

Input

Input is the first segment in the **Splunk data pipeline**. This is where Splunk ingests the (raw) data stream from its source, breaks it down into "64,000" blocks, and annotates each block with metadata keys. This includes the host, source, and source type of the data.

Parsing

The second segment within the Splunk data pipeline is **parsing**. Here, the data arrives from the **input** segment and is where **event processing** occurs (where Splunk analyzes data and puts it into logical components). Once the data has been parsed, it moves on to the next segment of the pipeline; that is, **indexing**.

Indexing

The process of parsing the events and writing them to disk on the system is called **indexing**. When the Splunk platform indexes raw data, it transforms the data into searchable events. Indexes reside in flat files on the indexer. There are two types of indexes: **events indexes** (these are the default type of index; they can hold any type of data) and **metrics indexes** (these hold only metric data — we will explore metrics indexers in a later section of this chapter).

The indexes residing in the disks of each of the indexers can be searched using Splunk's SPL. The efficiency of this process (the indexing rate) is critical and should be meticulously monitored.

> **Note**
> You can use Splunk's monitoring console or create your own metric indexer and search commands to monitor metrics such as the indexing rate. We will review creating a metric indexer later in this chapter and visit the monitoring console in *Chapter 14, Monitoring and Operability*.

Searching

This is the last segment of the Splunk data pipeline. By using Splunk's SPL, searching is designed to combine the best capabilities of SQL with the power of the Splunk data pipeline.

The most common use for Splunk's SPL to is to retrieve events from a Splunk index that match specific criteria. However, in addition to this, there are a vast number of statistical commands that can be used for calculating metrics and generating reports, searching within a rolling time range window, pattern identification, predicting future trends, and so on. Of course, you can also save searches as reports and use them to drive dashboard panels and alerts.

Splunk components

Now that we have introduced the Splunk data pipeline and have somewhat of an understanding of what it is, we can take a closer look at its three main/basic components:

- Forwarders
- Indexers
- Search heads

Forwarders are the components that are used for collecting data, **indexers** are the Splunk components that are used for indexing and storing data (coming from the forwarders), and the **search head** is the component that is used for searching and otherwise interacting with Splunk.

Forwarders work during the data input/collection segment of the data pipeline, indexers do their work during the parsing and indexing portion of the data pipeline, and finally, the search head component is used for (of course) searching.

The technology that's used by Splunk is effective in that it utilizes its indexers to store data. It also does not require any kind of formal database to organize and store data to have access to it.

This indexer architecture allows Splunk to scale and essentially be expanded to meet almost any capacity requirement you have before you, with proper planning.

This book is not meant to delve into the art or practice of proper Splunk capacity planning, but rather to help you understand how to discover and monitor the efficiency of a Splunk server environment and its resources.

> **Note**
> A good resource for getting started with understanding and estimating Splunk resource requirements can be found online at https://splunk-sizing.appspot.com/.

Understanding storage

Again, this book isn't going to attempt to provide hardware and/or sizing recommendations. All of that can be gleaned from the online product documentation at `https://docs.splunk.com/Documentation/Splunk/8.0.2/Admin/OptimizeSplunkforpeakperformance`.

Now, let's get back to Splunk indexers.

An indexer is actually a designated collection of directories that contains both the data and the index files organizing that data. These indexer directories are also called **buckets**, and a Splunk indexer typically consists of numerous buckets, organized by the age of the data in them. What's called an indexer cluster then replicates data on a bucket-by-bucket basis. Bucket size is a performance metric that is set, should be monitored, and can be changed as deemed appropriate.

By default, all data that's fed to a Splunk indexer is stored in a main index. At any point in time, you can create and specify as many other indexes for additional data inputs as you think you might need. Splunk manages this storage into buckets, first by sending data into a designated `db-hot` bucket and then by developing a list of target buckets to replicate the data to. Hot buckets are used for storing newly created indexed data with a predefined expiration or rollover date, which results in data being replicated at a certain point in time.

Each bucket has a bucket life cycle that's governed by a **bucket aging policy**. This is managed through attributes. This policy controls when a bucket transitions to the next stage in the life cycle. These stages are as follows:

- Hot
- Warm
- Cold
- Frozen
- Thawed

As time goes on, buckets age. As they age, a bucket goes from one stage to the next. As we mentioned previously, when data is indexed, it is saved into a hot bucket, which can both be searched and actively written to. An index can have multiple buckets that are hot at the same time.

Whenever certain circumstances are met (for example, a hot bucket reaches a certain size or Splunk gets restarted), the hot bucket will transition to the warm state, and a new hot bucket will be created in its place. Like hot buckets, buckets that are warm are still searchable, but they are no longer being actively written to. Also, similar to hot buckets, an indexer will most likely have many warm buckets.

Once further conditions are encountered (for example, the index reaches a set maximum number of warm buckets), the indexer begins to transition all warm buckets to cold, again always based upon their age (oldest to youngest).

Finally, after a set period of time, all cold buckets will be transitioned to frozen. To be able to make frozen data available for searching, it must be transitioned to thawed.

The number of hot buckets that can be created at any one time is a performance metric that can be set, should be monitored, and, as required, changed. Making changes to these metrics (and others) can produce a definitive result and consequences. For example, the number of hot buckets allowed and the previously mentioned bucket size can impact the pace at which buckets transition or roll to the next state. So, if the buckets are transitioning at too fast a pace, you'll end up with a lot of small buckets, and search performance will then be hampered when it comes to finding events. Due to this, Splunk will have to open and search more and more buckets.

A Splunk indexer can index a significant amount of data in a short period of time (actually, over 20 megabytes of data per second or over 1.7 terabytes per day), so understanding how data is ingested, stored, and made accessible is critical, as well as how to monitor these metrics.

Also, note that it is recommended (by Splunk) to utilize multiple indexers, as well as make an effort to distribute both data and searches to improve search performance. Splunk also states that it is more cost-effective to achieve high performance by using multiple machines with average storage, rather than just using a single machine with the absolute fastest resident storage possible.

In the next section, we will dig deeper into those metrics that are relevant to Splunk optimization and performance.

Storage metrics

In the Splunk platform, you use metric indexes to store and access metrics data.

Earlier in this chapter, we stated that there are two types of indexers (**events** and **metrics**); the metric indexer is a custom type of Splunk index that is configured for storing and retrieving metric data.

Storage metrics 59

A metrics index can only be used for metrics data, and you cannot convert an events index into a metrics index or vice versa.

You can access the default Splunk metrics indexer named _metrics, which is the metrics equivalent of the _internal event index. In addition (to the default metrics indexer), you can create your own metrics indexer, just like you can create your own event indexers. The easiest way to create a new Splunk metrics indexer is to use the Splunk web interface.

Creating a metrics index

Now, let's create a metrics index:

1. From the Splunk main page, click on **Settings**:

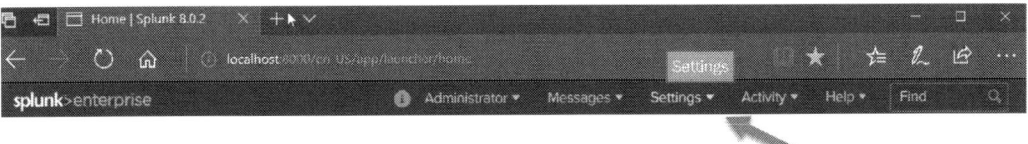

Figure 3.1 – Splunk main page illustrating the Settings menu option

2. Find and click on **Indexes**:

Figure 3.2 – Settings dialog indicating the Indexes option

3. On the **Indexes** page, you have the option to scroll down and locate the default `_metrics` index. However, instead, let's click on **New Index** (as shown in the following screenshot):

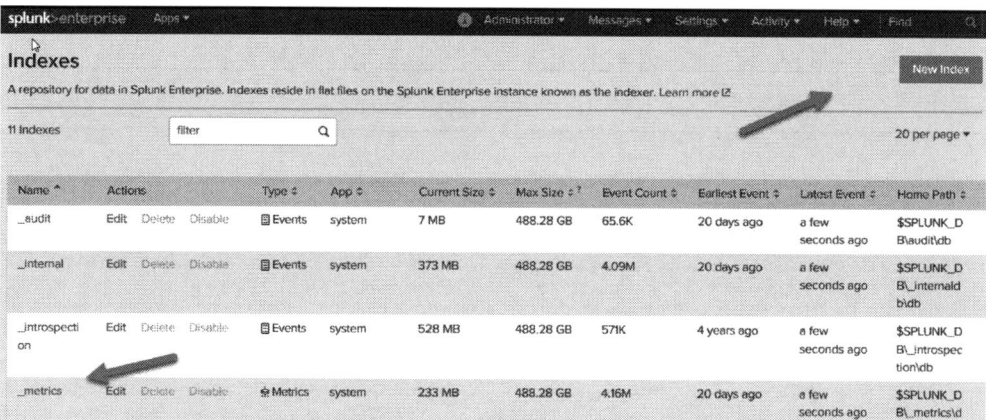

Figure 3.3 – Indexes page pointing out the default metrics index and the New Index button

4. On the **New Index** dialog (shown in the following screenshot), enter an index name for our new metrics index (I've used `jimssindex`). For **Index Data Type**, make sure you click **Metrics**. For this example, you can leave the default values for the remaining properties of the index. Finally, click **Save**:

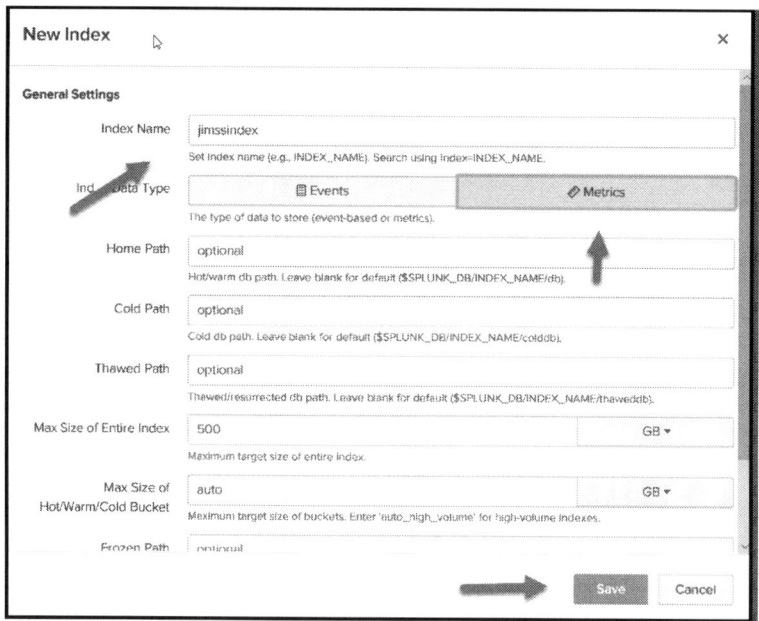

Figure 3.4 – Splunk's New Index dialog

5. Once you click **Save**, Splunk will create the new index. You should then be able to see the index listed under **Indexes**.

From the **Indexes** page, you can see vital information about all the indexes in the Splunk instance, such as its type (**Events** or **Metrics**), the app associated with it (**system**, **search**, or **custom**), its **Current Size**, **Max Size**, current **Event Count**, **Earliest Event**, **Latest Event**, **Home Path**, **Frozen Path**, and its **Status** (enabled/disabled).

The following screenshot shows the **Indexes** page and our new metrics index:

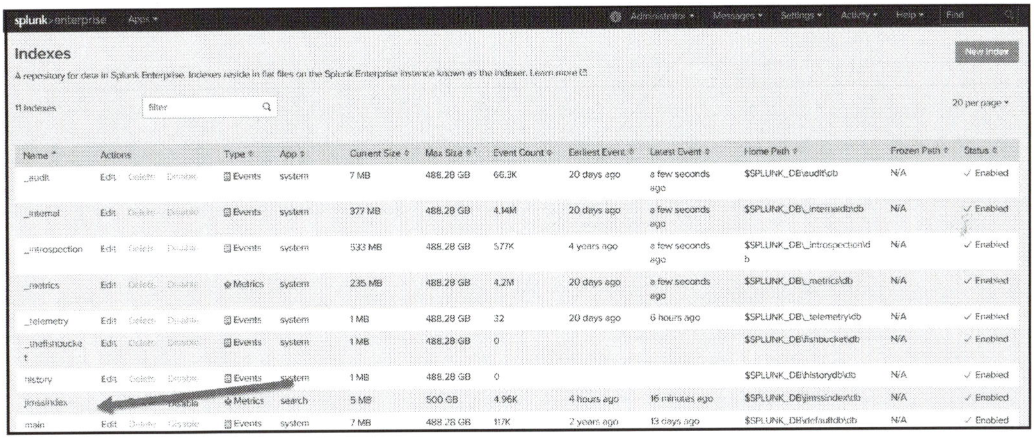

Figure 3.5 – Indexes page showing our new index

With that our new metric index has been created and is ready to use!

Metric indexers and user roles

When you run searches against a metrics indexer and you do not filter by that indexer (where `index=indexername`), Splunk will only see those indexers that have been assigned to your user role. If you have no default metrics indexers assigned to your role, then the metrics search runs over an empty dataset and will return no results.

In fact, it is always a good practice to assign default indexers to users. To do that, we can go to the Splunk main page and click on **Settings**, then **Roles**. The roles are then displayed. From there, you can click on **New**.

The **New Role** dialog will be displayed. Here, you can enter the information that's required for creating a new role (I've typed in `metricsrus`):

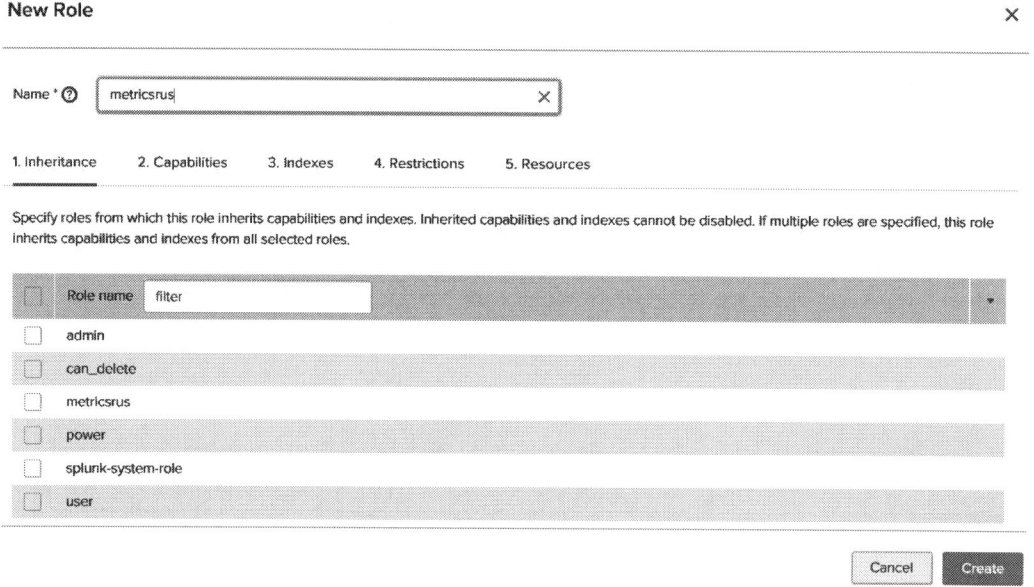

Figure 3.6 – Splunk's New Role dialog

The **New Role** dialog walks you through the steps of how to set up the new role. Right now, our main focus of interest is step 3; that is, **Indexes**.

If you scroll down through the list of available indexers, you should see both our default metrics indexer (`_metrics`), as well as the one we just created (`jimssindex`). Make sure you check both the **Included** and **Default** checkboxes for these indexes, and then click **Create**:

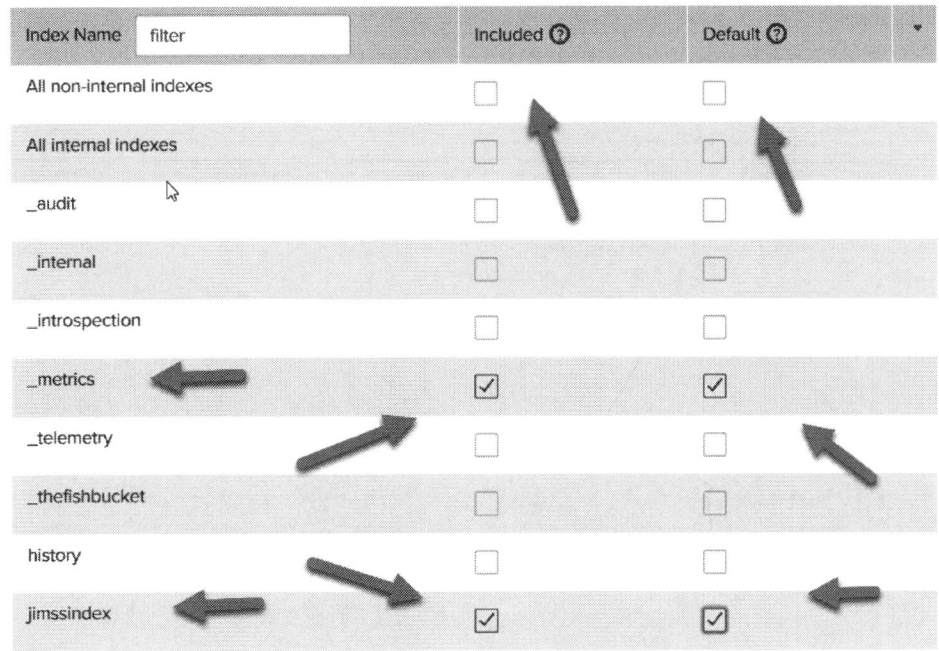

Figure 3.7 – Splunk's New Role dialog showing our selected options

Now that we have established a new role that has the capability to easily search both our metric indexers, all we have to do is assign ourselves to that role!

To do that, follow these steps:

1. Go back to the Splunk main page, click **Settings**, and then **Users**.
2. On the **Users** page, scroll down until you find our username and click on **Edit** (under **Actions**):

Figure 3.8 – User list

3. On the **Edit User** dialog, make sure you add the new role (metricsrus) to the selected items list on the right, and then click **Save**:

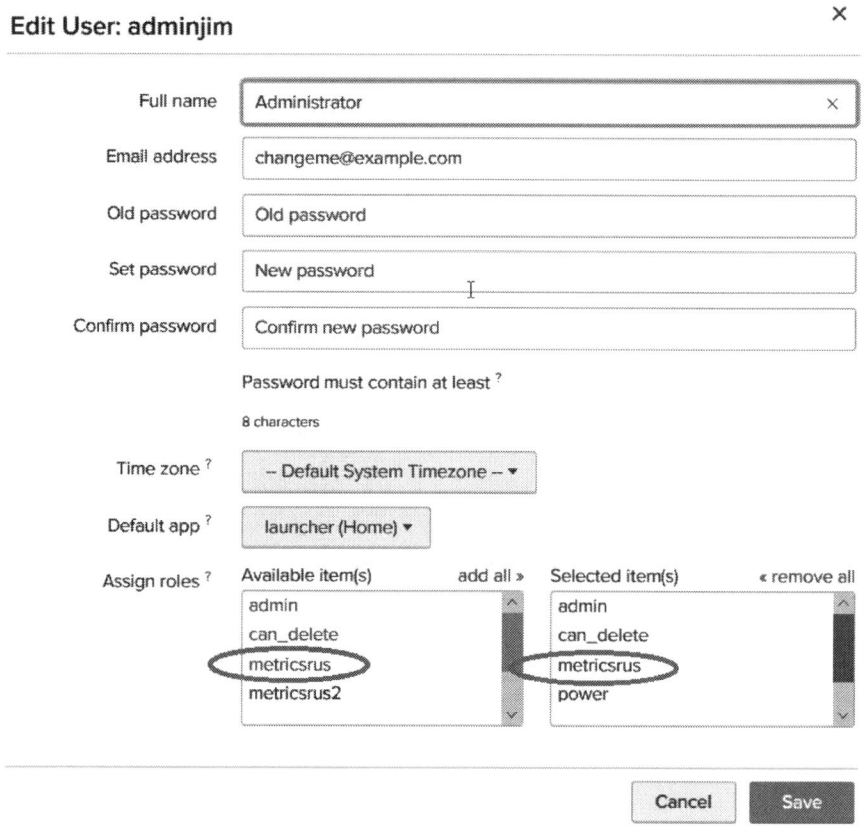

Figure 3.9 – Splunk's Edit User dialog

Searching metrics

Now that we have added our username to the new role, we can go ahead and try some simple metric-centric searching.

The most popular command that's used to search metric indexers and analyze metric data is the mstats command. This command automatically performs statistics for us on the metric data points (such as measurement, metric_name, and dimension) in a metric indexer.

> **Info**
>
> For more information on metric data point, please refer to `https://docs.splunk.com/Documentation/Splunk/8.0.2/Metrics/Overview`.
>
> Splunk offers metrics-specific commands such as `mstats`, `mcatalog`, and `msearch` that can be used on the metric data points in those metric indexes.

The `mstats` command also allows you to apply aggregate functions (`average`, `sum`, `count`, and `rate`) to metric data points. These are designed to help you diagnose and correlate problems from different data sources.

Let's try a few searches using our newly created metric index.

It's a good idea to start with a `mcatalog` search so that we can get an idea of what some of the default metrics are. From the **Search** page, type in the following:

```
| mcatalog values(metric_name) WHERE index=jimssindex
```

The results are shown in the following screenshot:

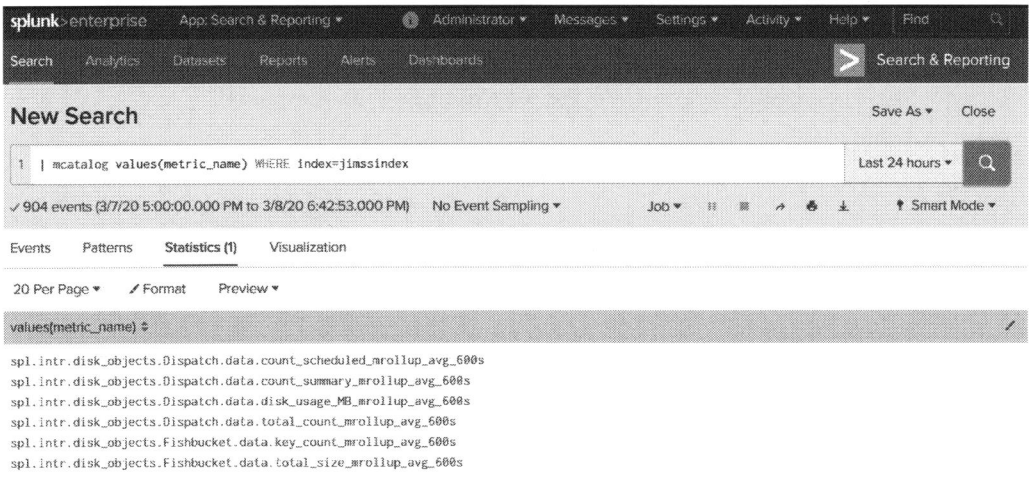

Figure 3.10 – Splunk's New Search page showing our search results

Another interesting search using the `mcatalog` command shows us the matrix's dimension values. Type in the following:

```
| mcatalog values(_dims) where index=* AND metric_name=*
earliest=-1h latest=now by metric_name
```

The following screenshot shows the values we received:

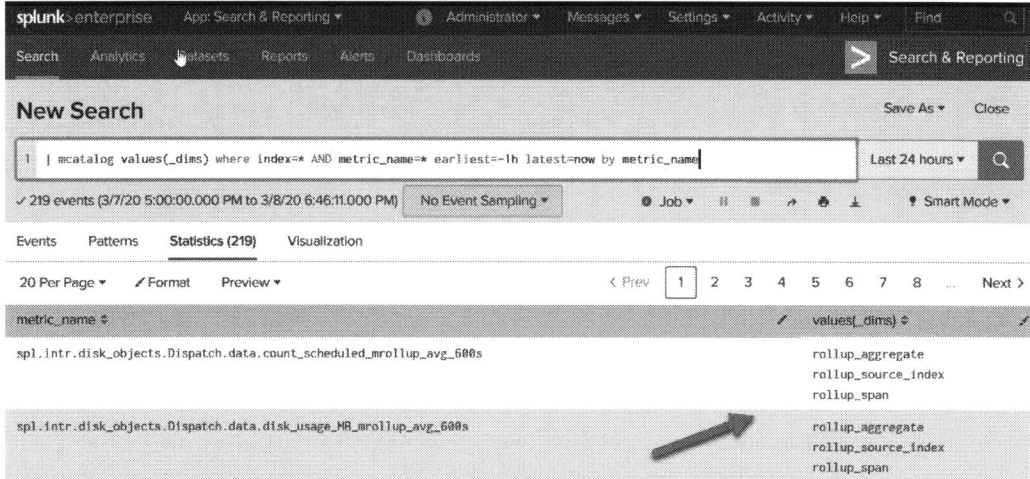

Figure 3.11 – Splunk's New Search page showing our search results

Alternatively, we can simply list the dimension names using the following command:

```
| mcatalog values(_dims)
```

The following screenshot lists the dimension names that were produced:

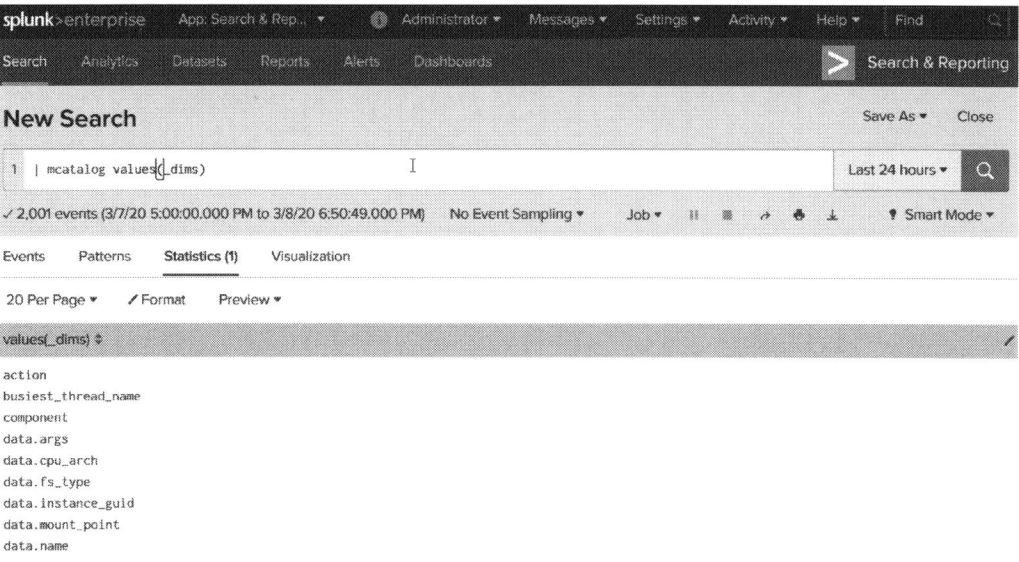

Figure 3.12 – Splunk's New Search page showing our search results

You get the idea. We will now try a few searches aimed at exploring `mstats`.

For example, let's type in the following:

```
| mstats avg(_value) where index=jimssindex AND metric_name=*
earliest=-1h latest=now by source, metric_name
```

Here, we've used the `avg` function to calculate the average value of each metric (`name`) within our new metric index. This orders the results by source and the name of the metric. When you are trying out these commands for yourself, remember to experiment with the time range to see different search results:

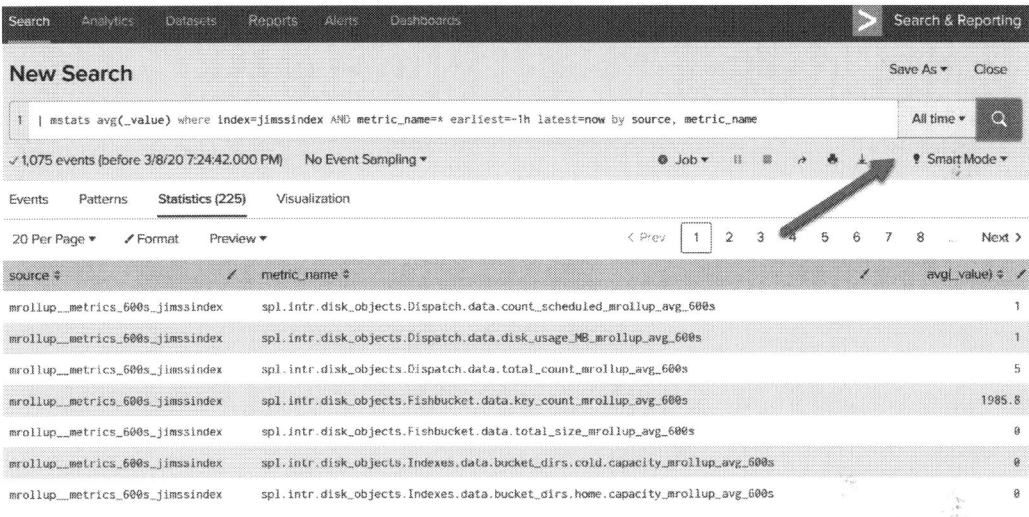

Figure 3.13 – Splunk's New Search page showing our search results

You can also change the aggregation you're using (`avg`) so that you can use others, such as `max` and `min`:

```
| mstats max(_value), Min(_value) where index=* AND metric_
name=* earliest=-1h latest=now by source, metric_name
```

You can even focus on a specific metric name:

```
| mstats avg(spl.intr.disk_objects.Dispatch.data.count_
realtime) WHERE span=30s
```

Alternatively, you can compare two metrics:

```
| mstats avg(spl.intr.disk_objects.Dispatch.data.count_realtime) avg(spl.intr.disk_objects.Dispatch.data.count_scheduled) WHERE BY host span=1m
```

To better understand the results of a metric search, it is always helpful to create a visualization (such as a timechart):

```
| mstats prestats=t count(spl.intr.disk_objects.Dispatch.data.count_realtime) span=1d | timechart span=1d count(spl.intr.disk_objects.Dispatch.data.count_realtime)
```

The following screenshot shows the visualization chart we've created:

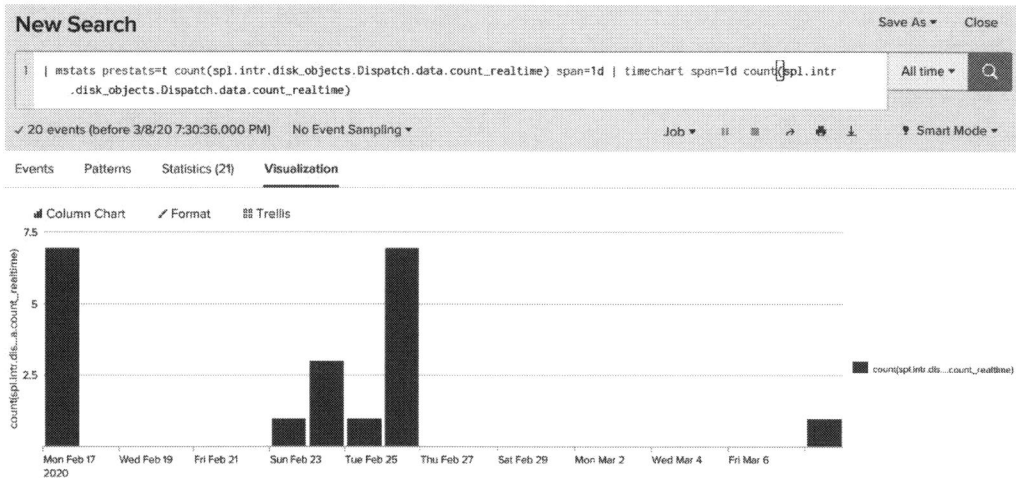

Figure 3.14 – Splunk's New Search page showing the Visualization tab

Finally, the following search uses the `msearch` command to return discrete data points from the `_metrics` index that match a precise filter (enter the search as shown):

```
| msearch index=_metrics filter="group=queue name=indexqueue metric_name=*.current_size"
```

The following screenshot shows the results of our search using `msearch`:

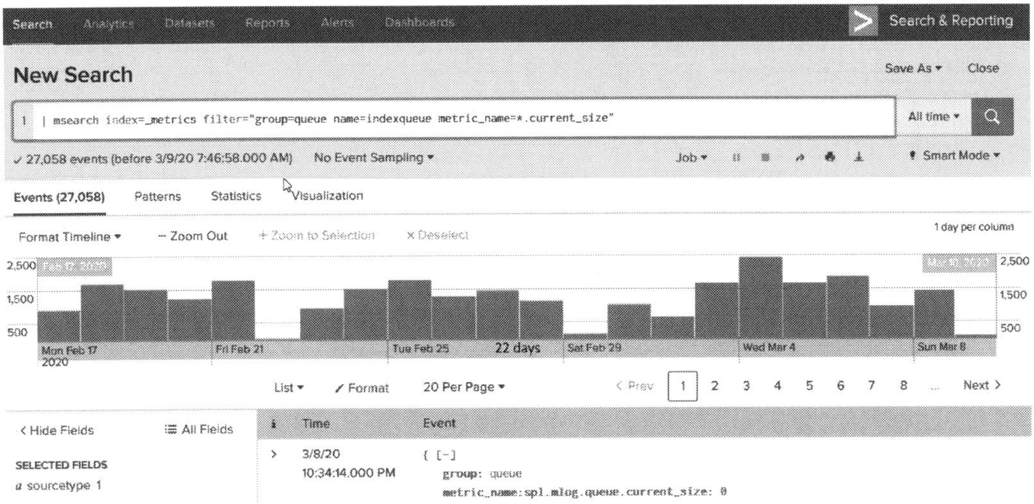

Figure 3.15 – Splunk's New Search page showing the Visualization tab

Now let's see the conversion of Log2Metrics.

Logs2Metrics

In addition to the available metrics data that we've just covered, you will often find that there are other metrics you may be interested in measuring. These typically exist within various unstructured or semi-structured logs.

Splunk can automatically translate this log data into metrics data and then insert that data into a specific metrics index. This conversion of Logs2Metrics can be set up by an administrator so that it occurs at the time the log data is collected (ingested) from the data source, or even at search time (when you want to search it).

The rule of thumb may be to consider if measuring log data is to ultimately become routine (if so, you'd want to set up the conversion so that it occurs upon ingestion) or if it's simply exploratory and you are just in investigation mode. (In this case, you would use the `mcollect` or `meventcollect` commands. These commands convert events data into metric data, thus inserting the metric data points into a specified metric index.)

Performance, Statistics, and Alerting in Splunk

You can only use the `mcollect` command if your role has the `run_mcollect` capability. You can add this capability to an existing role or create a new one using the same steps we covered in an earlier section of this chapter. In the following screenshot, you can see the **Edit Role** dialog being used to add this capability:

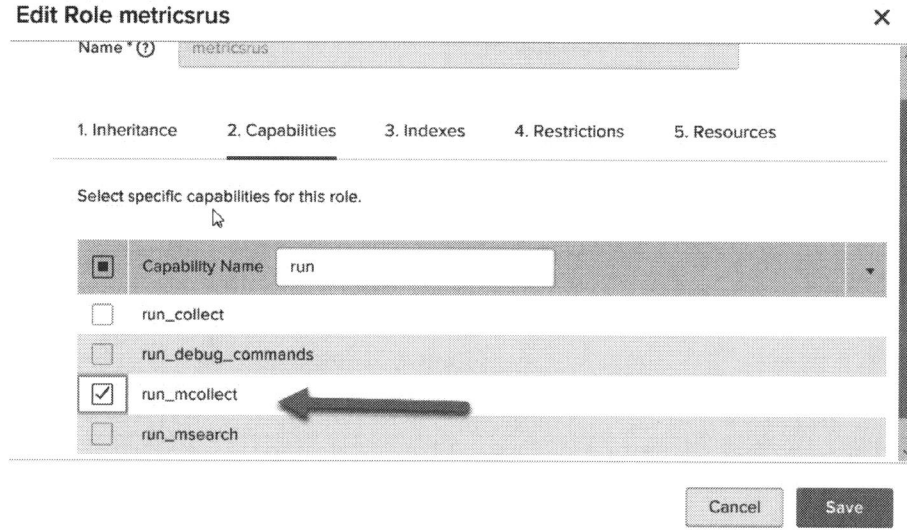

Figure 3.16 – Splunk's Edit Role dialog – Capabilities

Once you have set the capability to use these commands, you can give it a try.

Considering that Splunk stores all of its audit events in the audit index (`index=_audit`), it is reasonable to think that we might want to create a metric on some of that event data, such as the runtimes of jobs that are run in an instance.

In the following example, the search uses `split=true` to automatically convert event fields not otherwise identified as dimensions by `<field-list>` into metric data points.

The search also identifies `user` as a dimension:

```
index="_audit" info=completed
| stats max(total_run_time) as runtime max(event_count) as events by user
| mcollect index=jimssindex split=t user
```

The result is shown in the following screenshot:

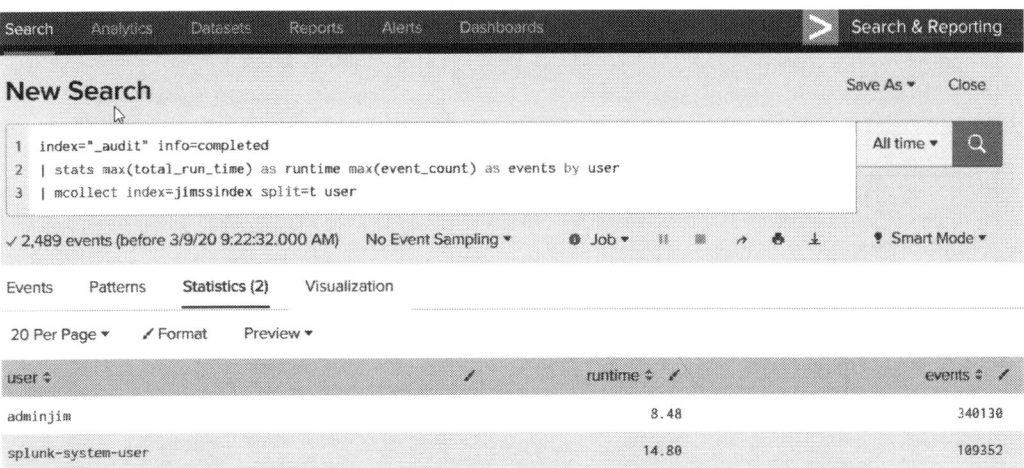

Figure 3.17 – Splunk's New Search page showing our search results

So, in effect, what the preceding command has done is use both the `stats` and `mcollect` commands to convert (unstructured) event data that is stored in the audit event indexer into measurable metric data points. It then writes them into the `jimssindex` metrics indexer so that we can see (and even visualize) the maximum runtimes (shown as **runtime** in the results) for all the jobs that are run by each user. `adminjim` and `splunk-system-user` seem to be the only usernames that have run jobs in this Splunk instance for this time range.

> **Note**
> `splunk-system-user` is the internal Splunk user that all system jobs run as.

Of course, these results show limited data, but in an actual production Splunk instance, there would be many users running many jobs. We might consider setting up this **Logs2Metric** conversion so that it occurs at data ingestion time.

The recommended next steps are for you to become comfortable with the various events where there might be opportunities for converting them into measurable metrics!

Alerting

Now, we'll wrap up this chapter by taking a brief look at the topic of Splunk Alerts. Splunk Alerts are created based upon a previously saved search that searches for events—in real time or on a schedule—and triggers when search results meet specific conditions. By doing this, Splunk Alerts can carry out various alert actions in response to when those alerts trigger.

There are two alert types; that is, **scheduled alerts** and **real-time alerts**. These alert type definitions are based on alert search timing. Depending on the situation, you can configure the timing, triggering, and other behaviors of both alert types.

Scheduled alert illustration

Suppose we want to identify the number of error events that have been recorded by Splunk within the last 24 hours. The following `search` command would achieve this:

```
index=_internal " error " NOT debug source=*splunkd.log*
earliest=-24h latest=now
```

After executing the preceding `search` command, we receive our results, as shown in the following screenshot:

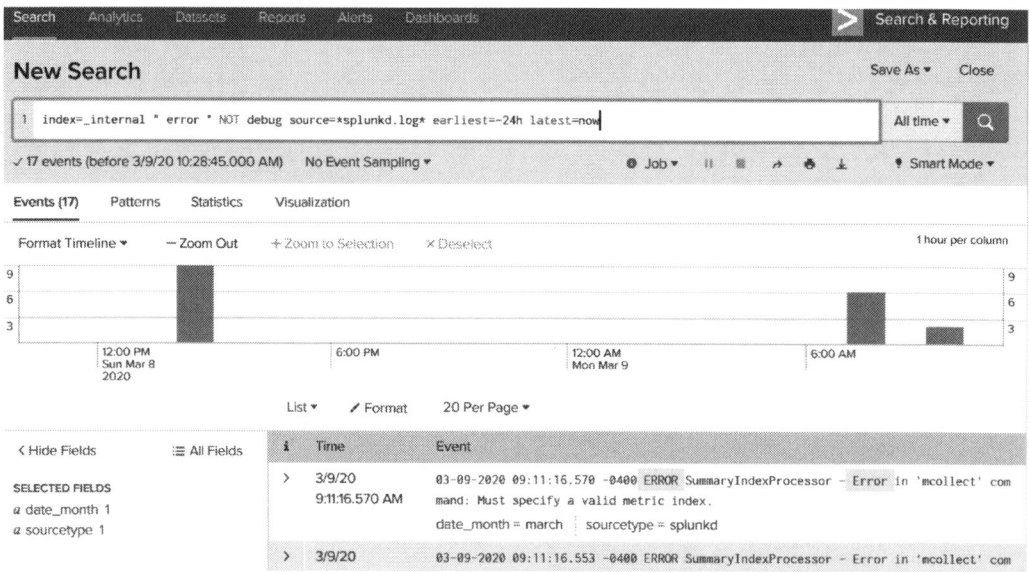

Figure 3.18 – Splunk's New Search page showing our search results

Now that we have a working search, suppose we want to search for these error events on a regular basis and trigger an alert action if the results meet the conditions that we specified (an error event was found). To do that, we can create a scheduled alert based upon our saved search command.

We just created and executed the preceding search, so, from the **Search Page**, click on **Save As** and select **Alert**:

Figure 3.19 – Splunk's New Search page saving a search as an alert

The **Save As Alert** dialog will be displayed. From here, you can set various alert options (you'll have to scroll down):

- **Title**: `Errors in the last 24 hours`
- **Alert type**: **Scheduled**
- Time Range: **Run every day**
- Schedule: **At 10:00**
- **Trigger condition**: **Trigger when number of results > 5**
- The following screenshot shows the preceding options that are listed:

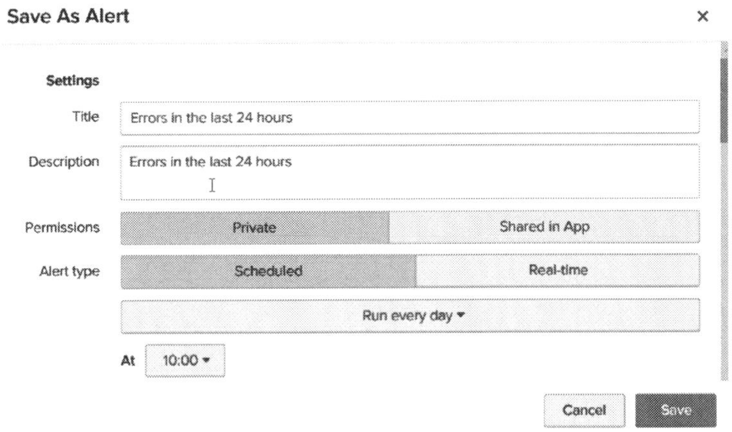

Figure 3.20 – Save As Alert dialog

Now that we have defined the alert settings, along with their trigger conditions, we can set an **Alert Trigger Action** by selecting **Send Email** as the alert action and then setting the required fields:

- **To**: *email recipient*
- **Priority**: **Normal**
- **Subject**: `Too many errors alert: $name$`
- **Message**: `There were $job.resultCount$ errors reported on $trigger_date$ and Include: Link to Alert and Link to Results (you can accept defaults for all other options)`

Finally, click **Save**. With that, we have just created a simple scheduled alert:

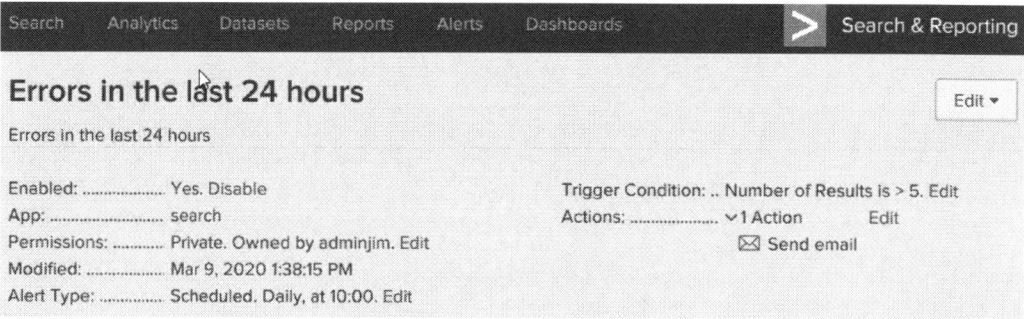

Figure 3.21 – Details of the saved alert

You can view, update, and remove all the alerts you have access to under **Settings** by selecting **Searches, Reports, and Alerts**:

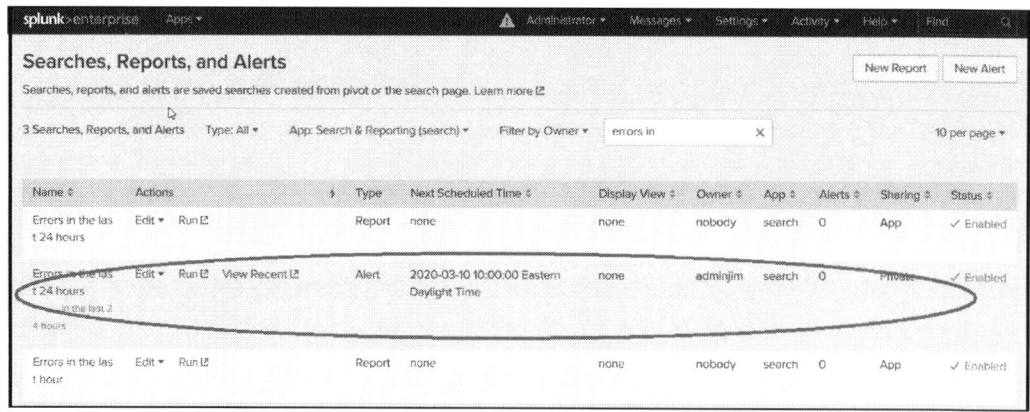

Figure 3.22 - Searches, Reports, and Alerts page showing our new alert

For the alert to run, **Next Scheduled Time** needs to be visible. If the alert conditions are met, you can expect an email.

Summary

In this chapter, we learned about storage as it pertains to the Splunk platform and how the continuous flow of the Splunk data pipeline is used to collect, parse, and index data so that it is ready for use in terms of efficiently searching through index types.

We also talked about indexer types (event and metric), created our own metric index, assigned it as a default index using a new user Splunk role, and then executed some simple metric queries to measure our storage performance. Finally, we saw how event log data can be easily converted into measurable metrics data using the concept of Logs2Metrics and finished up by creating a simple scheduled alert.

In the next chapter, we will cover the Splunk security enhancements that are included in version 8.0, including granular access controls and within-index controls, the latest user interface for roles management, and support for authentication tokens (the REST API and CLI with SAML).

4
Splunk Administration—Security

In the previous chapter, we discussed storage, the continuously flowing Splunk data pipeline, index types (event and metric), roles, and alerts. We also touched on the concept of **Logs2Metrics**.

In this chapter, the emphasis will focus on a review of how Splunk security works, and then point out the security enhancements in Splunk version 8.0, such as **granular access** and **within-index** control concepts, and the **latest interface for Roles management**. We will also touch briefly on authentication and **Authentication Tokens** (REST API and CLI with SAML).

This chapter will be broken down into the following sections:

- Security and security enhancements
- Granular access controls
- Role management
- Authentication

Security and security enhancements

For those readers who have little or no experience of Splunk, we'll begin this chapter with a general briefing on Splunk security.

You can administer Splunk security in Splunk Web from the main Splunk page by clicking on **Settings**. Under **Settings**, you will see the heading **Users and authentication**, which will list the following:

- **Roles**
- **Users**
- **Tokens**
- **Password Management**
- **Authentication Methods**

Roles

The concept of roles means the ability to manage permissions and capabilities of pretty much everything in most enterprise software applications. This concept is also used in Splunk security as well. You assign a role (or multiple roles) to each user in the system to determine the level of access that the user will have within the Splunk platform as well as each task that they can perform. Splunk comes with a set of default roles that you can use, and you can also create your own custom roles tailored to meet your specific requirements.

The default Splunk roles are as follows:

- **admin**: This role has the most capabilities.
- **power**: This role can edit all shared objects and alerts, tag events, and perform similar tasks.
- **user**: This role can create and edit its own saved searches, run searches, edit its own preferences, create and edit event types, and perform similar tasks.
- **can_delete**: This role allows deletion by keyword.

> Note
> The Splunk **can_delete** role only has the delete permission and this role should not normally be assigned to anyone.

Roles are typically set up to comprise many capabilities, providing access to specific parts of the Splunk platform, creating a profile that a user can easily be assigned to, rather than having to assign each of the capabilities to every new user that fits the profile. Each user that has a role assigned to them will have all of the capabilities that are associated with that role.

> **Information**
> The definition and management of roles can be simplistic or complex. The product documentation offers best practice tips and hints that should be reviewed and understood before creating new roles (or modifying existing ones). This information is available online at `https://docs.splunk.com/Documentation/CoE/ssf/Handbook/RolesResponsibilities`.

We will revisit the subject of roles in more detail a bit later in this chapter.

Users

Users are most easily added to Splunk from the main page by clicking **Settings**, and then **Users**. The **Create User** dialog requires you to provide a (user) **name** and **password** and a **role** (all Splunk users must be given at least one role). There are also optional fields available (**email address, default app** and **time zone**) that can add usability to the user. By default, Splunk assigns a new user the **user** role.

Tokens

(Authentication) tokens were added in version 7.3 and are a way of providing access to Splunk through the **Representational State Transfer** (**REST**) and the Splunk **Command-Line Interface** (**CLI**), without having to code or provide the standard types of credentials.

For example, rather than providing a (user) name and password, you can provide a token.

> **Hint**
> Tokens are *not usable* for gaining access to Splunk through the web interface.

Keep in mind that these tokens are credentials, so it is important that you *treat them securely*. To create and use authentication tokens, you must enable the functionality (from the main Splunk page, under **Settings**). As shown in the following screenshot, the **Token Settings** dialog allows you to change the **Default Expiration** (from **never**) as well as disable all of the tokens, should you need to:

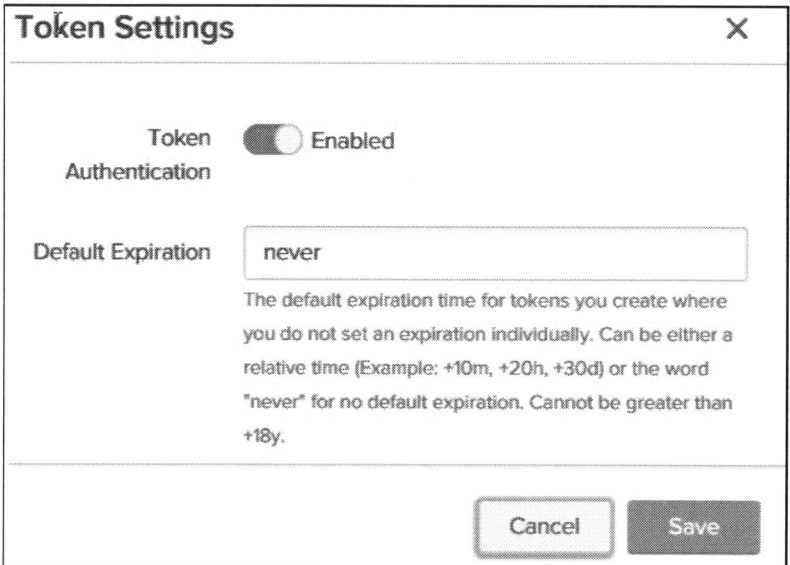

Figure 4.1 – Token Settings dialogue box

Creating a new token

If you are a Splunk administrator, you can go to the Splunk main page and click on **Settings**, followed by **Tokens**. From the **Tokens** page, you can click on **New Token**:

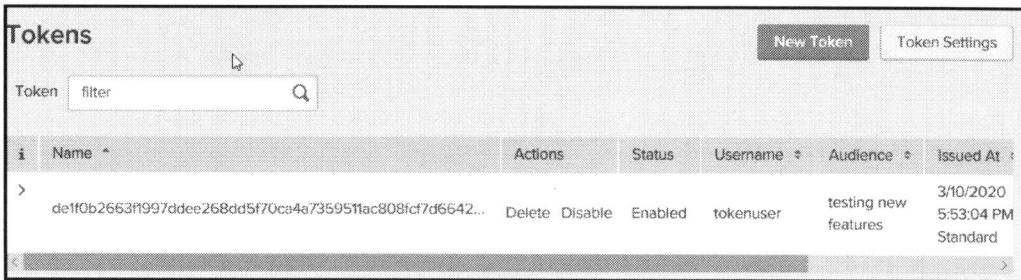

Figure 4.2 – New Token

From the **New Token** dialog (shown in the following screenshot), you can set the required token properties:

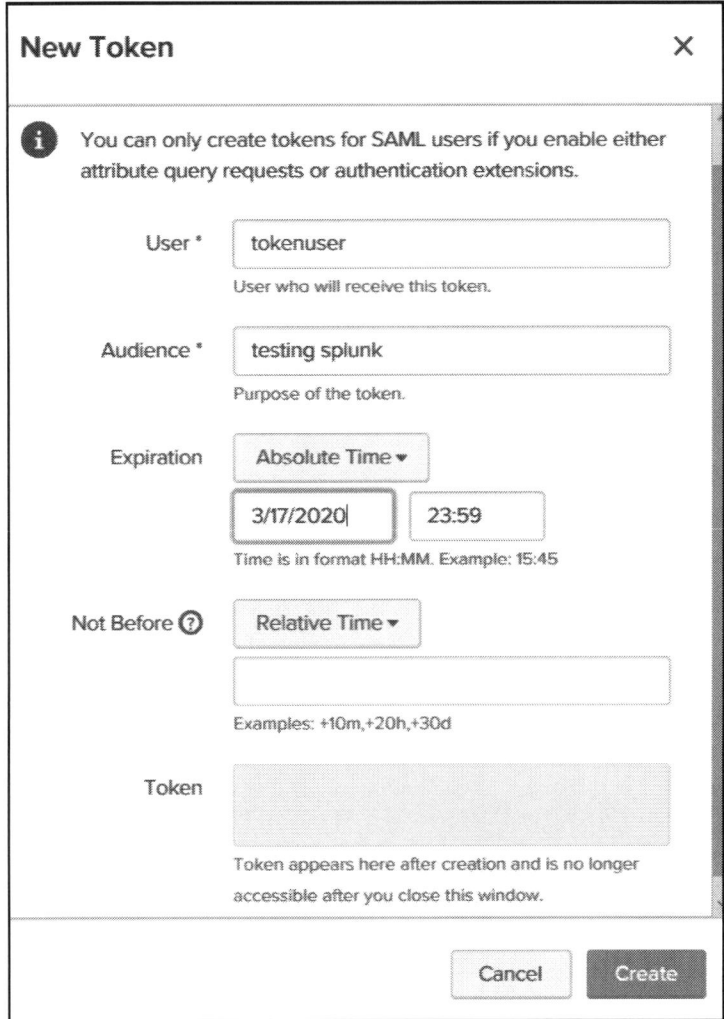

Figure 4.3 – Selecting properties under New Token

These properties (on the **New Token** dialog) are as follows:

- **User** (name) to receive (can use) the token. The user must already exist in Splunk.
- (Token) **Audience**, which is simply a label that indicates the token's purpose.
- **Expiration/Not Before**, which is how long the token will be valid for – when the user can start using it and when it expires.

Once you click **Create**, the token is generated, and you will be able to see it within the **Token** space (as shown in the following screenshot):

Figure 4.4 – A generated token

In the next section, we will discuss using tokens.

Using tokens

As mentioned earlier, you would use authentication tokens to simplify authentication when using the Splunk CLI (and REST). The Splunk CLI is the text-based interface to Splunk where you enter commands to run searches (and perform other tasks).

To run CLI commands in Splunk on an MS Windows platform, you use PowerShell or Command Prompt as an administrator. For a quick illustration, if you attempt to run a simple Splunk search using the CLI, Splunk will prompt you for a username and password:

```
PS C:\Program Files\Splunk\bin> ./splunk search '*'
Splunk username: adminjim
Password:
```

Once supplied, the search runs, and its output is as shown in the following screenshot:

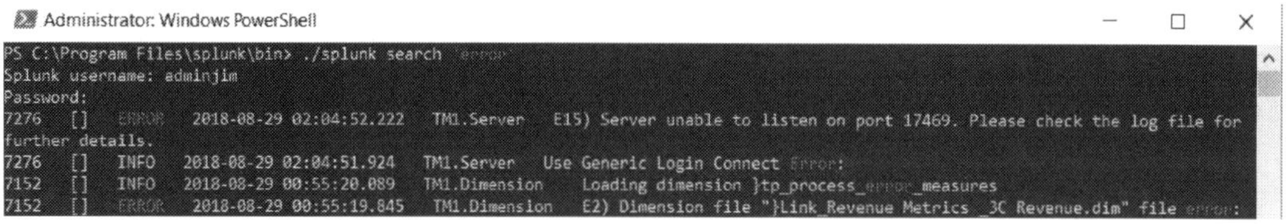

Figure 4.5 – Generated output

Using an established, valid Splunk token, the CLI command syntax would be as follows:

```
splunk search '*' -token <token>
```

Password management

Once users have been set up within Splunk with a proper password, those individuals can always access their account and change their password themselves (administrators are also able to reset any user passwords as well).

Password policy

If you are using Splunk native security (or **Splunk Authentication** as it is called in WebUI) and not **SAML** or **LDAP**, then you should set a **Password Policy**. Password policies are used to determine the standards and minimum requirements for all Splunk passwords.

To access and edit the Splunk password policy, an administrator can—from the Splunk main page—go to **Settings**, and then **Password Management**:

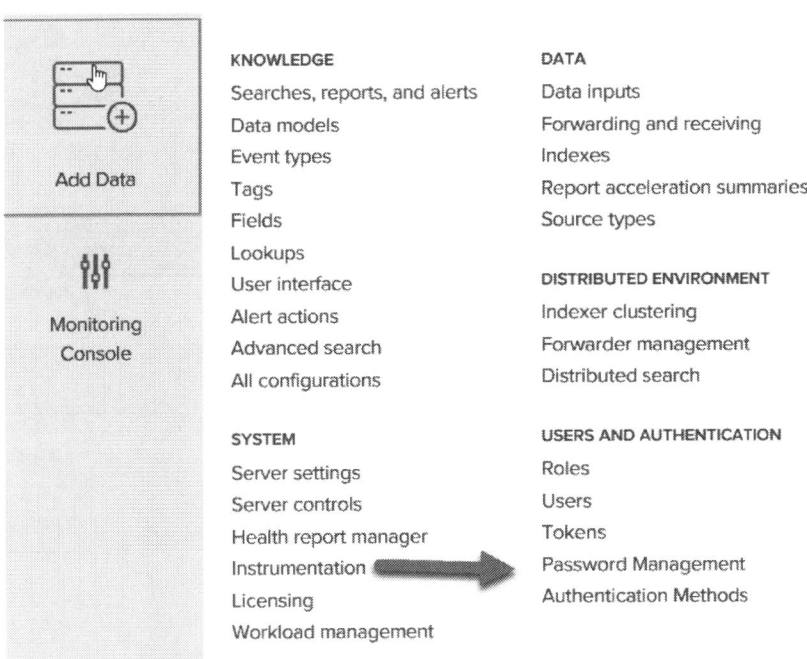

Figure 4.6 – Editing Splunk's password policy

From the **Password Policy Management** page (the top half of the page is shown in the following screenshot), an administrator can create and update the password policy used by Splunk instances:

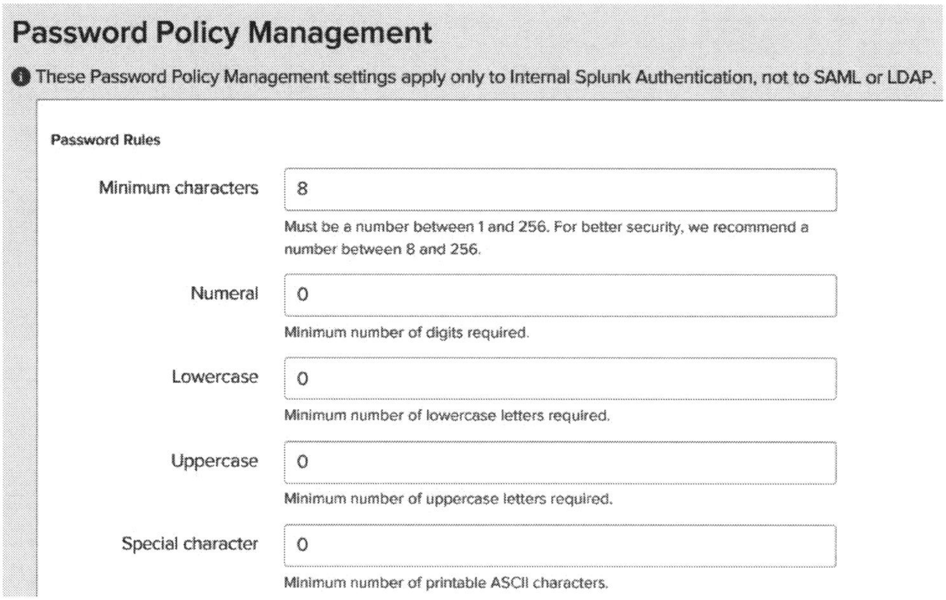

Password Policy Management

ⓘ These Password Policy Management settings apply only to Internal Splunk Authentication, not to SAML or LDAP.

Password Rules

Minimum characters: 8
Must be a number between 1 and 256. For better security, we recommend a number between 8 and 256.

Numeral: 0
Minimum number of digits required.

Lowercase: 0
Minimum number of lowercase letters required.

Uppercase: 0
Minimum number of uppercase letters required.

Special character: 0
Minimum number of printable ASCII characters.

Figure 4.7 – Password Policy Management

Splunk password policies are used to define the standards (as well as the minimum requirements) for passwords and login/lockout rules. The password policy changes are applied to the **Set Password** field on the **Create User** page.

> **Information**
>
> To see the complete list of parameters that make up the Splunk password policy, you can visit the product documentation online at `https://docs.splunk.com/Documentation/Splunk/8.0.2/Security/Configurepasswords`.

In the next section, we will discuss the implementation of Splunk security at a much more detailed level as well as an index within an index.

Granular access controls

A role-based Splunk security strategy provides an extremely flexible and effective security model that can be used to secure all data accessed via Splunk.

Splunk can hide data from users like any other RDMS that utilizes roles would but, in addition, Splunk offers additional layers of optional security that can be used to either further secure information or to provide ways to more easily manage security.

Having a thorough understanding and consideration of each applicable use case is a perquisite to implementing security in Splunk. That said, the good news is that you can certainly get started with a simple security design and build as you go since the Splunk architecture is very flexible.

For example, a single Splunk instance with admin and user roles may suffice initially, should there be a limited number of non-discretions required data sources. In other words, if you have access to Splunk, you have access to all data and control is only set for limiting administration to just a few key users.

Of course, the next step might be to control searches and results at the presentation layer (through a variety of methods) or even create total segmentations of data (usually done when the data is extremely sensitive or there are legal requirements in terms of accessing the data).

So, how secure must your data be? Typically, sort your needs into the following categories:

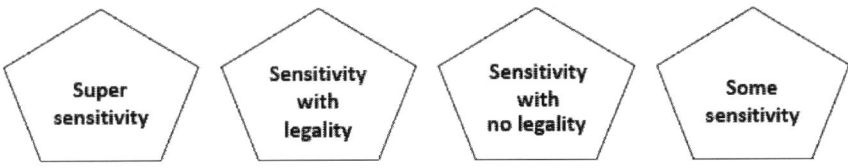

Figure 4.8 – The four categories

Super sensitivity

For environments where there is super sensitivity to data, you may want to consider actually having multiple instances of Splunk, with each instance accessing *only the data* for the appropriate audience.

This approach is not to be confused with a distributed deployment where each Splunk instance performs a specialized task and resides on one of three processing tiers corresponding to the main processing function.

Sensitivity with legality

If the data has super sensitivity and there are also potential *legal ramifications around exposing data*, then consider *creating indexes specifically* for privileged and non-privileged accounts and assigning them to roles created for each level of access.

We touched on the types of Splunk indexes and how to create and manage them in *Chapter 3, Performance, Statistics, and Alerting*. In that discussion, we were interested in the process of creating a metric index.

In this chapter, we are focusing on security and creating a separate event index that sources data based on (the data) sensitivity and managing the index so that it is only available to a particular role or group of roles.

Sensitivity with no legality

When there is **sensitivity** to the data, but there are **no legal concerns**, restrictions can be implemented using Splunk apps and static objects (such as dashboards or reports) and then assigning roles to only those apps. This method restricts data within the app and/or dashboard or report. It also relies on the administrator establishing access to the correct apps, dashboards, and/or reports, role by role.

A Splunk app is (of course) an application that runs on the Splunk platform and typically addresses a specific or unique need. An app will contain one or more views and numerous knowledge objects that are focused on a particular requirement. A Splunk app can easily be set up to only access a certain index or provide only filtered, and perhaps static, views of only appropriate data.

> **Information**
>
> Splunk knowledge objects are defined as a user-defined entity that enriches the existing data in Splunk. Splunk knowledge objects include saved searches, event types, tags, field extractions, lookups, reports, alerts, data models, transactions, workflow actions, and fields: `https://docs.splunk.com/Splexicon:Knowledgeobject`.

Some sensitivity

Finally, if there is only some sensitivity in terms of the data accessed by Splunk, then you may potentially meet your security needs through the use of **field encryptions** (optional feature), **search exclusions**, and **field aliasing**.

Field encryption or **obfuscation** can be accomplished via Splunk masking, which means simply replacing sensitive data strings with a mask, thereby preventing users from seeing through to the underlying real data, while search exclusions are a means of actually excluding certain data from a search result, and field aliasing can also be used to reduce exposure to certain information by providing alternate naming for selected fields.

Role management

Although Splunk users can log in to Splunk, they themselves *cannot have permissions and capabilities assigned to them directly*. Without roles, users wouldn't be able to do anything once they log in (actually, users must have at least one role assigned to them, most likely a new user would have the default role of user, which provides basic functionalities).

Roles (typically a Splunk user will have more than one role assigned to them) are used to *define how users* can interact with Splunk. As we've already mentioned, Splunk roles allow easy and efficient management of access to resources in Splunk.

You can assign roles to users to control the following:

- The scope of the tasks that they can perform (but you cannot use a role to exclude a task)
- The data that can be searched
- A limit in terms of the resources they can access on the platform

Permission granularity and customized roles

Along with the Splunk default roles (**admin**, **power**, **user** and **can_delete**), you can create customized roles to assign to your Splunk users. These customized roles allow you to make granular adjustments to control what resources users can access.

You can create and manage any roles, including the predefined ones, by either using Splunk Web or by editing directly the Splunk `authorize.conf` configuration file.

> **Note**
>
> If you are so inclined, you can add or modify Splunk roles by editing the local (`$SPLUNK_HOME/etc/system/local/`) version of the Splunk `authorize.conf` file and then restarting Splunk: https://docs.splunk.com/Documentation/Splunk/8.0.2/Security/Addandeditroleswithauthorizeconf
>
> Whenever you are making changes to the Splunk `authorize.conf` configuration file, you must perform a reload authentication configuration to have the changes take effect.

Reloading authentication configuration using Splunk Web

Form the Splunk main page, click on **Settings**, then **Authentication Methods**, and then click **Reload authentication configuration**. This will refresh the authentication caches, but will not disconnect current users:

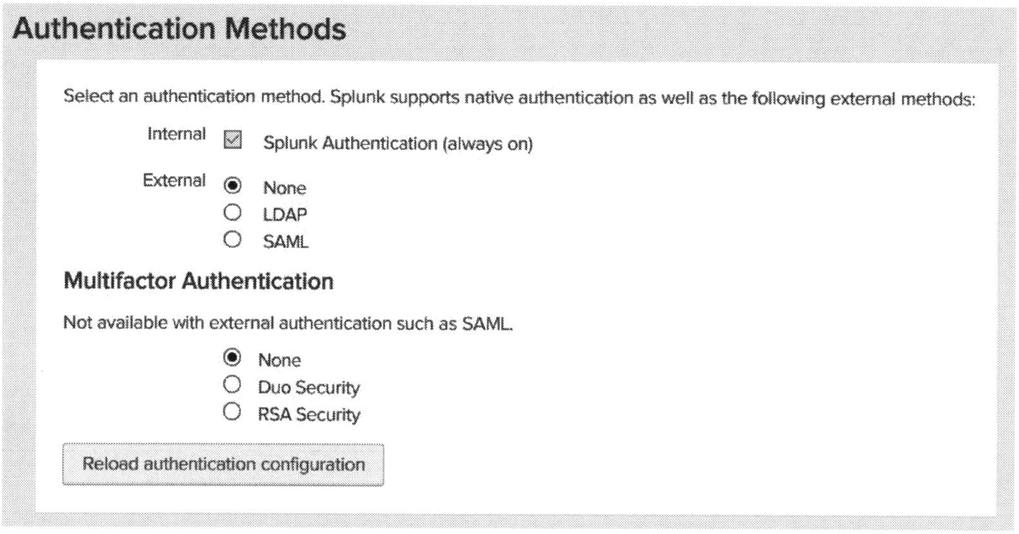

Figure 4.9 – Authentication methods

Reloading authentication configuration using the Splunk CLI

To reload authentication configurations using the Splunk CLI, you can perform the following steps:

1. On the Splunk instance where you want to reload authentication, open a shell prompt or PowerShell window.
2. Switch to the `$SPLUNK_HOME/bin` directory.
3. Use the CLI `./splunk reload auth` command (as shown in the following screenshot):

Figure 4.10 – Using the Splunk CLI to perform an authentication configuration reload

When setting up a new custom role, it is advisable (but not required) to leverage existing role capabilities though role capability inheritance. If you are using Splunk Web, this is easy—from the Splunk main page, click on **Settings**, then **Roles**, and then **New Role.**

In the next section, we will take a look at the detailed steps for configuring a new custom role.

Inheritance

From the **New Role** page, Splunk offers the new role workflow—steps 1 to 5—with step 1 being **Inheritance**:

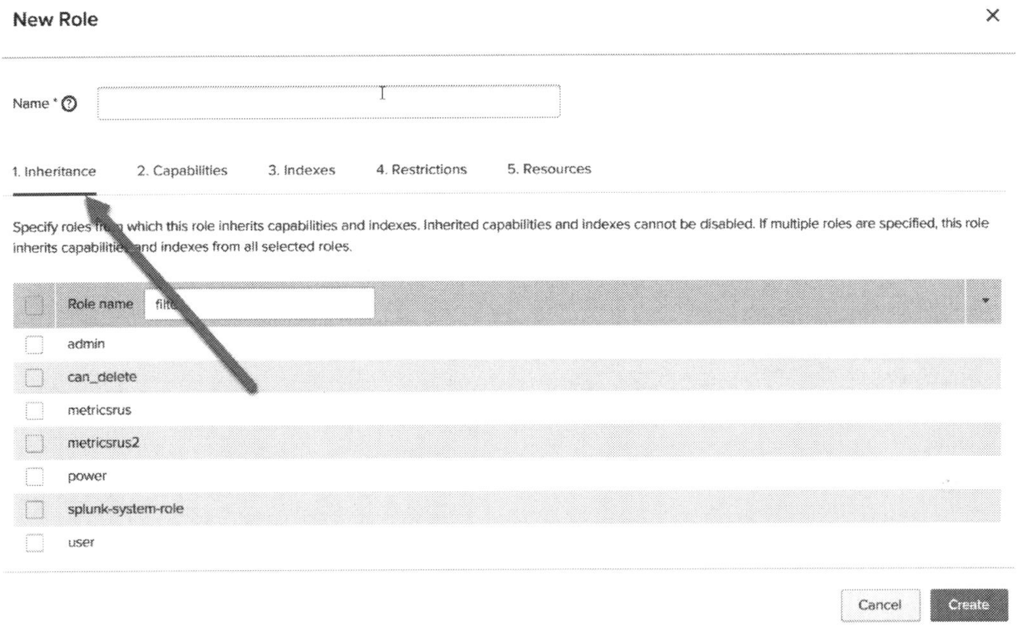

Figure 4.11 – New Role – Inheritance

90 Splunk Administration—Security

To have the new customized role inherit from an existing role, simply scroll through the existing roles and check the role (or roles) that you want to have this new role inherit form. For example, if I want my new customized role to be able to edit all shared objects (saved searches) and alerts, tag events, and other similar tasks, I can check next to the default role, **power**. In addition, I want this role to be able to search our metric index (that we set up in the previous chapter), so we click the checkbox next to the role name **metricsrus**:

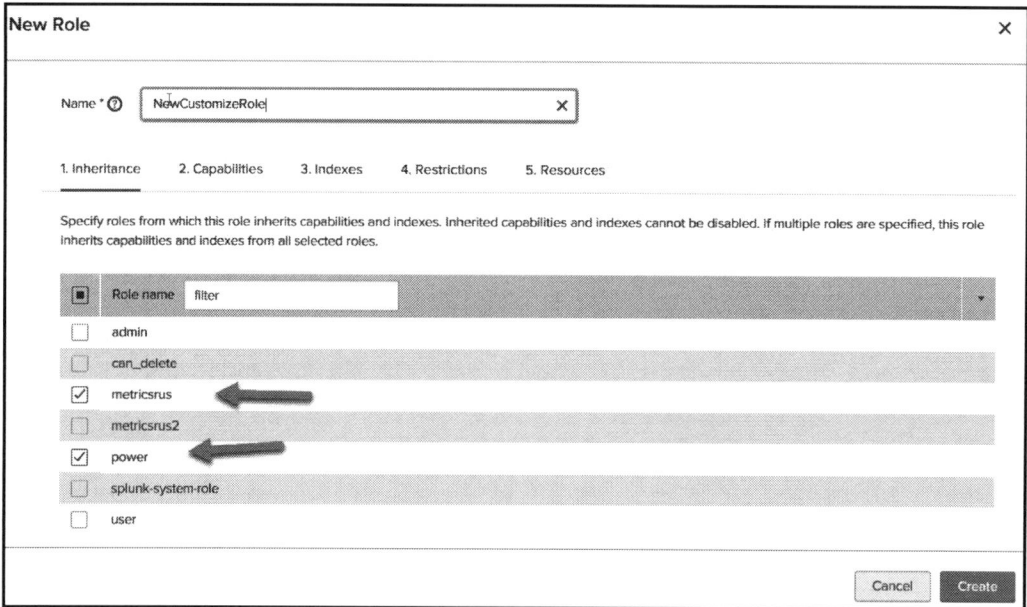

Figure 4.12 – The metricsrus role

Now, we have set our new role to have both the capabilities of the power role and the **metricsrus** role.

Capabilities

If we click on the next step in the new role workflow (**Capabilities**), we can examine each capability available to our new role. Similar to the prior (**Inheritance**) view, you can scroll through all available capabilities and specify which actions this role can perform. Notice that every capability that is being inherited is marked:

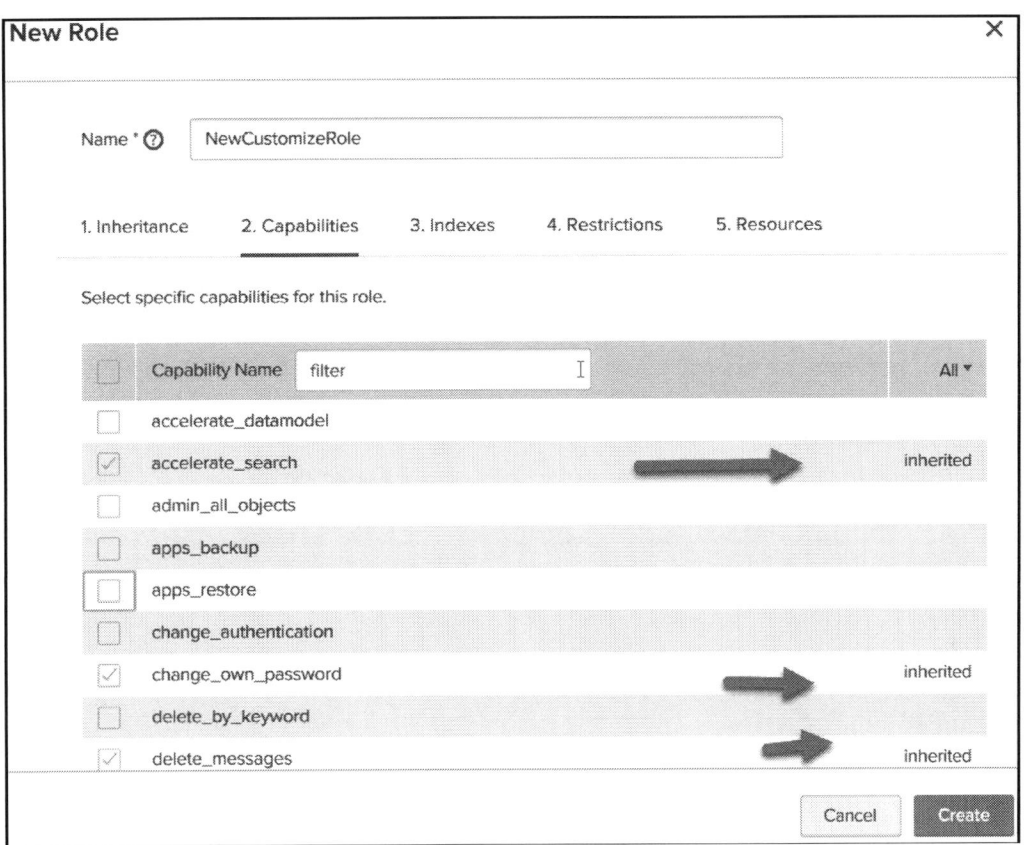

Figure 4.13 – New Role – Capabilities

Indexes

The next step is **Indexes**. Here, you can select each indexer that you want to be searchable for this role. You also set which index Splunk searches as its default index(s):

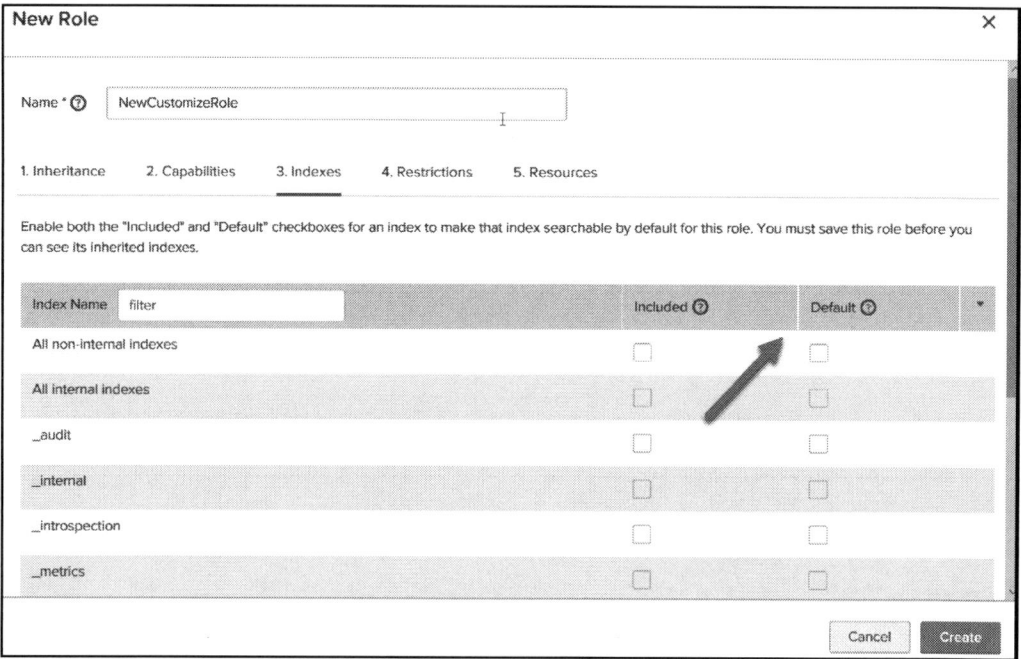

Figure 4.14 – New Role – Indexes

> **Note**
> When creating a new customized role, this view will not initially show any indexes as checked or selected. You have to save the role first before you can see its inherited indexes.

The following screenshot shows indexes checked. This view was obtained *after* the new role was created:

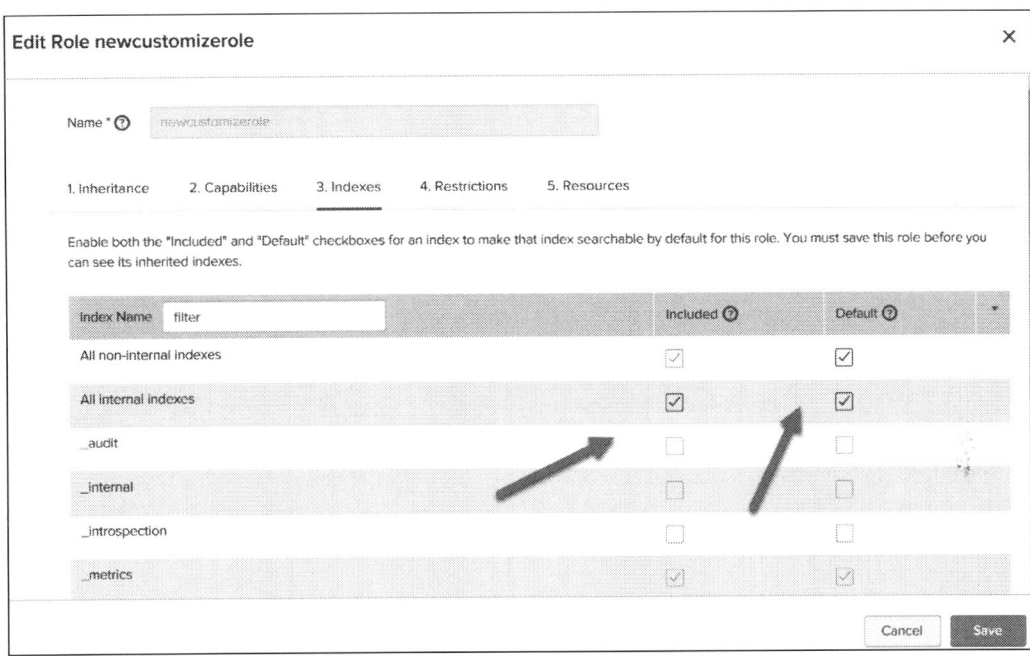

Figure 4.15 – Indexes checked after a new role has been created

Restrictions

Restrictions is the next step in the new role workflow. In addition to specifying which indexers are searchable for the role (set in the prior workflow step), you can also stipulate a search filter that limits what is visible in the search results for this role. For example, you can enter an SPL query or use the **SPL Search filter** generator on the **Restrictions** view to construct a restriction for this role:

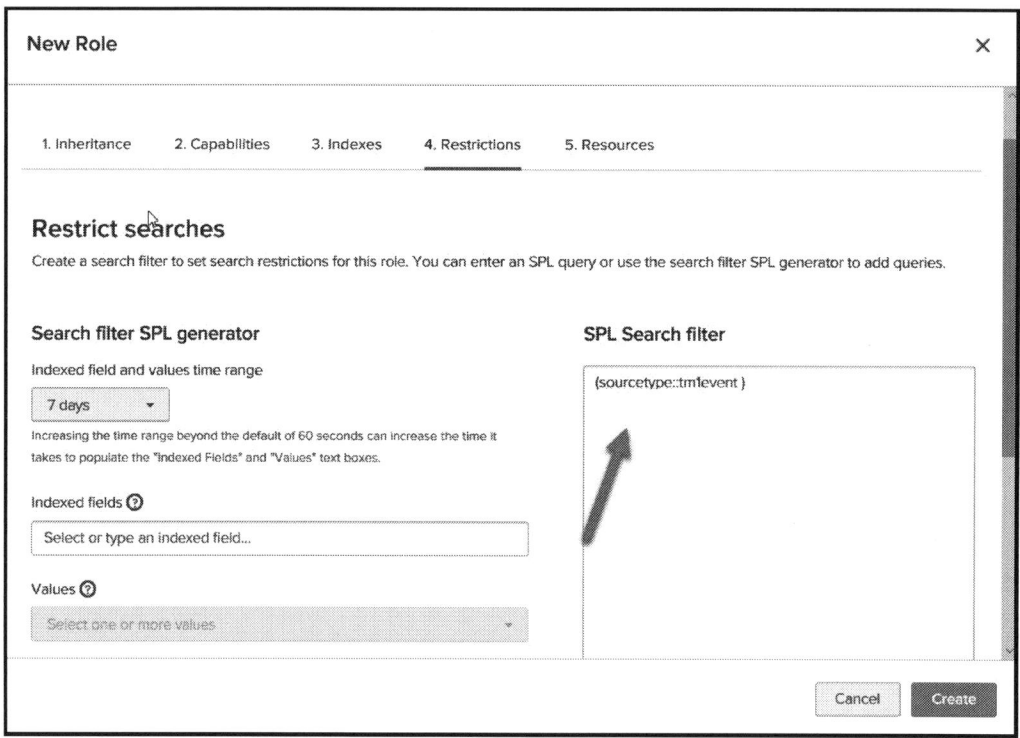

Figure 4.16 – New Role – Restrictions

In the preceding example, I am showing an **SPL Search filter** of (`sourcetype::tm1event`), which will limit this role to returning only results from the `sourcetype` of `tm1event`. If you are unsure about the restriction, Splunk provides the ability to preview the results. Clicking on **Preview search filter results** (from this view) will take you to the search page and run the query for you. This allows you to ensure that your restriction is correct and makes sense before you proceed to the next step in creating the new customized role:

Figure 4.17 – Preview search filter results

With the Splunk **Role Search filter** generator, you can create very complex search filters without concern for syntax and, as already mentioned, the preview search filter provides a chance to see what the search with this filter applied will look like, so that you can be 100% confident the role will provide the search results expected.

Resources

From an administration perspective, the **Resources** view might be the most important. In this view, you can control the number of standard and real-time searches (under **Role search job limit**) that this role can run at any one time, as well as individual limits for the role (under **User search job limit**). Finally, you can even restrict when the role can search jobs (under **Role search time window limit**), and how much disk space is available for search jobs that this role creates (under **Disk space limit**):

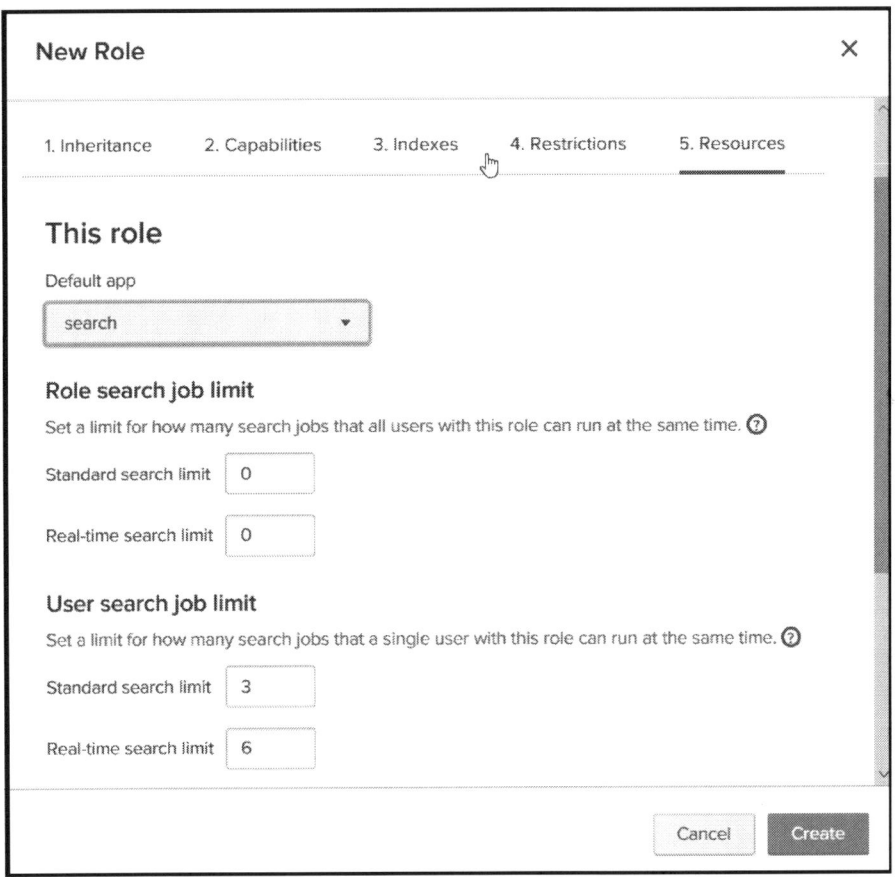

Figure 4.18 – New Role

More on inheritance

From the Splunk Web main page, you can click on **Settings**, and then **Roles**, to see the **Splunk Roles** page (as shown in the following screenshot):

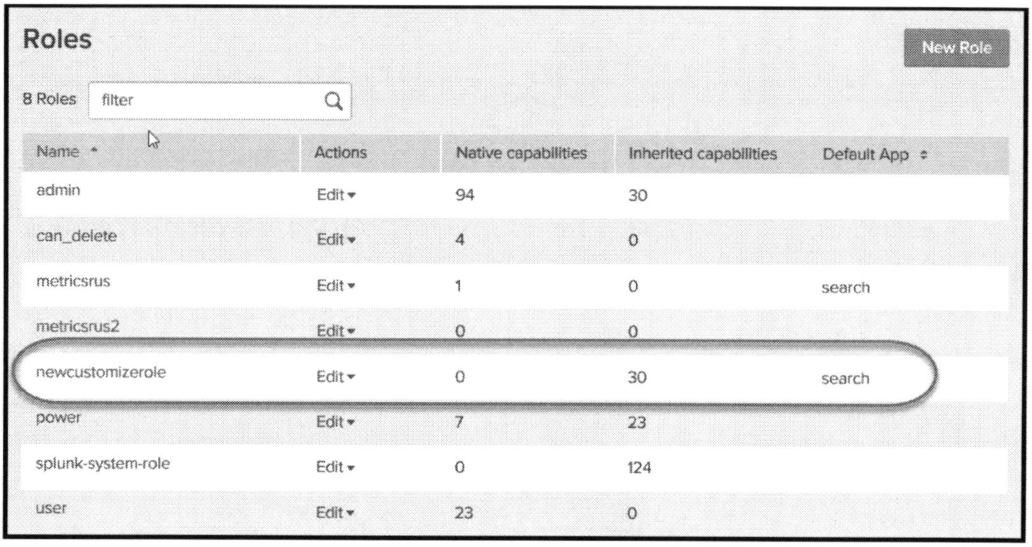

Name	Actions	Native capabilities	Inherited capabilities	Default App
admin	Edit ▼	94	30	
can_delete	Edit ▼	4	0	
metricsrus	Edit ▼	1	0	search
metricsrus2	Edit ▼	0	0	
newcustomizerole	Edit ▼	0	30	search
power	Edit ▼	7	23	
splunk-system-role	Edit ▼	0	124	
user	Edit ▼	23	0	

Figure 4.19 – Customized role

On this page, you can see the customized role we created (`newcustomizerole`) and we can also see the following information—**Native capabilities**, **Inherited capabilities**, and the **Default App** (for the roles). Notice that this role has a total of 30 inherited capabilities (based upon how we selected both the `power` and `metricsrus` roles).

A number of additional points regarding inheritance that the product documentation suggests reviewing are the following:

- Roles cannot be used to take away access; they only allow access.
- Users who are assigned to multiple roles inherit the permissions and capabilities of the role that has the most wide-ranging permissions. Be particularly careful with indexes. If you combine roles that have access to only specific indexes with a role that has **All non-internal indexes** or **All internal indexes** checked, the role with **All** checked will override and the role will end up with access to all indexers.
- Roles that have more permissions will supersede roles that have fewer permissions. Be super cautious when inheriting from roles such as **Admin**.

- If you want to limit a role's resources, you should create and assign roles that specifically set those limits, and do not let those roles inherit from roles that do not establish those limits.
- If a user is assigned roles with different search filters, Splunk combines the filters and applies the restrictions of each search filter.

Authentication

Splunk internal authentication (or native authentication) allows you to set up users and roles within Splunk (using Splunk Web or by editing the Splunk configuration files), which we've hopefully covered sufficiently within this chapter.

Authentication methods

In addition to native/internal, Splunk currently supports the following (considered the *typical* approaches) user authentication methods:

- External – LDAP or SAML
- Multifactor authentication
- Single sign-on

Even if additional methods are implemented, Splunk native is *always running* and will take precedence, meaning that upon a login attempt, Splunk attempts native authentication first.

External authentication

If an external authentication method (such as LDAP) has been enabled and, upon a login attempt, a native/local user (in other words, a Splunk user) *does not exist*, Splunk will then attempt an external authentication (meaning Splunk will try to authenticate the user using the external method).

Multifactor authentication

Multifactor authentication allows you to configure both a primary and secondary login for Splunk users. You can configure multifactor authentication using RSA Authentication Manager (for Splunk Web) or Two-Factor (DUO) authentication.

> **Hint**
>
> For more information on multifactor authentication, see `https://docs.splunk.com/Documentation/Splunk/8.0.2/Security/AboutRSAMultiFactorAuth`.

Single sign-on

Single sign-on (**SSO**) is a methodology that allows applications to use other, trusted sites to verify users. This means that there is no need to maintain user credentials in multiple locations. You can configure Splunk to use SAML authentication for SSO, using information provided by the identity provider you are using.

> **Hint**
>
> For more information on Splunk and SSO, including currently supported providers, see `https://docs.splunk.com/Documentation/Splunk/8.0.2/Security/HowSAMLSSOworks`.

Summary

In this chapter, we started off by providing information on how Splunk security works in general, covering roles, users, tokens, password polices, and management, and then discussed the layers of security, illustrating techniques that Splunk offers to provide the most granular access, including through search restrictions and within indexers. Finally, we concluded by mentioning the various authentication methods supported by Splunk and the precedence each holds.

In the next chapter, we will delve into advanced indexing, index clustering, the high availability of data, and disaster recovery.

5
Advanced Indexing

In the previous chapter, we focused on a review of how Splunk security works, and then pointed out the security enhancements in Splunk version 8.0. We also touched briefly on authentication and authentication tokens.

In this chapter, the discussion concentrates on developing an understanding of how Splunk **index clustering** works and the way it supports **High Availability** (**HA**) as well as **Disaster Recovery** (**DR**) in Splunk instances and indexed data.

This chapter will be broken down into the following main sections:

- Splunk deployment basics
- Understanding index clustering and replication
- Disaster recovery sites
- Special multi-site configurations – the site replication factor

Splunk deployment basics

In *Chapter 1, Overview of Splunk*, we explained that Splunk uses indexes (rather than a database) to access data sourced from almost anywhere, including data from websites, applications, servers, databases, operating systems, and more. A Splunk index is considered to be the **storehouse** used for storing data in Splunk and Splunk transforms incoming data into events and then stores it in those storehouses (indexes).

For smaller deployments, you typically start off with a single installation of Splunk with it performing all of the indexing of data, but also data input and search management, among other tasks. In this scenario, the same instance of Splunk performs indexing, forwarding, and searching. A single Splunk instance can have multiple indexes, perhaps each indexing from different data sources.

In a larger, or a *distributed*, Splunk deployment, you will often see the job of inputting data and search management assigned to separate Splunk **components**.

When you deploy separate instances of Splunk, each aimed to perform only a specific Splunk task, you create **specialized Splunk instances**. These *specialized instances* most likely will be on separate machines, or **Virtual Machines** (**VMs**). This type of deployment architecture helps with availability and concurrency issues. Each of these specialized instances are called **components**.

> Terminology check
>
> A Splunk component is a Splunk instance that performs a specialized task, such as indexing data. There are several types of components, to match the types of tasks in a deployment. Components fall into two broad categories: processing components and management components. A Splunk node is a Splunk instance grouped as a member of an indexer cluster and designated as the cluster's **master node**, **peer node**, or **search head**.

In the evolution from a smaller Splunk environment to a medium-sized deployment, you typically will need to increase both indexing and search capacities. For indexing, you can add additional indexers. For search, you can add search heads to service more users and provide more search activity.

Understanding index clustering and replication

As we've stated, Splunk stores its data in *indexes*, not **structured databases**, and indexes are nothing more than a group of subdirectories (called buckets) that hold both raw data files and index files.

Understanding index clustering and replication

After data has been added to an index, it cannot be updated in any way. You can, however (based on policy), perform the following actions:

- Delete all data (in that index).
- Delete individual index buckets.
- Archive individual index buckets.

In addition to the Splunk *preconfigured* indexes (which are **main**, **internal**, and **audit**), as an administrator, you can *create new* indexes, *edit* index *properties*, *remove indexes*, and *relocate* indexes. Administrators can perform these administrative tasks using **Splunk Web**, the **command-line interface**, as well as with configuration files (such as `indexes.conf`).

Another important ability that the Splunk administrator has is the ability to create **index clusters** (also known as **index replication**).

An **indexer cluster** is a *group* (or collection) of **indexers** configured to replicate (duplicate) each other's data, so that Splunk maintains duplicate copies of all data, thus preventing data loss and promoting **high (data) availability**.

If you have a designated set of nodes configured to work as a group to provide redundant indexing and search abilities, you have an *indexer cluster*.

The three types of nodes found in an index cluster are the following:

- The **master node**, which manages the nodes in the cluster
- Multiple **peer nodes**, which do the indexing work in the cluster
- At least one **search head node** to manage the searching

Splunk index clusters use what is called **automatic failover**, in that if one peer node fails for some reason, the next peer node in the cluster still indexes the data.

If there is a *peer failure*, the previously defined replication will ensure that all data coming in will get *indexed* and all indexed data continues to be *searchable*.

Just like with any other mission-critical application or database software, availability and disaster recovery planning are important with Splunk. Proper index clustering/replication is key in an effort to provide the highest resiliency to both the data and the functionality of the Splunk software:

- Index clustering supports **data availability** by making sure the already indexed data isn't lost, as well as ensuring that there is always an indexer available to index incoming data.
- Index clustering supports **data fidelity**, perhaps a new term, meaning that already indexed data *does not change*. This ensures that the data *sent to the cluster* is precisely the same when *stored in the cluster* and is available to be searched.
- Index clustering supports **data recovery**, meaning that the Splunk instance can endure index failures without data loss occurring.

In addition, in a multi-site environment, cross-site index clustering can be the epitome of proper **disaster recovery planning**. Obviously, if an entire data center is lost, having indexers and data copies in a separate, alternate location will allow Splunk to continue to operate and keep users happy.

Finally, index clustering supports **search affinity**. This means that a search head can access all of the data through their own site, which reduces long-distance trafficking over a network.

The cost of an encompassing Splunk index clustering schema is literally the cost of adding additional *storage* (and to some degree, some additional processing load while performing **replication activity**).

Since storage costs are relatively low, making the decision to create the appropriate index clustering/replication for a Splunk instance should be easy.

The **replication activity** of a Splunk index cluster will typically start by not requiring a lot of processing power, but should the replication factor increase, you can easily add indexers and storage to scale to meet the increasing requirements.

Because data replication is not resource-intensive, the multiple indexers in a cluster will actually increase the amount of data being ingested and indexed. Each indexer within a cluster can be a source peer and a target peer, indexing and storing copies of data (from other indexers in the cluster).

It stands to reason (and it is stated in the Splunk product documentation) that:

> *"the degree of data recovery that index clusters can possess (will be) directly proportional to the number of copies of data it is configured to sustain."*

More copies of data means higher storage requirements

The total number of copies (also referred to as **replicas**) of data maintained by an index cluster is known as the **Splunk replication factor**.

A Splunk replication factor equals *only one copy* of each row of data on one node. A replication factor of two means there will be two copies maintained per each row of data. In this case, each copy of data will be maintained on a separate node, and so on. A Splunk index cluster can handle a failure equal to one less than the peer node's replication factor.

You can affect the *recovery ability versus cost ratio* with the Splunk replication factor for each master node by configuring the exact number of copies (of data) that you want the index cluster to maintain. You do this by using the **Master Node Configuration** dialog (which we will cover in the upcoming *Enabling clustering* section of this chapter) or by editing the site replication factor within the `site_replication_factor` attribute in the master node's `server.conf` file.

> **Hint:**
> Using Splunk Web and the **Master Node Configuration** dialog is the recommended approach since the master node will not start if the `server.conf` file is incorrect.

How does this work?

We see that the *default replication factor* for a Splunk master node is three.

A replication factor of three means that the master node cluster will consist of three peer nodes, as illustrated in the following diagram:

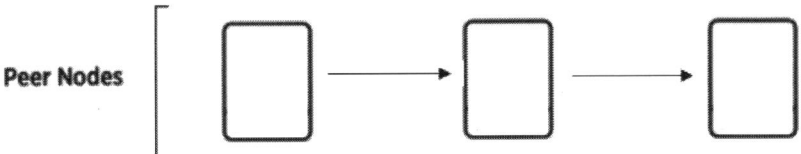

Figure 5.1 – Replication factor

A replication factor of three will ensure that three identical copies of each row of data are indexed in the cluster. Since we already stated that any Splunk index cluster can endure a failure of (replication factor minus one) peer nodes, then that means that the preceding cluster definition guarantees that Splunk can tolerate the failure of up to two peers at any time.

To be able to handle a greater number of peer node failures, you would need to increase the replication factor.

Keep in mind that this example shows a very basic version of peer replication within an index cluster. Here, we are assuming that all data is being ingested into Splunk through a single peer.

In most index clusters, each peer node can be both a source and a target (peer), meaning that they can each both ingest data and replicate data (from the other peers). Typically, each peer would be streaming copies of its data to two target peers, and at times, that set of target peers could possibly change.

With this in mind, a Splunk index cluster with a replication factor of three would most likely comprise many more peers than just three.

Enabling clustering

As previously mentioned, there are several methods for performing index cluster management.

> **Tip**
> The [clustering] stanza in the master node's `server.conf` file can be used to set up and manage index clustering. Refer to the product documentation online at https://docs.splunk.com/Documentation/Splunk/8.0.2/Indexer/Configuremasterwithserverconf.

The steps to enable clustering are as follows:

1. To use Splunk Web, you need to first (as an administrator) go to the Splunk main page, then click on **Settings**, and then **Index Clustering**. The message in the following screenshot should be displayed:

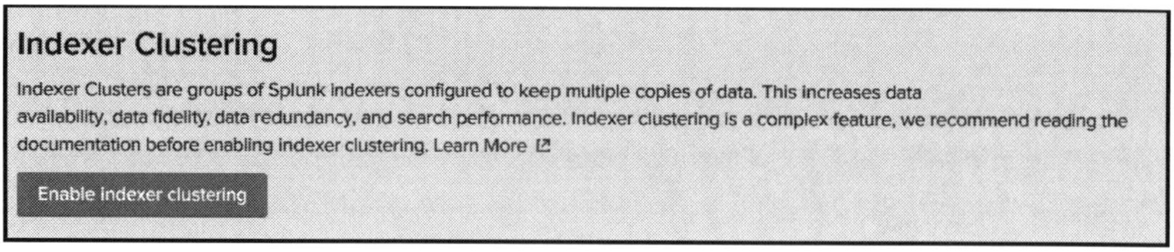

Indexer Clustering

Indexer Clusters are groups of Splunk indexers configured to keep multiple copies of data. This increases data availability, data fidelity, data redundancy, and search performance. Indexer clustering is a complex feature, we recommend reading the documentation before enabling indexer clustering. Learn More

Enable indexer clustering

Figure 5.2 – Enabling indexer clustering

2. Once you click on the **Enable indexer clustering** button, you'll need to enable **Master node** from the **Enable Clustering** dialog (shown in the following screenshot):

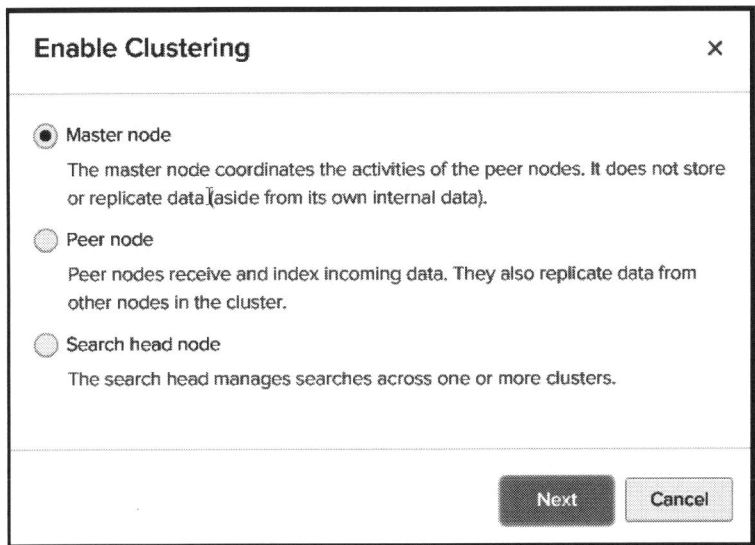

Figure 5.3 – Enabling Master node

By default, on the **Enable Clustering** dialog, **Master node** is selected. When defining a Splunk index cluster, understand that a cluster can only have one master node. As indicated by the preceding dialog, the cluster's master node coordinates all activities within the cluster, between the other nodes (the peer(s) and search head(s)). Additionally, the same Splunk instance cannot be configured to be both a master node and a peer node (or a master node and a search head node).

3. For illustration purposes, on the **Enable Clustering** dialog, we can leave the default checked and click the **Next** button to access the **Master Node Configuration** fields shown in the following screenshot:

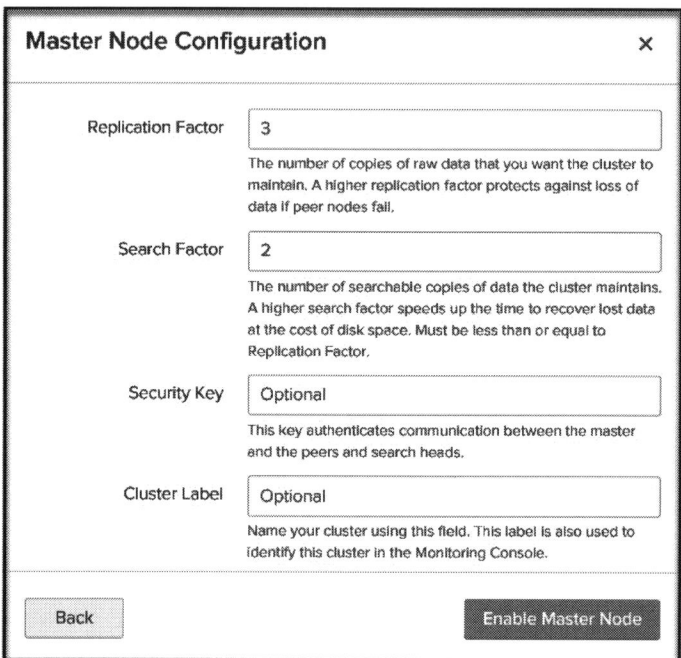

Figure 5.4 – Master Node Configuration dialog

There are four values to consider. Two values – the most critical (**Replication Factor** and **Search Factor**) – are required, while the other two (**Security Key** and **Cluster Label**) are optional. **Replication Factor** controls how many copies of data the cluster will maintain. For simple examples, you can assign 3 (the default value). **Search Factor** controls how many immediately searchable copies of data the cluster maintains; again, the easy answer is to assign 2 (the default value). You can skip the two optional fields.

> Note
> Once you proceed with clicking **Enable Master Mode**, Splunk will provide its own unique cluster label for you. Additionally, you will always have the ability to edit these master node configuration values as long as significant data has not already been indexed.

4. Lastly, click on the **Enable Master Nodes** button. Splunk will need to be restarted in order for your changes to take effect:

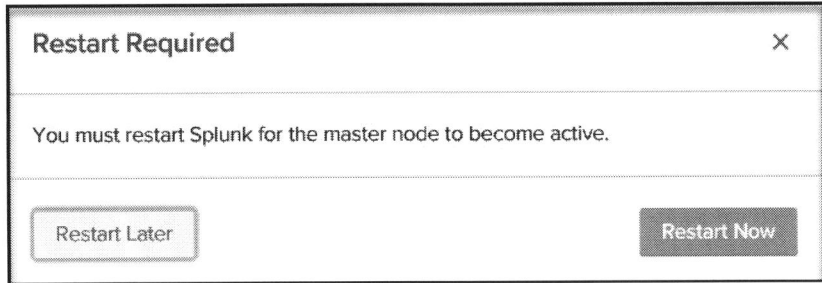

Figure 5.5 – Restart required after enabling master node

If you choose **Restart Later**, you can always go to **Settings** and then click on **Server Controls**, as shown in the following screenshot:

Figure 5.6 – Restarting Splunk

Once Splunk is restarted, by clicking on **Settings** and then **Index Clustering**, the master node dashboard (**Index Clustering: Master Node** page) will be displayed (rather than the enabled message), where you can access options and parameters to further configure this instance as a master node:

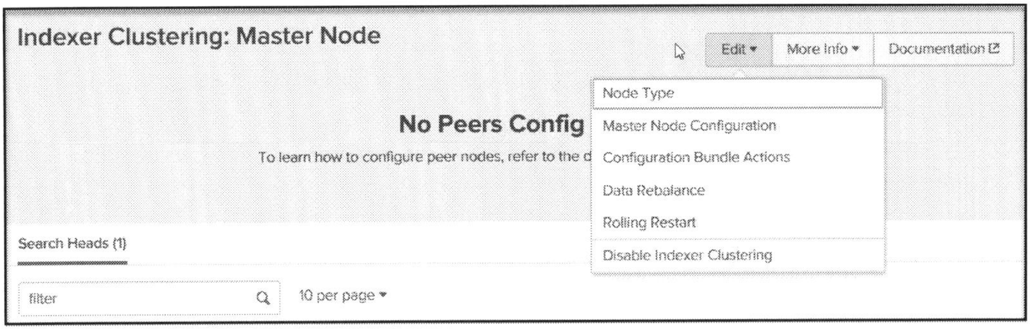

Figure 5.7 – Index Clustering: Master Node page

> **Tip**
> The previous information uses Splunk Web to perform index cluster management. To enable and manage index clusters using Splunk configuration files, you can visit the product documentation online at `docs.splunk.com/Documentation/Splunk/8.0.2/Admin/Indexesconf`.

Editing and configuring the master node

From the master node dashboard, you can edit the configuration of an existing master node. Clicking on **Master Node Configuration** returns you to the **Master Node Configuration** dialog, where you can view and/or edit the master node configuration values.

Configuring bundle actions

So, what is a Splunk bundle?

A **Splunk bundle** might also be simply defined as a **package** of Splunk **knowledge objects** that a search head node dispenses to all of its search peer nodes (within a designated cluster) so that each of the search nodes is able to process a **distributed** search (as opposed to a *standalone search head* search).

> **Reminder**
> Splunk knowledge objects are entities defined by users that enrich Splunk data, such as anything from the searches and event types to the lookups/field extractions, tags, reports, alerts, data models, transactions, workflow actions, and fields you develop and save.

With a distributed search, a Splunk search head distributes the search requests to its other search peers (within the configured search head cluster) that perform the actual searching, as well as the data indexing.

A search head cluster is a collection of Splunk search heads that serves as a central resource for searching. All search heads in the collection are meant to be identical, providing the ability to execute the same searches, view the same dashboards, and access the same search results from any member of the collection.

Since each search head (in the cluster) needs to be identical, from time to time, certain knowledge objects bundled together need to be *pushed* to each of the search head peers within a cluster. This **push** is the process of distributing each of the knowledge objects with a bundle to each of the search peers automatically, so as to keep everything *in sync*.

The act of distributing these objects is known as a **Bundle Push Operation**. This process includes both new as well as edited files and objects. The management of bundles includes various steps that an administrator needs to be comfortable with. These are as follows:

- Creation of the bundle
- Validation of the bundle (by the master node)
- Peer validation of the bundle
- Reloading and processing of the bundle by all peers
- The restarting of peers

In the `$SPLUNK_HOME/var/run` directory on the search head, there are what are known as **knowledge bundles**. These bundles have the extension `.bundle` (for full bundles), or `.delta` (for delta bundles). They are TAR-formatted files, allowing you to run `tar tvf` on them to view their contents.

> **Hint**
> A **TAR** (also known as **Tape Archive**) file is a common archive created by tar, a Unix-based utility that is used to package files together for backup or distribution purposes.

Bundles are validated first by the master node, and then at each peer node during a bundle push, to verify that what is included in the bundle is compatible with each search peer.

Administrators can perform the validation and check to see whether the bundle push will or won't require a restart without actually performing the push.

In Splunk Web, under **Settings**, and then **Index Clustering**, you can select **Configuration Bundle Actions** and perform **Validate and Check Restart**, **Push**, or **Rollback** separately, as shown in the following screenshot:

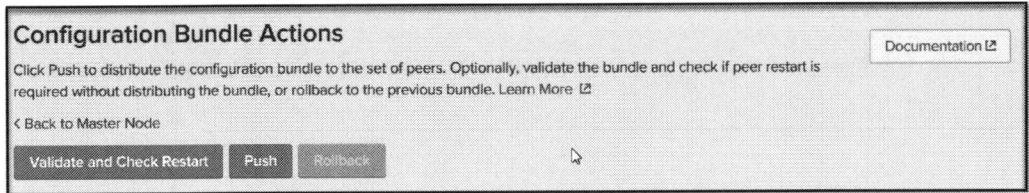

Figure 5.8 – Configuration Bundle Actions page

Once bundles are validated, peers may (or may not) need to be restarted to process the distributed bundle. Should anything fail during a bundle push, you can always roll back to the last valid bundle.

> **Note**
> Bundles are pushed, or replicated, based upon a replication policy.
> You can read more about replication policies online at `https://docs.splunk.com/Documentation/Splunk/8.0.2/DistSearch/Knowledgebundlereplication`.

Data rebalancing

The objective of data rebalancing is to try to best-balance storage across all of the peer nodes in an index cluster. This is done to ensure that each peer node has (roughly) the same number of searchable, non-searchable, and primary duplicates of the data.

There are two types of indexer cluster rebalancing—**primary rebalancing** and **data rebalancing**. Primary balancing attempts to balance the search load across the peers, while data rebalance looks to balance storage across the peers.

The easiest way to initiate (or periodically re-initiate) a rebalance process is through Splunk Web. Again, under **Settings**, and then **Index Clustering**, you can select **Data Rebalance**. From the **Data Rebalance** dialog (shown in the following screenshot), you can adjust the rebalance run parameters and then click **Start**:

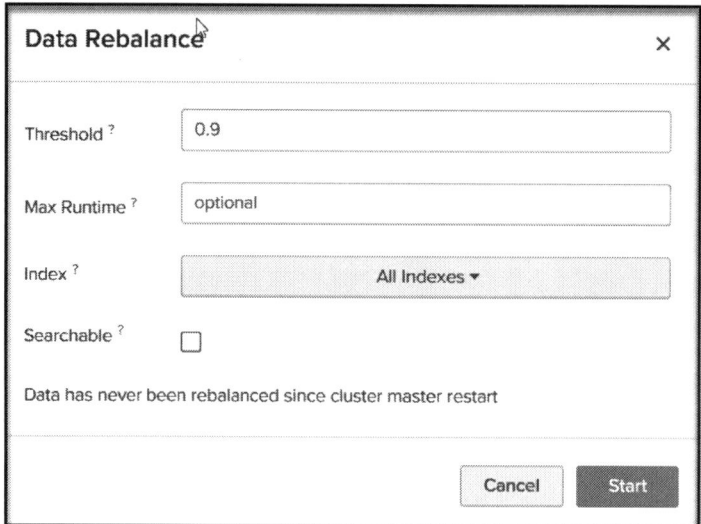

Figure 5.9 – Data Rebalance dialog

Let's look at the parameters:

- **Threshold**: This is actually a *balanced percentage* you set to determine however you want the index cluster to be balanced. For example, setting **Threshold** to 1.00 means you want the rebalancing to continue until the cluster is fully balanced, with each peer having the same number of copies. Values closer to 1 will cause the process to run the longest and use the most resources.
- **Max Runtime**: If you leave this field empty, the rebalancing process will continue until all peers are within the threshold limit, otherwise the process will complete when it reaches the threshold limit.
- **Index**: This indicates whether the rebalance process will run on a single index or across all indexes.
- **Searchable**: This enables a search-safe data rebalance. Data rebalance can take longer to complete in searchable mode.

> Note
> The process of data rebalancing involves substantial background processing, such as physically moving bucket copies between peer nodes. This can be a slow and prolonged process.

Performing an index cluster rolling restart

A rolling restart performs an incremental restart of all of the peer nodes within an index cluster. This is, by design, to ensure that the index cluster can continue to be available during the restart, since there will always be at least one peer node available during the process.

You can initiate an *index cluster rolling restart* in Splunk Web (the **Index Cluster Rolling Restart** modal screen is shown in the following screenshot), or with the rolling restart CLI command:

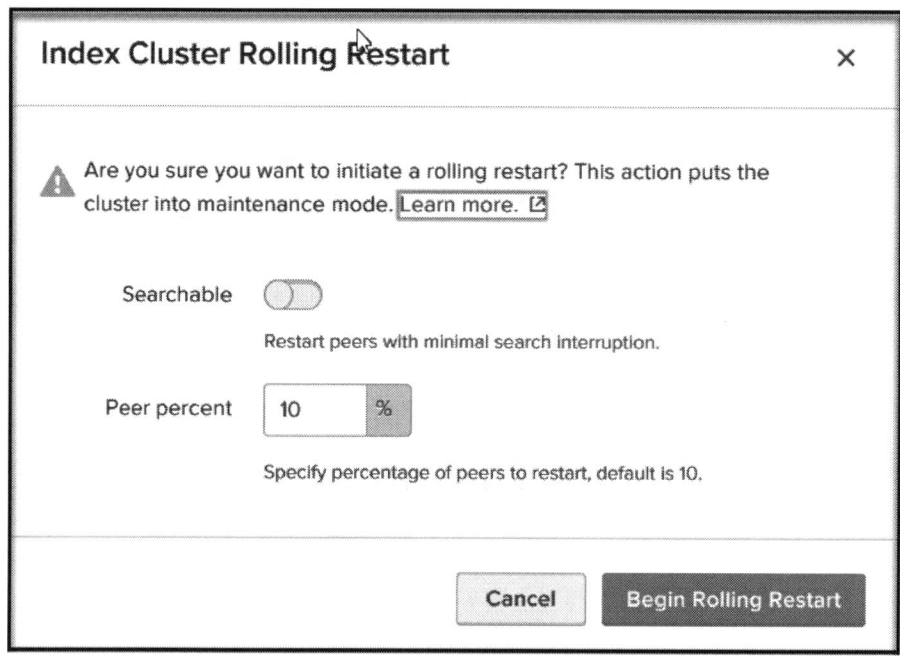

Figure 5.10 – Index Cluster Rolling Restart dialog

By default, the rolling restart command is issued to 10% of the cluster members at a time. The restart percentage is configurable through the preceding dialog (the peer percentage) or via the `percent_peers_to_restart` attribute in the `[shclustering]` stanza of `server.conf`.

Disabling clustering

Clicking on **Disable Clustering** turns off index clustering in the Splunk instance. Before proceeding with disabling clustering, you should make sure all the peers are disabled from the master.

In the next two sections, we will cover the concept of index clusters either within a single-site or multi-site instance, or within a distributed deployment Splunk environment.

Single-site index clusters

A Splunk single-site design is where, by design, there is only a single installation or instance (of Splunk), and one in which all nodes reside on that *single site*. This is also considered a *basic cluster configuration* and was the only configuration available in earlier versions of Splunk. In a Splunk single-site index cluster environment, naturally, all searches are limited to indexers within that site.

Multi-site index clusters

A multi-site index cluster environment differs from single-site index cluster designs. In a multi-site index cluster design, we have the following:

- Each node in a cluster will have a designated site.
- Replication of data occurs with *site awareness*.
- When possible, a search head will initiate their searches across local peers.

What is referred to as Splunk **site awareness** was introduced in Splunk version 6.1. This allows multi-site index clustering to improve or support high availability since multi-site index clusters provide site failover capability (in that clusters, and copies of data, span multiple sites).

Typically, DR and HA are discussed separately. DR is more about the ability to recover from a disaster event, while HA is about the ability to maintain an *acceptable* level of continuous service. DR equates to backup/archiving, while HA equates to data collection, indexing, and copying.

Additionally, **search affinity** affords the ability to manage whether a multi-site indexer cluster search head receives its search results only from peer nodes that exist on its local site or across multiple site peer nodes.

Disaster recovery sites

First, the basics of DR. You don't back up the *software*; you back up the *data* and the *configuration files*.

All of Splunk's configurations are stored within its configuration files. You need to make sure these files are periodically backed up and saved securely.

To back up the Splunk configuration files, you should routinely copy the entire, `$SPLUNK_HOME/etc/folder`.

The folder and all subfolders hold all of the settings for your Splunk installation, all apps, including saved searches, user accounts, tags, custom source type names, as well as other configuration details. A stop/restart of Splunk is not required in order to make a copy of this information.

Backing up the master node

We've spent some time going over index clustering/replication in this chapter.

If you have created index clusters, you should create copies/archives of each of the master node's configurations (its bundle of knowledge objects), just as you would do for the Splunk configurations mentioned in the previous section. We covered the details of master nodes in the *Configuring bundle actions* section. Creating archives of master nodes can be of specific use when configuring standby master nodes that can take over if the primary master fails.

Practicing recovery

No number of backups or archives performed will provide assurance that, in the event of a disaster, you will be able to fully recover unless you ensure that the backups are valid and clean, and you actually can use them to initiate a successful restore.

Therefore, it is recommended that you practice a full disaster recovery procedure end to end: backup/archive, validation, restore, and recovery.

These practices include the following steps:

- Creating a new Splunk instance on a new site
- Restoring the Splunk indexes
- Restoring the data/indexes
- Validation of the new instance

Special multi-site configurations – the site replication factor

A special point to consider with multi-site configurations is that a multi-site index cluster has its own version of a replication factor (known as the **site replication factor**).

This replication factor controls the number of data copies that the entire index cluster maintains, as well as the number of data copies that each site must maintain.

The multi-site index cluster replication factor overrides the replication factor we went over in an earlier section of this chapter. You specify the site replication factor on the index cluster's master node as part of the basic configuration of the cluster.

You set the site replication factor using the `site_replication_factor` attribute within the master node's `server.conf` configuration file. This attribute resides in the `[clustering]` stanza, instead of the single-site `replication_factor` attribute.

> **Tip**
> Be careful while updating this configuration file since the master node will not start if the `server.conf` file is incorrect.

Converting the multi-site index cluster

At some point, you may realize that some of your multi-site index clusters do not need to be multi-site index clusters. There are a variety of reasons as to why you may come to this conclusion. Typically, these decisions are based on performance, security, or data volume, but this can also be with a view to simplifying administration.

If you choose to convert a multi-site indexer cluster to a basic, single-site cluster, all peer nodes within the cluster index as well as the search heads in the index cluster become part of the same, implicit, single site.

To carry out the conversion, perform the following steps:

1. Perform a stop of all nodes in the cluster.
2. Edit the `server.conf` file on the master node and set `multisite` to `false`. Set the single-site `replication_factor` and `search_factor` attributes to implement the desired replication behavior. Then, delete the `site` attribute.
3. For each search head, edit `server.conf` and set `multisite` to `false`. Then, delete the `site` attribute.
4. For each of the peers, edit `server.conf`. Then, delete the `site` attribute.
5. Restart the master node.
6. Restart the peer nodes and search heads.

Converting the single-site index cluster

Should you want to convert a single-site index cluster to a multi-site index cluster, you can pretty much perform the same steps as in the previous conversion, this time editing the `server.conf` file of the cluster master node, except that in this case, you will only have one site defined and you'll need to add back the single-site attributes that had been removed. In addition, be sure that each peer node in the cluster is assigned to the same single-site attribute.

> **Final tip**
>
> You can examine in more detail how multi-site configuration differs from single-site configuration online at `https://docs.splunk.com/Documentation/Splunk/7.0.0/Indexer/Multisiteconffile`.

Summary

In this chapter, we jumped right into the science of index clustering/replication including the makeup of a cluster—master/peer/search nodes, what a replication factor is and how it affects storage, bundling between cluster peers, rebalancing data, and rolling restarts. We even touched a bit on single-site versus multi-site index clusters and wrapped things up by covering disaster recovery and high availability.

In the next chapter, we will discuss how Splunk can be easily integrated with other platforms and technologies, specifically looking at AWS and Azure.

6
Splunk Integration with Azure and AWS

Splunk can be easily integrated with other platforms and technologies, such as both the AWS and Azure cloud platforms. In this chapter, we will cover the topic of Splunk integration using Azure and **Amazon Web Services** (**AWS**) as working integration examples.

When we speak about *integrating Splunk*, we are usually referring to leveraging the functionality of the powerful Splunk engine so as to seamlessly search unstructured machine language or machine-generated data sourced from other technology platforms.

Integration can similarly refer to leveraging the functionality of Splunk from within another allocation; this is typically done through the Splunk Developer Program, REST APIs, **software development kits** (**SDKs**), and other developer tools that are available to you. In this chapter, we will focus on integrating data from other source platforms, specifically Azure and AWS.

Obviously, if your organization is already using Splunk to search and monitor application logs and other forms of machine generated data, then *broadening the net* (so to speak) to include log and message information (and other data) from other applications and technology platforms is a good thing and makes sense.

How do we approach this goal? With a proven strategy that can be evolved into a very specific plan.

This chapter will be broken down into the following main sections:

- Splunk integration strategy
- Integrating Azure
- Integrating AWS

Let's get started!

Splunk integration strategy

We are using the term **integration** as it generally consists of the ability to perform tasks such as **data on-boarding** for ingesting the data, **data cleaning and/or parsing** in a consistent way so that it can easily be interpreted and monitored, and **dashboard creation** or in other words, being able to present the data in a common, insightful manner, either as a report or in real time. The following diagram illustrates the stages in a Splunk integration strategy:

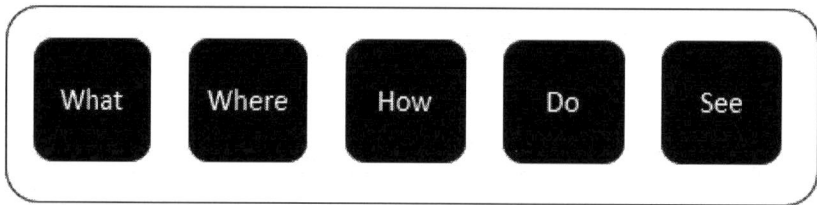

Figure 6.1 – Stakes in a Splunk integration strategy

Let's look at what each of these means:

- Identify **what** data you want to integrate
- Identify **where** the new data is sourced from
- Determine **how** to get data from the source (into Splunk)
- **Do** process/parse/transform/clean the data to ensure it makes sense (creating fields, events, transforms, and so on)
- Create reports and/or dashboards showing (**see**) the new data as insightful information within the Splunk interface

For each of these steps (actually, these are stages), you'll need to have a full understanding of the data you want to integrate, as well as what the final objective is supposed to be or needs to look like. To ensure this, each of the stages can take, and usually are, a significant amount of work.

Thankfully, there's a number of methods we can use to integrate data into Splunk. For example, the aforementioned Splunk Developer Program provides a REST API, SDKs, and various developer tools to help us easily and quickly connect Splunk to almost any business data source.

> **Hint**
>
> You can find information on the Splunk Developer Program information at `dev.splunk.com/enterprise/docs/welcome` and the SPLUNK REST API User at `docs.splunk.com/Documentation/Splunk/latest/RESTUM/RESTusing`.

Using an app

A Splunk app is an application that runs on the Splunk platform and is typically designed to solve a specific or focused use case or need.

> **Note**
>
> Generically speaking, a Splunk app might be more of a *concentrated configuration*, not necessarily an application in the purest sense of the word. However, the term *application* fits in this context.

A Splunk app contains one or more Splunk views and will usually include a number of Splunk knowledge objects such as reports, lookups, scripted inputs, and modular inputs. Apps may sometimes be contingent on one or more other add-ons (to Splunk) to provide specific functionality.

The point is, before breaking out the developer tool kits, why not cruise through **Splunkbase** and see what apps might have already been developed (and tested!) that may solve part or all our integration needs? In most cases, if you are looking to integrate Splunk with machine data generated from a mainstream application, then, most likely, there is an app for that!

> **Hint**
> Splunkbase is a site where users can post and share apps and add-ons. Check it out periodically at https://splunkbase.splunk.com.

Finding an app

As a rule of thumb or perhaps as a best practice, *never recreate the wheel*.

What this means is that if it has already been built, do not invest valuable resources building your own. Splunkbase offers a huge and ever-growing inventory of prebuilt functionality ready for download and use.

> **Information**
> Splunkbase has 1,000+ apps and add-ons from Splunk, our partners, and our community. You can find an app or add-on for most or any data source and user need at splunkbase.splunk.com.

As stated previously, to find a useful Splunk app, using your web browser, navigate to Splunkbase or, right from within Splunk, click on **Apps** and then **Find More Apps**, as shown in the following screenshot:

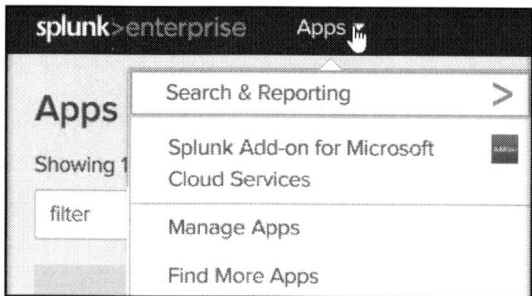

Figure 6.2 – Finding an app

From there, the **Browse More Apps** page will provide a simple and easy way for you to search Splunkbase for literally any functionality you have in mind:

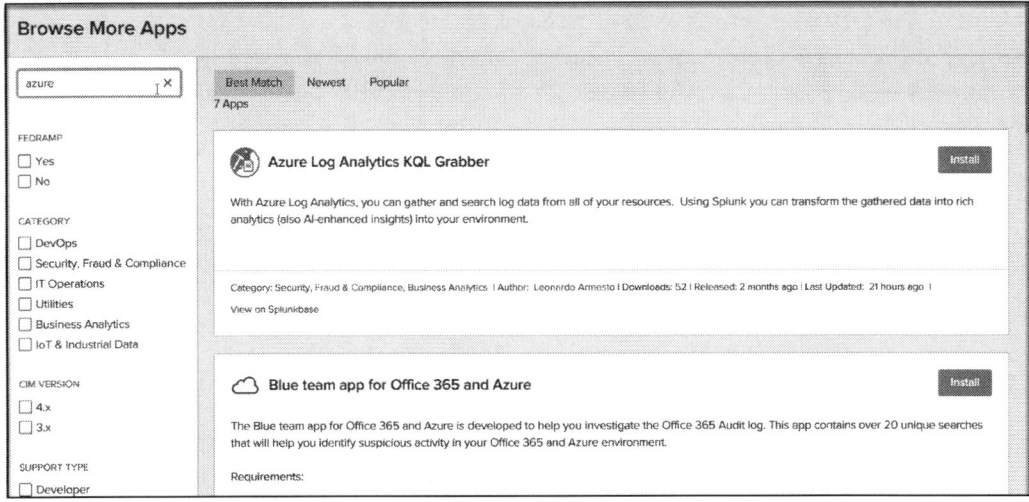

Figure 6.3 – Browsing for more apps

> **Hint**
> It is not uncommon to see different results when searching for apps within Splunk and on Splunkbase due to the version support that's recorded. There are plenty of cases where an app may not indicate support for a newer version (especially for apps containing only knowledge objects) but will still be completely functional, so it's helpful to be aware of this!

Integrating Azure

What is Azure? **Microsoft Azure** is an ever-expanding set of cloud services built to help organizations meet their business challenges. It provides us with the independence to build, manage, and deploy applications on an enormous, global network using tools and frameworks that we are already familiar with.

At its core, Azure is a public cloud computing platform with solutions including **Infrastructure as a Service** (**IaaS**), **Platform as a Service** (**PaaS**), and **Software as a Service** (**SaaS**) that can be leveraged for services such as analytics, virtual computing, storage, networking, and more.

What is an Azure instance? In simple words, an instance in Azure can be understood as a **VM**, also known as a **virtual machine**. Microsoft Azure websites have been defined as high-density and multi-tenancy platforms. Microsoft Azure does not use virtual machines as a *scale unit* but as a means of tracking processes.

It has been suggested that the future of Azure is as a platform for building and hosting web and mobile apps without any servers and providing virtual desktops (using MS Windows Virtual Desktop service). Azure is Microsoft's cloud platform and is one of the most popular cloud service vendors.

Global organizations are realizing great success with business solutions located in a cloud platform. They are redefining the way they do business with scalable and secure cloud-enabled enterprise applications.

> **Information**
> Globally, 90% of Fortune 500 companies are using Microsoft Azure to drive their businesses. Using deeply integrated Azure cloud services, enterprises can rapidly build, deploy, and manage simple to complex applications with ease. To learn about the 10 reasons why you should choose Azure, head over to `www.saviantconsulting.com/blog/10-reasons-why-choose-microsoft-azure.asp`.

Although our goal in this chapter is not to explain or instruct you about the objective of or the various uses for Azure, if you are not familiar with Azure, it is worth taking some time to understand some basic fundamentals. In fact, if you don't have access to Azure, you can create a free account by going to `azure.microsoft.com/en-us/features/azure-portal/`.

Enough background on Azure. Let's integrate.

Thinking back to the integration strategy we outlined at the beginning of this chapter, where are we?

Stage one: Identify **what** data you want to integrate. For this exercise, we are going to assume we are interested in Azure Microsoft cloud services-generated data, specifically the **Azure Activity log**.

> **Hint**
> The Azure activity (or subscription) log is actually part of the Azure monitor service/solution, which provides insight into subscription-level events that have occurred in Azure. The activity log captures activities that occur at the *subscription level* of Azure, including an assortment of data, from Azure resource manager operational data to updates on service health events.

Stage two: Identify **where** the new data is sourced from. Again, for this exercise, let's assume we have an Azure account and subscription to work with. Azure subscriptions allow for a single Azure instance (a VM) to separate costs and for you to bill in terms of *pay as you go* for what services and resources you need, when you need them.

> **Hint**
> The Azure portal (`https://portal.azure.com`) lets you easily manage all Azure services. In fact, if you do not have a current Azure account, you can create a **For Free** account here as well and then use it for this exercise.

Stage three: Determine **how** to get data from the source into Splunk. In this stage, we need to perform the steps that are required to *integrate* Splunk with Azure data. Referring to our earlier advice (*never recreate the wheel*), we will use an already built and tested Splunk app, the **Splunk Add-on for Microsoft Cloud Services** (`https://splunkbase.splunk.com/app/3110`).

> **Hint**
> Splunk recommends installing Splunk-supported add-ons across the entire Splunk deployment, then enabling/configuring inputs only where they are required. See the following link for more details: `https://docs.splunk.com/Documentation/AddOns/released/Overview/Wheretoinstall`.

The steps are as follows:

1. From the **Splunk** main page, click **Apps**, then **Find More Apps**.
2. Then, search for **Azure**.
3. When you scroll through the apps listed and find the app, click on **Install**:

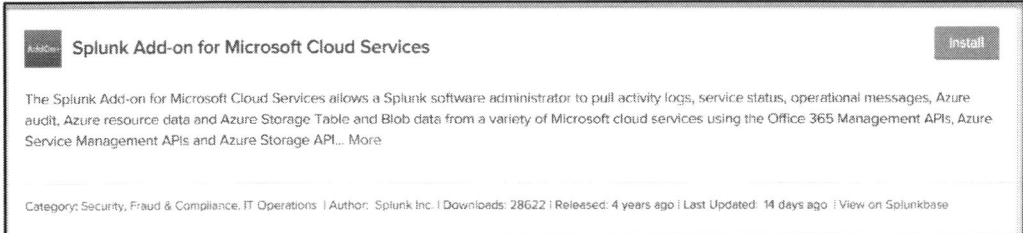

Figure 6.4 – Installing Azure

Once the app has been installed, you should see it show up on the main page, as shown in the following screenshot:

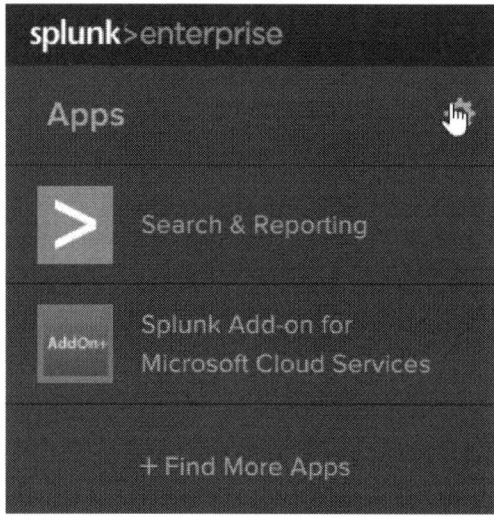

Figure 6.5 – Installed apps list

Now that we have installed the app, let's move on to the next step.

Connecting to the Azure app account

Once the **Splunk Add-on for Microsoft Cloud Services App** has been installed in your Splunk instance, you need to configure the app so that you can start ingesting your Microsoft cloud services data into the Splunk platform.

Like most Splunk configuration changes, you can configure the app using **Splunk Web** (recommended) or using the configuration file settings (you can edit $SPLUNK_HOME/etc/apps/Splunk_TA_microsoft-cloudservices/local/mscs_azure_accounts.conf).

We will use Splunk Web in this case. The steps for this are as follows:

1. First, click on the app:

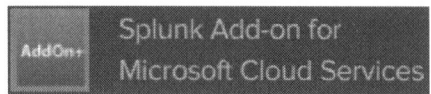

Figure 6.6 – Connecting to the app

Integrating Azure   125

2. Next (from within the app), click on **Configuration**. The app configuration page will be displayed. Click on the **Azure App Account** tab. There will be no items listed yet, so click on the green **Add** button. Once done, you will get the **Update Azure App Account** dialog, as shown in the following screenshot:

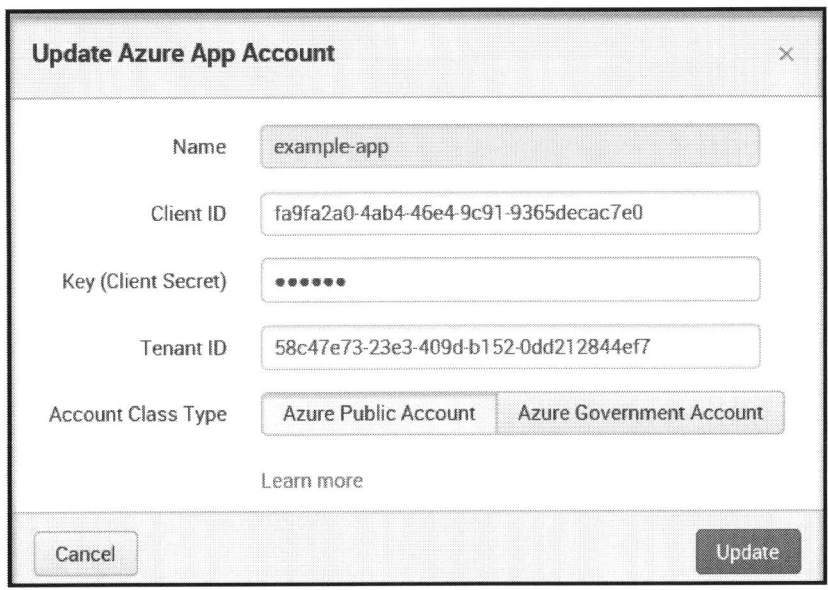

Figure 6.7 – Update Azure App Account dialog

3. On the **Update Azure App Account** dialog (shown in the preceding screenshot), you'll need to enter or select the following parameters:

    a) **Name**: This is just a friendly name used to identify your Azure app account.

    b) **Client ID**: Use the Client ID that Azure AD *automatically assigned* to your Azure integration application.

    c) **Key (Client Secret)**: This is the secret or password you established for the Client ID.

    d) **Tenant ID**: Enter the Tenant ID that was established when the Azure application was created.

    e) **Account Class Type**: Just select **Azure Public Account**.

4. Click **Add**. You should now see your app listed:

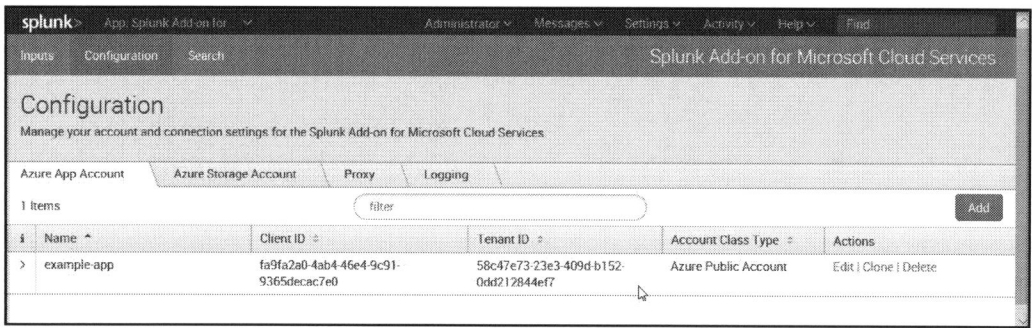

Figure 6.8 – Adding the app

5. Now, we need to define a new input for the app. From within the app, click on **Inputs**. It may take a moment or two to load, but you should then see the app's **Inputs** page. From there, click on **Create New Input**. You should see a drop-down list where you can select **Azure Audit**. You should then see the **Update Azure Audit** dialog (as shown in the following screenshot):

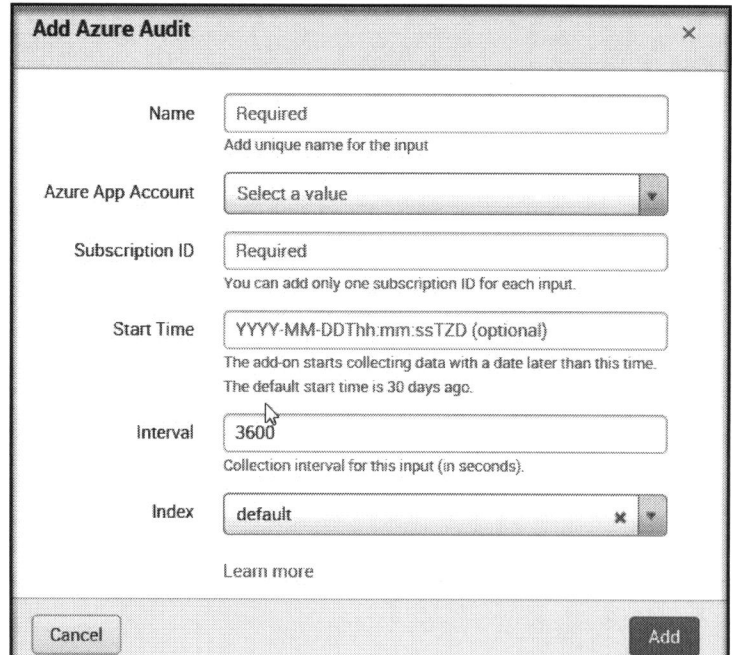

Figure 6.9 – Updating the Azure audit configuration

In this dialog, you can enter the following parameters:

- **Name**: Again, this is just a friendly name you can make up and type in.
- **Azure App Account**: You cannot enter this value. Instead, you'll need to select it from the drop-down list when you click on the field. Since we already did our configuration step, you should be able to see and select our configured Azure app:

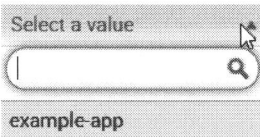

Figure 6.10 – Selecting the app

- **Subscription ID**: This is the ID of your Azure subscription.
- **Index**: Practically speaking, a non-default index would be used; we're just using the default as an example.

The dialog should now look like this (shown in the following screenshot) and you can then click **Update**:

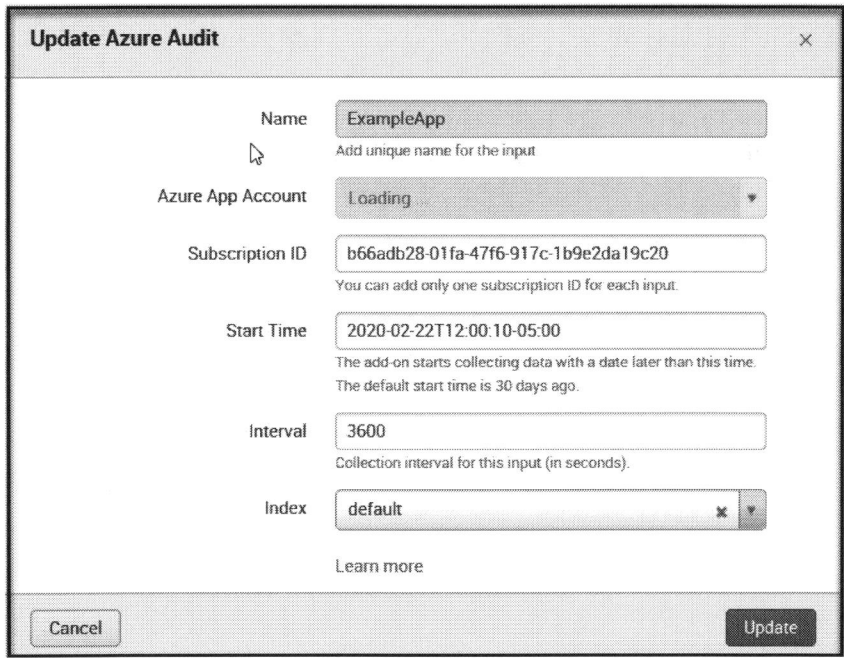

Figure 6.11 – Updated Azure Audit configuration

Back on the **Inputs** page, you should now see our input listed:

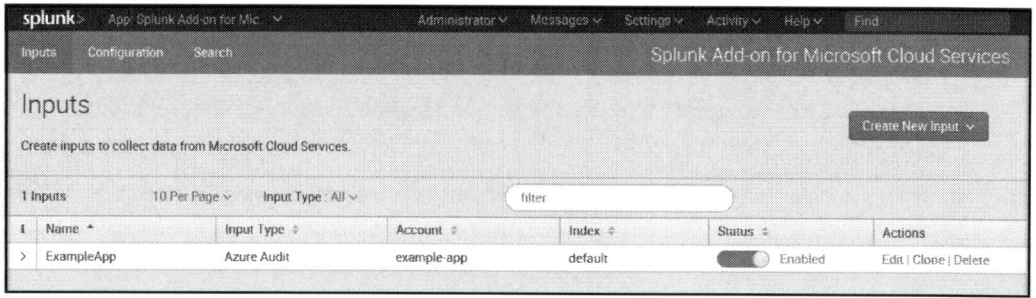

Figure 6.12 – Input updated

Now, our app has been configured and ready to be used. This brings us to the next stage in our integration strategy.

Stage four: **Do** process/parse/transform/clean the data to ensure it makes sense (create fields, events, transforms, and so on).

As we covered in *Chapter 3, Performance, Statistics, and Alerting in Splunk*, when Splunk indexes data, it breaks out the incoming data automatically into **events**, based on timestamps. Additionally, the term **indexing** is used in Splunk to refer to the entirety of event processing, encompassing both parsing the data (into events) and indexing the data.

So, what this means is that Splunk has us covered in that, through the use of our recently installed app, we should be ready to do some searching through the Azure activity logs without having to think about parsing and transforming it first.

In fact, we can now go and click on **Search** within our app:

Figure 6.13 – Searching within the app

This brings up the **Search** page shown in the following screenshot, where you can click on **Data Summary**:

Integrating Azure   129

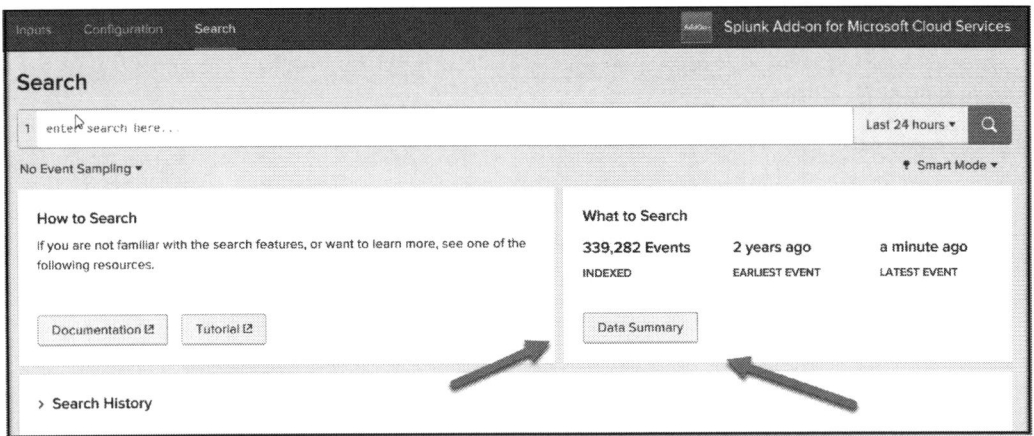

Figure 6.14 – Checking the data summary

On the **Data Summary** page (shown in the following screenshot), click on **Sourcetype**:

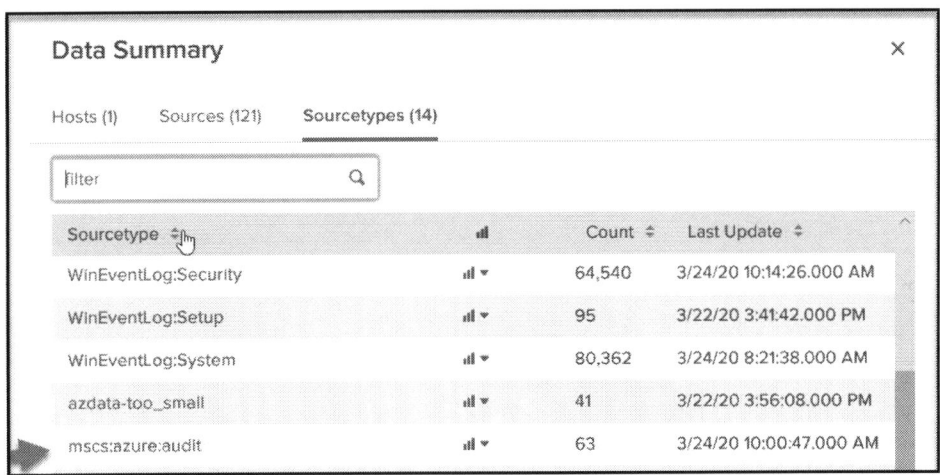

Figure 6.15 – Selecting the sourcetype

On the **Data Summary** page, scroll down until you find the `mscs:azure:audit` source type and click on it.

> **Hint**
> The source type (**Sourcetype**) is a default field that Splunk assigns to all incoming data. It tells Splunk what type of data you have so that it can format the data logically during indexing.

After clicking on our new Azure source type, the **New Search** page will be displayed with `sourcetype="mscs:azure:audit"` already set for you (as shown in the following screenshot):

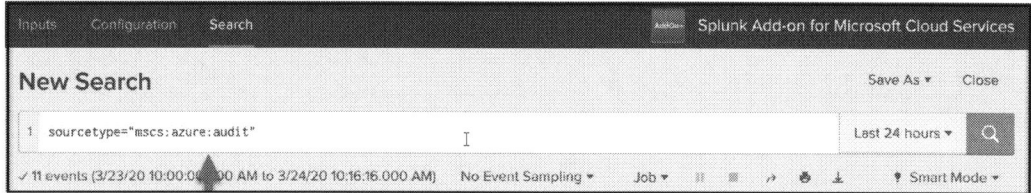

Figure 6.16 – New search page

The search time range is defaulted to **Last 24 hours**, but you can change it to **All Time** so that you can search over more Azure activity data. If you go ahead and click on the search icon, you'll notice that you now have access to and are, in fact, searching Azure activity log data:

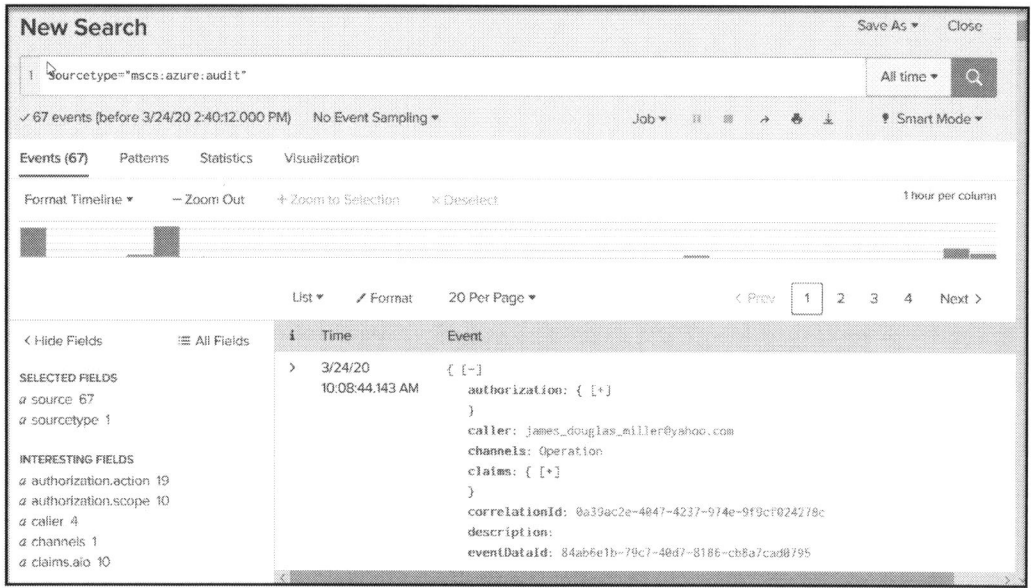

Figure 6.17 – Azure activity log data

Stage five: The last stage in our integration strategy is to create reports and/or dashboards showing (**see**) the new data as insightful information within the Splunk interface.

As a bit of validation, if we were to log into the Azure portal and access our Azure account, we could navigate to the **Activity log** view for a selected Azure name space that had been already set up within our subscription and query and view the activity log directly.

> Hint
>
> To view the activity logs through the Azure portal menu, you can select **Monitor**, then **Activity log**. This will show a summary of all recent operations. A default set of filters is applied to the operations, which you can use to filter by a particular type of event.

For example, after experimenting with the filters (shown in the following screenshot), we can see that two **'audit' Policy action** events were recorded in the activity log for this namespace on **Tue March 24**:

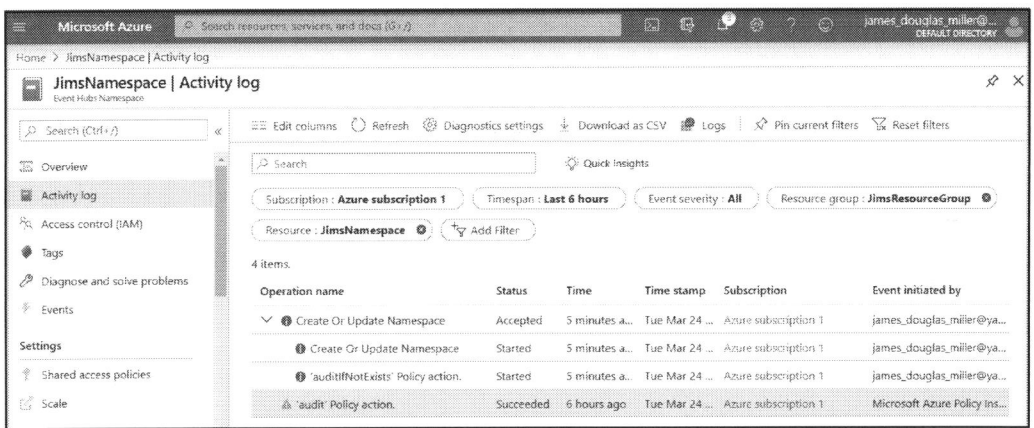

Figure 6.18 – Filtering the activity log

Going back to Splunk, from our installed app, we can enter the simple search command known as `sourcetype="mscs:azure:audit" audit`.

We will see a similar result (two events):

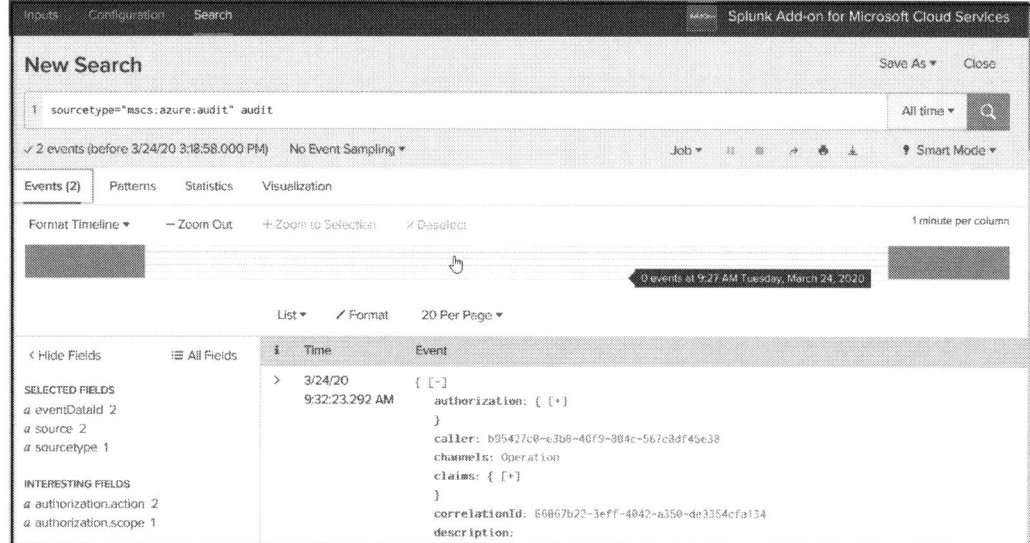

Figure 6.19 – Simple search result

Anytime someone makes changes to role assignments or role definitions within an Azure subscription, those changes get logged in the Azure Activity log. You can view the activity logs periodically, or, as an exercise, you can go ahead and set up a Splunk **Alert**, with the intention of having Splunk run the search against the Azure activity log once every 24 hours and perform an **Alert Action** if the number of results (the number of change events) is greater than a certain threshold limit.

For example, if *authorization action* is an update to any policy assignments, you could create and save (as a Splunk alert) a search command similar to `sourcetype="mscs:azure:audit" "authorization.action"="Microsoft.Authorization/policyAssignments/write"`.

The following screenshot is the Splunk search results showing two events with a matching authorization action:

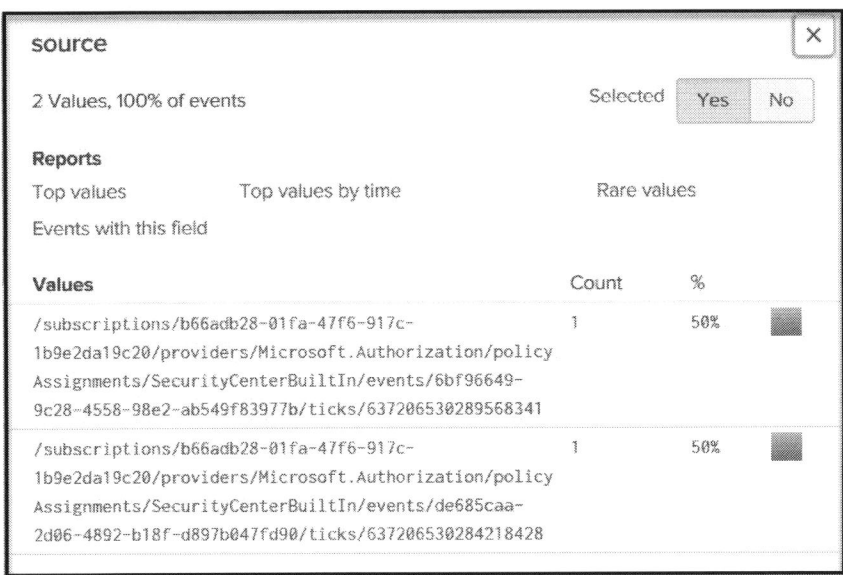

Figure 6.20 – Splunk search result

And then, you would have Splunk monitor the Azure logs and let you know when there is a significant amount of activity. You can set up an alert like so:

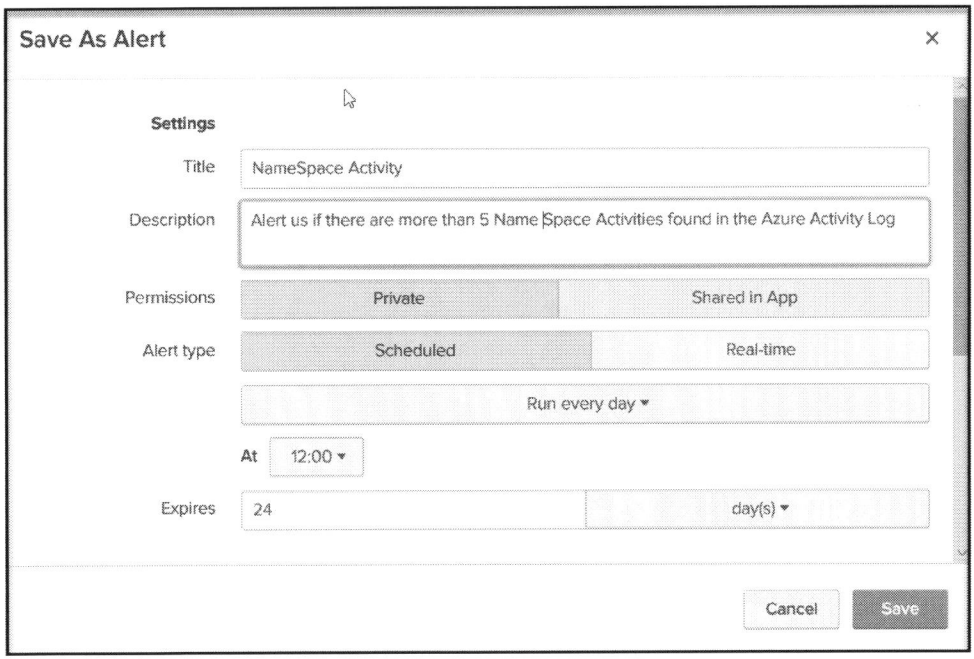

Figure 6.21 – Save As Alert screen

With that, we have seen how easy it is to connect and integrate Splunk with Azure. In the following sections, we will cover integrating with AWS.

Integrating with AWS

Somewhat similar to Azure, AWS is a secured cloud-based services platform that offers computing resources, data/database storage, content delivery, and additional functionalities to help businesses scale and grow. With AWS, you can run web and application servers in the cloud to host dynamic websites.

Both AWS and Azure provide long-running and reliable storage services. AWS has services such as AWS S3, EBS, and Glacier, whereas Azure storage services offers Blob Storage, Disk Storage, and Standard Archive.

AWS is advertised (by Amazon) as the *world's most comprehensive and broadly adopted* cloud platform, offering over 175 fully-featured services from data centers globally.

Integration

Once again, we can take the *app approach* to integrating (in this case) AWS log data with our Splunk environment. If you follow the same procedure we outlined earlier in this chapter (to locate, download, and install the Azure App Add-on), you can now locate, download, and install to your Splunk instance using the **Splunk Add-on for AWS**. Once installed, you should see the app from the main Splunk page, similar to what is shown in the following screenshot:

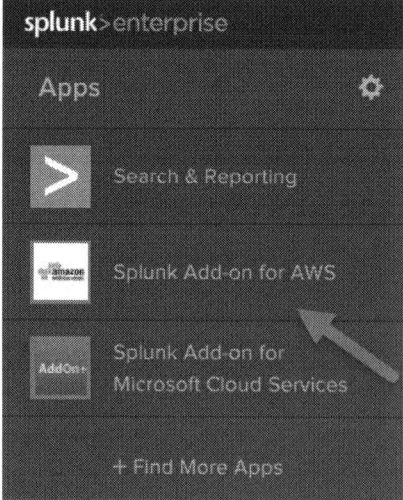

Figure 6.22 – Installing AWS in Splunk

> **Hint**
> Before you can configure Splunk to work with your AWS data, you must set up and configure an account in AWS.

Once installed, we can configure the add-on in much the same manner as we did for the **Microsoft Cloud Services** add-on.

Configuration

Perform the following steps to configure AWS in Splunk:

1. Start by clicking on **Configuration**, which you can find under the **Splunk Add-on for AWS** banner:

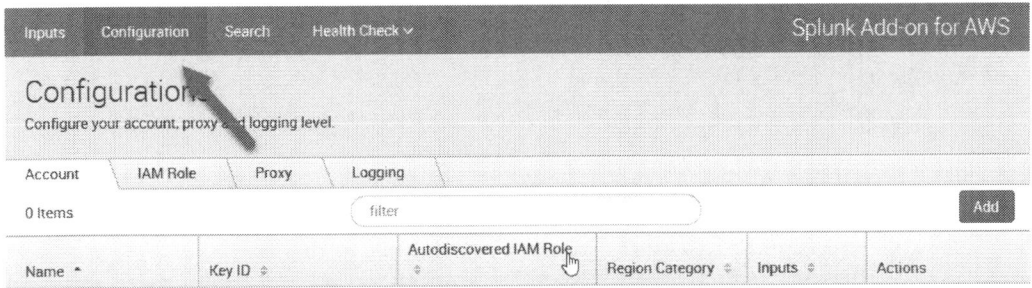

Figure 6.23 – Configuring AWS in Splunk

> **Note**
> For this step, you'll need to have an active AWS account that has administrator-level access. If you do not have an active account, you can set one up at https://docs.aws.amazon.com/polly/latest/dg/setting-up.html.

2. Click on the **Account** tab. When you get to the **Add Account** dialog (shown in the following screenshot), you will need to enter a **Name** for your new account, a **Key ID**, a **Secret Key**, and, finally, select a **Region Category**:

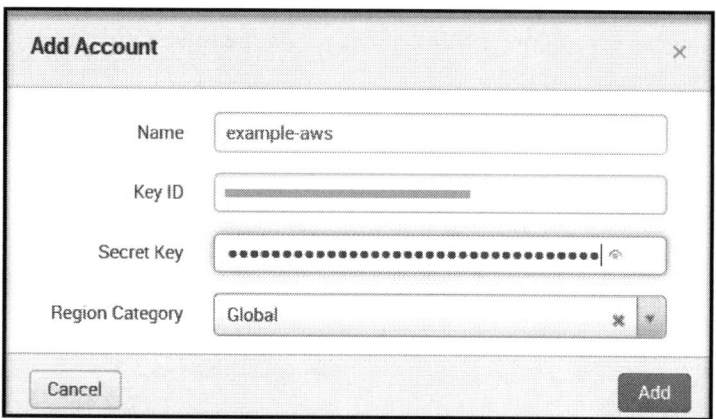

Figure 6.24 – Adding your AWS account

The **Name** parameter is just a friendly name to refer to the account. Key ID is the AWS account ID, while Secret Key is the ID you would have to generate for your AWS account. You use these secret access keys to make programmatic calls to AWS API operations in order to use AWS CLI commands. In this case, the key will be used by the AWS Add-on for Splunk. Lastly, on this dialog, select **Global** as the value for **Region Category**.

3. Click **Add**. Once you click **Add**, the new account will be authenticated and then listed within the AWS add-on under **Configurations**, as shown in the following screenshot:

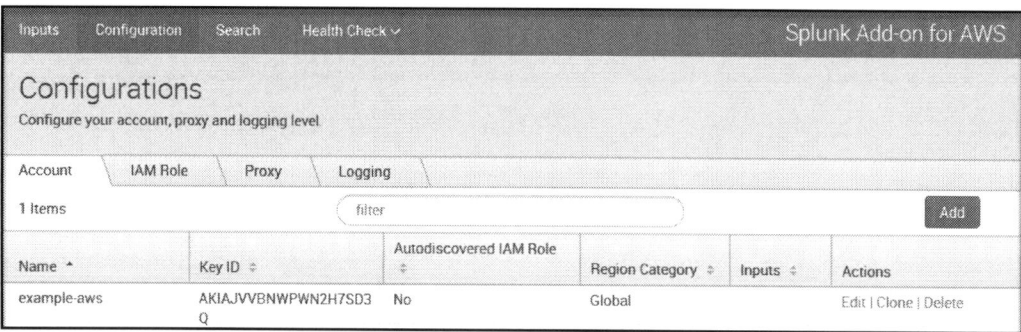

Figure 6.25 – New account added

Integrating with AWS 137

4. Now that we have a *valid AWS account* set up within our AWS Splunk add-on, just as we did with the Splunk add-on for Microsoft Cloud Services, we will need to set up a new input, so click on **Inputs**:

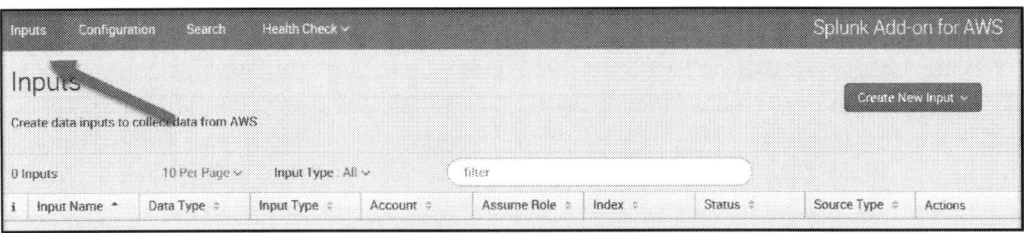

Figure 6.26 – Setting up a new input

5. Next, click on the **Create New Input** button and then select **VPC Flow Logs** and **CloudWatch Logs**:

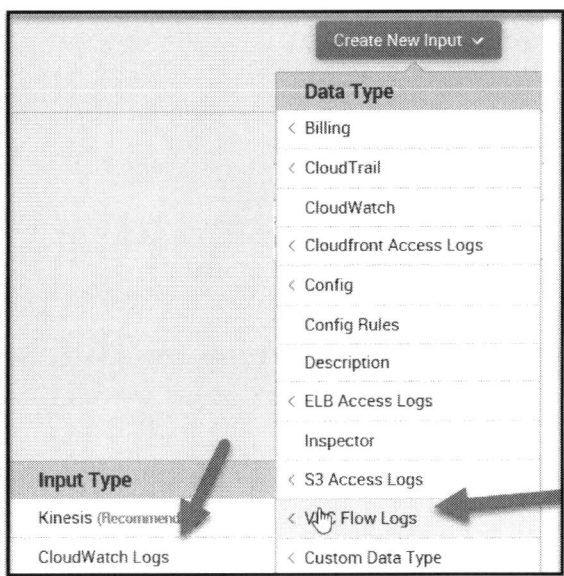

Figure 6.27 – Creating new input

> **Note**
> **Virtual Private Cloud** (**VPC**) flow logs capture information about the IP traffic going to and from network interfaces in **VPC Flow Logs**. **CloudWatch Logs** store information about your resources, applications, and services in near real time.

You can see that the Splunk Add-on for AWS supports many data types as input sources. For our exercise, we will focus on **CloudWatch Logs**.

AWS CloudWatch Logs enable the centralization of the logs from all AWS systems, applications, and services you are currently using into a single (highly scalable) location.

AWS has a lot of information to absorb and use. If you are not familiar with AWS, that's okay, at least for this exercise. There are, however, a few concepts you do need to understand, such as **Flow Logs**. An AWS flow log is just one option within **CloudWatch** that allows you to monitor activities on various AWS resources. A flow log generally monitors traffic within the different AWS resources, capturing various pieces of information based on traffic and events into and out of an AWS resource. With flow logs, you can view things such as the IP address of the source and destination, along with the port numbers of the source and destination. In our example, we will use an Amazon **Virtual Private Cloud** or **VPC** to track our flow log, and then integrate that data source with Splunk.

> **Hint**
> For information on setting up your own VPC, see www.awsbeginner.com/flow-logs-basics.

Setting up the input

Follow these steps to set up the input in your AWS Add-on for Splunk:

1. On the **Create New Input** dialog (shown in the following screenshot), we need to fill in the following parameters:

    a) **Name**: This is just a friendly name for our new input. I've used `example-aws-Log`.

    b) **AWS Account**: This should be a drop-down selector that you will be able to use to select the AWS Account that we set up earlier under **Configuration**.

    c) **AWS Region**: This should be a drop-down selector where you need to select the AWS Region that your AWS account is using.

    d) **Log Group**: This is the name of the AWS log group you set up in AWS and are streaming **CloudWatch Logs** to:

Integrating with AWS   139

Figure 6.28 – AWS Input Configuration screen

2. The parameters under **Splunk-related Configuration** can be left with their default values. One thing to take note of is that the **Source Type** has been automatically set for you to `aws:cloudwatchlogs:vpcflow`:

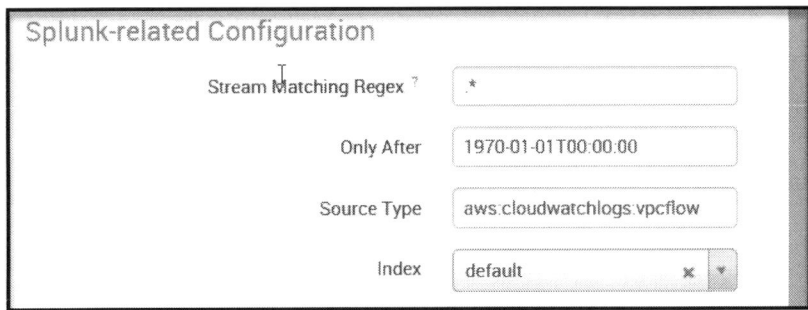

Figure 6.29 – Splunk-related Configuration screen

3. Finally, click **Save**. You should now see your new AWS input listed on the **Inputs** page, as shown in the following screenshot:

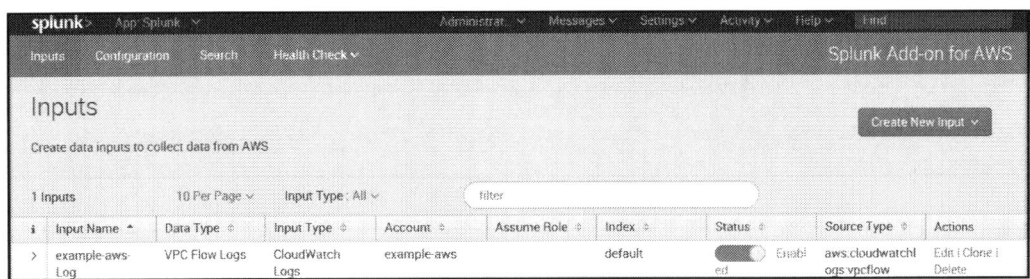

Figure 6.30 – New AWS input listed

Now that we have finished with the setup, let's move on and start searching AWS logs in the following section.

Getting ready to search AWS logs

So, now, just as we did with the **Splunk Add-on for Microsoft Cloud Services**, we have completed the initial setup required to integrate AWS log data into our Splunk instance and we are now ready to search it. The steps for this are as follows:

1. To accomplish this, click on **Search**:

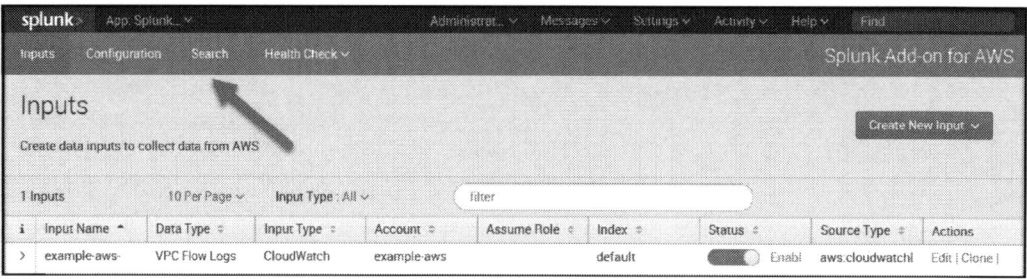

Figure 6.31 – Searching on AWS

2. On the **Search** page (shown in the following screenshot), click on **Data Summary**:

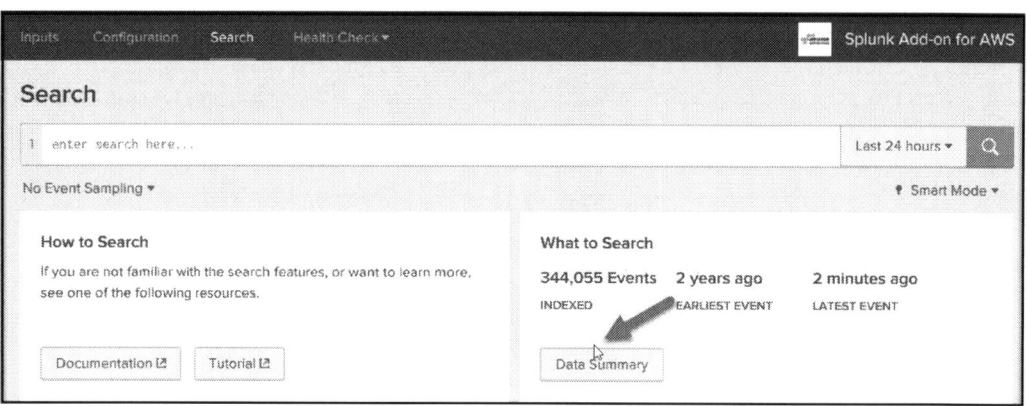

Figure 6.32 – Data Summary

3. On the **Data Summary** dialog (shown in the following screenshot), click on **Sourcetypes**:

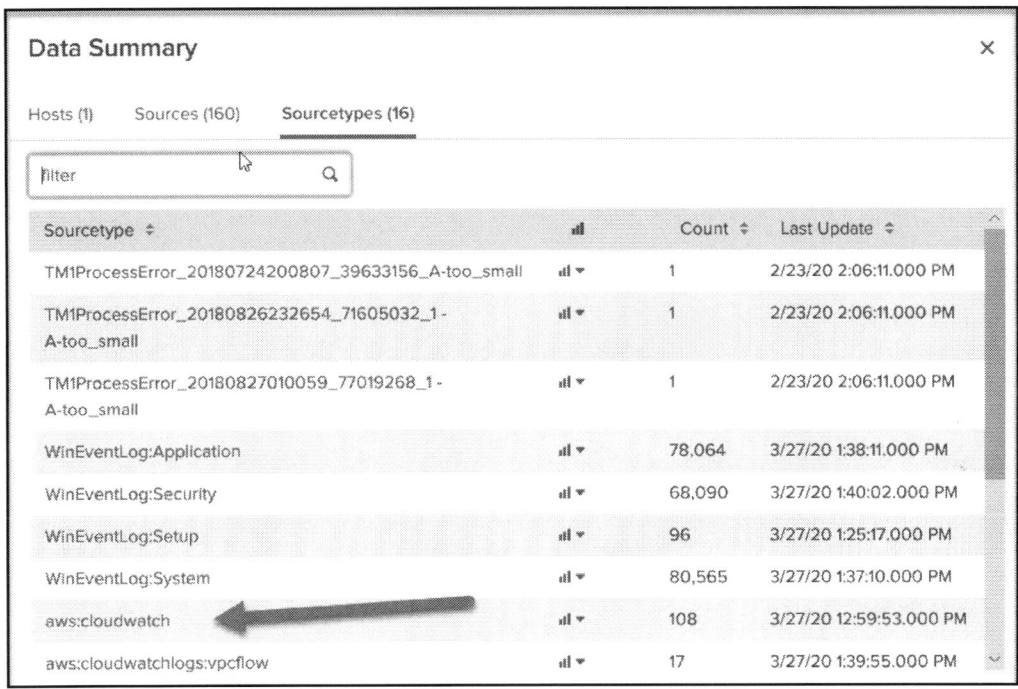

Figure 6.33 – List of Sourcetypes

4. In the **Sourcetypes** list (shown in the preceding screenshot), scroll down until you find the `aws:cloudwatch` source type and click on it.

This will take you to the **Search** page with `"sourcetype="aws:cloudwatch"` already entered in the **Search** line for you. Splunk should automatically run the search and display the results:

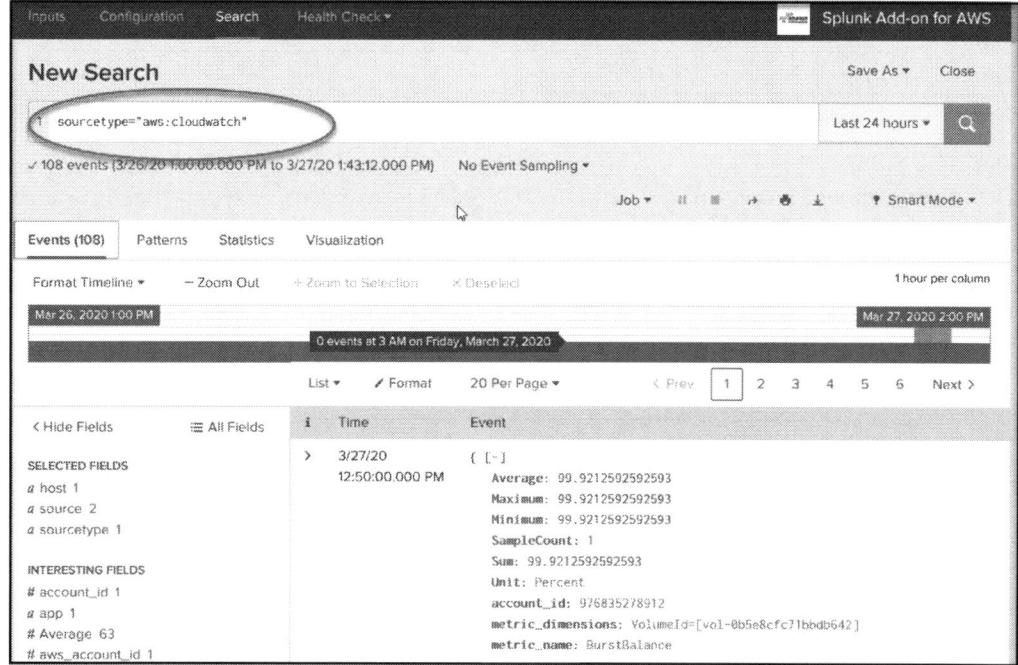

Figure 6.34 – Search result

Take some time to explore the fields listed on the left of the page. For example, if you click on the field named `app`, you will see the following dialog. Note that the only value for the `app` field is `aws:cloudwatch` (as shown). This makes sense since we have only set up one input for our Splunk add-on, `aws:cloudwatch`:

Integrating with AWS 143

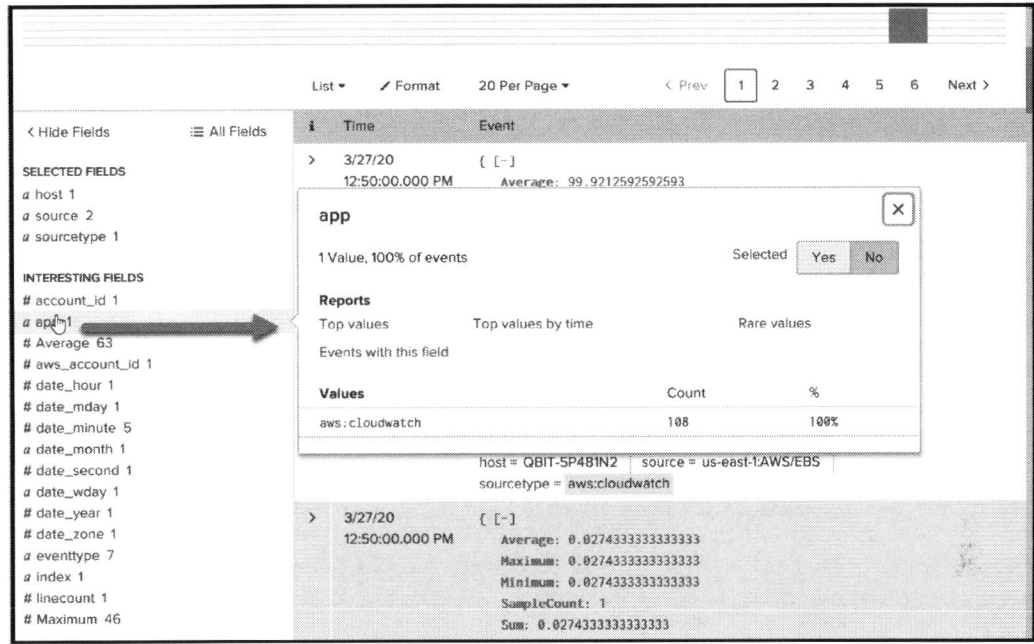

Figure 6.35 – Exploring fields

With our Azure integration example, we created a Splunk alert as the last step in the stated integration strategy (create reports and or dashboards showing (**see**) the new data as insightful information within the Splunk interface). In this example, we can easily create a **Splunk Bar Chart** visualization showing the event types that have been recorded in our AWS logs:

1. To do this, you can enter a **New Search** using the following command:

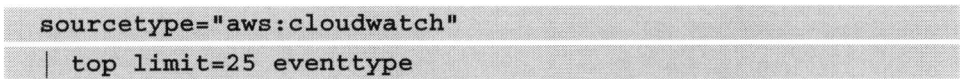

```
sourcetype="aws:cloudwatch"
| top limit=25 eventtype
```

2. Then, click on the search icon, as shown in the following screenshot:

Figure 6.36 – New search

3. Once you execute the search, click on **Visualization**:

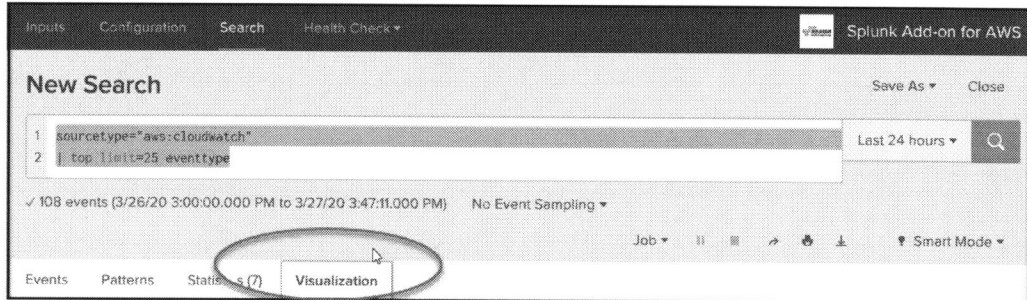

Figure 6.37 – New search visualization

Splunk will create the following bar chart:

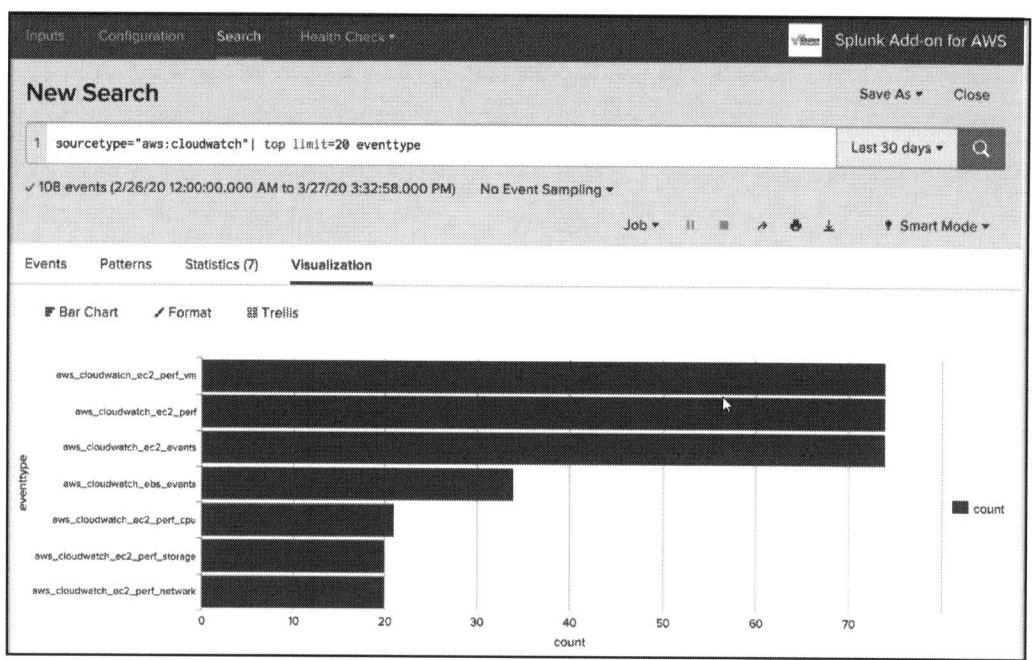

Figure 6.38 – Bar chart

At this point, we have connected to and integrated AWS data with Splunk. It may be worth mentioning that these examples represent only one way to bring data into Splunk from Azure and AWS, and that there are other options that may be preferred in other scenarios (such as using HEC, for example).

Summary

In this chapter, we indicated that Splunk offers a variety of methods for integrating data from other platforms. We outlined a common data integration strategy and elected to use Splunk add-ons to integrate both Azure and AWS data into our Splunk instance. We successfully searched that data and then presented it. We have seen how easy it is to leverage the functionality of the powerful Splunk engine to seamlessly search data generated by these technology platforms.

In the next chapter, we will show you how to create categorical charts (line, column, area, time-column) and run analytical operations on metrics and accelerated datasets using reference lines to metrics data. We will do this to make comparisons and perform analysis using the latest features within the Splunk analytics workspace.

Section 3: Advanced Reporting and Dashboards

This section covers all the advanced features that could help you deal with reporting and dashboards.

This section comprises the following chapters:

- *Chapter 7, Advanced Reporting – Analytics Workspace*
- *Chapter 8, Advanced Reporting – Histogram Metric Data Types*
- *Chapter 9, Search Performance Considerations*
- *Chapter 10, Advanced Reporting Using Macros*
- *Chapter 11, Dashboards – Advanced Data Analytics*
- *Chapter 12, Dashboards – Correlating Events*
- *Chapter 13, Dashboards – Workflow Actions*
- *Chapter 14, Dashboards – Monitoring and Operability*
- *Chapter 15, Dashboards – Custom Visualizations*

7
Advanced Reporting – Analytics Workspace

In the previous chapter, we indicated that Splunk offers a variety of methods for integrating data from other platforms. We outlined a common data integration strategy and elected to use Splunk add-ons to integrate both Azure and AWS data into our Splunk instance, and successfully searched that data and then presented it. We have seen how easy it is to leverage the functionality of the powerful Splunk engine to seamlessly search data generated by these technology platforms.

In this chapter, the reader will learn how to create categorical charts (such as line, column, area, and time-column) and run analytical operations on metrics and accelerated datasets using reference lines to metrics data for comparison and analysis using the latest features within the **Splunk analytics workspace**. The Splunk analytics workspace is a built-in module that aims to enable easy monitoring and analysis of metrics and trends in data without having to create and use search commands. In this chapter, you will learn how to access and use the workspace to easily monitor and track metrics using the most popular charts and visualizations.

This chapter will be broken down into the following main sections:

- Workspace review
- Categorical charts
- Running analytical operations
- Adding reference lines
- Streaming alerts
- Expanding the time-range picker

Let's get started!

Workspace review

The Splunk analytics workspace provides a *built-in* user interface that enables you to monitor and analyze metrics and other time series in data without having to create or write your own **search processing language** (**SPL**). Its intention is to allow you to select a data source and then create interactive visualizations (within the workspace), apply filters and aggregations to the data, and rapidly gain insights.

The analytics workspace helps you to identify and then respond to issues or anomalies in data you are interested in, find correlations much quicker than if you had to build your own search statements, apply filtering and aggregations, and then create visualizations.

The analytics workspace comes with a set of built-in analytic functions and operations to help you make sense of your data. Depending on your data source, the following operations are available in the workspace:

- `Aggregations` summarize data points into meaningful values.
- `Time shifts` modify the time range of a series.
- `Splits` show results for a specific dimension.
- `Filters` include or exclude certain results.

You can access the Splunk analytics workspace from the Splunk main page by clicking on **Search & Reporting** and then **Analytics**:

Figure 7.1 – Splunk Analytics

Now let's look into the workspace and understand the layouts.

Workspace layout

Once the workspace loads, you will see that the workspace is divided into three main *panels*, as shown in the following screenshot:

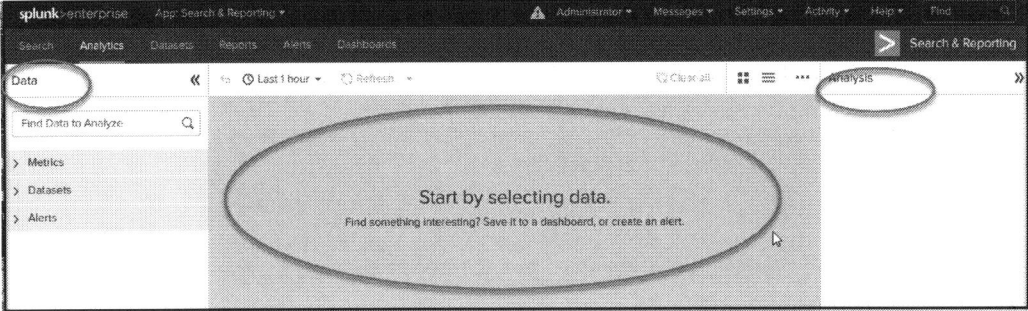

Figure 7.2 – Splunk workspace

The panels are as follows:

- **Data**: The data panel is located on the left-hand side of the workspace and lists all data sources that are available for analysis within the workspace.

- **Main panel**: The main panel is in the center of the workspace and is where you see your data represented as visualizations.

- **Analysis**: The analysis panel is on the right-hand side of the workspace and lists the aggregations and analytic functions that you can apply to your data in real time.

Using the analytics workspace

The workspace is all about metrics. Therefore, to best understand how it works, think about how metrics are generally interpreted. For example, think of a metric as a data point that you want to monitor and measure overtime. An example of a metric might be a company's inventory level for a popular product. Now, suppose that you might want to compare the inventory level for this product from different warehouse locations, on different days, this is considered an overtime.

With this product inventory scenario in mind, the metric data you would typically maintain are the following data points: *metric name*, a *value*, a *location*, a *day*, and a *time*, or Product A, 4000, PA, 2/23/20, 10:00 AM EST. Building on this idea, suppose that you have invested in a multilocation, 24-hour, self-service kayak rental business that allows individuals to check out, use, and then re-dock kayaks themselves using a slick new smart phone app. To gain a better insight into how your business is doing, you want to analyze the following metrics:

- Kayak inventories
- Kayak availability checks using the phone app
- Social media mentions of your business
- The general *user sentiment*

Suppose you have had metrics collected and saved into a **comma separated values** (**CSV**) file in the following format:

- `metric_timestamp` (a unique ID for the metric record)
- `metric_name` (the metric descriptive name)
- `_value` (the value for this metric)
- `city` (the location, in this case, city name)
- `day` (the day (of the week) that the metric value was recorded)
- `date` (the date that the metric value was recorded)

Loading the data

To use our data work in the Splunk analytics workspace, you need to create a metrics index for the data first. We created metrics indexes in an earlier chapter, so this should be simple. As a refresher, we will list the steps again:

1. From the Splunk main page, click on **Settings** and then **Indexes**.
2. Click **New Index**.
3. For **Index Name**, type `kayaks`.
4. For **Index Data Type**, click **Metrics**.
5. For the remaining properties of the index, just use the default values.
6. Click **Save**.

Now that we have our metric index created, we can tell Splunk to load and index our metric data (into that index). The steps are as follows:

1. From the Splunk main page, click on **Settings** and then **Add Data**:

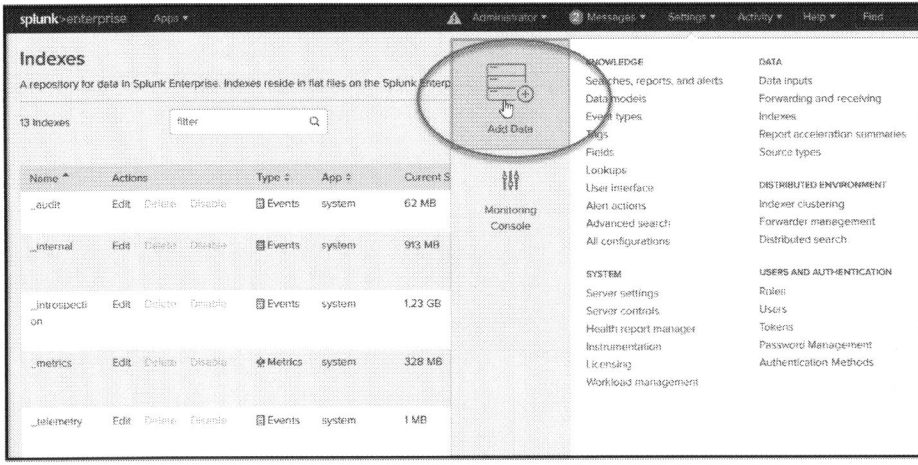

Figure 7.3 – Adding data

2. Scroll down and click **Upload files from my computer**:

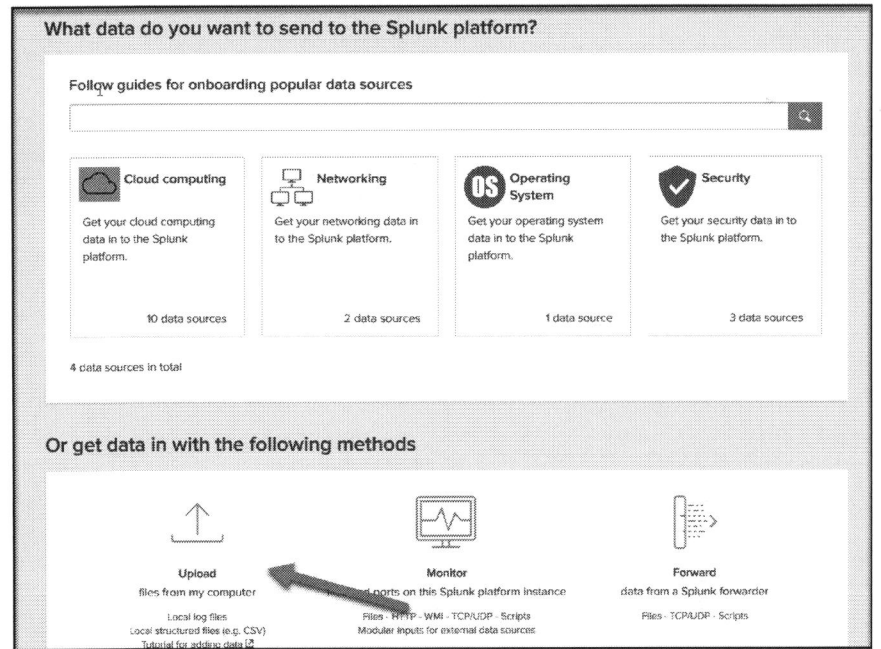

Figure 7.4 – Uploading data

3. Under **Select Source**, click **Select File**:

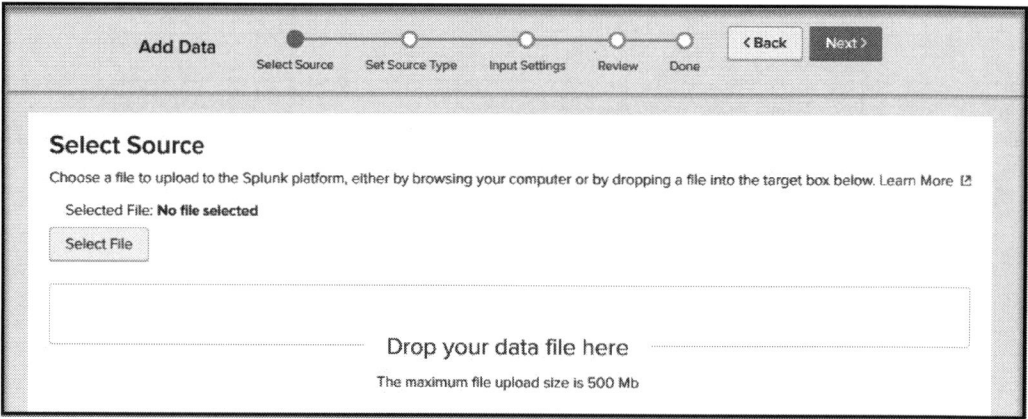

Figure 7.5 – Selecting files

4. Locate the `metrics-example-kayaks.csv` file and click **Open**. After the file finishes uploading, click **Next**:

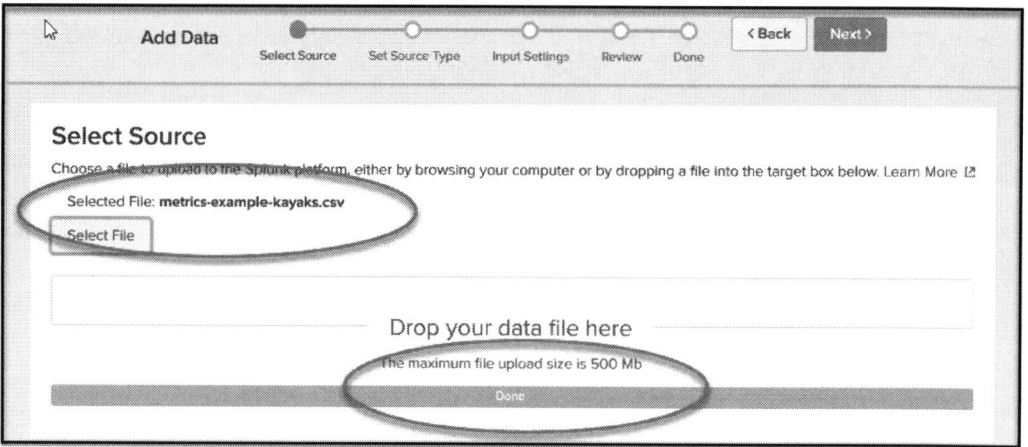

Figure 7.6 – Uploading metrics-example-kayaks.csv

5. Under **Set Source Type**, click the **Source type** drop-down list, click **Metrics**, then `metrics_csv`, and then click **Next**:

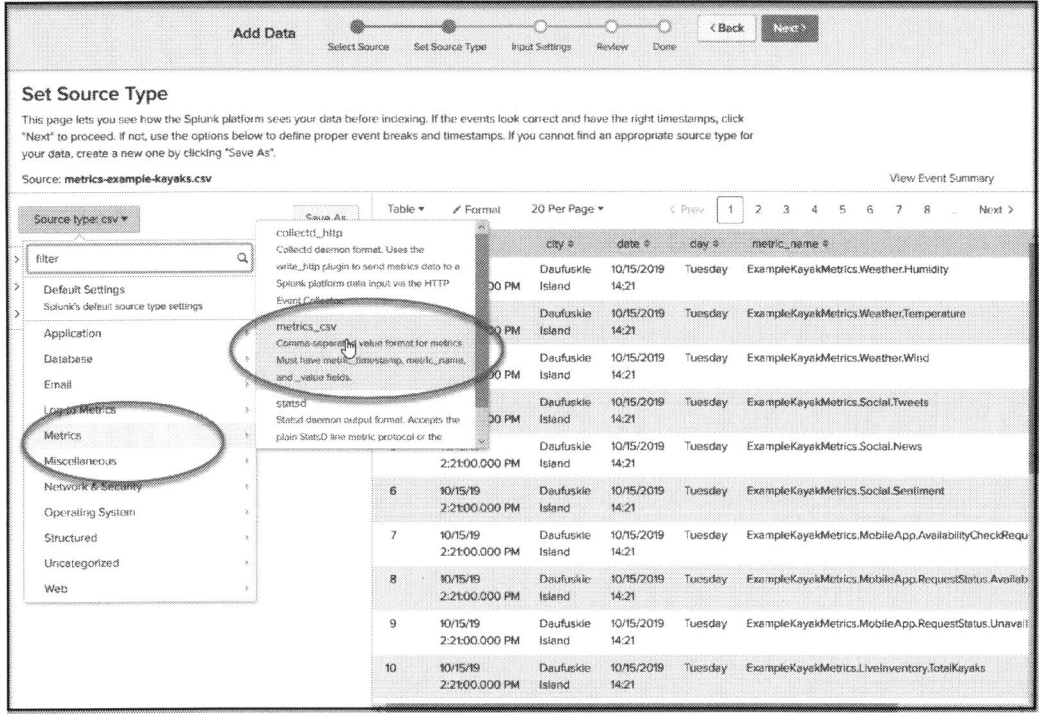

Figure 7.7 – Setting the source type

6. On the **Input Settings** page, under **Index**, select **kayaks** and then click **Review**:

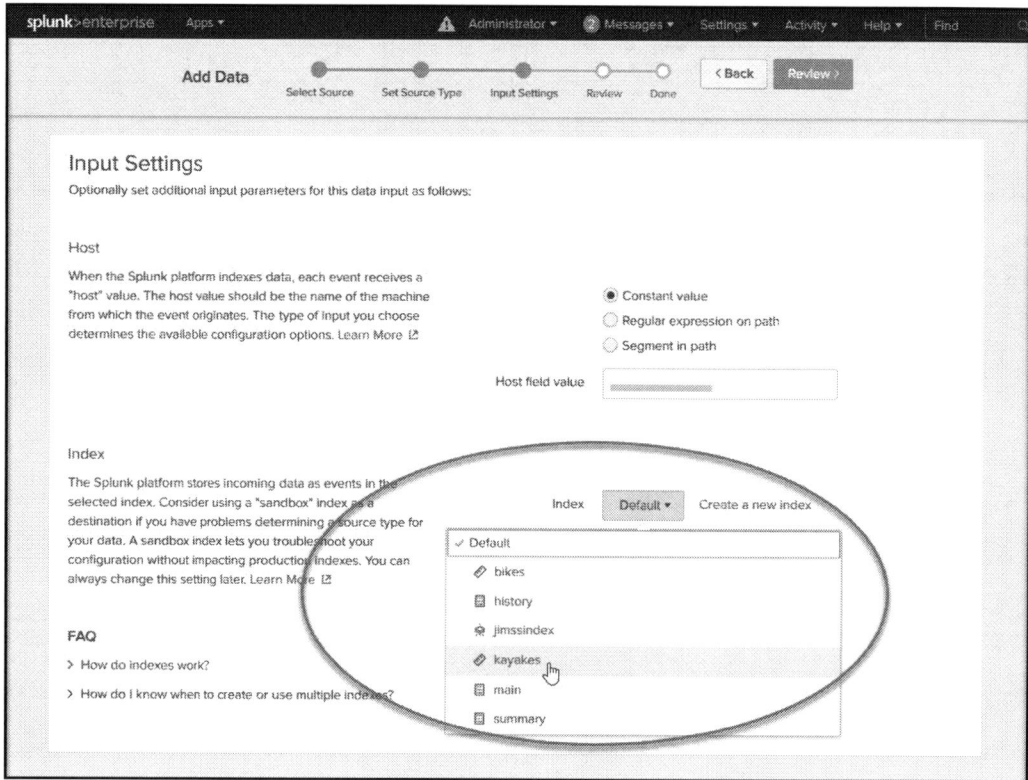

Figure 7.8 – Input Settings

7. Click **Submit**:

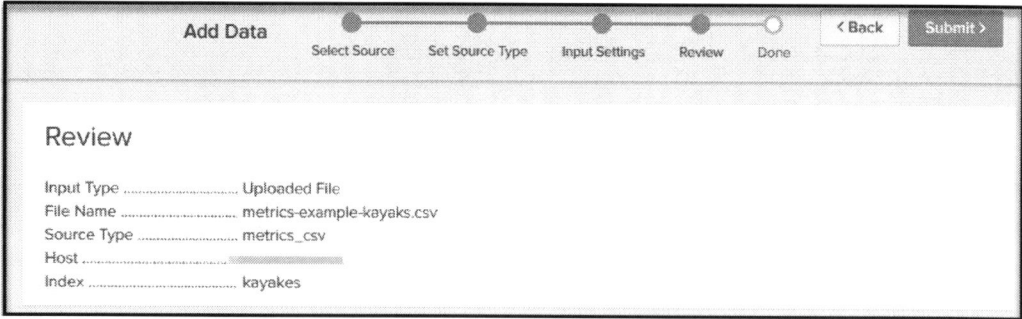

Figure 7.9 – Review

Now we are ready to see the analytics workspace in action!

If you open the analytics workspace (from the Splunk main page, click on **Search & Reporting**, and then click on **Analytics**), you can click **Metrics** in the data panel.

This will display a list of available metrics data. Locate **ExampleKayakMetrics** from within the list of metrics data sources:

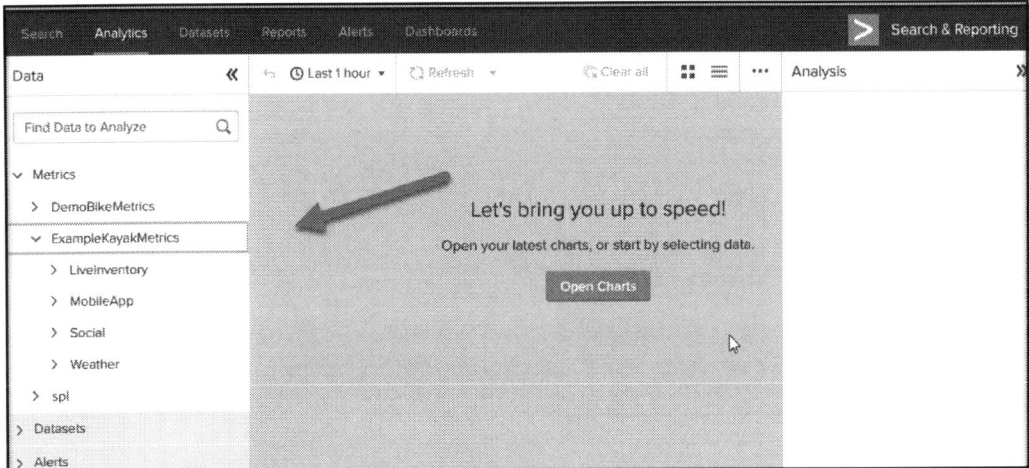

Figure 7.10 – Locating ExampleKayakMetrics

Analyzing with the workspace

Now, with just a few clicks, you can view dynamic charts within the workspace. For example, try the following:

- To view a chart showing checked-out kayak inventory over time, click on **Metrics | ExampleKayakMetrics | LiveInventory | CheckedOut**. To adjust the workspace time range, in the global actions bar, click the time range picker, and then select **Last 48 hours**.

- To view a chart showing the number of times the phone app was used to check kayak availability over time, click **Metrics | ExampleKayakMetrics | MobileApp | AvailabilityCheckRequests**.

- To view a chart showing social media mentions over time, click **Metrics | ExampleKayakMetrics | Social | News**.

- To view a chart showing user sentiment over time, click **Metrics | ExampleKayakMetrics | Social | Sentiment**.

158   Advanced Reporting – Analytics Workspace

Using Split By

To view how your metrics vary based on city, click on any chart in the workspace (to select the chart) and then, in the **Analysis** panel, under **Split By**, select **city**.

(You can repeat this process for each of the other three charts in the workspace if you like).

In addition, you can also do the following:

- View the workspace in a grid layout by clicking the grid icon ⸬ in the global actions bar.
- Change the **Chart type** property by clicking **Chart Settings** and then selecting a different chart type.

Without writing an SPL or creating visualizations, the workspace creates and displays some pretty interesting charts automatically:

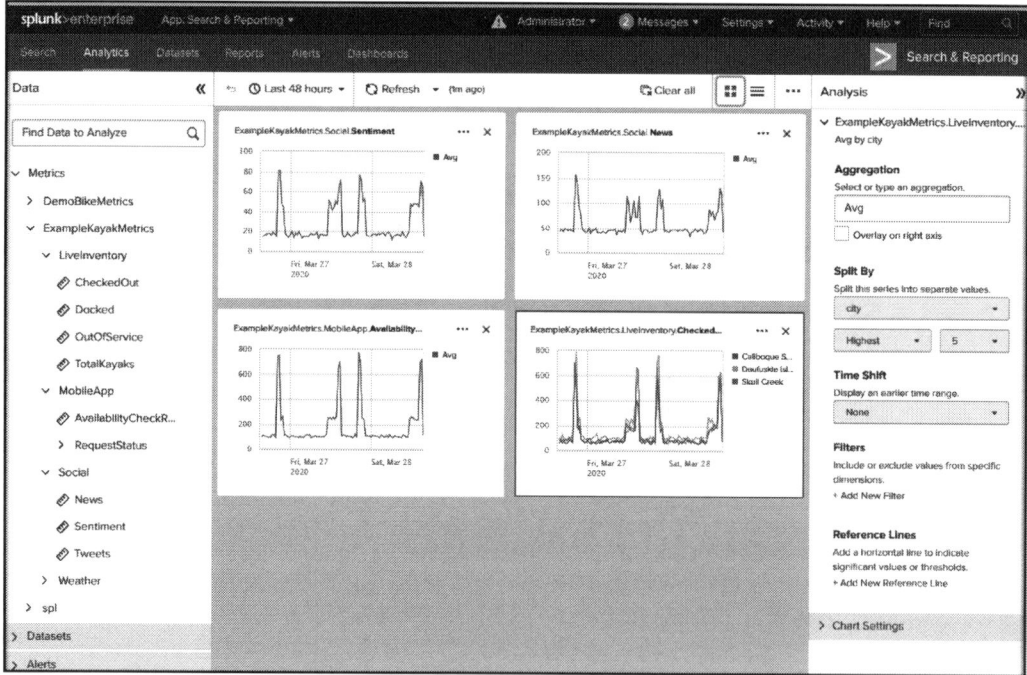

Figure 7.11 – Grid view of the workspace

> **Hint**
> You can always *hover* over any data point on any chart generated in the workspace to view the equivalent values in the chart legend.

Categorical charts

By default, the Splunk analytics workspace **Analysis** panel (shown in the following screenshot) offers a **Chart Type** area where you can choose a chart type based on your requirements. The selection list is divided into two types — TIME CHARTS (**Line**, **Area**, and **Column**) and CATEGORICAL CHARTS (**Column** and **Stacked Column**):

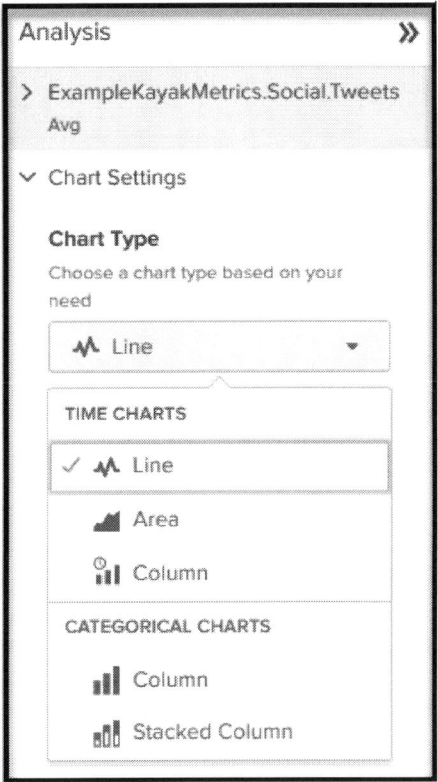

Figure 7.12 – Types of charts

While time charts visualize data over time, allowing you to identify trends in your data, categorical charts show data over time and grouped by data dimensions, allowing you to analyze and compare the different dimensions across multiple metrics (both of these chart types allow the data to be split by dimensions).

Multiple metrics

You can add additional metrics to a workspace chart to analyze correlations in the data:

1. To do this, select an existing chart from the main panel of the **Analytics** workspace by clicking on it:

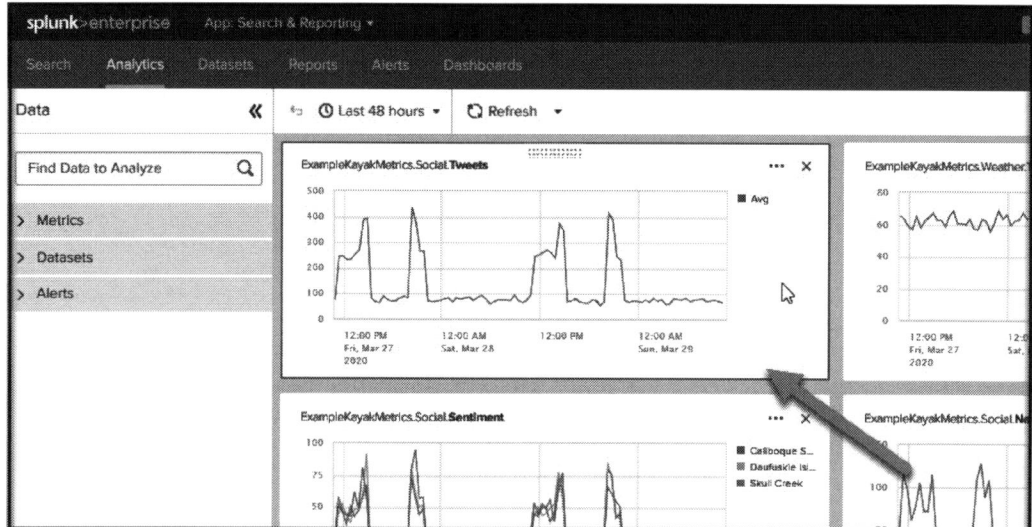

Figure 7.13 – Selecting an existing chart

2. Next, within the Splunk **Analytics** workspace data panel, search or browse for the data source that you want to add to the selected chart and *hover over* the data source that you want to add to the chart. The **Add to selected chart** ( ) icon will appear (as shown in the following screenshot):

Categorical charts   161

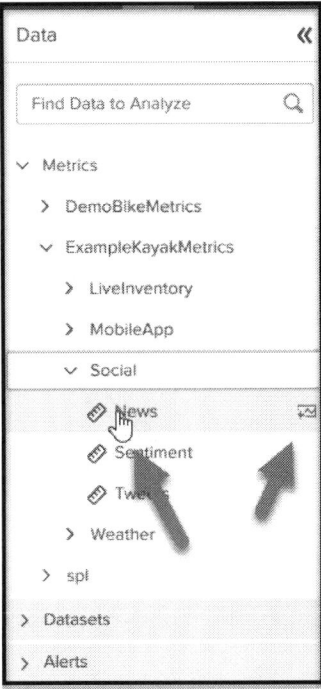

Figure 7.14 – The Add to selected chart icon

3. Click the **Add to selected chart** ( ) icon to add that data source to the selected chart. The new data source will now appear as an added time series on your selected chart. In our example (shown in the following screenshot), we have added social media news to the chart that originally only displayed social media tweets:

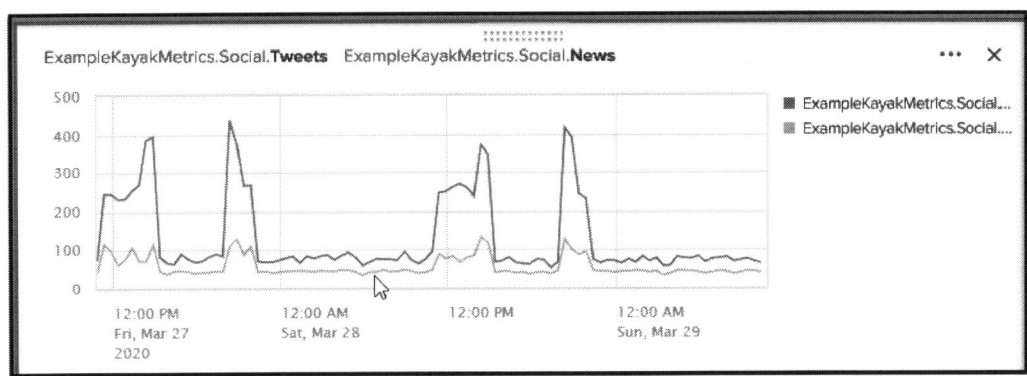

Figure 7.15 – Additional metric added

Looking at the preceding updated chart, there may be some correlation between the number of tweets and news.

You can always eliminate the added (or any) time series metric from an existing chart, as shown in the following screenshot:

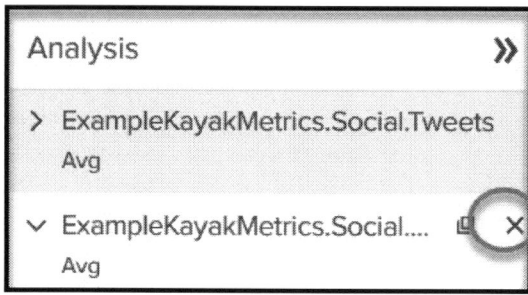

Figure 7.16 – Eliminating the added metric

To do so, locate the name of the time series that you want to eliminate (in the **Analysis** panel) and click the **X** icon located next to the name of the time series.

Running analytical operations

Once you assembled one or more analytical charts within the Splunk **Analytics** workspace, you can configure analytic functions and operations available in the analysis panel to do much more with the charts. Keep in mind that each of these functions automatically generate SPL (in the background) so you don't have to.

Aggregation

Charts created within the Splunk **Analytics** workspace contain time series based on aggregated data. To calculate those aggregations, Splunk categorizes data points within roughly the same time frame into what they call **buckets**. Aggregations are calculated from the data points within the same bucket, so in other words, once Splunk has grouped the data points within a bucket (a time range) it can then easily execute the average aggregation function on them.

Selecting an aggregation

To execute an aggregation operation (or any analytical operation) on a chart within the **Analytics** workspace, you always first select the chart that you want to update, and then use the **Analysis** panel to select and configure the operation. Let's look at a simple example. In the following screenshot, we have a chart in our main workspace panel showing a visualization of the average temperature during a specific time frame (**Last 48 hours**):

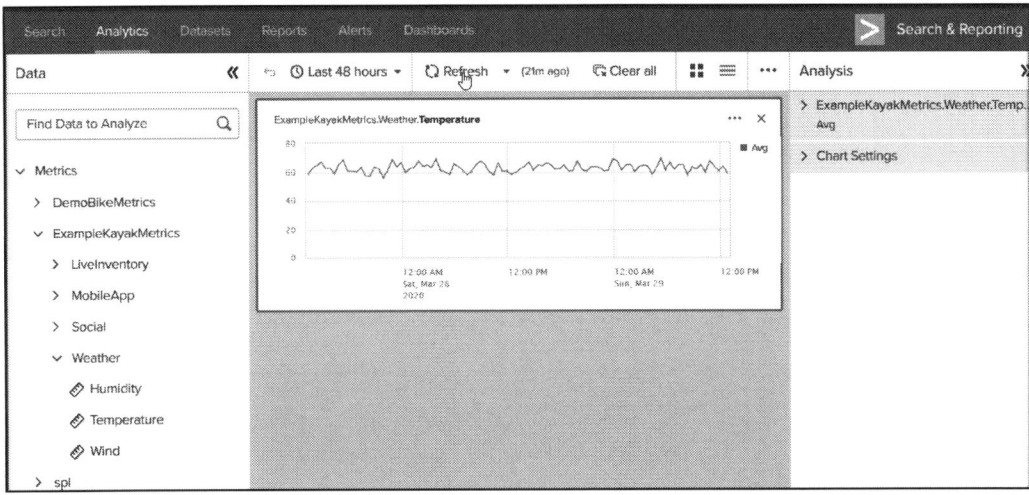

Figure 7.17 – Chart of the average temperature during a specific time frame

Suppose we want to add another aggregation on the measure to show the maximum temperature during that same time range. To do that, you can perform the following steps:

1. In the **Data** panel, hover over **Temperature** and click the **Add to selected chart** icon. Splunk will add the measure as **(2)** to the **Analysis** panel:

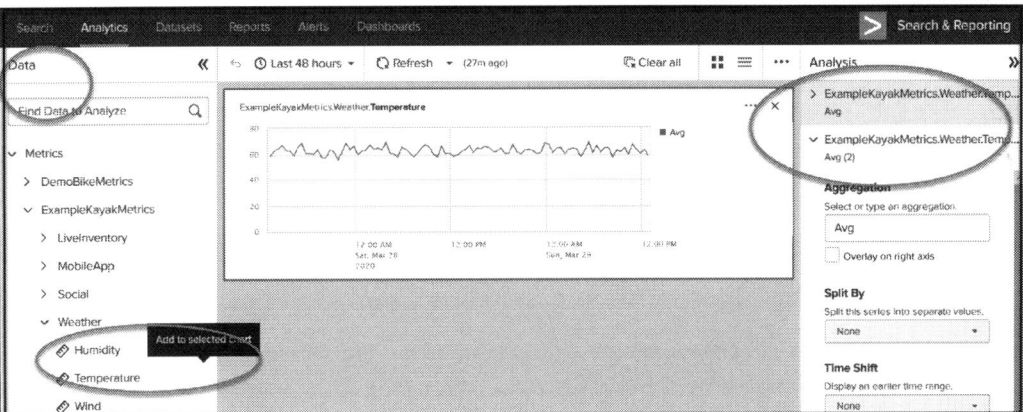

Figure 7.18 – Adding another aggregation

2. Next, you can now click on the measure (again on the **Analysis** panel) and then select **Max** as the **Aggregation** operation. Splunk will add the new time series to the selected chart and update it for us:

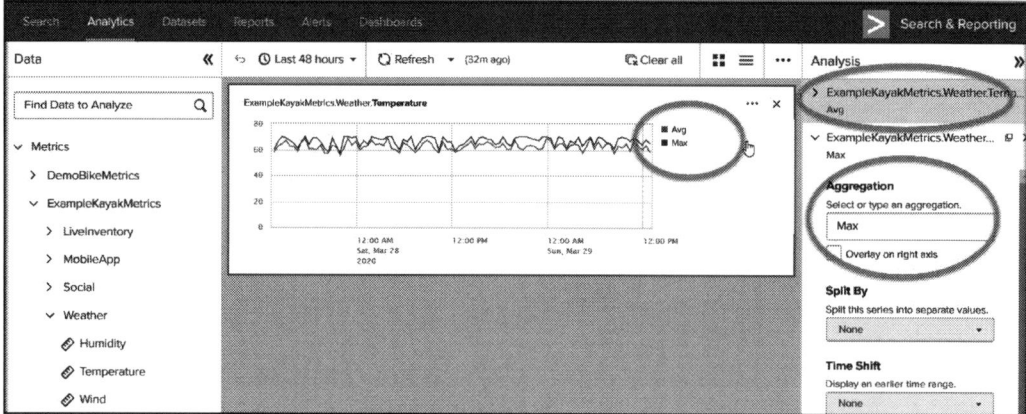

Figure 7.19 – Adding Max aggregation

You can see the result in the preceding screenshot. Both the **Avg** and **Max** temperatures are displayed for comparison!

Comparing time range

The Splunk **Analytics** workspace makes a comparison of changes in data over time very easy by offering a (chart action) clone function and the time shift analytical operation.

To perform a quick time range comparison, you can perform the following steps:

1. In the main panel of the Splunk **Analytics** workspace, select the chart that you want to configure, click on the ... icon, and then select (from chart actions) **Clone this Panel**:

Running analytical operations   165

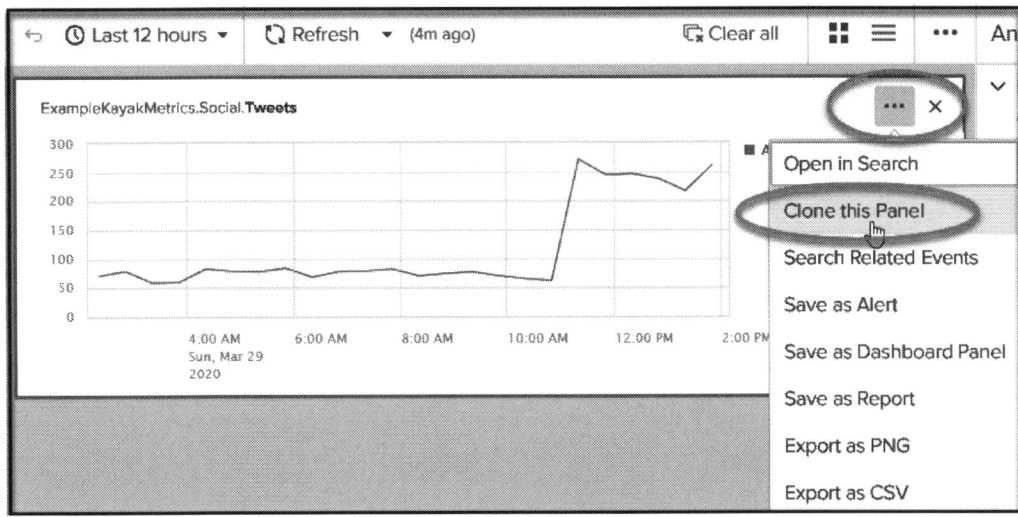

Figure 7.20 – Cloning panel

2. Once Splunk has made a clone (a copy) of the selected chart, you can then click on **Time Shift** and select a time frame shift value. In this example, I have selected **24 hours ago** and Splunk has shifted the cloned chart accordingly so I can compare (in this example) the average number of tweets in the last 12 hours, as compared to the average number of tweets during a 12-hour time period 24 hours ago:

Figure 7.21 – Comparing the time range

> **Note**
> The time-shifted series appears as dotted lines on the cloned chart. To remove a time shift, just select **None** as the time shift value.

Filtering data

Another analytical operation supported in the Splunk **Analytics** workspace is the ability filter data displayed in a chart by a specific dimension value.

If you have already added **Split By** (we did this earlier in the chapter) to a workspace chart, you can then use a filter to add or remove (exclude) time series data for selected dimension values:

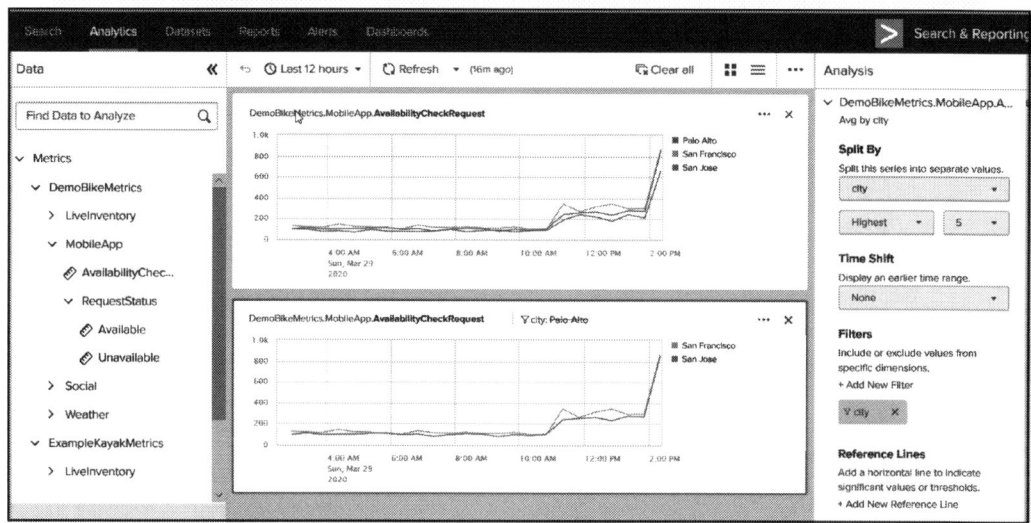

Figure 7.22 – Filtering data

> **Hint**
> To filter from the chart legend, you can click the name of the dimension value that you want to filter and then click either **Keep Only** or **Exclude** from the options that appear.

Stacking time series

You can stack the time series on an area chart to see how each series relates to the chart's data as a whole. Stacking time series in an area chart shows the sum of dimension values. In an area chart, each series appears as a filled-in area on the chart. To switch to a chart type of area, you can perform the following steps:

1. In the main panel of the **Analytics** workspace, select the chart that you want to stack the series for.
2. In the **Analysis** panel, click **Chart Settings**.
3. From the **Chart Type** drop-down menu, select **Area**.

Adding reference lines

A **reference line** (also known as a **base line**) is a user-defined vertical or horizontal line in a graph or visualization. You can use reference lines to compare, reference, or measure against the data values displayed in the visualization.

You can easily add reference lines to charts created in the Splunk **Analytics** workspace. To add a reference line to a chart, you use the **Reference Lines | + Add New Reference Line** feature in the **Analysis** panel.

Here is an example of using a reference line in the Splunk **Analytics** workspace to establish a base line for wind speed during a time series:

1. In the **Analytics** workspace, click on **Weather** and then **Wind** in the **Data** panel of the workspace. Splunk will create a chart showing the average wind speed for the time range. Adjust the time range to **Last 7 days**:

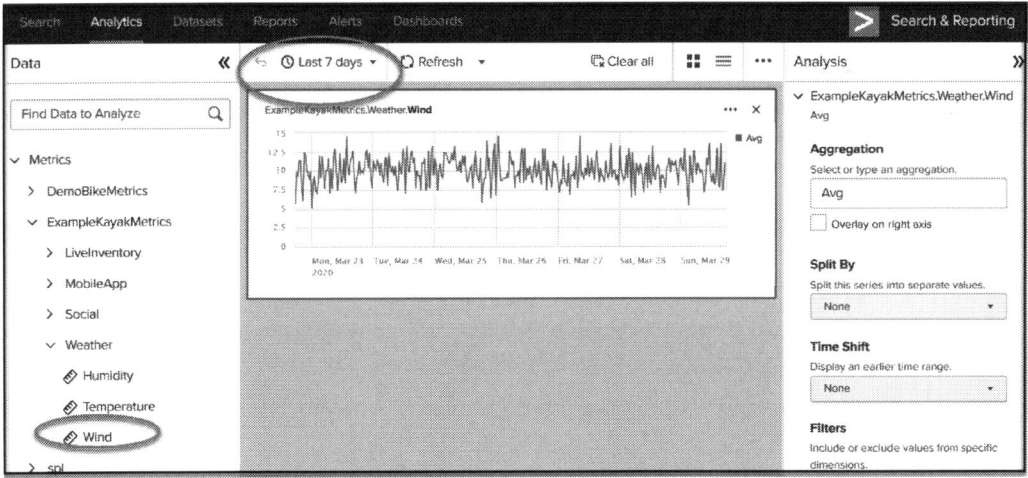

Figure 7.23 – Wind speed data

2. Now, using the **Analysis** panel, change **Aggregation** to **Max**, and then scroll down and, under **Reference Lines**, click **+ Add New Reference Line**.

168   Advanced Reporting – Analytics Workspace

3. Under **Add a New Reference Line**, click the radio button that says **Raw Data** and for **Value**, select **Avg**. For **Label**, type Average Wind Speed:

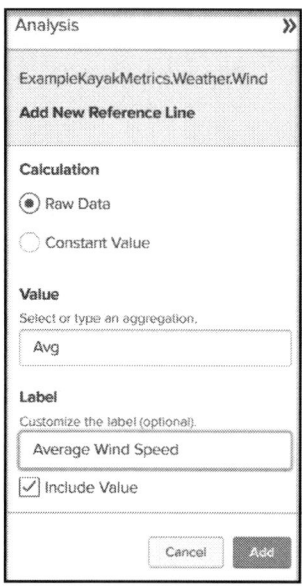

Figure 7.24 – Adding new reference line

> **Hint**
> If no label text is provided by you, the aggregation name is used for the reference line label.

4. Finally, click **Add**. Splunk updates the chart with the reference line (as shown in the following screenshot):

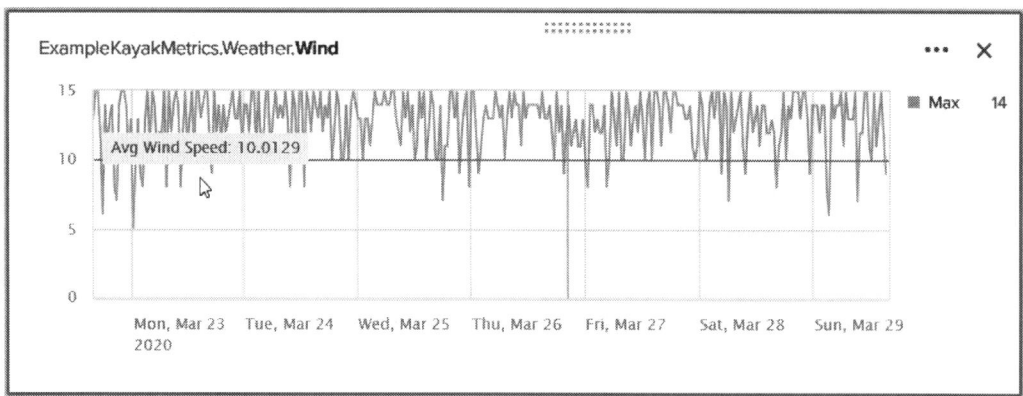

Figure 7.25 – New reference line added to the wind speed data

Now, by using the *average wind speed* base line as a reference, we can see that over the last 7 days, the wind speed was typically always above average.

Streaming alerts

Splunk alerts use saved search commands to look for specific events (in real time or on a schedule) that occur in data. The alert will trigger when the search results meet specific conditions. The idea is to set up an alert and use it to monitor and automatically respond to a behavior in data.

Splunk **Analytics** workspace alerts also use saved searches and are configured to automatically trigger when search results meet specific conditions but are based on a specific workspace chart. A workspace alert is made up of settings, trigger conditions, and trigger actions. You can create and maintain workspace alerts from within the workspace.

As an illustration, let's create a workspace alert based upon our test kayak data. Assuming that we have already created a chart showing the average number of kayaks that are unavailable over the last 48 hours, let's create an alert to monitor this metric and do something should the number of kayaks be unavailable.

In the **Analytics** workspace, click on the chart to select it and then click on the ... icon (chart actions) and select **Save as Alert**:

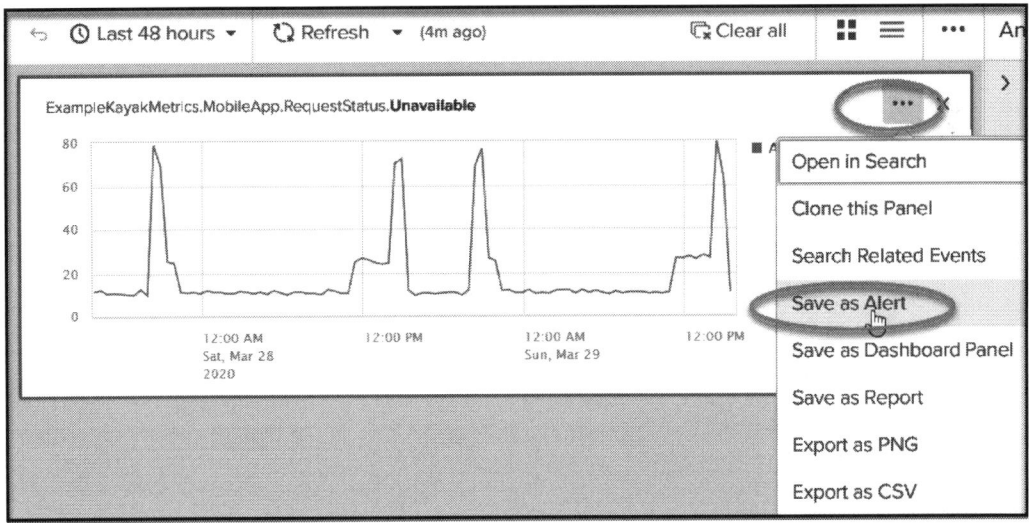

Figure 7.26 – Saving an alert

The **Save as Alert** dialog appears:

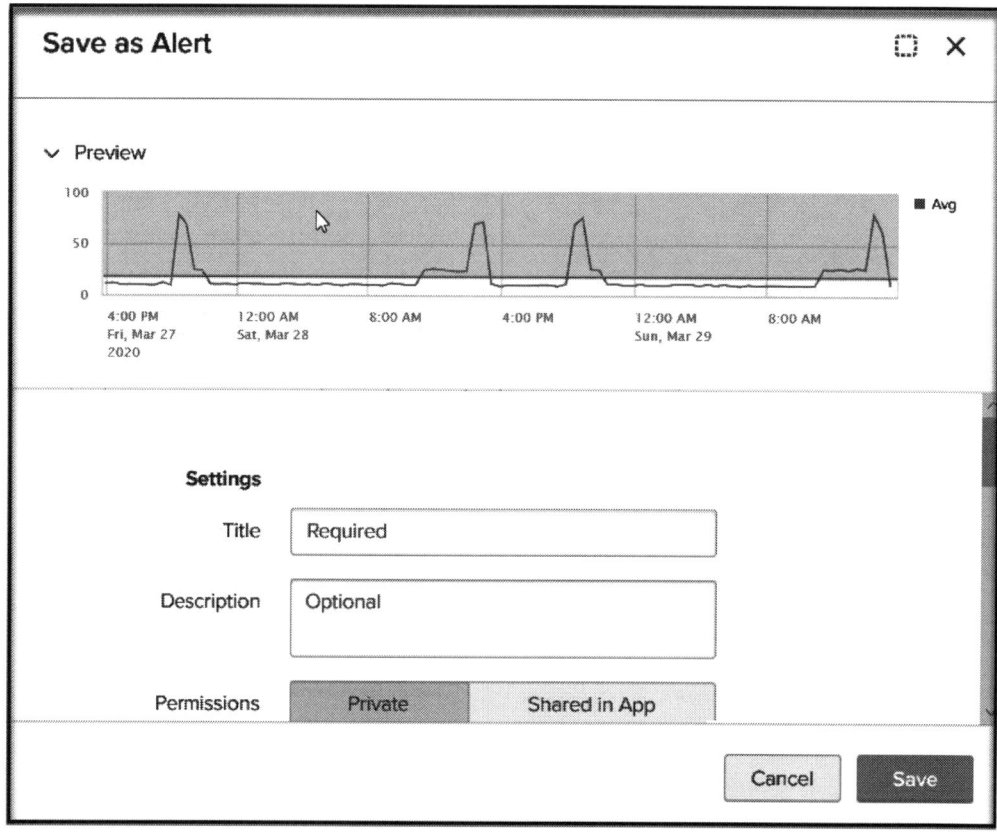

Figure 7.27 – Save as Alert dialog box

You can scroll through and configure the three alert sections, starting with **Settings**:

- **Title** (friendly name, enter `Unavailable Alert`)
- **Description** (enter `An Alert Example`)
- **Permissions** (indicates whether the alert is private or shared in the workspace, select **Private**).
- **Alert Type** (**Scheduled** alerts periodically search for trigger conditions. **Streaming** alerts continuously search for trigger conditions. Select **Streaming**).
- **Evaluate every** (How often do you want to check the alert conditions? Enter `1` and `Hours`)

You set the alerts trigger conditions next. You set the alert to trigger if the metric value is greater or less than a certain value and in the last minutes/hours/days/weeks. You can enter the following: **Is greater than 15 in the last 1 hour**.

Leave the **Throttle** checkbox checked and enter `30 minutes` for the **Suppress Triggering** option.

This tells Splunk that the alert does not have to trigger for 30 seconds after the trigger condition is met.

Finally, we need to tell Splunk what to do if the alert is triggered. You can select an option from the **Trigger Actions** drop-down list. We can select **Output results to lookup**. You will need to supply some additional details depending upon which action you choose; for example, we would have to provide a valid filename for this option.

Lastly, once you have filled out the **Save as Alert** dialog, you can click on **Save** and your alert is ready to go and will be listed under **Alerts** in the **Data** panel of the Splunk **Analytics** workspace (as shown in the following screenshot):

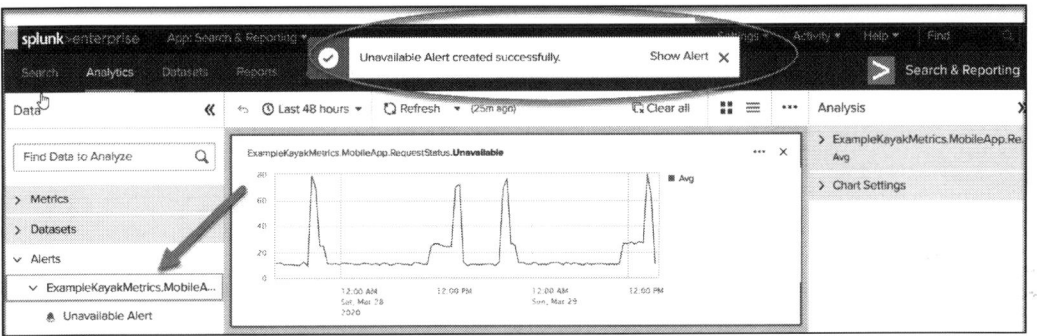

Figure 7.28 – Alert created successfully

Management of alerts

You can conveniently view all of the alerts that you created using the Splunk **Analytics** workspace to monitor and respond to alert activity. You can display any alert in the **Analytics** workspace by clicking on **Alert** in the **Data** panel.

When you add an alert this way, it will show in the same time range as the other charts currently displayed in the workspace. If you change the time range, then all of the charts, as well as the alerts, will reset to that new time range.

As you can see in the following screenshot, the alert is displayed at the top of the **Analytics** workspace main panel and is set to **Last 24 hours** (rather than the original **Last 48 hours**):

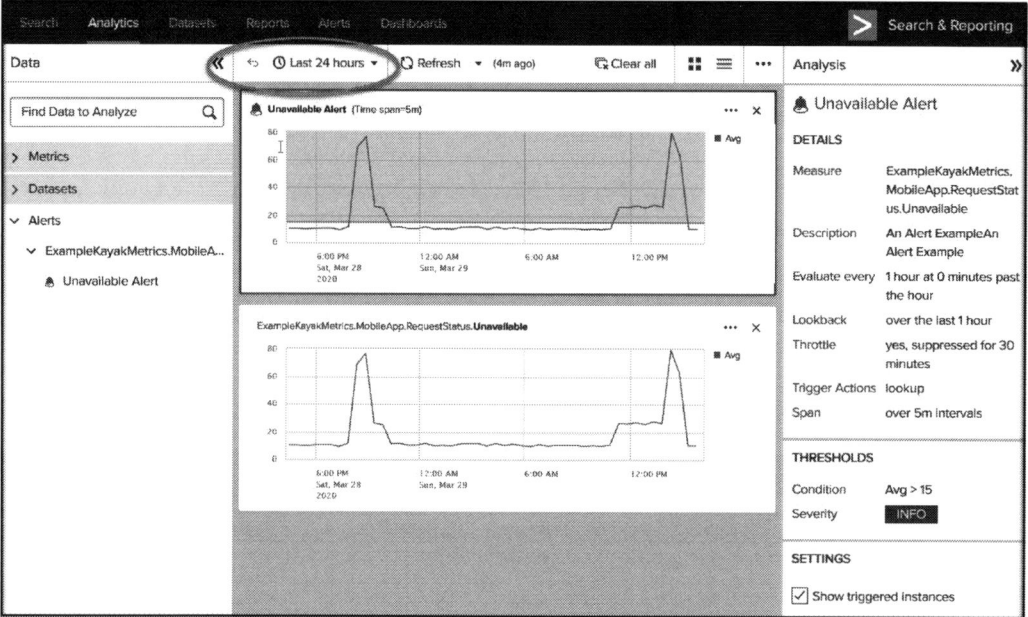

Figure 7.29 – New alert set and displayed

You will also see that if you click on the alert, its configuration details are displayed on the right, in the **Analysis** panel. To edit the alert, click on the ... icon (chart actions) in the top-right corner of the alert chart and select **Edit Alert** (as shown in the following screenshot):

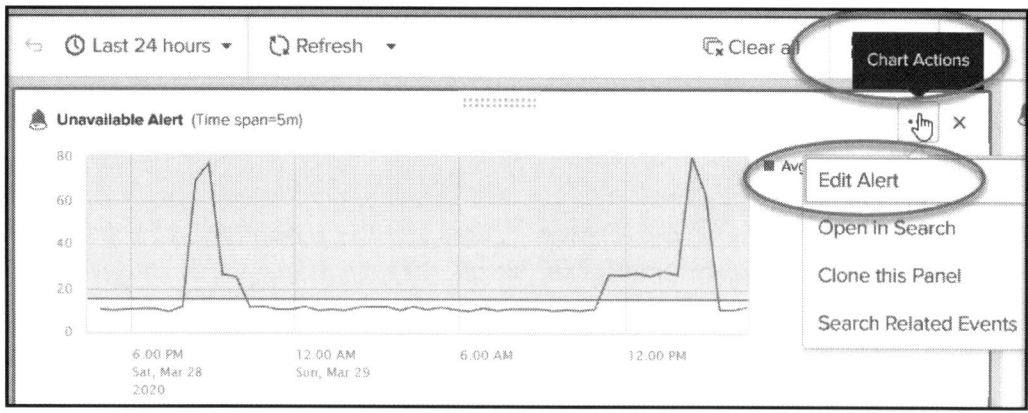

Figure 7.30 – Editing an alert

> **Hint**
> If you select the chart action **Open in Search**, Splunk will show the SPL that drives the alert in the **Search & Reporting** page.

Expanding the time range picker

Just like in the Splunk **Search & Reporting** page, the Splunk **Analytics** workspace has its own time range picker (located at the top of the **Main** workspace panel, on what is called the **global actions bar**), and it works in the same fashion. The default time range for the workspace is always 1 hour.

To change the time range using the picker, perform the following steps:

1. Click on the time range picker.
2. Select a preset time range from the list or select **Custom**. If you select **Custom**, the **Custom Time Range** dialog (shown in the following screenshot) is displayed:

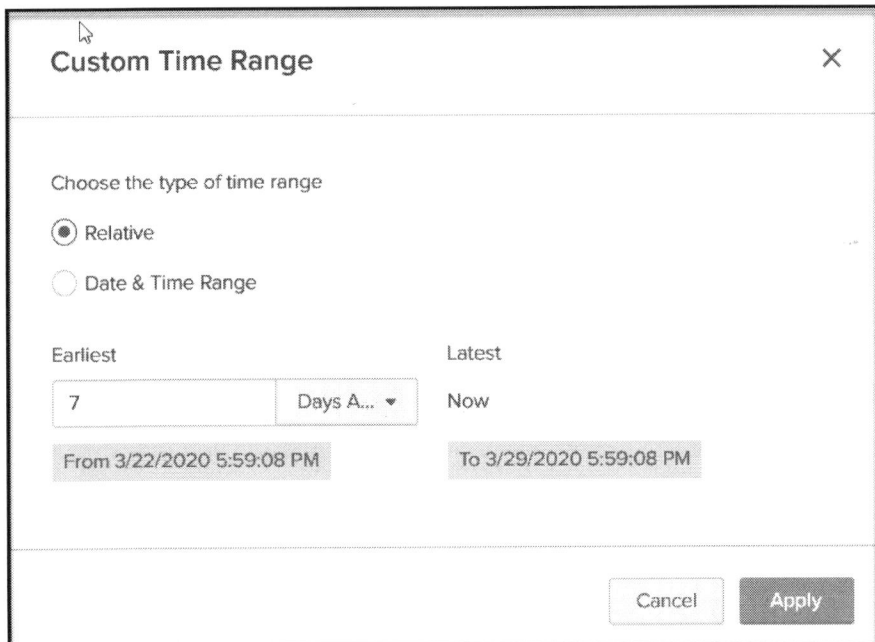

Figure 7.31 – Setting custom time range

You can use the **Relative** option to specify a custom time range that is relative to the *current time*. You can use the **Date & Time Range** option to specify a *specific* custom time range.

3. For viewing metrics in a time range *relative* to *right now*, you select **Relative** and enter the **Earliest** date and time you want to view.

4. For viewing metrics in a *specific* time range, you select **Date & Time Range** and enter the start and end dates and times. Then, click **Apply**.

Zooming to a time range

In addition to utilizing the time range picker, you also can *zoom in to* a custom time range from a specific time period by clicking and dragging your cursor over the time period you want to view. The following screenshot is an example of a workspace chart showing the time series of **Last 7 days**:

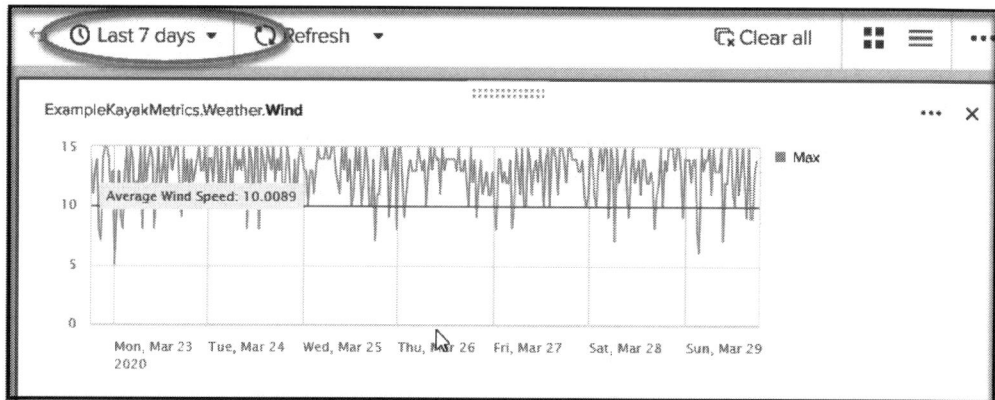

Figure 7.32 – Example of time range for last 7 days

After the click and drag operation, we see that the time range has been updated to **25th - 28th Mar**:

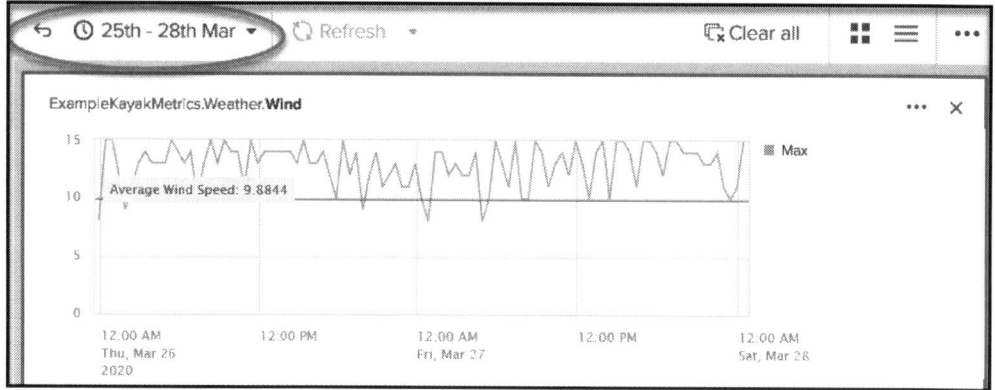

Figure 7.33 – Custom time range

> **Hint**
> To undo any zoom, you can click the back arrow in the top-left corner of the **Main** panel. The time range will then be reverted to the previous setting.

The following are some answers to analytics workspace time range FAQs:

- The default time range for the workspace is always 1 hour.
- To help you compare time series, all charts in the workspace will always show the same time range.
- You can *hover over* any chart to view a shared hairline.
- You can always adjust the time range to gain more insight from your charts.
- You set the time range through either the time range picker or by zooming in on a chart.

> **Hint**
> If you notice a significant change in your data around an approximate time, you can narrow the time range. If you want to see a broader selection of data, you can expand the time range.

Now you can access and use the Splunk analytics workspace and use what we've covered in this chapter to create interesting, dynamic visualizations to easily monitor operational or other metrics within your organization.

Summary

In this chapter, we explored in detail the Splunk analytics workspace, performing exercises to illustrate how to create categorical charts, run analytical operations, add reference lines, understand and create streaming alerts, and expand the time range of a time series using the time range picker (and by clicking and dragging on a chart).

In the next chapter, we will be exploring the now supported histogram metric data type, which enables you to bucket metric data into a time series of histograms.

8
Advanced Reporting – Histogram Metric Data Types

In the previous chapter, we explored the Splunk Analytics Workspace, performing exercises to illustrate how to create categorical charts, run analytical operations, add reference lines, understand and create streaming alerts, and expand the time range of a time series using the time-range picker (and by clicking and dragging on a chart).

In this chapter, the focus will be on exploring the newly supported histogram metric data type, which enables you to bucket this more complex metric data into a time series of histograms.

This chapter will be broken down into the following main sections:

- Understanding Splunk metrics data types
- Histogram metrics
- Histogram time series

Before getting into histogram metric data types, let's have a bit of a discussion around Splunk metrics and the Splunk metric datatype.

Understanding Splunk metrics data types

Metrics is a feature mostly aimed at system administrators and IT and service engineers that concentrates on collecting, investigating, monitoring, and sharing various metrics (or measurements) from infrastructure, security systems, and business applications in real time.

In Splunk, you use metrics indexes to store metrics data. This index type is optimized for the storage and retrieval of metric data. This means that when designating an index as a metrics index, you let Splunk know the kind of data it will be indexing (metrics) so it can collate and organize that data effectively. (We covered Splunk metrics and Splunk metric indexes in *Chapter 3, Performance, Statistics, and Alerting in Splunk*, earlier in this book.)

Metrics in Splunk uses a specific custom index type, again that is optimized specifically for metric storage and retrieval. Splunk even offers *metrics-specific* commands such as `mstats`, `mcatalog`, and `msearch` that can be run on the metric data points in those defined metric indexes.

For example, the `mstats` command lets you apply Splunk aggregate functions such as `average`, `sum`, `count`, and `rate` to those data points, helping you separate, correlate, and describe issues from different data sources.

Other examples you can use to describe patterns found in univariate data include looking at the mean, mode, median, range, variance, maximum, minimum, quartiles, and standard deviation.

This, then, is the objective of the metric; to be able to identify a measurement and then fully understand it, so that perhaps an actionable decision can be made, based upon that metric.

As an example, during a particular time series, a metric search may ask, *what is the average memory consumed by a web server?* This is accomplished by doing the following:

1. Accumulating the data points to be measured, by time period
2. Then applying an aggregation (such as average)
3. And finally, visualizing the result to establish a clear understanding

In the next section, we will discuss how histograms can be used with metric data.

Histograms

The purpose of a histogram is to graphically summarize the distribution of a **univariate** dataset, which is data consisting of *one variable* or *one type of data*.

An example of a data point or metric that can be considered univariate is a counter. A **counter** is a cumulative metric that represents a value that can only increase or be reset to zero on restart. For example, you can use a counter to represent the number of requests served, tasks completed, or errors that have occurred (again within a time frame or time range).

It is recommended to use a histogram when the dataset consists of 100 values or more. A histogram consists of contiguous (adjoining) boxes. It has both a horizontal axis and a vertical axis.

The following diagram shows a simple, sample histogram:

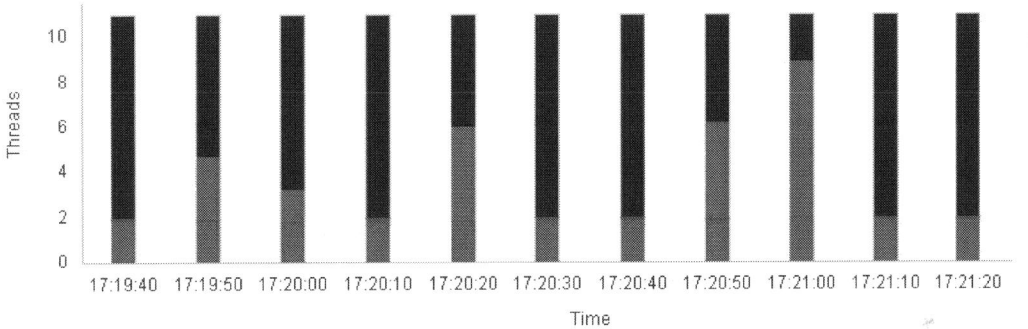

Figure 8.1 – A sample histogram

Now that we have learned the basics of histograms, let's explore and learn how to work with histogram metrics.

Histogram metrics

What can we understand about what a histogram metric is?

Histogram metrics are categorized as being more complex than standard metric data types. **Histogram data points** (**HDPs**) define a set of differently sized data stacks.

> **Hint:**
> We use the term **data stack** here to mean accumulating a group of like-data intersection points, such as login attempts on a certain day. The stack can also be referred to as a **bucket** of sequentially organized measurements. We are not using the term *stack* to imply that the measurements can be inserted and deleted from a structure programmatically.

Histogram metrics answer questions about the distribution of measurements—such as request durations or response sizes—across those data stacks at a given point in time. A histogram of an individual data stack might be the number of logins attempted over a period of time, for example; a set of these stacks can show the number of logins attempted for each day in a week, and this becomes the histogram metric:

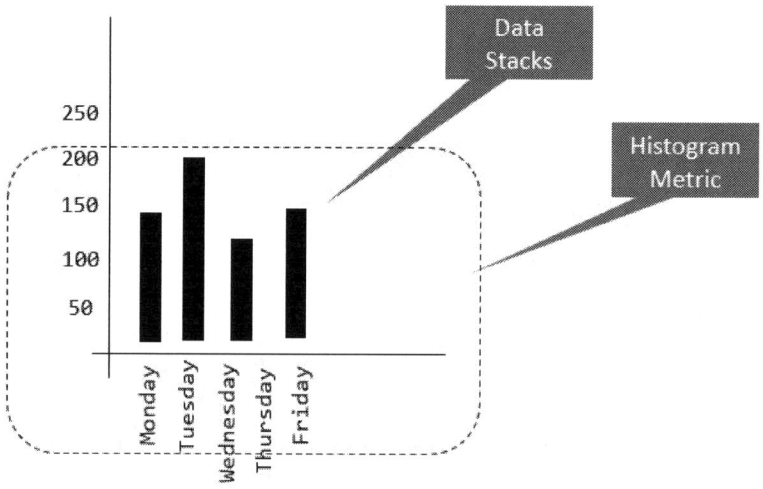

Figure 8.2 – Histogram metric

In the preceding diagram, you can see the data stacks are the total number of measurements on a given weekday, and adding a set of data stacks (**Monday** through **Friday**) makes up a histogram metric.

Typically, histogram metrics can be used to establish insights such as what the number (count) of a measurement (of a metric) is that is less than, greater than, or equal to the value that is the maximum boundary of a data stack. This number or count includes all of the data points that fit into the particular data stack. In other words, using our diagram example, the data stacks would be all measurements recorded that fit into the **Monday** data stack, **Tuesday**, **Wednesday**, and so on.

Additionally, other insights of interest include the sum of all of the measurements that have been recorded (for a metric) and the full count/total number of the measurements that have been recorded (for the metric) as well as limitless others.

Example of histogram metric use cases

Since histogram metrics are different than other metrics, perhaps more easily understood or common metrics, it is a good idea to take some time to review a few real-world use cases.

There are many things you can do with the information gleaned through histogram metrics, including the following:

- Establish averages.
- Build threshold alerts.
- Calculate percentiles.

Averages established through histogram metrics are common. For example, the total number of customer service calls (during a period of time) and the total duration of each call are typically used to calculate the average length of customer service calls.

With Splunk, it is also often typical to implement alerts that will be triggered for specific histogram metric values. Using the previous example, you could build a Splunk alert that sends an email if the number of customer service calls surpasses an established average number of calls in a set period, or the average call length begins to exceed a calculated average call duration time.

Again, using the same example use case, histogram metrics can be used to automatically calculate various percentiles, such as the percentage of calls handled in less than 10 minutes.

With histogram metrics, the overall objective should be to provide a value (a result) that's appropriate to base an engineering, business, or other decision on.

Ingesting histogram metrics

To use histogram metrics within Splunk, you need to ingest histogram-formatted metric data from an application such as **Prometheus** or a similar metrics monitoring client that utilizes an **HTTP Event Collector** (**HEC**).

The Splunk HEC is an effective method to send data to Splunk. This methodology enables you to send data over HTTP (or HTTPS) directly to Splunk from another application.

HEC was fashioned for the mindset of the application developer, such that it takes only a minimal number of lines of code to be added to an application to enable the app to send data. Also, HEC is token-based, so you never need to hardcode Splunk credentials into an app or supporting files to support authentication.

The Splunk HEC provides a new way for developers to send application logging and metrics directly to Splunk via HTTP in a highly efficient and secure manner.

To enable the HEC using Splunk Web, perform the following steps:

1. From the Splunk main page, click on **Settings**, then **Data Inputs**.
2. On the **Data Inputs** page, scroll down and click on **HTTP Event Collector**.
3. On the **HTTP Event Collector** page (shown in the following screenshot), click on **Global Settings**:

Figure 8.3 – Setting up the HEC

4. On the **Edit Global Settings** dialog (shown in the following screenshot) you need to select **Enabled** for **All Tokens**. All of the other following configurations here are optional:

    a) **Default Source Type** is the Splunk source type that will be used for HEC tokens. You can also type in the name of the source type in the text field above the dropdown before choosing the source type.

    b) **Default Index** is the defined Splunk index to be used for all HEC tokens.

    c) **Default Output Group** is the defined output group to be used for all HEC tokens.

    d) **Use Deployment Server** is to handle configurations for HEC tokens.

    e) **Enable SSL** is to have the HEC listen and communicate over HTTPS rather than HTTP.

    f) **HTTP Port Number** is the port number for the HEC to listen on (note that the default port is `8088`).

5. Finally, click **Save**:

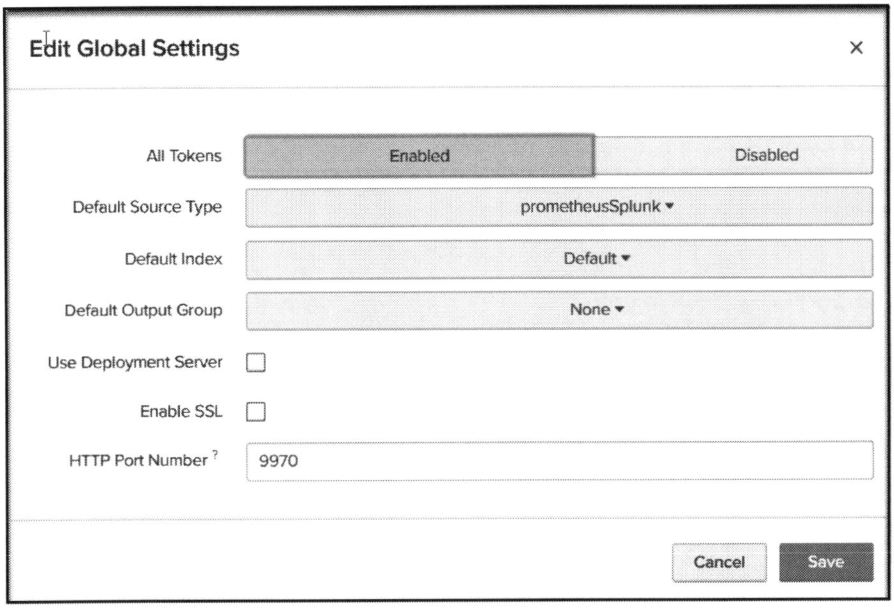

![Edit Global Settings dialog showing All Tokens Enabled, Default Source Type prometheusSplunk, Default Index Default, Default Output Group None, Use Deployment Server unchecked, Enable SSL unchecked, HTTP Port Number 9970]

Figure 8.4 – The Edit Global Settings dialog

Now that we have enabled the HEC, let's begin creating the event collector tokens.

Creating an event collector token

Now that the HEC has been enabled, to actually use it, you need to configure at least one token. To create a token, perform the following steps:

1. From the Splunk main page, click **Settings** and then click **Add Data**.
2. Click **Monitor**:

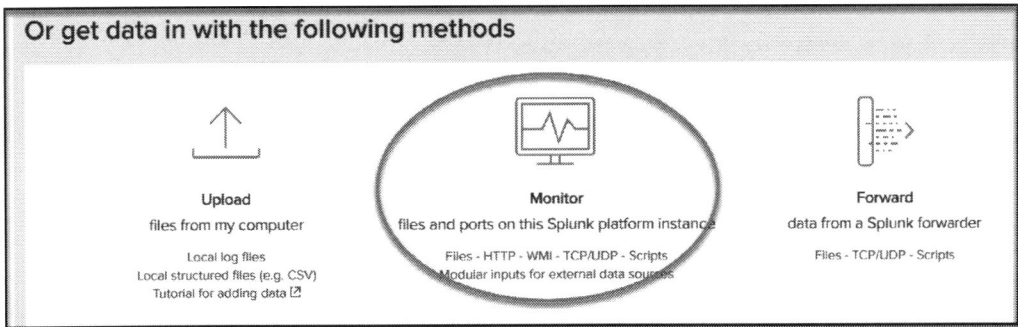

Figure 8.5 – Creating an event collector token

3. Click **HTTP Event Collector**. The following will be displayed:

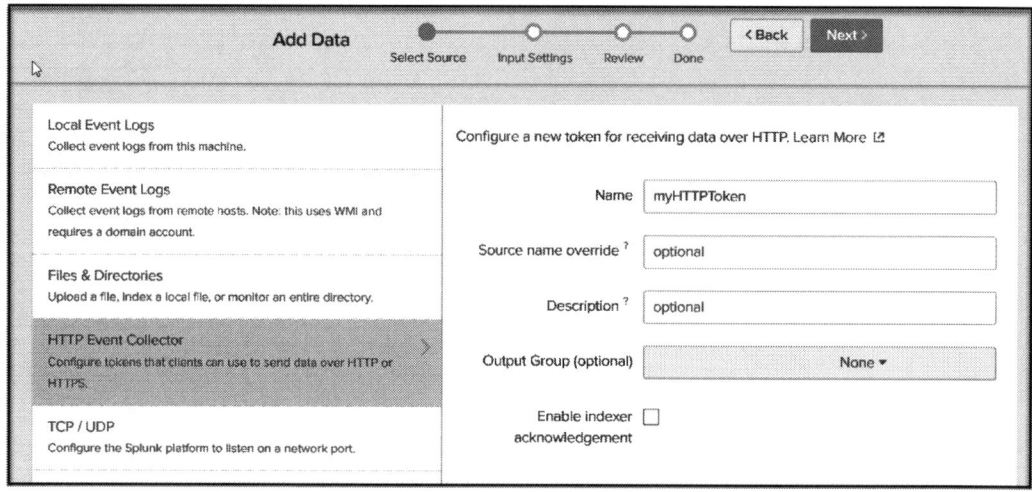

Figure 8.6 – Configuring the new token

4. In the **Name** field, enter a name for the token. Again, all of the other configurations (**Source name override**, **Description**, **Output Group**, and **Enable indexer acknowledgment**) are optional, so leave the defaults as they are.

5. Click **Next**.

6. The next step (confirming the source type and the index for HEC events) is optional as well, so just click **Review** and then confirm that the settings for the endpoint you see are what you expected, then click **Submit**.

7. (Optional) Copy the token value (something like `10da7e6a-df4c-4455-8d38-e62b32515144`) that Splunk Web displays and paste it into another document for reference later.

Enabling the HEC within Splunk allows the use of the Prometheus (or another application) remote-write feature to continuously push metric data to Splunk.

When installed, enabled, and correctly configured, this will add a new listening port to the Splunk server that can be the remote write target for a Prometheus server.

Validation

Once you have the HEC enabled (using the preceding process), it is a good idea to validate that it is actually working. The good news is that the HEC writes usage data to log files that you can search in Splunk to explore usage trends system-wide, per token, per source type, and more, as well as to appraise HEC performance.

HEC usage data is written whenever **HTTP Event Collector** is enabled (again, as we just did in the previous section). In addition to using Splunk to search this data, you can also view the HEC error logs data in the `splunkd.log` log file, but the easiest and perhaps the most straightforward method to validate that the HEC is working correctly is to review the HEC log itself.

All HEC metrics are written to the `http_event_collector_metrics.log` file located at the following path:

`$SPLUNK_HOME/var/log/introspection/`

An example of the path to the file is shown in the following screenshot:

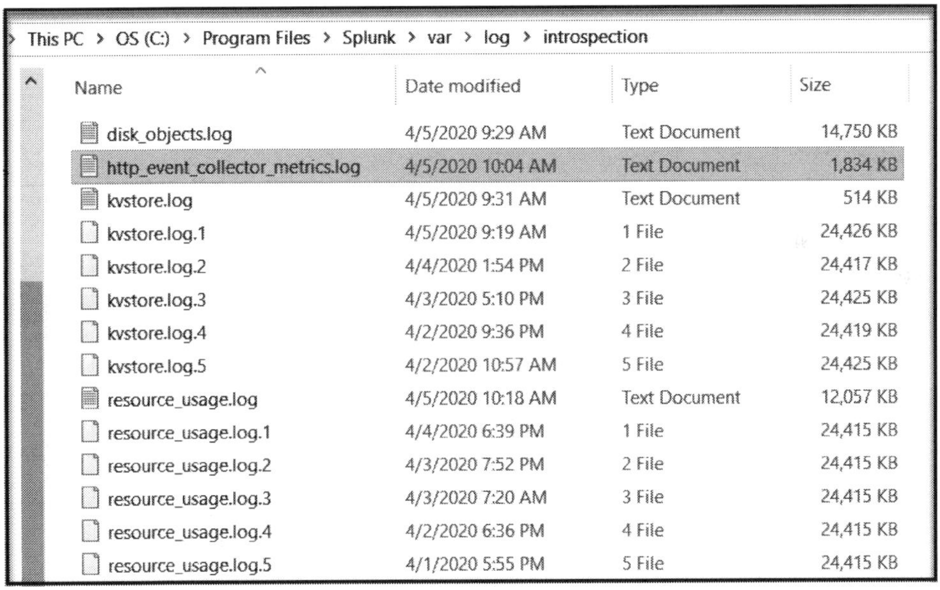

Figure 8.7 – File path to the introspection directory

> **Hint:**
> You configure the logging frequency of HEC metrics in the `limits.conf` file. 60 seconds is the default frequency.

Advanced Reporting – Histogram Metric Data Types

All HEC data is recorded to the log in JSON format (to ensure that it is both easily human-readable and consistent with other Splunk formats). However, it is also pretty easy to open and view the log file with **Notepad** or another text editor as shown in the following screenshot:

```
{
"datetime":"04-01-2020 12:00:09.795 -0400",
"log_level":"INFO",
"component":"HttpEventCollector",
"data":{
"series":"http_event_collector",
"transport":"http",
"format":"json",
"total_bytes_received":0,
"total_bytes_indexed":0,
"num_of_requests":0,
"num_of_events":0,
"num_of_errors":0,
"num_of_parser_errors":0,
"num_of_auth_failures":0,
"num_of_requests_to_disabled_token":0,
"num_of_requests_to_incorrect_url":0,
"num_of_requests_in_mint_format":0,
"num_of_ack_requests":0,
"num_of_requests_acked":0,
"num_of_requests_waiting_ack":0
}
}
```

Figure 8.8 – JSON format log file

Notice, in the record displayed, the -0400 code. This is the HTTP status code for the logged record. This value indicates that for this record, there was no data retrieved by the HTTP request.

> **Hint:**
> For a full list of possible HEC status codes, refer to the documentation at https://docs.splunk.com/Documentation/Splunk/8.0.2/Data/TroubleshootHTTPEventCollector#Detecting_scaling_problems.

Histogram metrics before and after indexing

HDP structures are made up of several individual metric data points. Each line (or record) of a histogram data point follows the following format:

```
<metric_name>
{<dim0>=<dim_value0>,<dim1>=<dim_value1>,...,<dimN>=<dim_valueN>}
<_value>
<timestamp
```

A raw histogram data point (using Prometheus) that deals with HTTP request durations in seconds (for example) should look something like the following lines of data example before being ingested into Splunk:

```
prometheus_http_request_duration_seconds_bucket{handler="/metrics",instance="localhost:9090",job="prometheus",le="0.1"} 1183 1568073334000
prometheus_http_request_duration_seconds_bucket{handler="/metrics",instance="localhost:9090",job="prometheus",le="0.2"} 1183 1568073334000
prometheus_http_request_duration_seconds_bucket{handler="/metrics",instance="localhost:9090",job="prometheus",le="0.4"} 1184 1568073334000
prometheus_http_request_duration_seconds_bucket{handler="/metrics",instance="localhost:9090",job="prometheus",le="1"} 1184 1568073334000
prometheus_http_request_duration_seconds_bucket{handler="/metrics",instance="localhost:9090",job="prometheus",le="3"} 1184 1568073334000
prometheus_http_request_duration_seconds_bucket{handler="/metrics",instance="localhost:9090",job="prometheus",le="8"} 1184 1568073334000
Prometheus_engine_query_durration_seconds_sum{instance="localhost:9090",job="prometheus",slice="inner_eval"} 12.7 1568073334000
prometheus_engine_query_duration_seconds_count{instance="localhost:9090",job="prometheus",slice="inner_eval"} 3 1568073334000
>
```

Advanced Reporting – Histogram Metric Data Types

As mentioned earlier, to use histogram metric data types, you'll need to ingest them from an external data source. We've used Prometheus since it is referenced throughout the Splunk documentation and is open source.

Prometheus requires that the **bucket-boundary** dimension be named le (an acronym for *less than or equal to*) as seen in our raw data. Note that you can use a different name for the dimension within Splunk.

> Hint:
> See more information about using Prometheus at docs.splunk.com/Documentation/Splunk/8.0.3/Metrics/Histogramdatatype.

After ingesting the histogram data into Splunk, the HDP records should evaluate to something like the following table matrix (note that for Server, we are translating localhost:9090 to 9090):

Metric Name					
prometheus_http_req_dur_sec_bucket	prometheus_http_req_dur_sec_sum	prometheus_http_req_dur_sec_count	le	Server	Endpoint
1183			0.1	9090	1568073334000
1183			0.2	9090	1568073334000
1184			0.4	9090	1568073334000
1184			1	9090	1568073334000
1184			3	9090	1568073334000
1184			8	9090	1568073333

Figure 8.9 – Table of HDP records

Each individual metric (that is represented within the preceding table matrix) is a component of the overall histogram metric data point and is actually composed of three types of metrics, each providing some detail about the measurements that have been recorded for the metric as of the timestamp.

In the preceding example, we have the following metrics:

- `prometheus_http_req_dur_sec_bucket`
- `prometheus_http_req_dur_sec_sum`
- `prometheus_http_req_dur_sec_count`

> **Hint:**
> Each of these is also an example of an accumulating counter metric, which means their values do not decrease over time.

Going back to an earlier section in this chapter, we said that histogram metrics answer questions about a distribution of measurements—such as request durations or response sizes—across data stacks at a given point in time.

A histogram of an individual data stack might be the number of logins attempted over a period of time, and for example, a set of these stacks could show the number of logins attempted for each day in a week, becoming the histogram metric.

Here, in our simplistic raw data example, we can align to that concept by understanding that `prometheus_http_req_dur_sec_bucket` is a data point such as *response size* and where `prometheus_http_req_dur_sec_sum` and `prometheus_http_req_dur_sec_count` might be used to determine the average `prometheus_http_req_dur_sec_bucket` value.

Histogram count boundaries

Although our simple example in the previous section showed only one, there are usually multiple count records in an HDP, forming a sequence of simultaneous measurement counts with larger and larger bucket boundaries, defined by the `le` dimension.

The first count only represents measurements with relatively small values, then the next count represents the measurements from the first count plus measurements with slightly larger values. This sequence continues until the final count, corresponding with the `le` dimension value of `+Inf` (meaning **infinite**).

This means that the final bucket captures all of the measurements that were captured by the preceding bucket and any measurements that exceed the preceding bucket.

The count for `+Inf <metric_name>_bucket` should be equivalent to the value of the `<metric_name>_count` field.

Both of these fields provide a count of all of the measurements categorized by the histogram data point (as of the histogram's timestamp).

The following is an example of Prometheus histogram count data points, showing `le=+Inf`:

```
prometheus_http_request_duration_seconds_bucket
{handler="/static/*filepath",instance="localhost:9090",job=
"prometheus",le="0.1"} 3
prometheus_http_request_duration_seconds_bucket
{handler="/static/*filepath",instance="localhost:9090",job=
"prometheus",le="0.2"} 3
prometheus_http_request_duration_seconds_bucket
{handler="/static/*filepath",instance="localhost:9090",job=
"prometheus",le="0.4"} 3
prometheus_http_request_duration_seconds_bucket
{handler="/static/*filepath",instance="localhost:9090",job=
"prometheus",le="1"} 3
prometheus_http_request_duration_seconds_bucket
{handler="/static/*filepath",instance="localhost:9090",job=
"prometheus",le="3"} 4
prometheus_http_request_duration_seconds_bucket
{handler="/static/*filepath",instance="localhost:9090",job=
"prometheus",le="8"} 4
prometheus_http_request_duration_seconds_bucket
{handler="/static/*filepath",instance="localhost:9090",job=
"prometheus",le="20"} 4
prometheus_http_request_duration_seconds_bucket
{handler="/static/*filepath",instance="localhost:9090",job=
"prometheus",le="60"} 4
prometheus_http_request_duration_seconds_bucket
{handler="/static/*filepath",instance="localhost:9090",job=
"prometheus",le="120"} 4
prometheus_http_request_duration_seconds_bucket
{handler="/static/*filepath",instance="localhost:9090",job=
"prometheus",le="+Inf"} 4
```

Prometheus

Since we are utilizing Prometheus, what is Prometheus?

Prometheus is an open source system monitoring and alerting toolkit originally built by SoundCloud.

> **Hint:**
> Introductory documentation for Prometheus can be found online at `https://prometheus.io/docs/introduction/overview/`.

Prometheus collects metrics from monitored targets by scraping metrics from HTTP endpoints on these targets. Since Prometheus also logs some data about itself, it can also scrape and monitor its own activities.

It's pretty easy to get started with Prometheus by downloading the latest release, and then extracting and running it. If you want to get comfortable with Prometheus logging and pushing to HTTP collectors, you can configure it to monitor itself.

To configure Prometheus, you need to locate, edit, and update the `Prometheus.yml` file.

Once configured, you can start up the **Prometheus** server and verify that **Prometheus** is serving up metrics about itself by navigating your web browser to its metrics endpoint at `localhost:9090/metrics`.

The **Prometheus** metrics page looks something like the following screenshot:

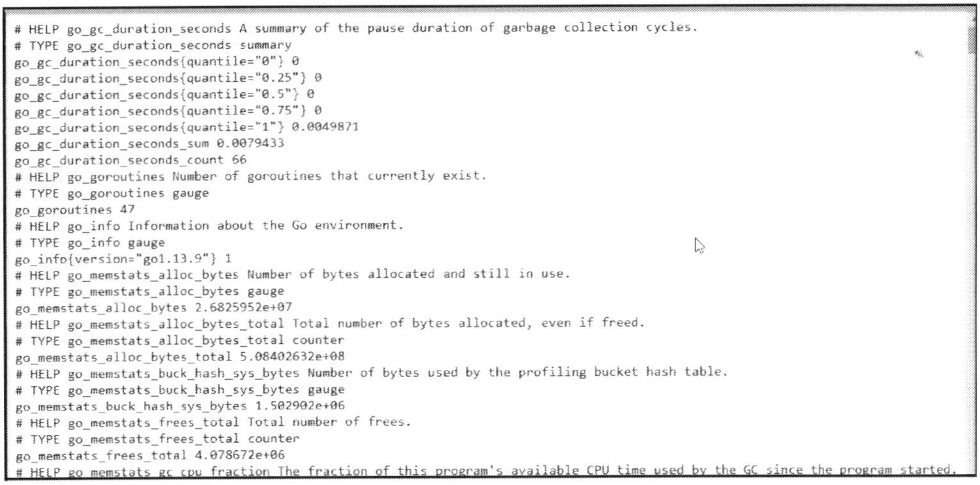

```
# HELP go_gc_duration_seconds A summary of the pause duration of garbage collection cycles.
# TYPE go_gc_duration_seconds summary
go_gc_duration_seconds{quantile="0"} 0
go_gc_duration_seconds{quantile="0.25"} 0
go_gc_duration_seconds{quantile="0.5"} 0
go_gc_duration_seconds{quantile="0.75"} 0
go_gc_duration_seconds{quantile="1"} 0.0049871
go_gc_duration_seconds_sum 0.0079433
go_gc_duration_seconds_count 66
# HELP go_goroutines Number of goroutines that currently exist.
# TYPE go_goroutines gauge
go_goroutines 47
# HELP go_info Information about the Go environment.
# TYPE go_info gauge
go_info{version="go1.13.9"} 1
# HELP go_memstats_alloc_bytes Number of bytes allocated and still in use.
# TYPE go_memstats_alloc_bytes gauge
go_memstats_alloc_bytes 2.6825952e+07
# HELP go_memstats_alloc_bytes_total Total number of bytes allocated, even if freed.
# TYPE go_memstats_alloc_bytes_total counter
go_memstats_alloc_bytes_total 5.08402632e+08
# HELP go_memstats_buck_hash_sys_bytes Number of bytes used by the profiling bucket hash table.
# TYPE go_memstats_buck_hash_sys_bytes gauge
go_memstats_buck_hash_sys_bytes 1.502902e+06
# HELP go_memstats_frees_total Total number of frees.
# TYPE go_memstats_frees_total counter
go_memstats_frees_total 4.078672e+06
# HELP go_memstats_gc_cpu_fraction The fraction of this program's available CPU time used by the GC since the program started.
```

Figure 8.10 – Prometheus metrics page

Finally, you can view the various data points that **Prometheus** is collecting by using Prometheus's built-in expression browser.

To view the **Prometheus** expression browser, navigate your web browser to `http://localhost:9090/graph` and then choose the **Console** view within the **Graph** tab:

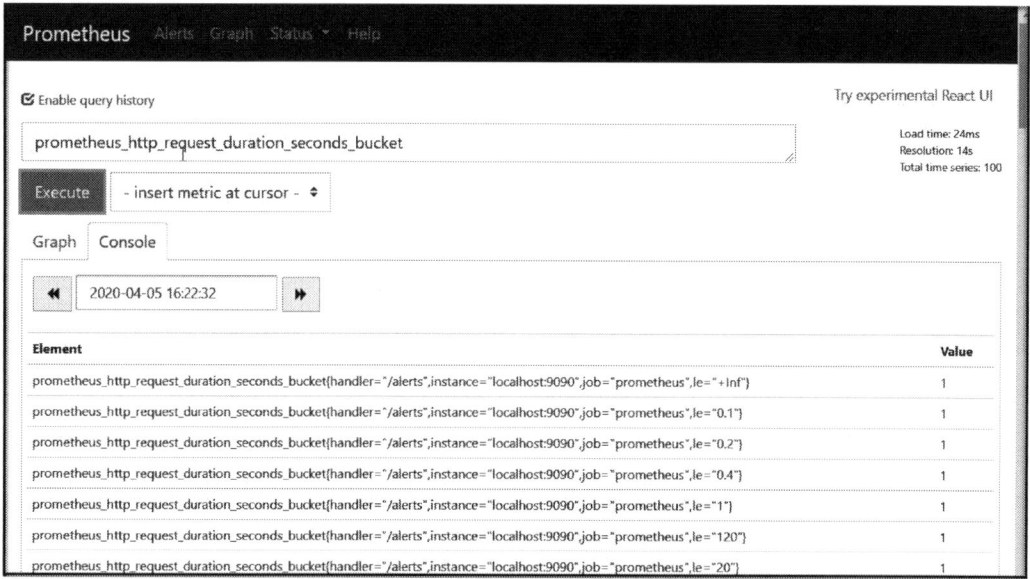

Figure 8.11 – Steps to view the Prometheus expression browser

> **Hint:**
> You can find the **Getting started** documentation for Prometheus online at `https://prometheus.io/docs/prometheus/latest/getting_started`.

Searching histogram metrics

So now that we have at least a reasonable understanding of histogram data structures and how to ingest them into Splunk, let's consider how we can search that data.

Since histogram metric data points contain interconnected data stacks or sets of counter metrics (as we've illustrated in the previous sections of this chapter), Splunk provides the `rate(x)` function (introduced in Splunk version 7.2.x) in combination with the standard `mstats` function, both of which can be used to expose the bucket distribution for a given time span.

The `mstats` command is a metrics analysis function, performing statistics on a given measurement, such as the following, for example:

```
| mstats avg(prometheus_http_req_sec_bucket) WHERE
index=myHECMetricData span=30s
```

The `mstats` command in conjunction with the `rate` function looks as follows:

```
| mstats rate(Prometheus_http_req_dur_sec_count) as rate_hits
  where index= myHECMetricData name=indexerpipe processor=index_
  thruput span=1h
```

The `_timeseries` field is also essential. This field lets you group by various dimension fields in commands that follow your `rate(x)` calculation.

The `_timeseries` field enables you to perform calculations comparable to those that the Prometheus client allows, where every stats-like operation implicitly does something such as `by _timeseries` when there is no explicit `by` clause.

Counting and summing

Each HDP has a count of all of the measurements that have been recorded as of the histogram timestamp, as well as a sum of the values of all of those measurements. Recall the following from our previous example:

- `prometheus_http_req_dur_sec_count` is the count of all of the measurements on the histogram data structure.
- `prometheus_http_req_dur_sec_sum` is the sum of the values of all of those histogram data structure measurements.

You can use these histogram dimensions to calculate the average measurement during a given period of time, so here we could calculate the average value of `prometheus_http_req_dur` for a given period of time.

Alerts

We covered Splunk alerts in *Chapter 3, Performance, Statistics, and Alerting in Splunk*. In the *Alerting* section, we stepped through how to create a simple scheduled alert based upon a previously saved search.

As with just about any saved search, you can use histogram metrics to design a Splunk search command and save it as an alert that is triggered when, for example, your HTTP request service rate dips below a certain threshold.

For example, say you have a **Service-Level Agreement** (**SLA**) to serve 95% of HTTP requests within a certain time allotment. You could configure a histogram that has a bucket with an upper boundary for the maximum stated time allotment.

The following **Search Processing Language (SPL)** command statement is from the Splunk knowledge base and calculates the relative number of requests served within 300 ms by a job over the last 5 minutes. You can use this search in the definition of an alert that triggers when the `percent_requests_served` metric for a job is less than 95:

```
| mstats rate(http_req_dur_sec_bucket) as bkt_req_per_sec where
index="metrics" AND le=0.3 AND earliest="-5m" by _timeseries,
job | stats sum(bkt_req_per_sec) as sum_bkt_req_per_sec by
job | appendcols [ | mstats rate(http_req_dur_sec_count) as
req_per_sec where index="metrics" AND earliest="-5m" by _
timeseries, job | stats sum(req_per_sec) as sum_req_per_sec by
job ] | eval percent_requests_served=sum_bkt_req_per_sec / sum_
req_per_sec | fields job, percent_requests_served
```

The preceding search command is just one example of how alerts can be used with histogram metric types.

Percentiles

Earlier in this chapter, we indicated that one of the many things you can do with histogram metrics is to calculate percentiles.

The Splunk `histperc` macro (no, it's not a Splunk function) enables you to easily calculate percentile values for histogram metrics.

Remember, a Splunk macro is a reusable block of SPL that you can use over and over to accomplish an objective or goal.

The `histperc` macro accounts for (bucket) boundaries and the rate of increase of its counters, and estimates the value associated with the specified percentile based on the linear interpolation between histogram boundaries.

The `histperc` macro takes four different parameters using the following syntax:

```
histperc(<perc>, <rate_field>, <bucket_upper_boundary_
dimension> [, <groupby-fields>])
```

The parameters are defined as follows:

- `perc`: The desired percentile value.
- `rate_field`: This is the name of the field containing the output of the (previously mentioned) `mstats rate(x)` commands.

- `bucket_upper_boundary_dimension`: This is the name of the histogram dimension that represents the inclusive upper boundary of the buckets in the histogram data structure.
- `groupby-fields`: This specifies the dimension(s) to be grouped by during the percentile calculation.

histperc example

Suppose you have a histogram macro named `http_req_dur_sec` that provides the distribution of HTTP request duration measurements in terms of seconds.

You could use the `histperc` macro to calculate the request duration within which you have served 95% of requests—otherwise referred to as the P95 value for the request service.

This search calculates the HTTP request duration within which you have served 99% of requests. It groups the results by `_time` for charting purposes:

```
| mstats rate(http_req_dur_sec_bucket) as requests_per_sec
where index="metrics" by _timeseries, le span=5m | stats
sum(requests_per_sec) as total_requests_per_sec by _time, le |
`histperc(0.99, total_requests_per_sec, le, _time)`
```

Again, the preceding search command is just another example of using histogram metric types.

Summary

In this chapter, we started out by reviewing the Splunk metric datatype and metric indexers, then introduced histograms and histogram metrics. We then went over how to ingest histogram metrics into Splunk with the HEC and tokens, enabling the Splunk HEC and then validating that it is working.

The later sections covered details on how histogram metrics look and work; and suggested using an open source monitoring toolkit named **Prometheus** before touching on how to search histogram metrics, create alerts, and calculate percentiles.

In the next chapter, we jump into building advanced searches and move beyond a single installation of Splunk and see how distributed search can provide substantial increases in performance.

9
Search Performance Considerations

In the previous chapter, we explored the newly supported Splunk **histogram metric data type**. In this chapter, the focus will be on approaching advanced searches and reporting from a performance perspective, starting with some general advice on identifying, avoiding, and addressing items that can cause diminished search performance.

Over time, adding additional users and data sources can begin to strain any Splunk environment deployment. Adding additional servers to an existing deployment is typically the most efficient approach to what is referred to as *scaling to demand* and the best part is that this approach doesn't require rebuilding a Splunk environment from scratch.

> **Note**
> A word of caution here. Splunk users may want to set up dynamic scaling, as you might with a web service in AWS, but scaling doesn't work the same way in Splunk.

Moving beyond an original single installation of Splunk and implementing an environment that supports *distributed searching* has the potential to provide considerable increases in search performance as well as overall response times while running Splunk reports.

This chapter first looks at some common areas that can affect search performance, and then covers two proven approaches—adding indexers and search heads—to scale a Splunk deployment to ensure acceptable search and reporting performance.

The chapter will be broken down into the following main sections:

- Gauging performance
- Adding indexers
- Additional search heads
- Search head clustering

Gauging performance

Whether you are beginning to experience diminished performance or are now planning for increased Splunk usage, users, data, and so on, it is a good idea to first understand what are the potential causes of poor Splunk performance.

Let's take a look at some of the common causes in the following section

Some typical causes

Many factors affect search performance, including the following:

- File size/last updated (ingesting larger and larger files)
- Event sizes
- Custom data model definitions
- Concurrent searches
- Overall deployment architecture
- The number and type of apps
- Hardware
- Event field extractions

File sizes

After adding files as input for Splunk to index, it is a good idea to monitor the physical size of these files as well as how often they are being updated. Typically, input files will be logs generated by applications and other machines. As files grow larger and larger, searches executed against the data may slow down for a variety of reasons, that is, depending upon the time ranges searched, and the bigger the file, the more events to process.

You can use the SPL commands to review information about these files, including current sizes. For example, in one Splunk instance, if we have a number of IBM TM1/planning analytics logs being monitored, we could use a search command like this:

```
source="*tm1*.LOG" | eval esize=len(_raw) | stats sum(esize) by sourcetype
```

This yields the following results:

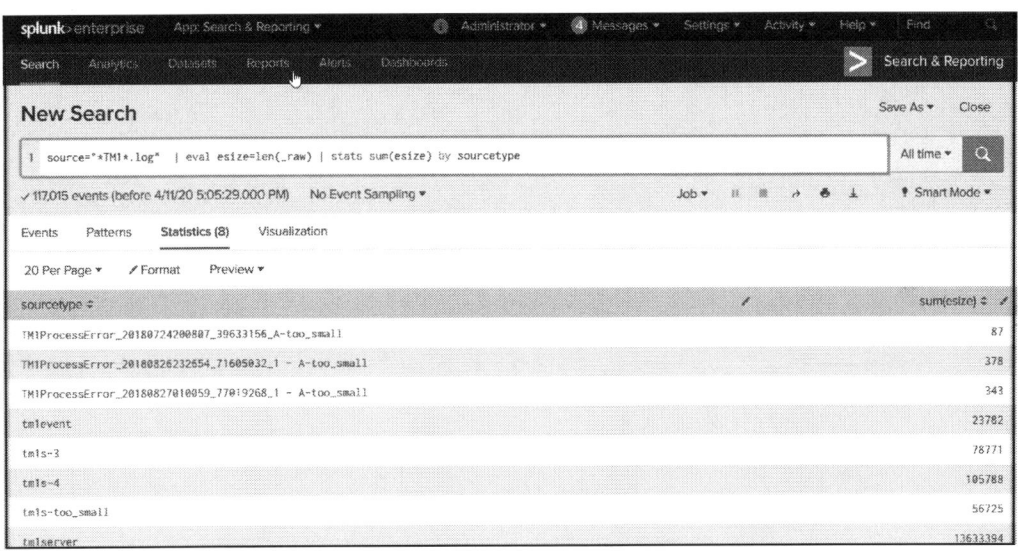

Figure 9.1 – Monitoring file size

> **Hint**
> Typically, starting a search command with leading wildcards should be avoided wherever possible since they most often result in search performance problems. We've used them here as a simple illustration.

A useful app

The Splunk **File/Directory Information Input** app is a handy app that can be downloaded and configured to provide a new data input for indexing file metadata (such as size and last modified dates) in your Splunk instance, making it easier to search and monitor—rather than building your own individual search commands.

> **Hint**
> You can find the **File/Directory Information Input** app online at `https://splunkbase.splunk.com/app/2776/`. It's worth checking out!

To install the app (or any app) using Splunk Web, you can perform the following steps:

1. Click on the **Apps** menu, and then click on **Manage Apps**.
2. Click **Install app from file**.
3. In the **Upload app** window, click **Choose File**.
4. Locate the `.tar.gz` file you previously downloaded, and then click **Open** or **Choose**.
5. Click **Upload**.
6. Click **Restart Splunk**, and then confirm that you want to restart.

After you install the new app, you will find a new data input available named `File Meta-data` (as shown in the following screenshot):

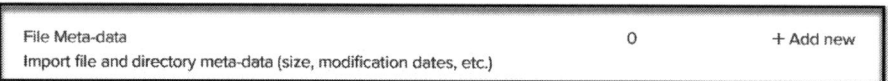

Figure 9.2 – Adding a new app

With this new source type (`file_meta_data`), you can use the UI provided with the app to configure new data inputs. In the following screenshot, we have configured the `GO_scorecards` folder as the input source for Splunk to monitor at 1-minute intervals, using this new source type:

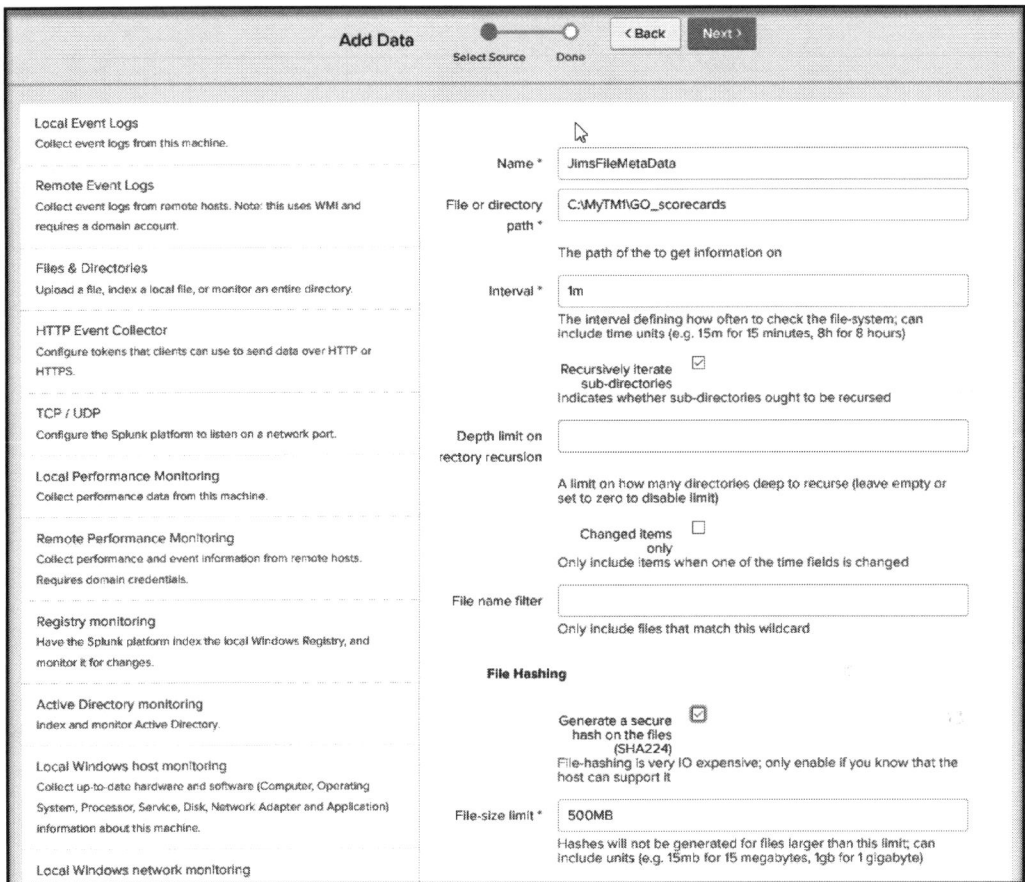

Figure 9.3 – App configuration

> **Note**
> When defining a new input source, you should be cognizant that it could generate a lot of data, with potentially limited value, so keep the intended use case in mind when defining the source.

Once we have set the configurations and click on **Next**, we are ready to begin searching:

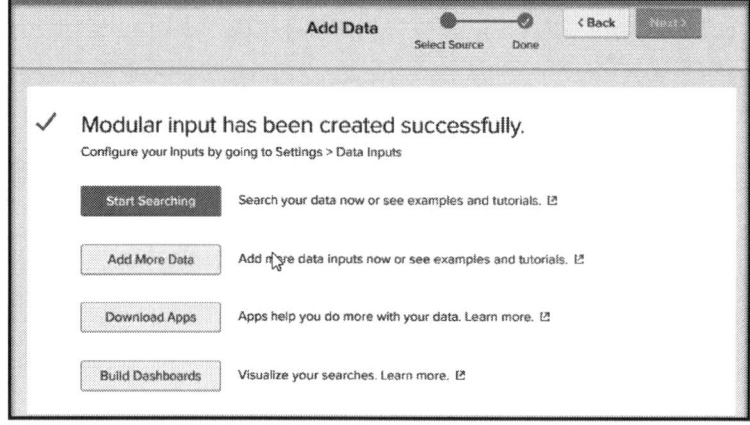

Figure 9.4 – Modular input

Now we can use the SPL `table` command to review the last updated times for files monitored by Splunk using our new source type and the `path` and `mtime` fields:

```
Sourcetype="file_meta_data" | table path, mtime
```

This will yield the following result:

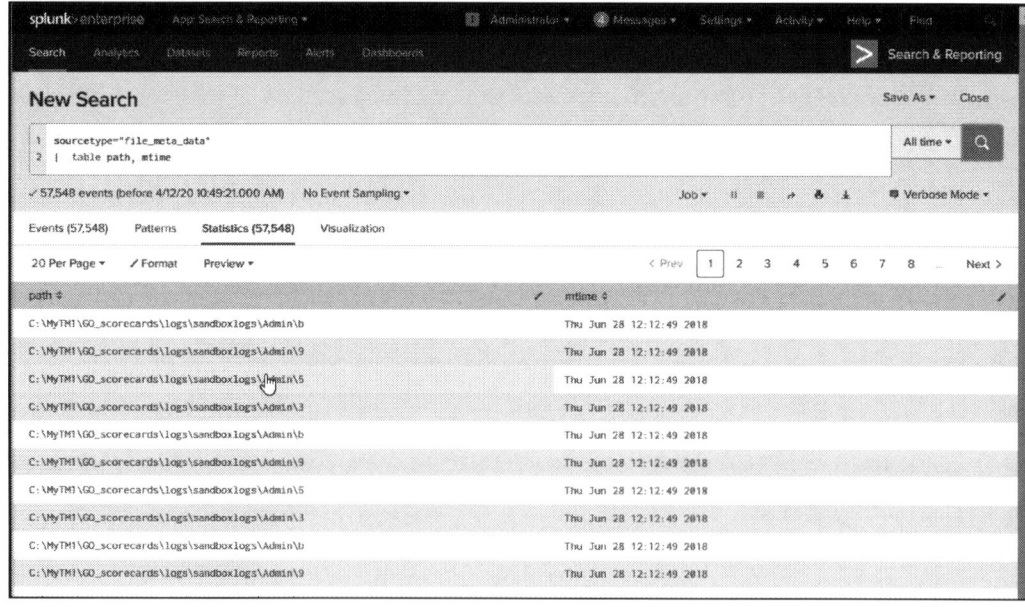

Figure 9.5 – Search results using the table command

Evaluating the current landscape

The Splunk `dispatch` directory folder should be reviewed on a routine basis. It stores artifacts about nodes where searches are run. The nodes include search heads, search peers, and standalone Splunk instances. This folder is scanned by Splunk, so if it becomes very large, search performance is usually impacted to some degree.

The location of the Splunk `dispatch` directory is `$SPLUNK_HOME/var/run/splunk/dispatch`:

Figure 9.6 – Splunk dispatch directory

If Splunk finds that it is taking too long to scan the folder, the following error may be issued:

```
Too many search jobs found in the dispatch directory
(found=3692, warning level=2000). This could negatively impact
Splunk's performance, consider removing some of the old search
jobs.
```

If you see the preceding error, you can manually purge sub-folders from the `dispatch` folder starting with the older ones first. A good practice is to monitor the `dispatch` folder for size and last update date and remove the oldest data found.

Since the data saved in the `dispatch` folder still exists within the Splunk summary index, any data you remove from the `dispatch` folder will be automatically regenerated during the next execution of a search that requires this information.

> **Hint**
> It is recommended that after purging data from the `dispatch` folder, Splunk should be stopped and restarted. Since restarting Splunk causes buckets to roll from hot to warm, which can have implications on retention and search performance, you should plan for any required Splunk restart.

File compression techniques

Generally, Splunk routinely compresses raw data to about half its original size.

How the compression of raw data works is known as the **compression ratio** and can affect overall search performance. Typically, the Splunk compression ratio is set to *strike a balance* between speed and space or, in other words, how much of the data ingested actually gets compressed.

For example, if there is 100 GB of raw data, that most likely will compress to about 50 GB, with a split of 35 GB for index files and 15 GB of compressed data.

It should be understood that the Splunk **compression rate** is typically pretty close to being identical for hot, warm, cold, and frozen buckets. However, when a bucket is frozen, all of the metadata is removed, and only the *raw data* remains.

> **Hint**
> Remember that Splunk stores its indexed data in buckets, which are simply directories containing both the data and index files into the data. An index typically consists of many buckets, organized by the age of the data.

Just as a point of information, Splunk uses `gzip` (by default) for compression, but also supports `lz4` and `zstd` and can handle different buckets compressed using different compression algorithms.

> **Information**
> More information on how Splunk calculates its storage needs can be found online at `https://docs.splunk.com/Documentation/Splunk/8.0.3/Capacity/HowSplunkcalculatesdiskstorage`.

The bottom line on compression is that although it may affect Splunk performance, it is probably not a root cause. Splunk support would most likely be the best place to start should you be interested in evaluating compression rates or alternative compression algorithms.

Gauging performance   205

Event sizes

Splunk events are a solitary piece of data, similar to a single record in a log file or other data input. When data is ingested into Splunk and indexed, it is automatically separated into individual events. Each of those events is assigned a timestamp, host, source, and source type.

Keeping track of the events being indexed within Splunk is always recommended. What you are interested in is the minimum, maximum, and average event size over a period of time.

Splunk does apply limitations to extremely large events when it comes to line breaking and segmentation. Splunk breaks lines over 10,000 bytes into multiple lines of 10,000 bytes each during the indexing process.

Generally, the more events to process and/or the more times that the number of events approaches the line limit, the slower the searches. Periodically reviewing this information can allow you to better manage how data is being ingested and indexed and better predict search times.

Like an earlier section of this chapter (*A useful app*), a downloadable app can make the process of monitoring even details a bit easier. I've installed the **Meta Woot!** app, which lets us run the following search:

```
index=_internal sourcetype="splunkd"
| eval eventSize=len(_raw)
| table eventSize _raw
| sort - eventSize| stats max(eventSize), min(eventSize), avg(eventSize)
```

This yields the following output:

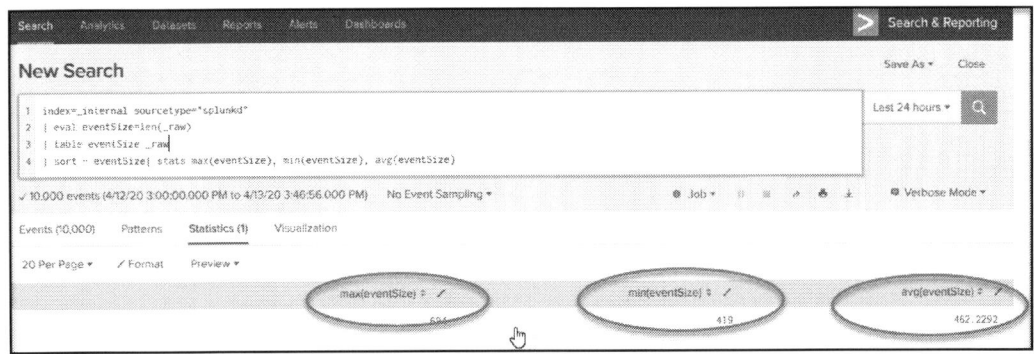

Figure 9.7 – Searching with Meta Woot!

> **Hint**
>
> You can check out the details and download **Meta Woot!** online at `https://splunkbase.splunk.com/app/2949/`.

Custom data model definitions

Splunk data models are defined as *hierarchically structured search-time mappings of semantic knowledge about one or more datasets*. Another way to think about a data model is that it is a *mini database* organizing the informational schema—or the searches and fields—for some existing Splunk data.

You create a data model to enable acceleration and improve search performance. For example, if there are frequent reports using the same fields within the same dataset, you can create a data model and enable data model acceleration. This will cause Splunk to run search jobs in the background to build a separate index for your data model and improve the speed of searches on the data.

Simply, a Splunk data model is just a JSON document defining the searches and fields that make up a specific model. You can use the `datamodel` command to return the JSON for all or a specified data model and its datasets:

```
| datamodel
```

This yields the following output:

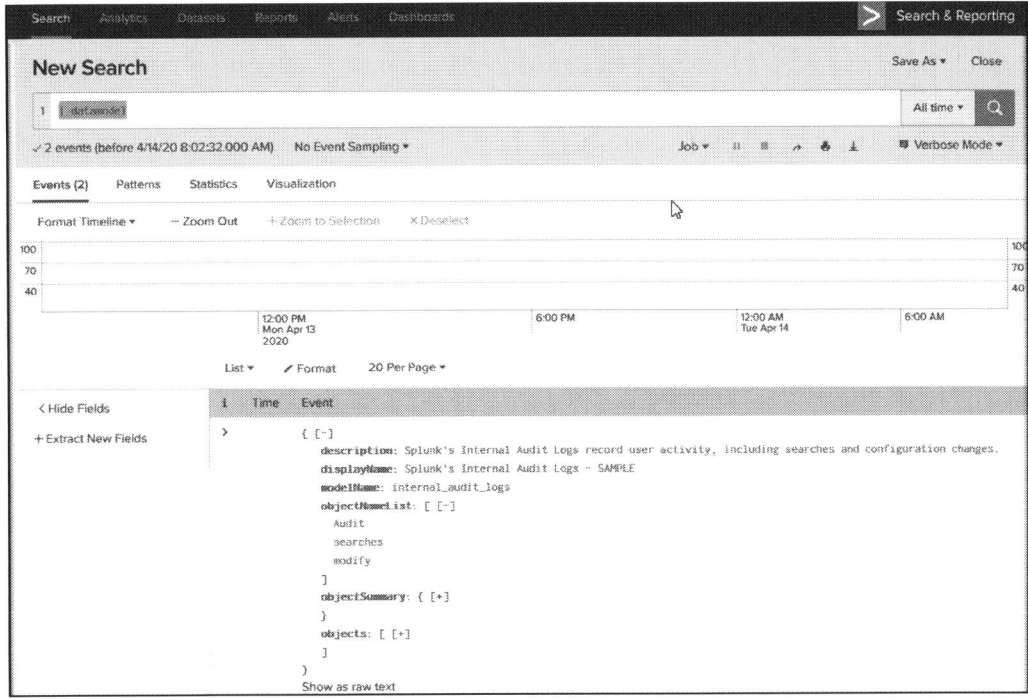

Figure 9.8 – Custom data model search

Concurrent searches

When you run searches, Splunk limits the number of concurrent searches (searches that are running at the same time) in order to improve the performance of each individual search. In fact, Splunk states that the largest *performance factor* in a Splunk deployment is the number of concurrent users and the number of concurrent searches.

The limit for concurrent searches is set by the `base_max_searches` settings in the `limits.conf` file.

> **Note**
>
> As a default, with a Splunk 16 core system, Splunk can run 22 searches at any given time. That number is calculated via the following formula:
>
> $max\_hist\_searches = max\_searches\_per\_cpu$ (default of 1) x $number\_of\_cpus$ (16) + $base\_max\_searches$ (default of 6)

With Splunk Web, you can also set search concurrency limits by going to **Settings** and then clicking on **Server Settings**. From there, you will see the **Search preferences** page (shown in the following screenshot) where you can view and modify the **Relative concurrency limit for scheduled searches** and **Relative concurrency limit for summarization searches** settings:

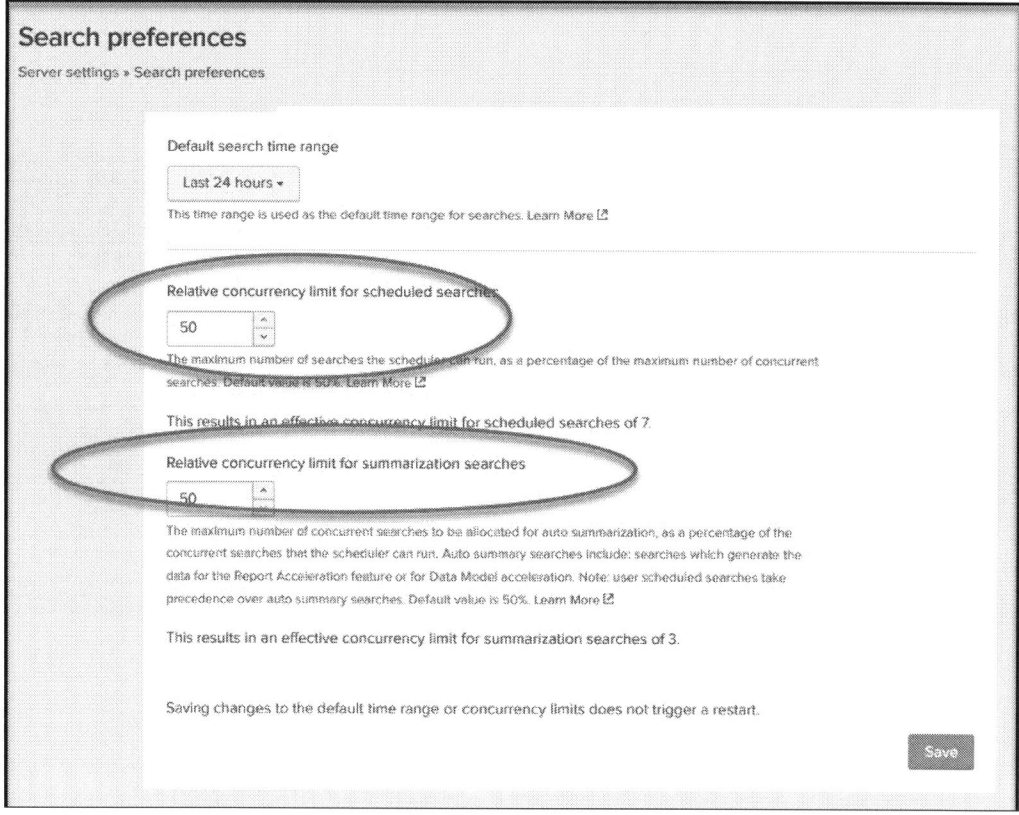

Figure 9.9 – Setting concurrency limits

Overall deployment architectures

How Splunk is installed and deployed can certainly effect search performance and, ultimately, the ongoing success of the use of Splunk within an organization.

To that point, **Splunk Validated Architectures**, or **SVAs**, are proven blueprint architectures designed and proven as being stable, efficient, and repeatable Splunk deployments. These architectures are built on five foundational pillars:

- Availability
- Performance
- Scalability
- Security
- Manageability

Using the SVAs, you can decide with confidence whether you'll require a single server or distributed deployment. We'll touch more on this distinction later in this chapter.

> **Information**
> SVA resource: `https://www.splunk.com/en_us/blog/tips-and-tricks/splunk-validated-architectures.html`.

Number and type of apps

A single Splunk indexer can run numerous apps simultaneously. In fact, Splunk includes several default apps that it runs at the same time. **Search & Reporting** is actually a default Splunk app.

Apps (also sometimes referred to as **add-ons**) are typically used to provide custom configurations or data inputs or otherwise extract/transform parts of data that are meaningful to a particular objective.

> **Note**
> Although **apps** and **add-ons** are, from time to time, loosely referred as being the same, technically, they can be different. Both (apps and add-ons) are examples of knowledge objects.

Apps, by nature, are designed to make accessing information easier by using summarizing and accelerating searches and sometimes utilizing searches that run in the background. The more background processing of this type an app requires, the more likely it is that overall performance will be impacted.

Splunk apps and resource requirements

Simply put, an app will typically execute a number of saved searches to deliver its functionality/functionalities. Executing a large number of saved searches will use larger amounts of CPU resources and can impact performance and even overwhelm a single-server Splunk instance.

In some cases, the details of the apps' system requirements are not provided, and it isn't clear of the resource usage until performance is already compromised.

The bottom line is that a Splunk environment that heavily uses apps (depending upon on the apps being used and how they're written to work) may require migration to a distributed type of deployment.

Hardware

Finally, the hardware configuration where Splunk is installed can certainly affect Splunk performance. Splunk supports utilization on several computing environments.

Requirements will change based on where you're planning a single or distributed deployment and, of course, on projected use.

> **Hint**
> You can learn about the supported environments and recommended hardware at `https://docs.splunk.com/Documentation/Splunk/8.0.3/Installation/Systemrequirements`.

Addressing search performance through architecture

You can expand (scale) your Splunk architecture to meet almost any capacity requirement your organization may have. Taking advantage of this Splunk scaling capability first requires an understanding of the base architectural scenarios.

The simplest architectural scenario is the one you get by default when you first install Splunk on a machine—a separate instance that performs both indexing and searching. Users log in to Splunk on this instance, configure data inputs, and use this same instance to search, monitor, alert, and report on incoming data. This is a **standalone deployment**.

Beyond this initial architectural scenario, Splunk can also be deployed as specialized instances of Splunk across multiple machines to address any additional load and availability requirements. These specialized instances are referred to as **Splunk components**. In this scenario, for example, search work can be spread across multiple Splunk components. This is a **distributed deployment**.

In the next sections, we will examine evolving a Splunk standalone deployment into a distributed deployment by adding indexers, search heads, and clustering.

Adding indexers

Indexers index data and perform searches on the data. By default, all full Splunk instances serve as indexers.

In standalone Splunk deployments, there is a single indexer that indexes incoming data and also handles search management (accepts search requests and performs the searches) functions.

In a distributed Splunk deployment, indexing is separated from the data input function and sometimes from the search management function as well. In these deployments, the indexer might reside on its own machine and handle only indexing, along with the searching of its indexed data. In those cases, other Splunk components assume the non-indexing roles.

Scaling up

Adding an additional indexer to a Splunk deployment is considered to be a routine but important step in *scaling up* a Splunk deployment. This process includes both installing and then configuring an indexer to receive data from other Splunk instances.

At a glance, installing an indexer is straightforward:

1. Prepare a host that meets or exceeds the Splunk system requirements.
2. Take note of the hostname/IP address for the host that you are preparing.
3. Confirm that no firewall blocks relevant network traffic into or out of this host.
4. Download the Splunk software onto the host.
5. Install the correct version of the Splunk software (based on the operating system that the host runs).
6. After installation, confirm that the Splunk software functions by starting, logging into, and then performing a simple search.

Configuring the indexer

Once you have your new indexer set up, you need to configure the forwarding and receiving settings on both the original Splunk install (indexer) as well as the new indexer.

To access these settings, from the Splunk main page, you click on **Settings** and then **Forwarding and receiving**:

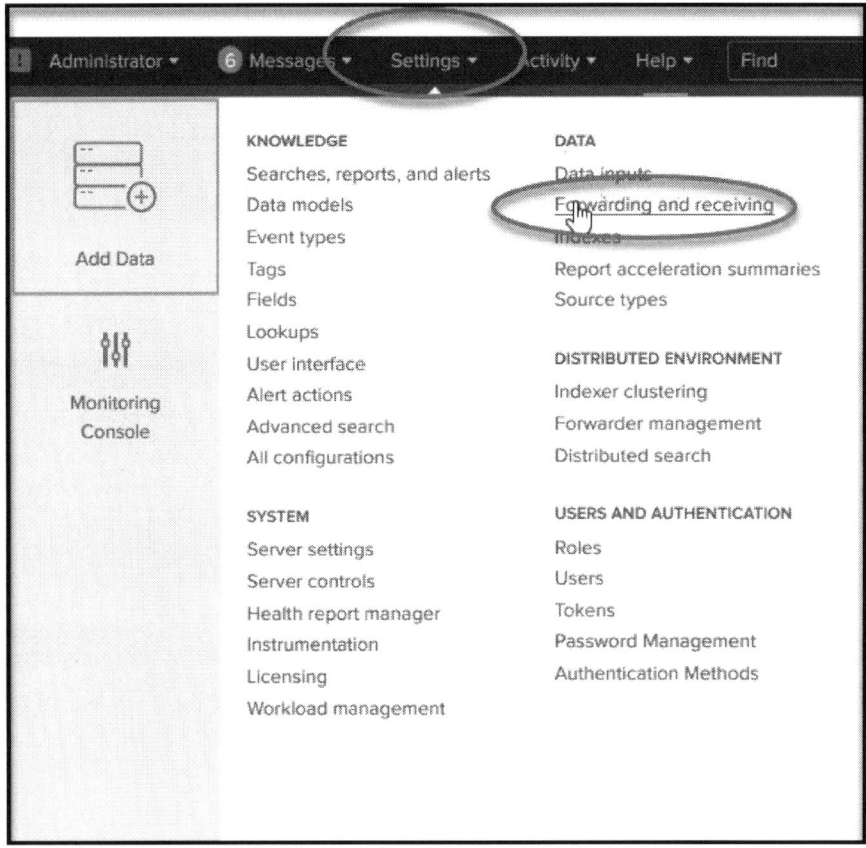

Figure 9.10 – Configuring the indexer

The **Forwarding and receiving** page is shown in the following screenshot:

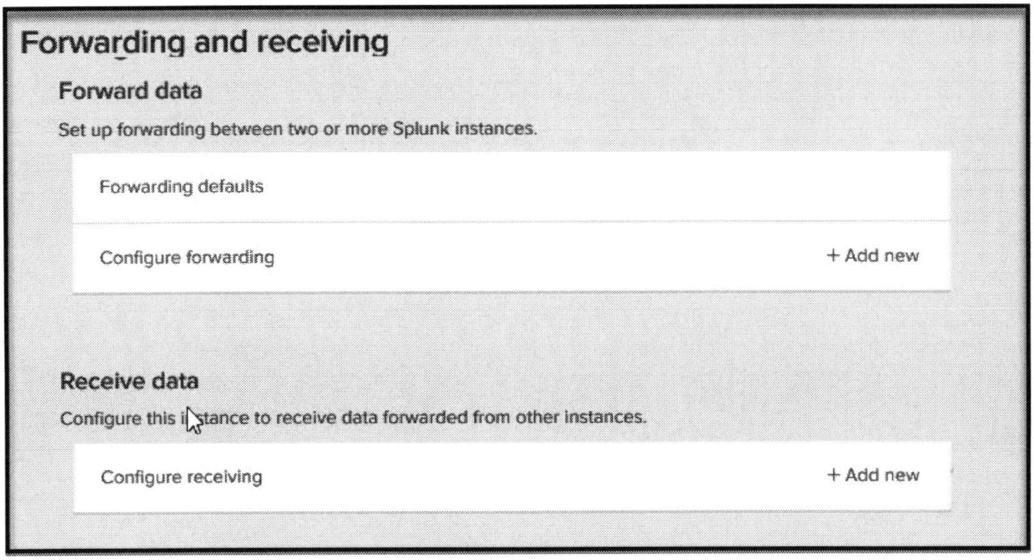

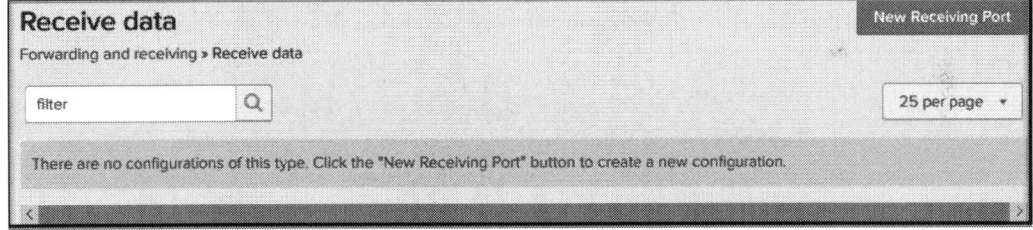

Figure 9.11 – Configuring forward and receive data

For the original Splunk instance (indexer), you click on **Configure receiving**. The **Receive data** page will be displayed (as seen in the following screenshot):

Figure 9.12 – Configuring receiving

214　Search Performance Considerations

Click on the **New Receiving Port** button. On the **Add new** page (shown in the following screenshot), you need to enter the **Listen on this port** value. This will be the port number that you want Splunk to listen on for incoming data from other Splunk instances. Splunk indicates that the conventional port number is 9997:

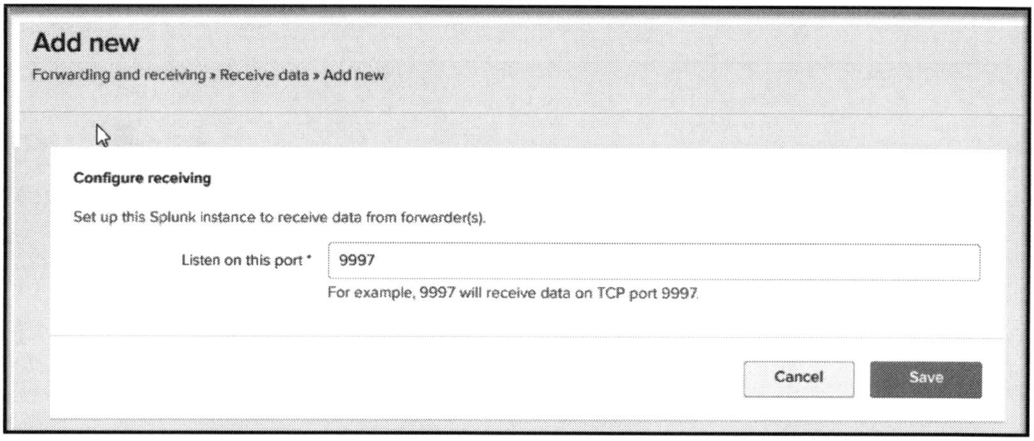

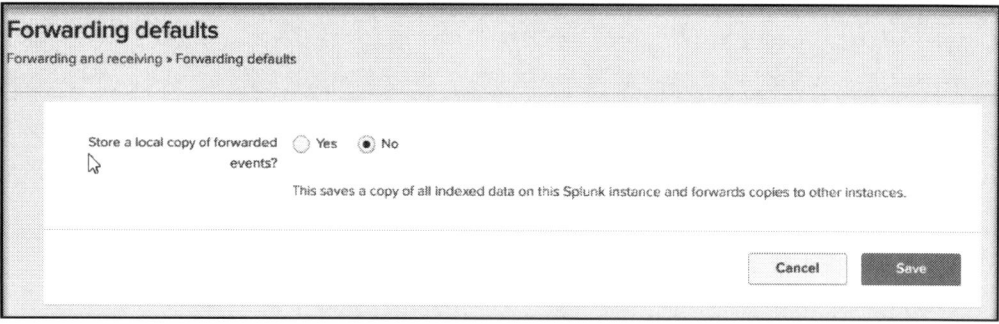

Figure 9.13 – Setting the listening port

For indexers, you generally would not configure forwarding, but to continue our exercise, let's do it.

Now, for the new indexer, under **Forwarding and receiving**, you click on **Forwarding defaults**. On the **Forwarding defaults** page (shown in the following screenshot), you can select to save a (local) copy of forwarded events that the new forwarder indexes (or not). For this exercise, just leave the default setting:

Figure 9.14 – Setting defaults

Back on the **Forwarding and receiving** page, click on **Configure forwarding**:

Figure 9.15 – Configuring forwarding

On the **Forward data** page (shown in the preceding screenshot), click on the **New Forwarding Host** button. The **Add new** page (shown in the following screenshot) is displayed:

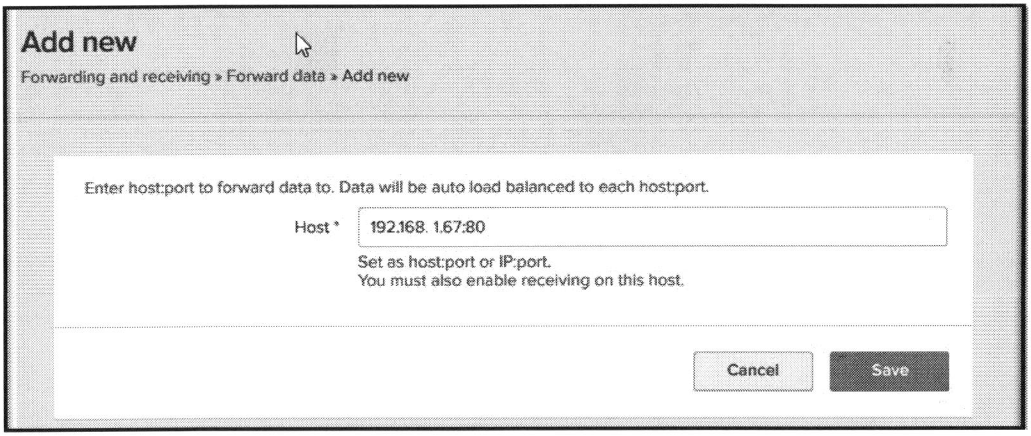

Figure 9.16 – Setting the host

On this page, you need to enter the IP:port value of the original Splunk indexer.

Using multiple indexers to improve performance

It is a common belief (and seems to make good sense) that the more indexers you have, the better your overall Splunk performance will be.

So, in the previous section, our intention was to split out the data input function from the search management function by adding the new indexer on a separate machine. Our original Splunk installation will be where the users log in and submit searches, while we'll set up the data inputs on the new indexer to handle all of the data ingesting and indexing.

> **Note**
> When adding indexers, each could end up with data (assuming the new indexer receives events) and potentially increase license usage and also (possibly) result in duplicate events returned when searching.

As a next step, we might go ahead and add an additional new indexer so that we can further split the data ingesting and indexing:

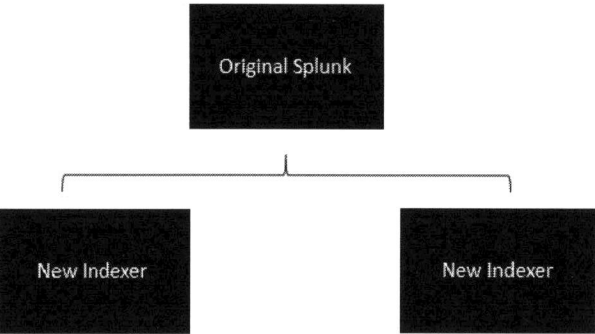

Figure 9.17 – Multiple indexers

Indexers play an important role in Splunk deployments.

In the preceding scenario, we simply added two additional indexers to our Splunk deployment, expecting each to have its own list of data inputs. We would now have three installed instances of Splunk.

In fact, we opted to not save a (local) copy of forwarded events when we set up our additional indexers. In this scenario, the indexers are independent and are not considered to be part of an index cluster (as we covered in *Chapter 5, Advanced Indexing*).

As a reminder, in *Chapter 5, Advanced Indexing*, we explained that an indexer cluster, or the Splunk implementation of index replication, is a group of indexers configured to replicate the data of other indexers in the cluster group (to ensure the system has redundant copies of all data). In our preceding scenario, our intention is that the additional indexers do not replicate each other's data.

Single search head

The next step in configuring our simple three instances' deployment is to define the *original* Splunk instance as the **single search head** of the deployment.

> **Note**
>
> An indexer cluster has one, and only one, master node to coordinate the activities of all the defined peer nodes within the cluster. To have a successful index cluster, you must define a master node. See `https://docs.splunk.com/Documentation/Splunk/8.0.5/Indexer/Enablethemasternode`.

One approach to accomplishing this task is by logging in to that instance and, from the main page, clicking on **Settings**. From there, click on **Indexer Clustering**. On the **Indexer Clustering** page (shown in the following screenshot), click on **Enable indexer clustering**:

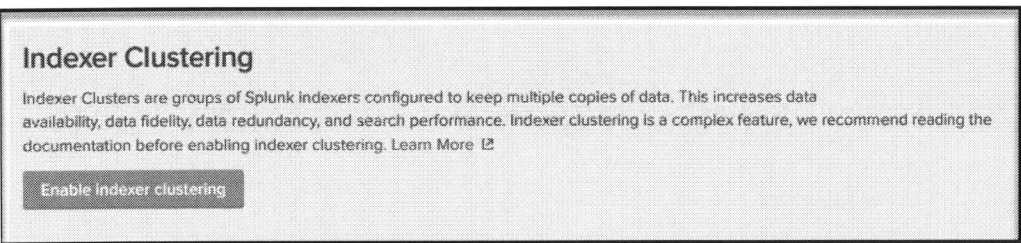

Figure 9.18 – Enabling indexer clustering

On the **Enable Clustering** dialog (shown in the following screenshot), select **Search head node** and then click **Next**:

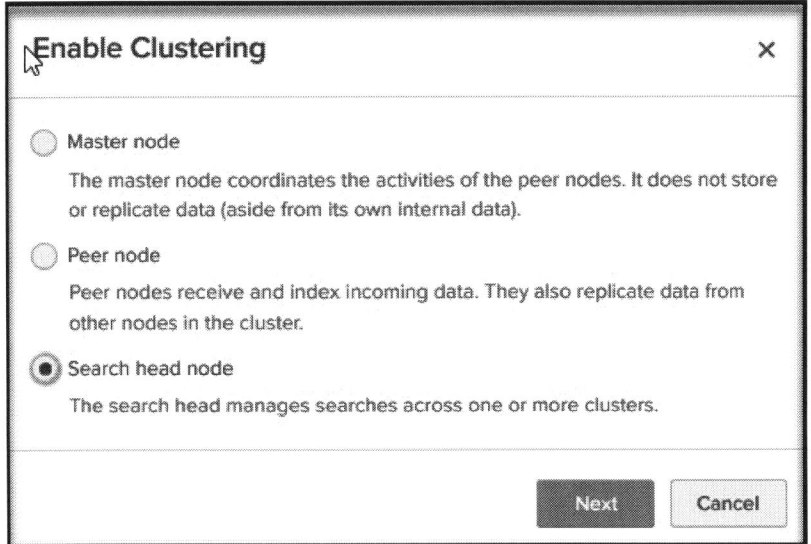

Figure 9.19 – Selecting the search head node

Then, the following dialog box will appear:

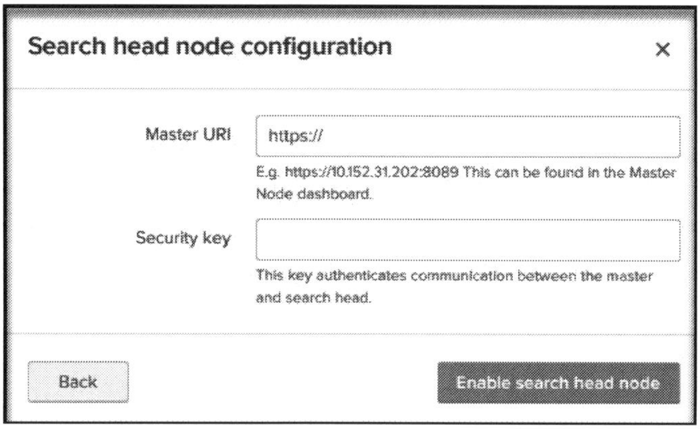

Figure 9.20 – Search head node configuration

On the **Search head node configuration** dialog (shown in the preceding screenshot), there are a few items to fill out:

- **Master URI**: This is the search head's URI identifier, including its port. The syntax for this entry is `https://10.152.31.202:8089`.
- **Security key**: This is the key that is used to authenticate the communication between the search head and the indexers. The key must be the same across all nodes.

> Information
>
> For information on how to establish the security key, refer to `https://docs.splunk.com/Documentation/Splunk/8.0.3/DistSearch/Setsecretkey`.

Once the preceding information is added, you click **Enable search head node**. At this point, we should have a working multi-instance Splunk deployment!

Additional search heads

Another way to scale up a Splunk deployment is by adding an additional search head to the deployment. Going from a single search head deployment to multiple search heads is referred to as **adding search peers**. Adding an additional Splunk instance and designating it as a search head is as straightforward as adding additional indexers; however, before an indexer can function as a search peer, you must change its password from the default value.

> **Note**
> Best practice emphasizes that indexers should be added before search heads to improve performance, otherwise you'll see environments with a bunch of search heads and too few indexers.

Adding an additional search head

Once you have selected a separate Splunk instance to be a search head peer, you can perform the following steps:

1. Log in to the selected Splunk instance and, from the main page, click on **Settings**, and then click on **Distributed search**. The **Distributed search** page (shown in the following screenshot) is displayed:

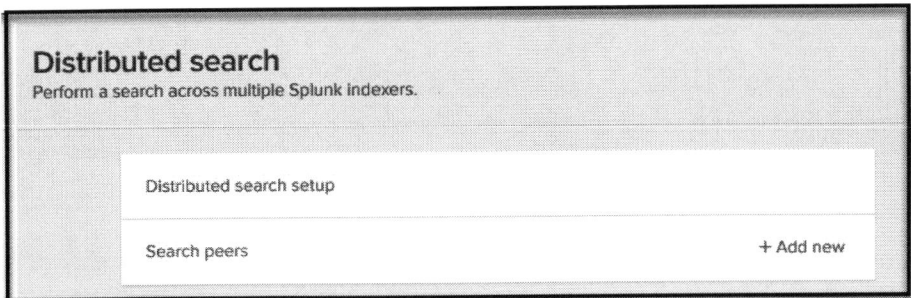

Figure 9.21 – Distributed search page

2. Click **Search peers**. On the **Search peers** page (shown in the following screenshot), select **New Search Peer**:

Figure 9.22 – Search peers page

3. On the **Add new** page (shown in the following screenshot), enter the search **Peer URI**, along with any authentication settings. Note: you must precede the search peer's hostname or IP address with the URI scheme, either `http` or `https`, and then click **Save**:

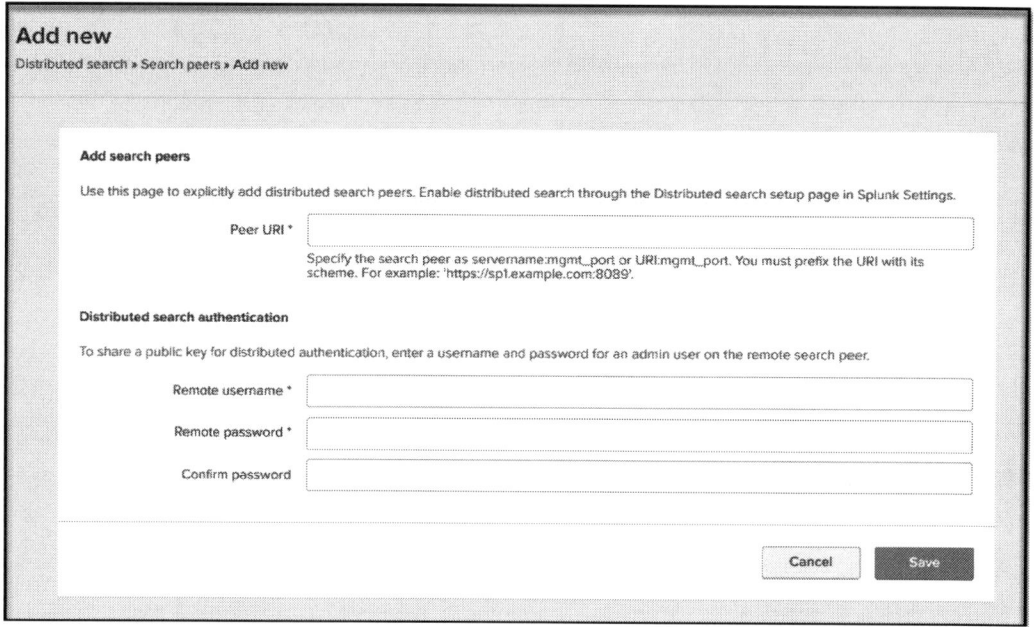

Figure 9.23 – Adding a new search peer

You have successfully added a new, independently operating search head peer!

Search head clustering

A search head cluster is two or more Splunk search heads that serve as a central source for all searching. The goal of a search head cluster is to make all search heads in a cluster interchangeable. You should be able to run or access the same searches, dashboards, knowledge objects, and so on from any member of the cluster. To achieve this interchangeability, the search heads in the cluster must have the same essential configurations, apps, search artifacts, and job loads.

> **Hint**
> Each search head in the search head cluster stores unique configurations made outside of the deployer as well as configurations merged by the deployer in their own local `server.conf` files, located under `$SPLUNK_HOME/etc/system/local/`.

The essential configurations should be set for each Splunk instance at *startup* when you initially configure each search head. Although there is a large number of configurations available, you should always try to change only those that are *essential*. If you change any setting for a single search head, all Splunk instances in the deployment should be restarted.

The following are the minimal essential configurations that must be correctly set:

- The member's URI
- The member's replication port
- The cluster's replication factor
- The cluster's security key
- The deployer location
- The cluster's label

Summary

In this chapter, we spoke about some of the reasons for potentially diminished performance and offered recommendations for combating these issues by adding indexers and additional search heads and implementing search head clustering.

In the next chapter, we'll continue to discuss advanced reporting with the why(s) and how(s) of using SPL within Splunk macros to create effective and efficient searching.

10
Advanced Reporting Using Macros

In the previous chapter, we spent time going over many common causes of dimensioned search performance, and then went over migrating from a single standalone Splunk instance to a distributed environment by adding indexers and then an additional search head.

In this chapter, we will discuss the why(s) and how(s) of using Splunk macros to create effective and efficient searching solutions.

The chapter will be broken down into the following main sections:

- Understanding macros and SPL
- Creating a macro

Understanding macros and SPL

A **macro** in computer science is a **pattern of code** or a number of commands or statements that are written in the correct syntax and saved to be executed later independently or as part of another pattern.

Similarly, Splunk search macros are *reusable blocks* of SPL that you create, save, and then insert into other searches. These macro *code sets* can be used when you want to use the same search logic on different parts of or values in a dataset dynamically, or in other words, without having to *paste* or type the additional SPL commands into a working search.

Splunk search macros can be either full SPL search commands that can be run as is, or a portion of a search command that can be run as part of another query. Macros can even be a specific part of a search command such as an eval expression or function. Not all macros use arguments (parameters) but some do.

To insert a previously defined macro within a search command, you do not have to paste in the actual lines of code or expressions; you simply wrap the name of the macro with the *backtick* character.

> **Hint**
>
> The backtick character (`) typically is located on the same key as the tilde (~). You can reference a search macro within other search macros using this same syntax.

To illustrate the proper syntax, if you have a search macro named `mymacro`, you would code your search as follows:

```
sourcetype=mysourcetype_* | `mymacro`
```

Splunk does not automatically expand or display the macro's contents if it is within quotes. In the following example, the `mymacro` macro is not expanded:

```
"ILOVESPLUNK`mymacro`ALOT"
```

Macro previewing

You can check the contents of any macro (that you have access to) from the Splunk **Search** bar by using the *Ctrl + Shift + E* keyboard combination (on Linux and Windows) and *Command + Shift + E* for a Mac.

You can use this method to view a macro, including macros embedded within a search, without actually running the macro or the search. When you run a preview, the feature expands the macro in question, or all of the macros within the search, if more than one was included. The preview will include all macros that are nested within other macros.

To preview a macro, you can perform the following steps:

1. Navigate to the Splunk **Search** page. In the **Search** bar, type the default macro name, `'audit_rexsearch'`, as shown in the following screenshot:

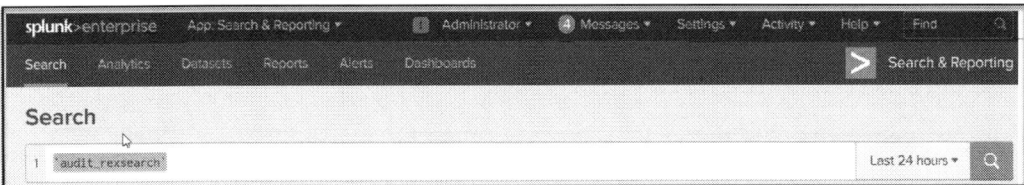

Figure 10.1 – Preview of macro

2. Use the *Ctrl* + *Shift* + *E* keyboard shortcut (on Linux or Windows) to display the macro preview in the **Expanded Search String** dialog as shown in the following screenshot:

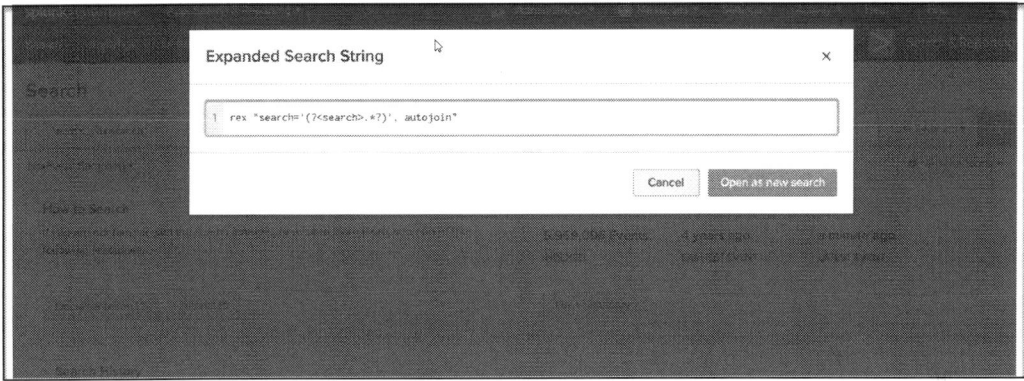

Figure 10.2 – Expanded Search String

3. The **Expanded Search String** dialog will display colored syntax highlighting and line numbers if those features are enabled (which they are by default):

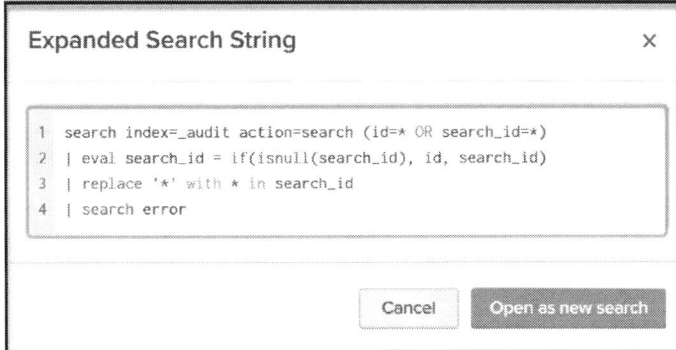

Figure 10.3 – Expanded Search String code

Macros and generating commands

A Splunk **generating command** is a type of command that generates events or reports from one or more indexes without transforming the events it returns.

When you use a Splunk macro in a search string, you need to consider whether the macro expands to an SPL string that begins with a generating command such as the following:

- from
- search
- metadata
- inputlookup
- pivot
- tstats

If it does, Splunk requires that you add the | pipe character before the search macro. This means, for example, we create a macro (named mytstats) with the idea that we want to be able to embed it in a search, and the macro uses tstats to, say, calculate the count for events with host=MySplunkServer:

```
| tstats count WHERE host=MySplunkServer
```

(Page note: item 4 above — In the **Expanded Search String dialog**, you can copy a portion of the search and/or click on **Open as new search** to run the expanded search (in a new browser window).)

Understanding macros and SPL 227

Refer to the following screenshot:

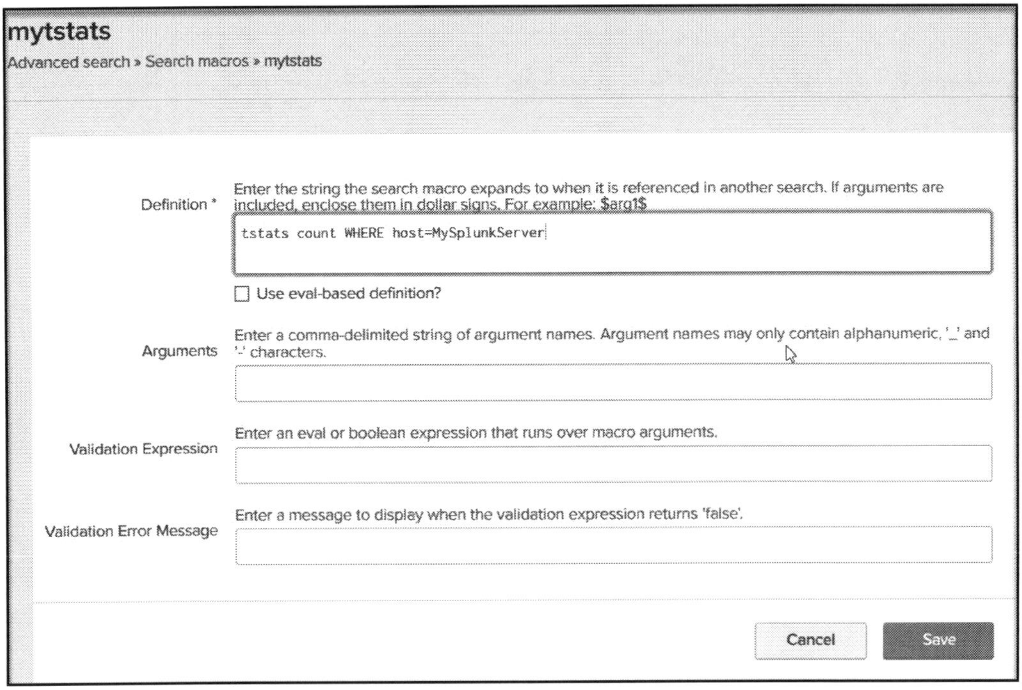

![Configuring a search macro screenshot]

Figure 10.4 – Configuring a search macro

You would run the macro using | `'mytstats'` as follows:

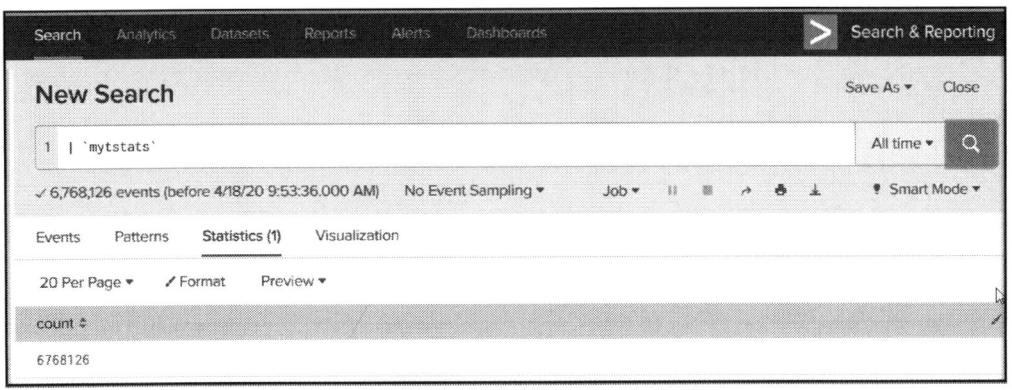

Figure 10.5 – Running a macro

Then, we can embed the macro into a simple search as follows (still using `| 'mytstats'`) by source:

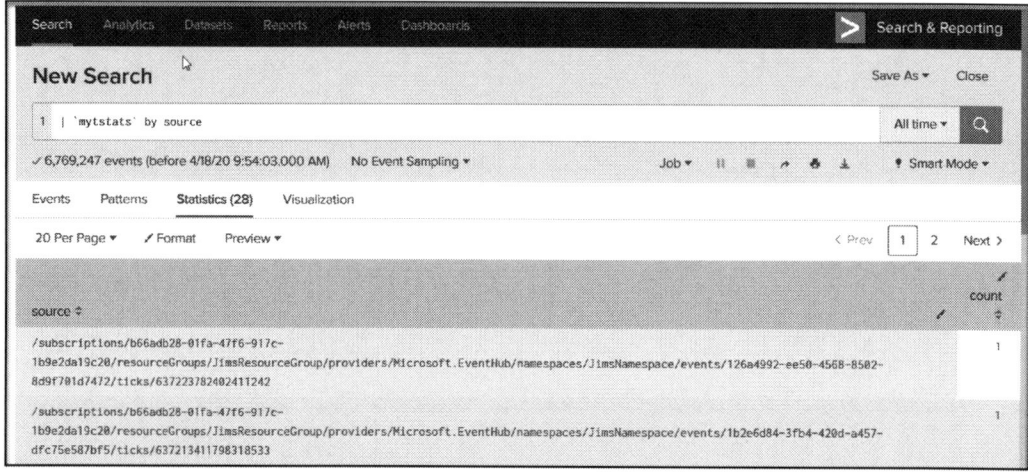

Figure 10.6 – Embedding the macro into a search

Let's now begin exploring search macro arguments.

Search macro arguments

To make Splunk macros even more effective, they can be created to accept one or more runtime parameters or arguments.

Adding arguments to a macro definition is easy. When you define the macro, you enter those argument names as a comma-delimited string containing the argument names in the **Arguments** text field (as shown in the following screenshot). Argument names may only contain alphanumeric characters, along with `'_'` and `'-'`:

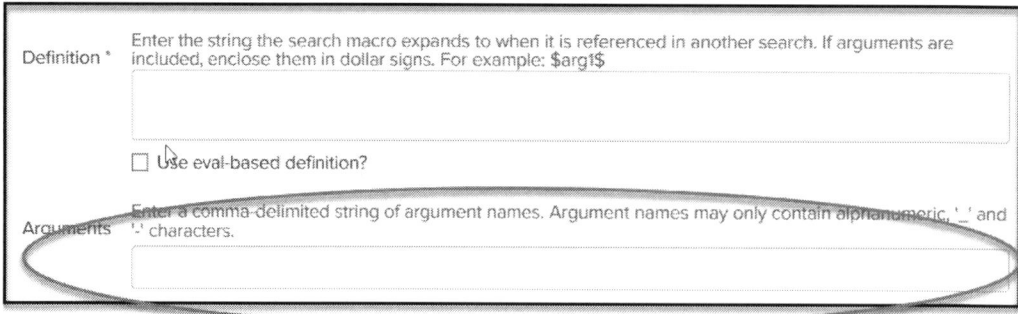

Figure 10.7 – Search macro arguments

To embed a macro that accepts arguments, you would insert the macro into a search string as `'argmacro(120,300)'` (in this example, the `argmacro` macro takes two numeric arguments).

If the macro argument includes quotes, you need to escape the quotes when you call the macro in a search.

For example, if you pass a quoted string as the argument for your macro, you use `'mymacro("He said \"hello!\"")'`.

Splunk macro definitions can include the following:

- A validation expression that determines whether the arguments you enter are valid
- A validation error message that appears when you provide invalid arguments

Argument example

Let's start with a search string that we have used in the past!

The search is used to perform some analysis on trip data. An event driving service concludes that customer satisfaction may be based loosely on the level of tip that was given. The firm wants to do some searching and see what measure might be directly affecting the tip grade. For example, could it be that certain types of events are better?

The following search charts the average (numeric) `Tip Grade` by `Event Type`:

```
sourcetype="csv" | chart avg(Tip Grade) BY "Event Type"
```

Although this is a pretty simple search command, let's create a macro that accepts `BY` as an argument.

The name of the macro will be `TipAnalysis(1)` (notice we are indicating that the macro will expect one argument) and the macro definition will be entered as follows:

```
sourcetype="csv" | chart avg(Tip Grade) BY $ByMeasure$
```

We need to do one more thing in this macro – set the arguments. There will be only one, named `ByMeasure`.

Our macro definition is shown in the following screenshot:

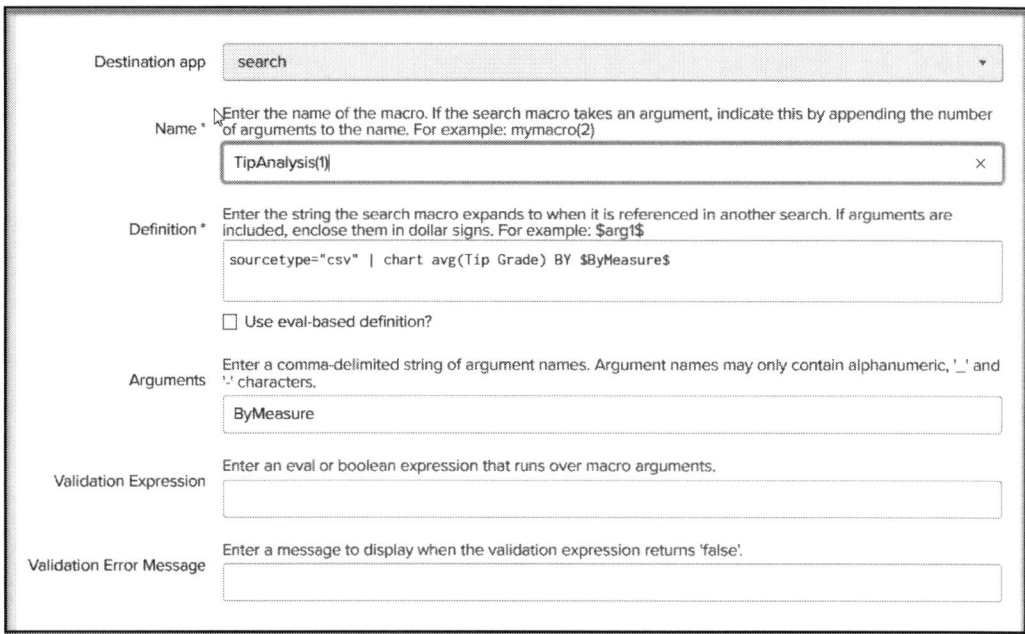

Figure 10.8 – Setting the search macro arguments

Now, the fun part: running the macro from the **Search** bar!

We can now run the macro and analyze the average tip grade by any measure (the event field).

The first test of our macro is to use `"Event Type"` as the `"by measure"` argument, `'TipAnalysis("\"Event Type"\")'`:

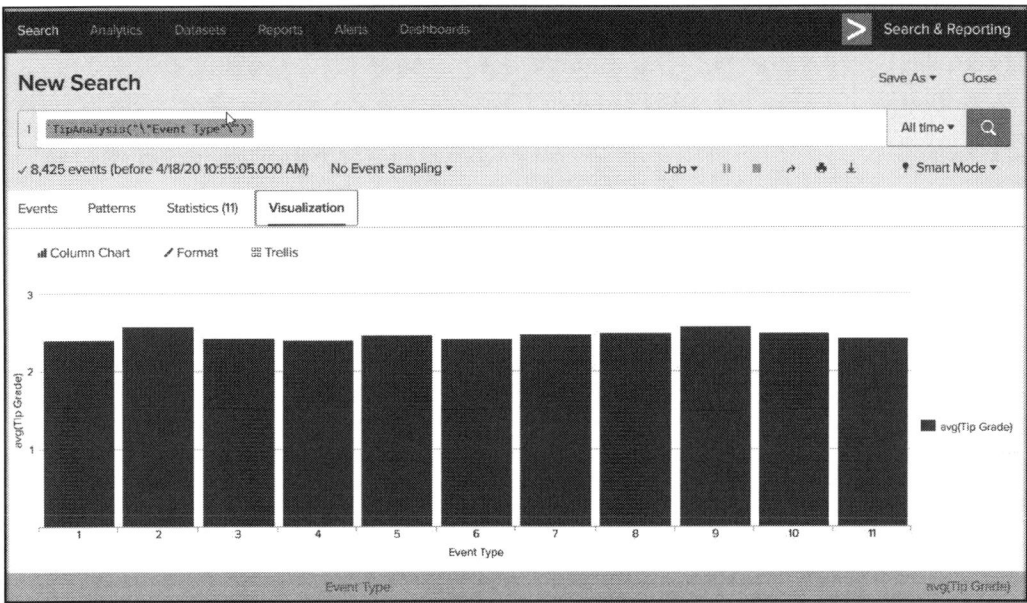

Figure 10.9 – Running the macro from the Search bar

Another variation of search using the macro might be as follows:

`'TipAnalysis("\"Vehicle Type"\")'`

We could also have the following:

`'TipAnalysis("\"Payment Type"\")'`

You can perhaps see how adding an argument (or two) to a macro definition tends to make the macro much more effective and easier to use, and adds to its value.

Macro definitions

Every macro that is defined is automatically written to and stored in the Splunk `macros.conf` configuration file.

The file containing your macro definitions can be found at `C:\Program Files\Splunk\etc\users\admin\search\local`.

The following screenshot is a view of the `macros.conf` file that was generated by Splunk for the macros we've created (so far) in this chapter:

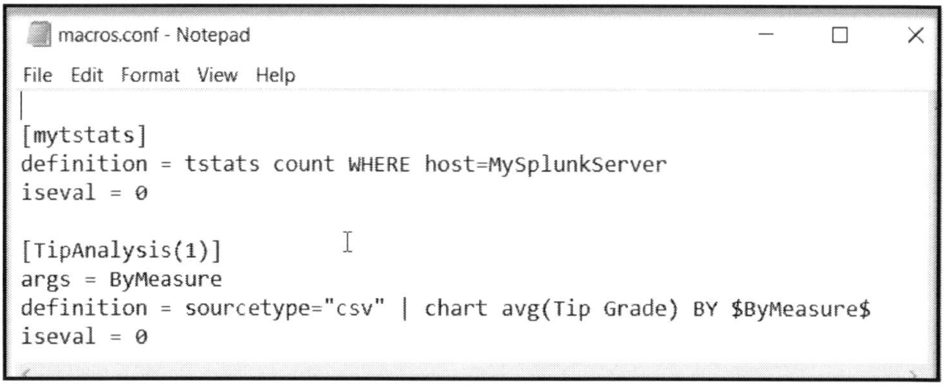
macros.conf - Notepad
File Edit Format View Help
[mytstats]
definition = tstats count WHERE host=MySplunkServer
iseval = 0
[TipAnalysis(1)]
args = ByMeasure
definition = sourcetype="csv" | chart avg(Tip Grade) BY $ByMeasure$
iseval = 0

Figure 10.10 – The macros.conf file

In the next section, we will walk through the step-by-step process required to create a Splunk macro.

Creating a macro

We have already created two somewhat simple (but illustrative) Splunk macro examples in this chapter.

In this section, we will show the specific steps to create a Splunk macro:

1. From the main Splunk page, go to **Settings**, then click on **Advanced search**:

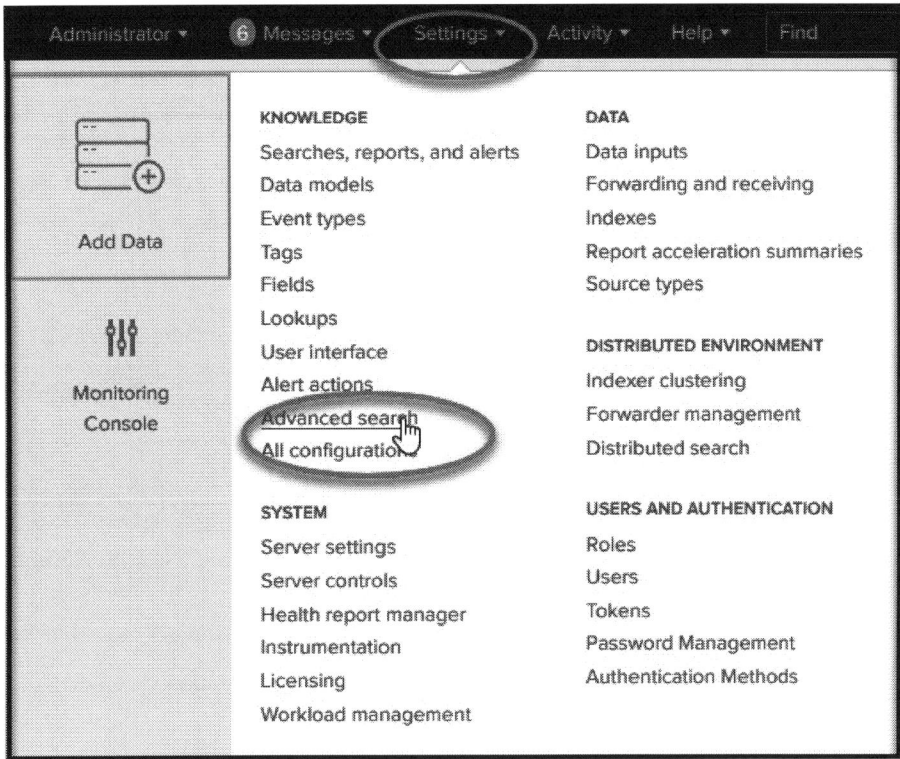

Figure 10.11 – Creating a Splunk macro

2. On the **Advanced search** page, click on **Search macros**:

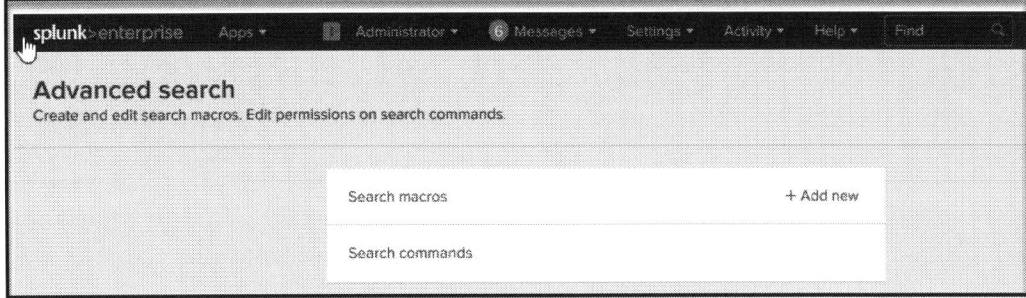

Figure 10.12 – Searching for existing macros

234 Advanced Reporting Using Macros

3. Next, on the **Search macros** page, click on **New Search Macro**. If you have access to any macros at this point, they would be listed here:

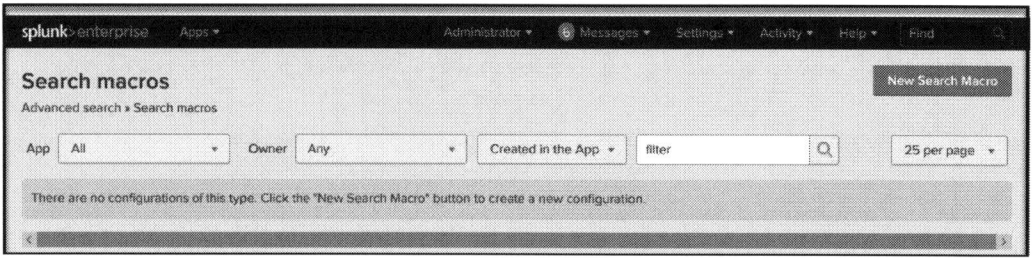

Figure 10.13 – Adding a new search macro

4. In the **Add new** dialog (shown in the following screenshot), enter the appropriate information about the macro we are defining:

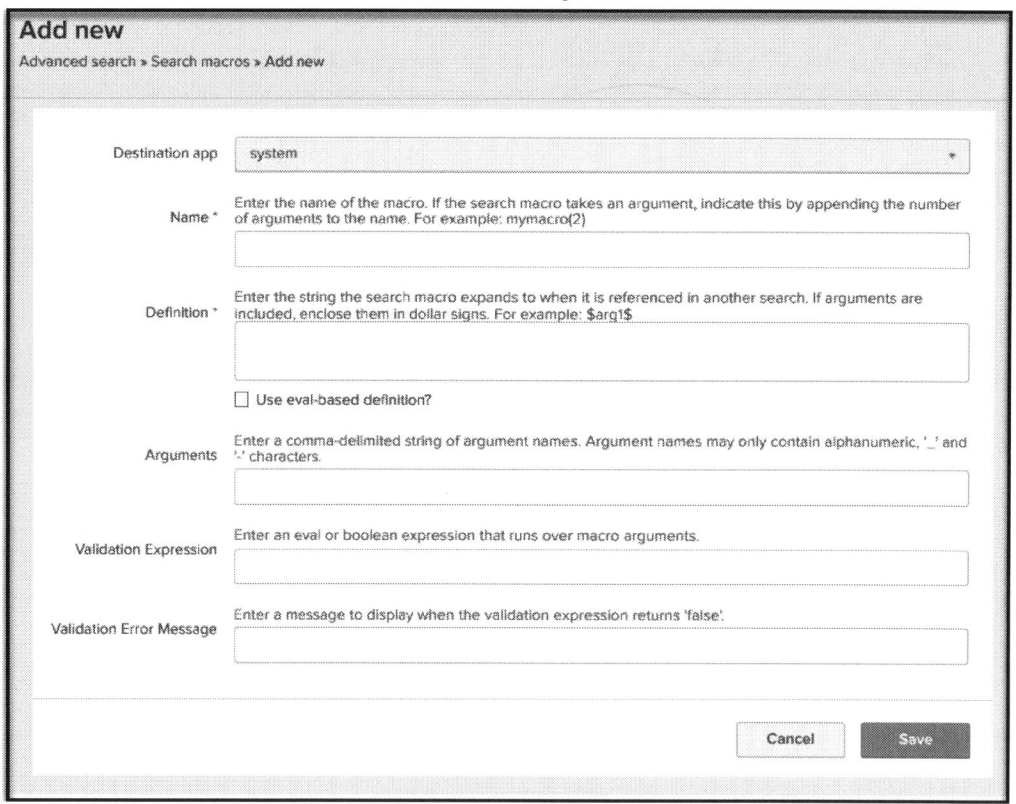

Figure 10.14 – Configuring a new search macro

Now that we have learned how to create macros, let's look into the macro definition specifics.

The following are the macro definition specifics from the preceding screenshot:

- **Destination app**: This indicates where the macro will be restricted to. You can click on the field and select a different app from the list if you need to restrict your search macro to a different app.
- **Name**: You need to enter a unique name for the macro. If you are defining any arguments to be used by the macro, you also need to indicate this in the macro's name. In the preceding section, we used "TipAnalysis(1)". In this example, the macro expected one argument.
- **Definition**: This is the actual search command that the macro expands to when you execute it or embed it in another search.
- **Use eval-based definition?**: This checkbox is used to indicate whether the macro is an eval expression that will return a string value that the search macro expands to.

    Here is an example. In the following macro definition, we have the name set to splunk_domain(1) and the argument set to splunk_domain. This indicates that our macro will expect an argument named splunk_domain.

    The objective of this simple eval-based macro example is to return a valid hostname in our search, rather than having to know the actual host IDs. In other words, we simplify the search command by allowing the user to search the "corp" or "local" host Splunk servers.

    The macro definition uses the Splunk case function and is case("$splunk_domain$"=="corp", "CorpSplunk", "$splunk_domain$"=="local", "MySplunkServer", "$splunk_domain$"=="remote", "Flex", true(), "*").

Our macro definition would look something like this:

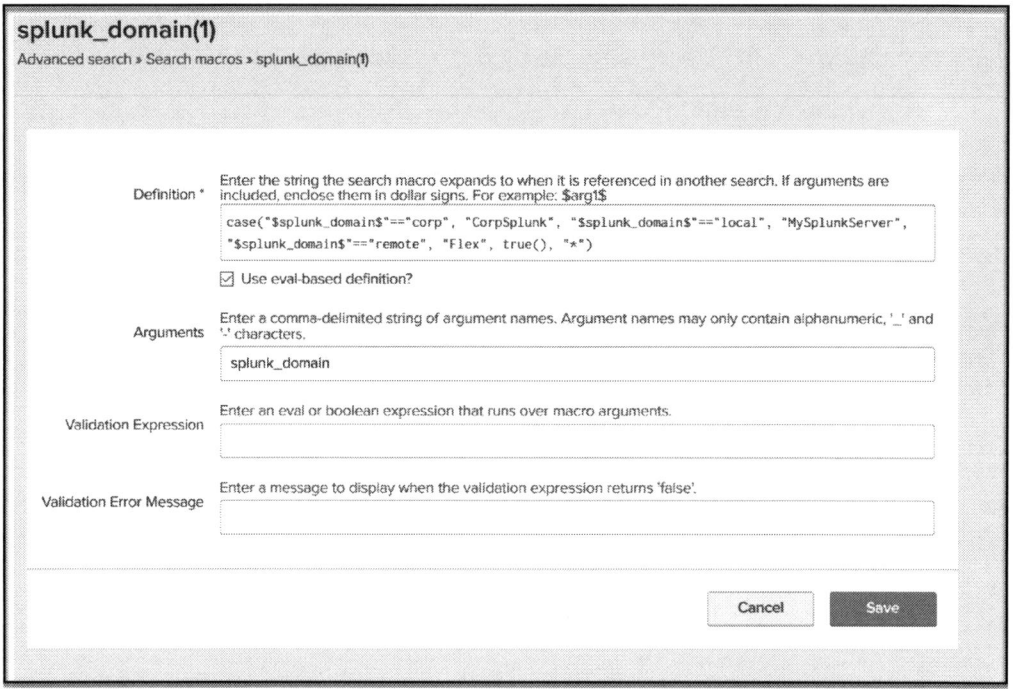

Figure 10.15 – Macro definition using a case function

Note that in this macro definition, we were sure to check the **Use eval-based definition?** checkbox!

Now, once we save our macro, we can return to the search page and type `sourcetype="csv" host='splunk_domain(local)'`:

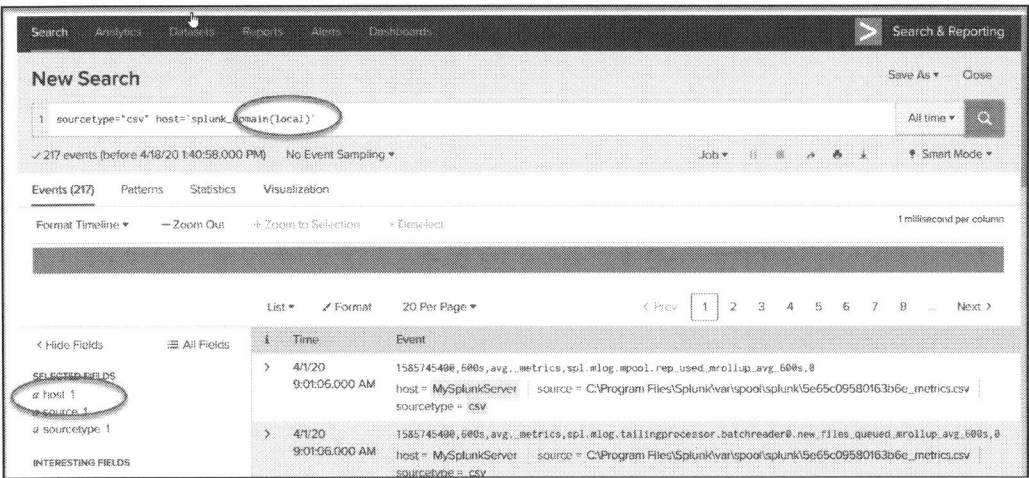

Figure 10.16 – Running the new search macro from the search bar

Notice, in the preceding search results, that the macro transformed the string value from `local` to `MySplunkServer` and returned the event results for that host (also notice that the **host** field only has one distinct value now).

- **Arguments**: This is where you list the arguments the macro will expect as a comma-delimited string of argument names. Argument names may only contain alphanumeric characters (a–z, A–Z, 0–9), underscores, and dashes. The string cannot contain repetitions of argument names.

- **Validation Expression**: When you add arguments to a Splunk macro, you can (and should) set up an expression that will validate that the argument values used to invoke the search macro are acceptable and what the macro expects. The validation expression is an eval expression that evaluates to a Boolean or string value. A common validation expression involves the use of the `isnum` function.

  For example, in a macro definition, to verify that the `dummy` argument is a number, you might type `isnum($dummy$)` into the **Validation Expression** field.

- **Validation Error Message**: This is a handy setting if you defined a validation expression for your macro (as we did in the preceding example). This is the message that will appear if the argument value used fails the validation expression.

238   Advanced Reporting Using Macros

To have some fun using the preceding validation expression, we could enter a message such as `Yo! Thats not a number!` into the **Validation Error Message** field in our macro definition.

Our macro definition would look something like this:

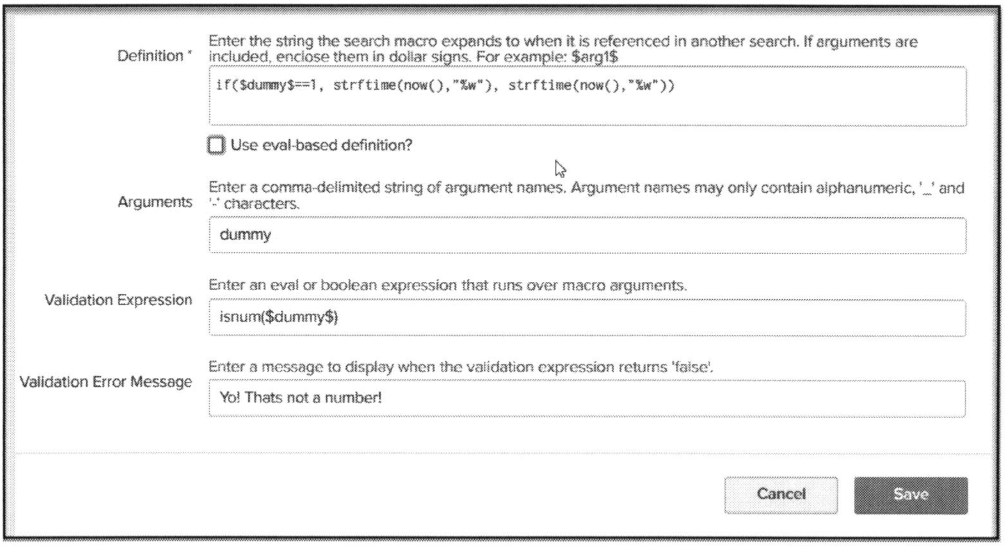

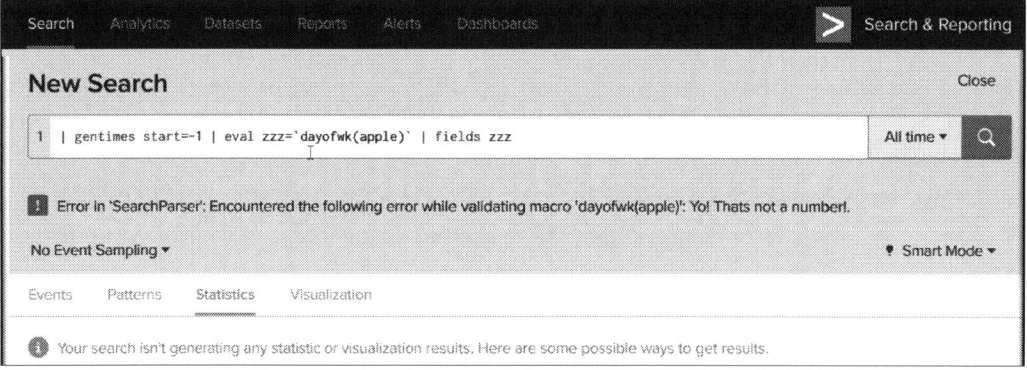

Figure 10.17 – Macro definition

Now, if we run the search using this macro and purposely supply a non-numeric argument (in this case, `apple`) in `| gentimes start=-1 | eval zzz='dayofwk(apple)' | fields zzz`, we will see the following result:

Figure 10.18 – Running the macro with a non-numeric argument

When you have entered valid values for all of the preceding specifics, click **Save** to save your search macro.

Your new macro should now be listed on the **Search macros** page (shown in the following screenshot):

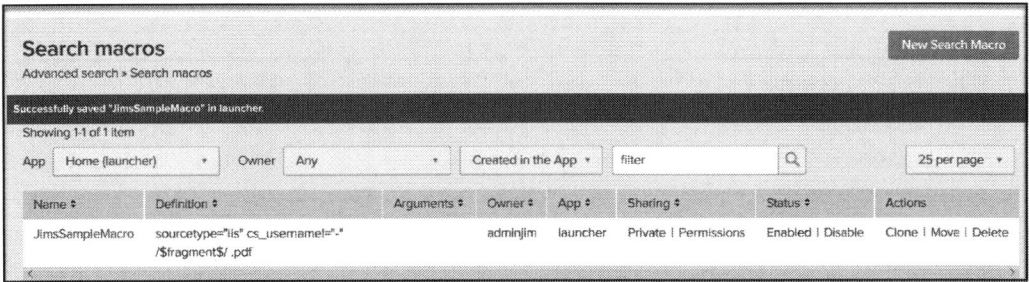

Figure 10.19 – Saving the new macro

Once you have created your macro, don't forget to click on **Permissions** and ensure you provide access to it! This is shown as follows:

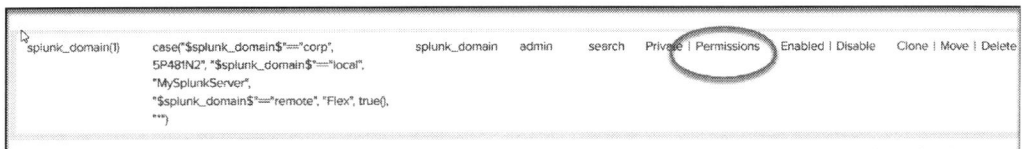

Figure 10.20 – Providing access permissions to the macro

Now that we have become comfortable with the idea of Splunk macros, you can consider creating and sharing a macro any time you want to use the same search logic on different parts of or values in your data.

Summary

In this chapter, we went over what a Splunk macro is, the value provided by using macros, and the steps necessary to create and use them.

In the next chapter, we will cover advanced data analytics techniques used to enhance productivity and gain advantages from data using Splunk.

11
Dashboards – Advanced Data Analytics

In the previous chapter, we discussed the *why(s)* and *how(s)* of building reusable Splunk macros to create effective and efficient searching solutions.

In this chapter, we will cover advanced data analytics techniques used to enhance productivity and gain advantages from data using Splunk.

We will start with a discussion on the fundamentals of an analytics framework, look at various tips and examples aimed at exploring data using Splunk datasets, take a look at the **table editor** and **pivot tool**, and finish off the chapter by touching on transactional analysis.

The chapter will be broken down into the following main sections:

- Fundamentals of analytics frameworks
- Explanatory data analysis—exploring data
- Transactions and transactional analysis

Fundamentals of analytics frameworks

To start, what is an analytics framework?

Analytical frameworks are designed to add structure to an analyst's way of thinking and to promote logical thinking in a systematic manner. In short, analytical frameworks are **models** that aim to guide and facilitate the process act of acquiring an understanding of something seemingly complex. In most cases, analytical frameworks are often presented in a visual way.

Sometimes breaking a concept down into individual components helps develop a better understanding. For example, let's define **Analytics** and **Framework**:

- **Analytics**: Defined as the process of breaking a problem into smaller, simpler parts and then using inferences based on data to drive decisions. Analytics is not a tool or a technology; rather it is a way of thinking and acting.

- **Framework**: A framework is an essential supporting structure of something (an example is a body's skeletal system). Combined with the word analytics, a framework could be the functionalities and features of a tool like Splunk.

Analytics projects

With any analytics project, it can be difficult to know where to start, as well as how to proceed. There are common challenges and considerations present in every project—even those employing proven analytical frameworks.

For an analytics framework to add value, it must meet the following challenges or at least address these critical areas:

- **Deciding on the metrics**: Before beginning any analytical project, it is critical to decide on what metrics are the most meaningful to the success of the project. Once you have those identified, eliminating the extraneous noise will streamline the workflow of the project and simplify the visualizations generated, allowing the focus to be on only metrics that are relevant to the objective(s) of the project.

- **Data modeling**: In order to gain actionable insights from all of the raw data collected, you need to be able to transform your raw data into a data model that is easy to understand, flexible, and easy to work with.

- **Dashboarding**: Visualizations are by far the most effective method to present and consume data, particularly for non-technical users. You should be able to create, edit, and distribute dashboards designed with visualizations that display relationships between highlighted information points, provide context, and ensure that key stakeholders can understand them at a simple glance.

Exploratory data analysis—exploring data

Exploratory Data Analysis (**EDA**) refers to the critical process of performing initial investigations on data so as to discover patterns, to spot anomalies, to test hypotheses, and to check assumptions with the help of summary statistics and graphical visualizations. From this investigation, you establish and formulate the correct questions to ask the data, how to manipulate the data sources to get the required answers, and so on. The objective is to understand (and possibly fix) the data first, gathering as many insights from it as possible. The data may be comprised of various sources.

Determining the data details

This means determining the base facts of the data, which are listed as follows:

- What is the dataset type? A table? A CSV? A JSON-formatted file?
- What is the source(s) of the data?
- What are the permissions? Public or private? Owned by whom?
- How fresh is the data? What is the last modified date/time? What is the refresh rate?
- What are the relevant fields in the data?

Establishing relevancy

This is to find out whether the dataset actually contains information you want:

- Is the data at the right level? Summarized or detail level?
- What is the time range of the data? (Daily? Weekly? Monthly?)
- Do the contents of the data match the needs of the project?
- What is the context of the data? For example, is the data factual/actual or a forecast/prediction?

Performing EDA with Splunk

To illustrate how well Splunk covers EDA, or perhaps supports the analytical framework, let's walk through a working use case.

Our case involves analyzing crime activity recorded over time, to satisfy governmental budgeting—should we cut or increase funding for crime enforcement? We are going to explore crime activity data provided to us. We have already been given an initial CSV file and as time progresses, we'll have additional files provided. Since they are being provided from the same source and, presumably, they will be formatted consistently, we can set up a data input to continuously monitor a folder where files will be dropped. Once we have the new data input set up, we can explore the first file and create a Splunk dataset for use by ourselves and other analysts.

Setting up the data input

The steps for setting up the data input are as follows:

1. From the Splunk main page, we can click on **Settings**, then **Data Inputs**. Then click on **New Local File & Directory**:

Figure 11.1 – Creating new data input

2. Next, we will set **File or Directory** to the location where we expect to be periodically dropping new crime activity files:

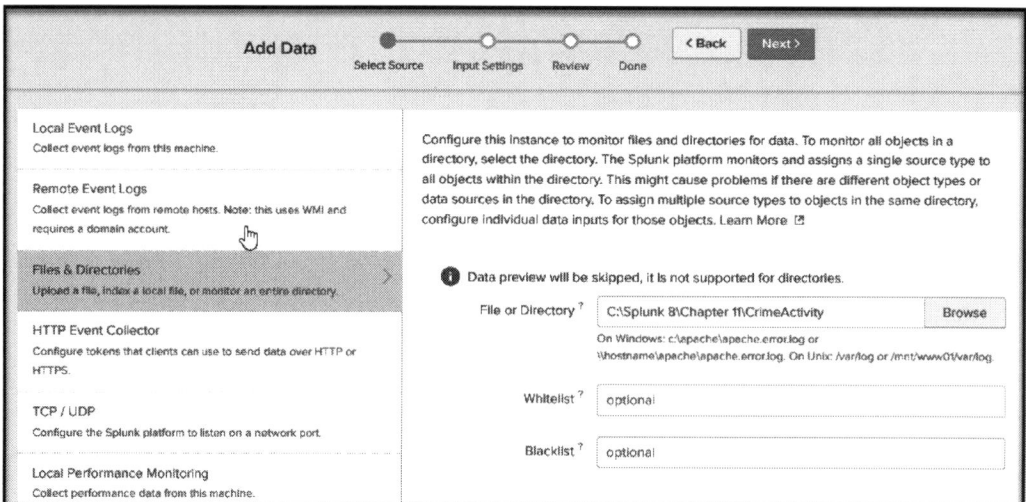

Figure 11.2 – Setting the file or directory

Exploratory data analysis—exploring data 245

3. Then select the settings for our new input—**Source type: CSV**, **App context: Search & Reporting**, **Host**: `MySplunkServer`, and **Index: Default**:

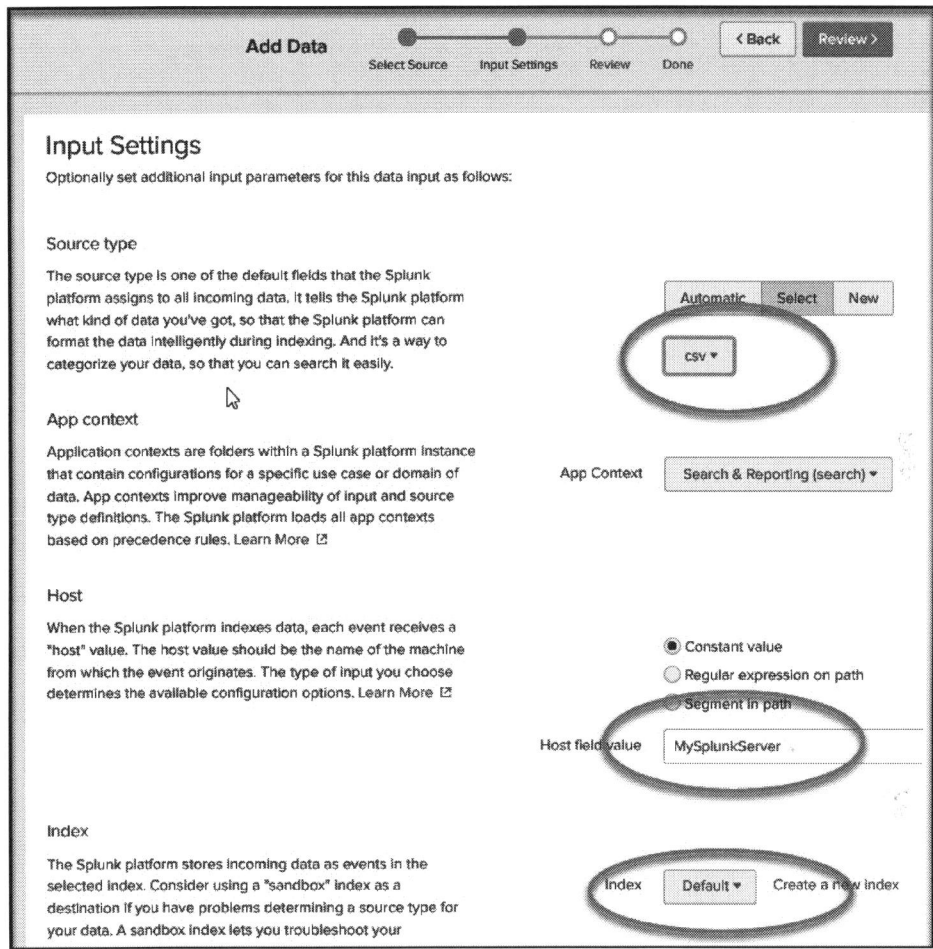

Figure 11.3 – Configuring the settings for the new data input

4. After clicking **Review** you can click **Submit**, and see our input's summary:

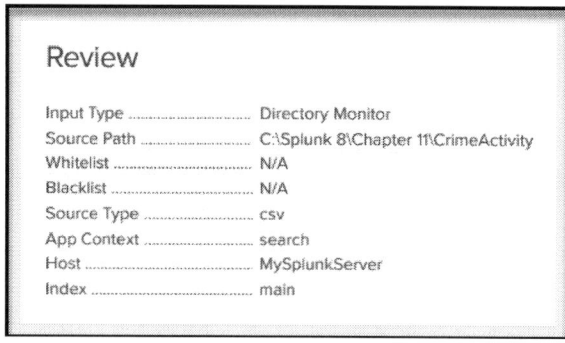

Figure 11.4 – Input summary

5. After the new input is successfully created, you can click **Start Searching** (as shown in the following screenshot):

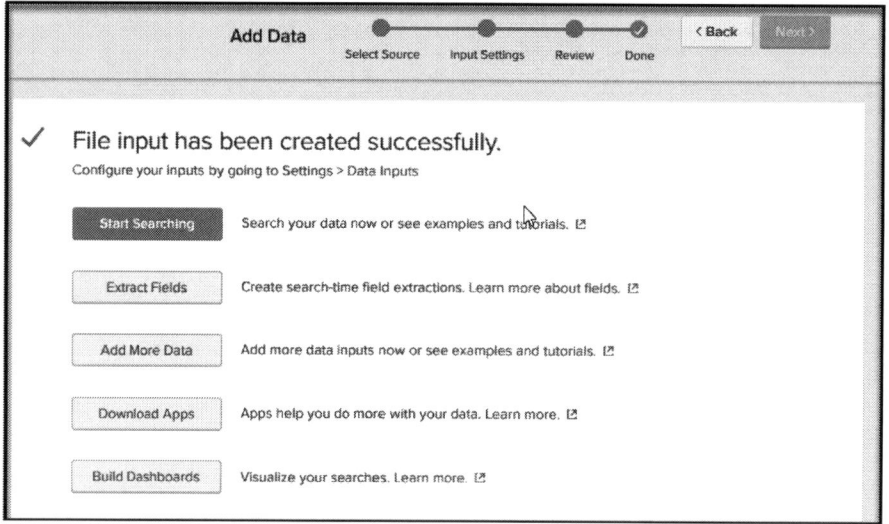

Figure 11.5 – Searching with the new data input

Exploratory data analysis—exploring data   247

We see that an initial search against our new input has returned results (shown in the following screenshot):

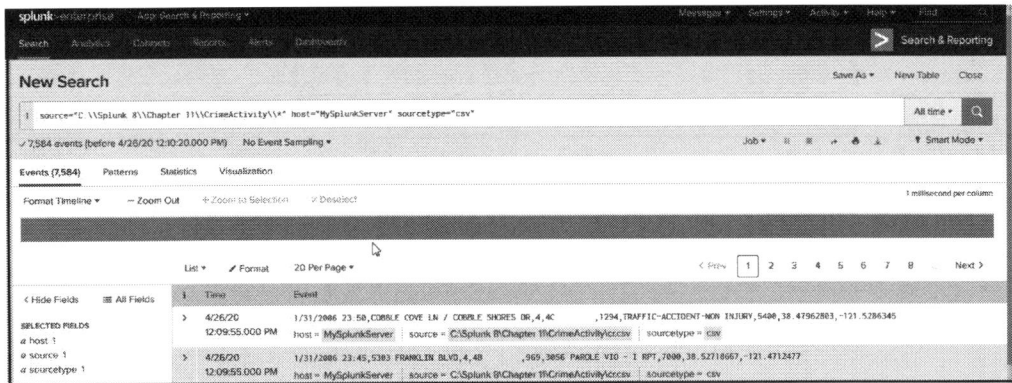

Figure 11.6 – Search results

Rather than using specific Splunk data exploration commands here, let's move on and use this input to create a data model.

Creating a data model

A **Splunk dataset** is a collection of data that you define and maintain for a specific business purpose. It is represented as a table, with fields for columns and field values for cells. You can view and manage all of your datasets from the **Datasets** listing page using the following steps:

1. From the **Search & Reporting** menu bar, click on **Datasets**:

Figure 11.7 – Accessing the dataset management page

2. Once you have access to datasets, from the **Datasets** listing page, you can *expand* a dataset row to quickly see some of the data details we mentioned earlier in the chapter, such as the fields contained in the dataset and the date the dataset was last modified. For this exercise, let's jump right into creating a new dataset (using our crime activity data) by clicking on **Create New Table Dataset**:

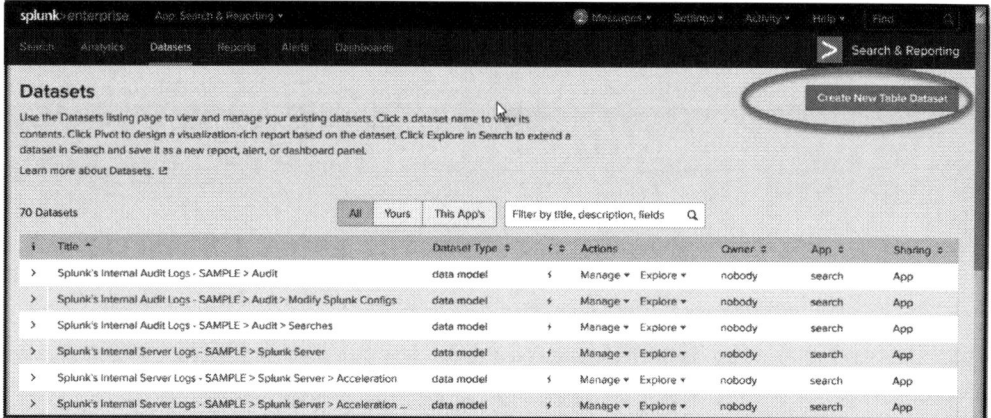

Figure 11.8 – Creating a new table dataset

3. On the **New Table Dataset** page (shown in the following screenshot), you can click on the **Indexes & Source Types** icon, which will list all indexes on the left of the page. Recall that our crime activity data input was set to use the main index, so click on `main` to select it:

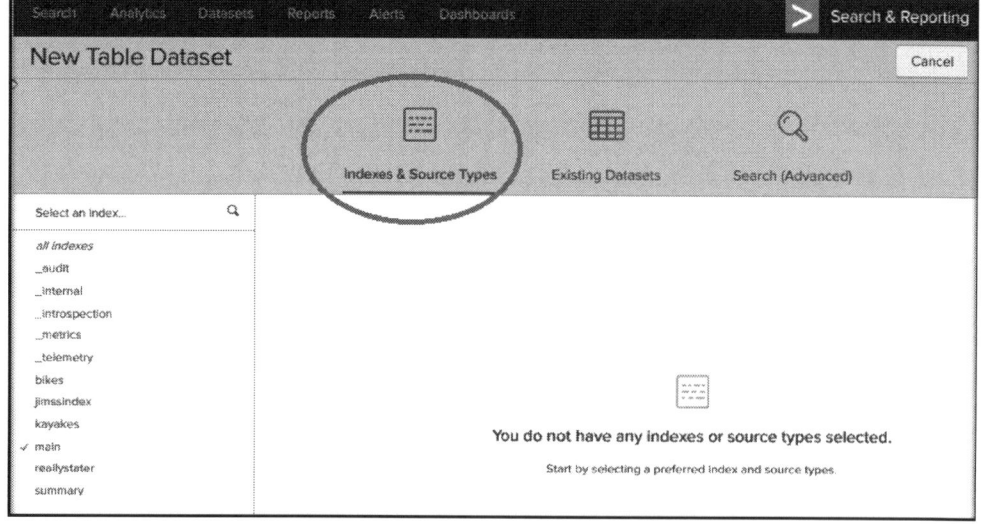

Figure 11.9 – Listing the indexes of the dataset

Hint:

The **Existing Datasets** icon allows you to select an existing dataset, make a copy of it as a starting point for a new dataset, or extend that dataset by adding to it or modifying it. The **Search (Advanced)** icon can be used to enter search commands that allow you to create a very customized, specifically focused list of fields to build into a new dataset.

4. Next, select the source type (Splunk lists the source types available to the selected index), then scroll down, click on `csv`, and then **OK**:

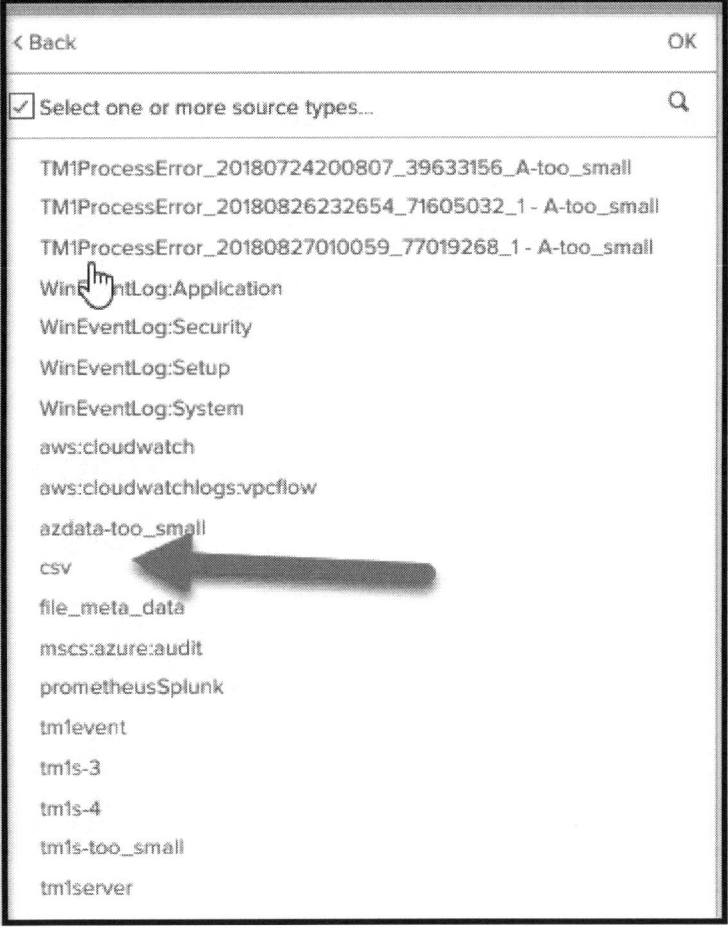

Figure 11.10 – List of source types

5. Splunk will run a search using `index=main` and `soucetypes=csv` and then display all of the available fields (down the left of the page) as well as the selected fields' values in the center. Note that, initially, Splunk selects the internal fields `_time` and `_raw` from our data:

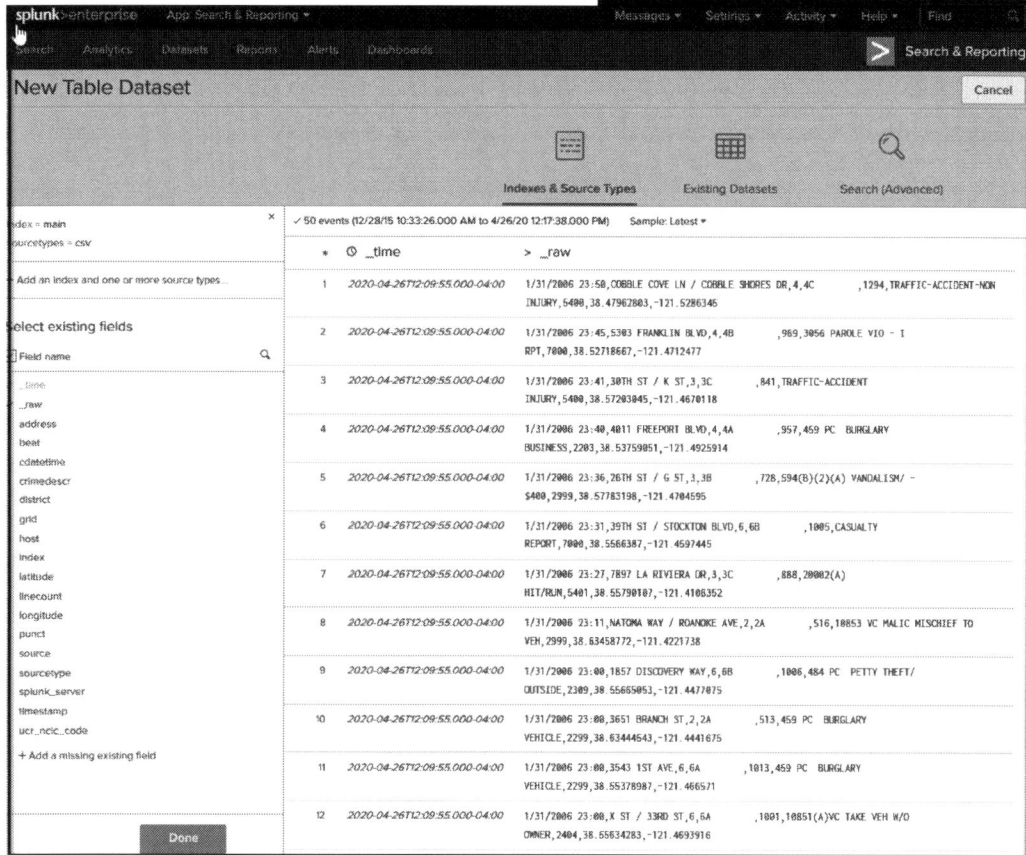

Figure 11.11 – List of the new search results

Although we could just search and explore this raw data, the point of using the raw data to create a dataset is to make subsequent exploration and analysis of the data easier and more efficient. So, we can unselect `_raw` (you cannot unselect `_time`) and then select the fields we think are relevant to our analysis.

Exploratory data analysis—exploring data   251

6. To make this field selection process a little easier, if you hover over a field name, Splunk provides a popup of descriptive details for that field, for example, **Top 10 Values** and **%**:

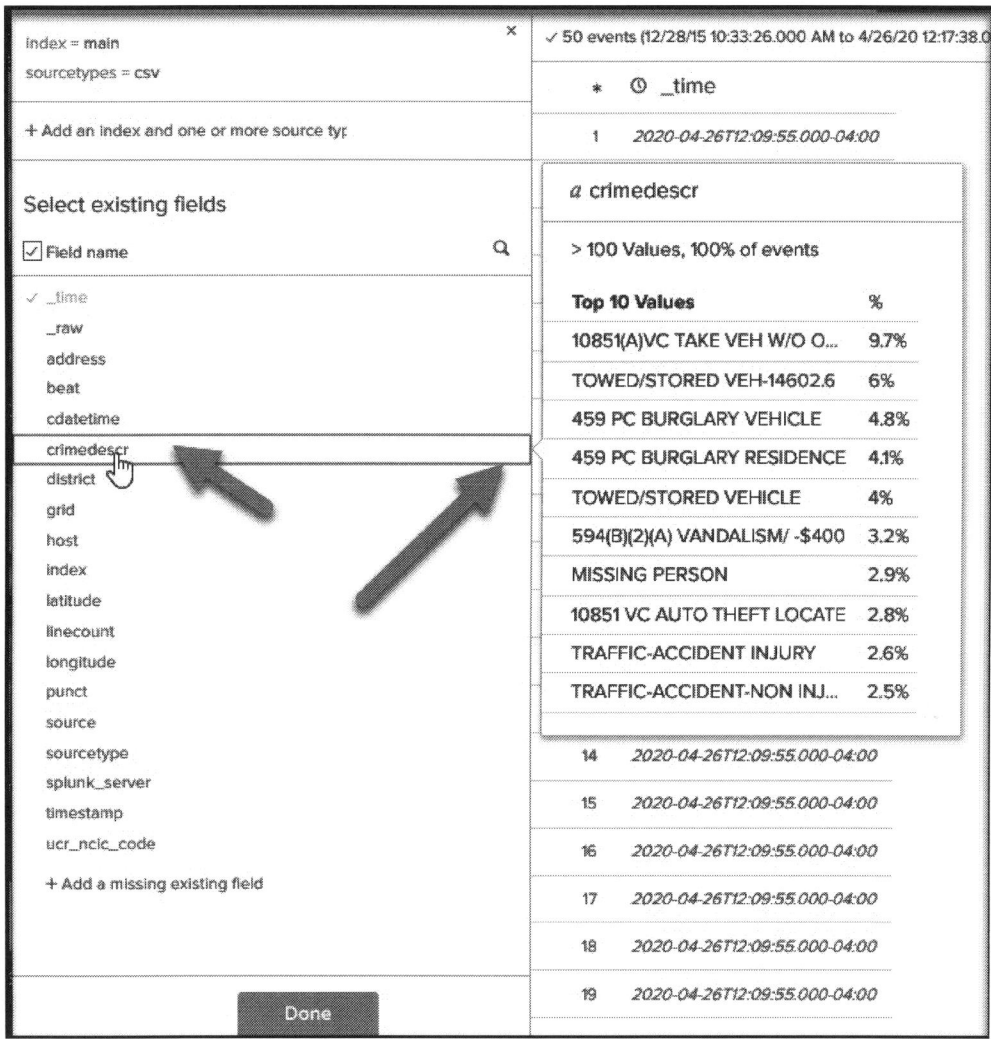

Figure 11.12 – Popup description of fields

7. Select the following fields—`address`, `beat`, `cdatetime`, `crimedesc`, `district`, and `grid`. Note that even though we've added another `time` to our selected field list (`cdatetime`, which is the date and time that the criminal activity took place, and is formatted a bit more nicely), we still cannot remove the Splunk `_time` field, since that is what Splunk is using to uniquely qualify the events within the indexed raw data. Once our field selection is completed (as shown in the following screenshot), we can click on **Done**:

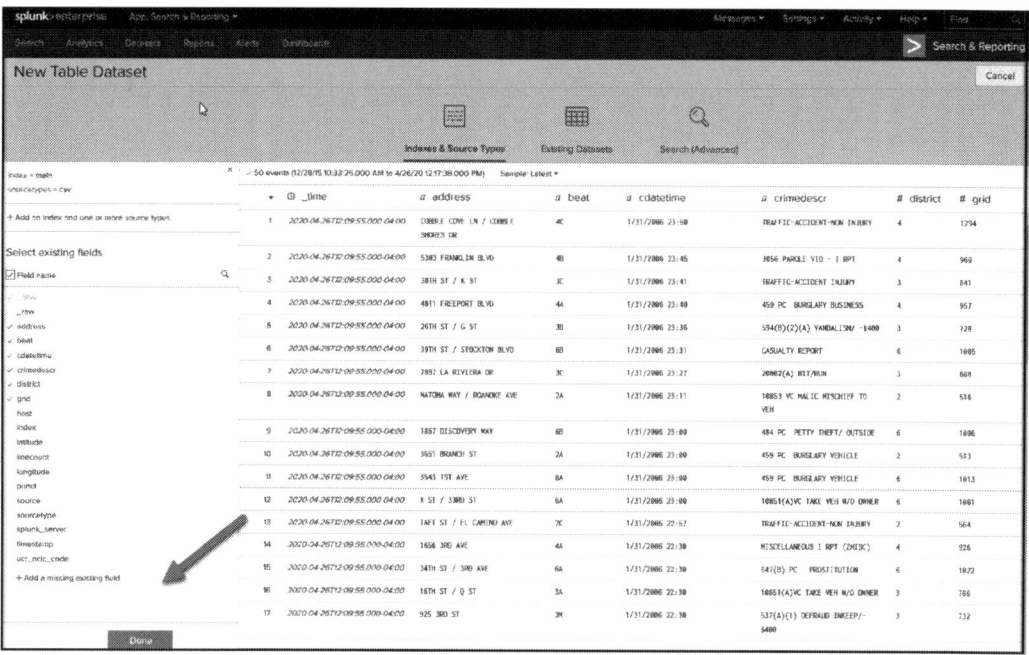

Figure 11.13 – Selecting multiple fields

8. Once you click on **Done**, you can preview rows and/or summarize the fields with the data in the Splunk table editor (see the following screenshot). Clicking on **Preview Rows** provides a simple row and column view and allows you to **Edit**, **Sort**, **Filter**, **Clean**, **Summarize**, and **Add New** (fields):

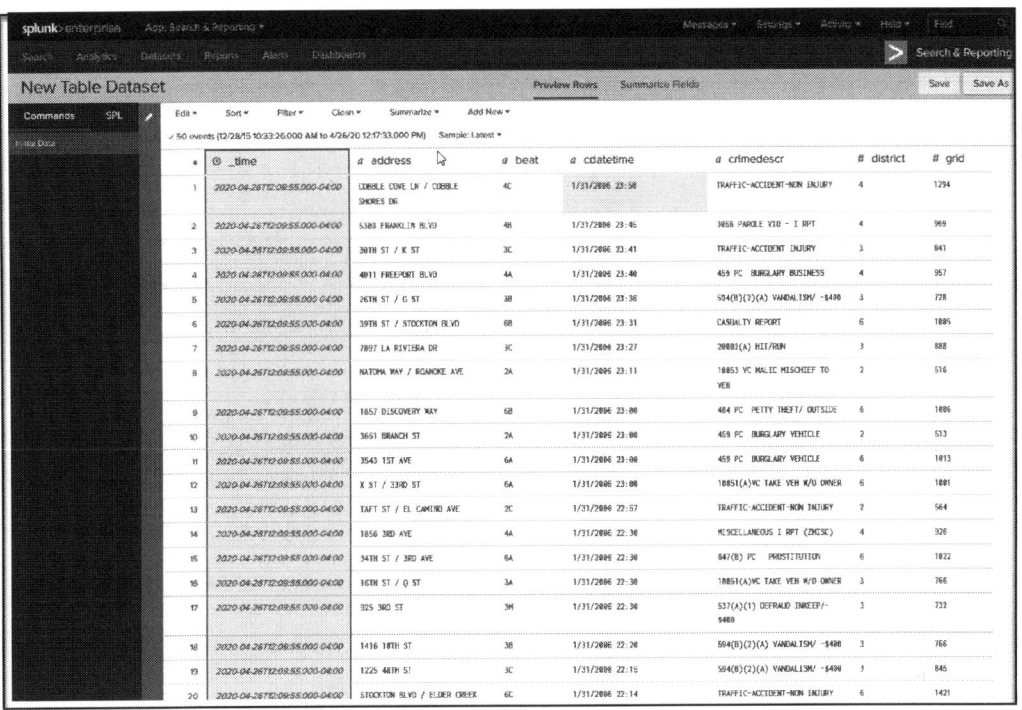

Figure 11.14 – Splunk Preview Rows view

9. Clicking on **Summarize Fields** instantly and automatically calculates and displays each field's vital statistics, such as matched/mismatched types and null percentages; single, multi, and unique value counts; as well as the top value percentages:

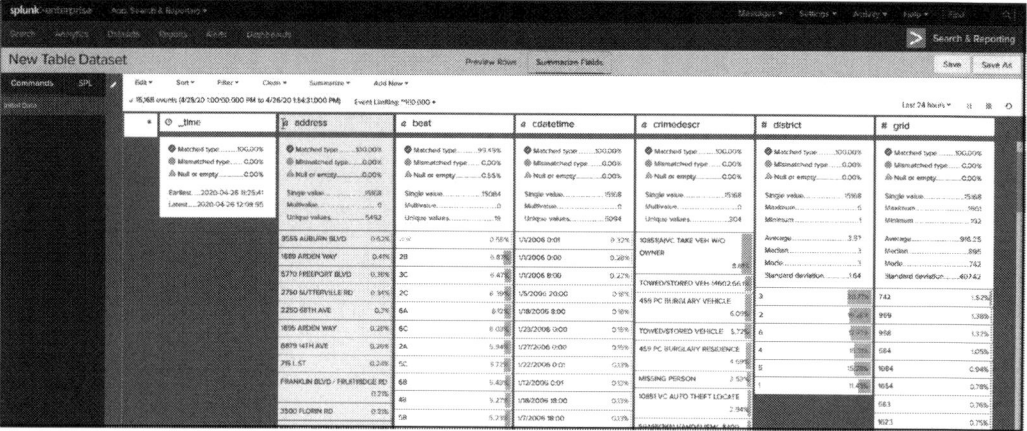

Figure 11.15 – Splunk Summarize Fields view

What is super nice is that we haven't had to write any SPL commands to garner these stats and gain a unique understanding of our crime activity data.

Also, within the table editor, you can apply actions to the table that filter events, add fields, edit field names and field values, perform statistical data aggregations, and more.

As an example (of a useful action), we mentioned the field `cdatetime`. If we double-click on that field's column header, we can type in a more descriptive value, `crimedatetime`, then click outside of the cell to complete the field name change:

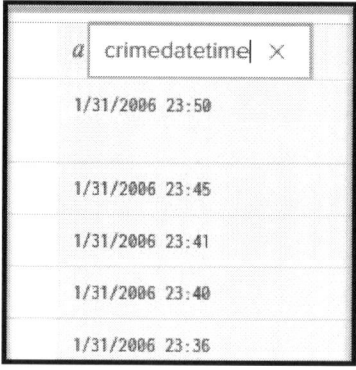

Figure 11.16 – Adding a description to the field's column headers

In police or crime prevention terminology, a **beat** is a territory and time that police officers patrol. If we look at our statistical view and check each field we selected to include in our dataset, we notice that the `beat` field has a higher percentage of null values, which may make further analysis messy. We can use the table editor to clean the null values out of the data by replacing all null values in the `beat` field with `zz`.

To do this, we can click on the column to select it, scroll down, and double-click on a field with `null` and type `zz`, and finally, click outside of the cell to complete the field replacement. Every instance of the field value `null` in the field's column will be changed! This is called **applying actions through direct table editing**:

Figure 11.17 – Applying actions through direct table editing

There are a good number of other types of edits you can perform using this method. In addition, you can perform actions such as making basic edits (changing field types, renaming fields, moving and deleting fields), as well as sorting, filtering, cleaning, summarizing, and adding new data through the Splunk table editor menu.

Once you are happy with your dataset (remember you can always edit and/or extend it later), you can perform a **Save As** to begin using it. On the **Save As New Table** dialog (shown in the following screenshot), you can provide a **Table Title**, **Table ID**, and (optionally) a **Description**:

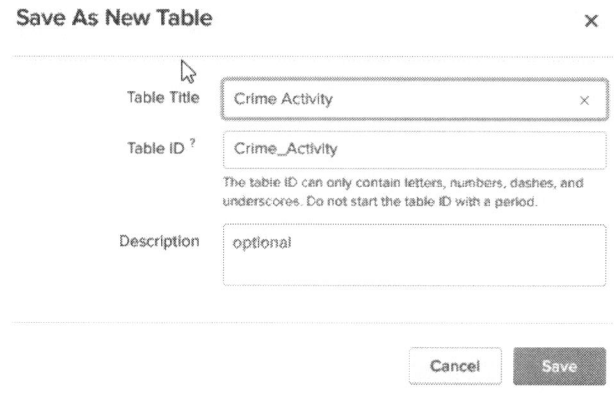

Figure 11.18 – Adding table properties

Once the new dataset has been successfully saved, Splunk will ask you if you would like to set permissions (see the following screenshot), **Continue Editing**, or **Explore Dataset**:

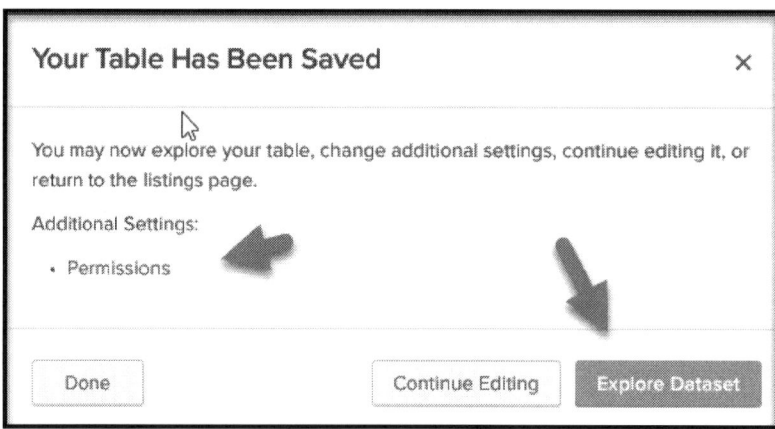

Figure 11.19 – Additional options for table

Exploratory data analysis—exploring data   257

> **Note**
> You can set permissions to restrict or expand access to objects in your Splunk deployment. Read more about permissions at https://docs.splunk.com/Documentation/Splunk/8.0.6/Knowledge/Manageknowledgeobjectpermissions.

Let's just click on **Explore Dataset**! Splunk will open our **Crime Activity** dataset ready for us to start exploring:

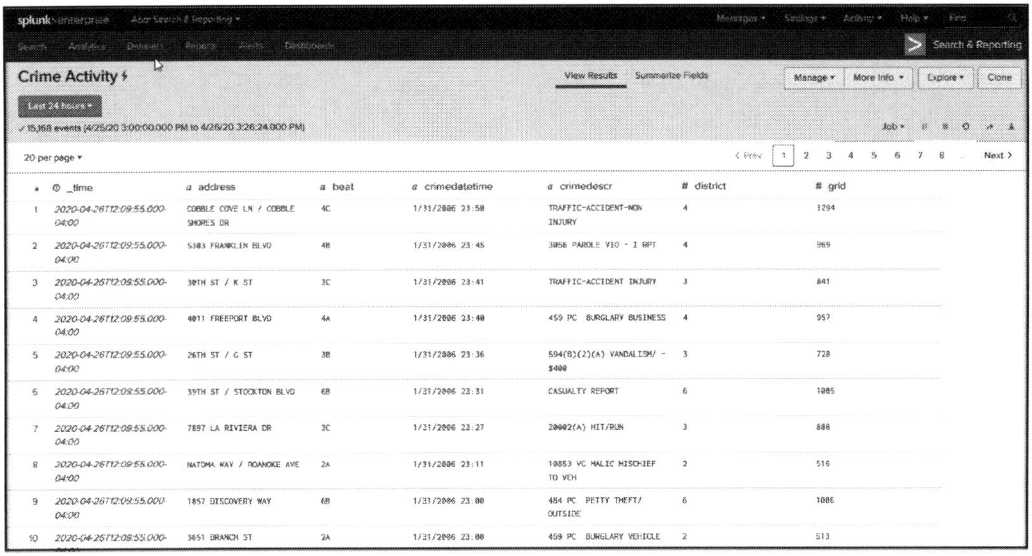

Figure 11.20 – Exploring the dataset

From here, we can adjust the time range with the time picker (on the left) or perform several other actions by clicking a button (on the right):

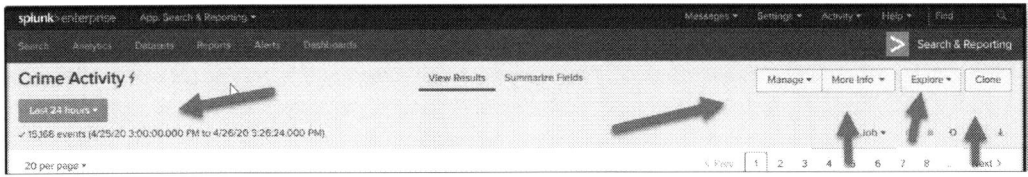

Figure 11.21 – Options to action on a dataset

We can use **Manage** to manage the dataset (go back and edit it with the table editor, add a more detailed description for the dataset, add/edit permissions, extend the dataset, or delete the dataset). We can also use **More Info** to see the updated dataset details, make a copy of the dataset (using **Clone**), or perform some detailed investigative analysis of the data through the use of **Explore**, **Search**, or **Pivot**.

Let's click on **Explore**, then **Visualize with Pivot**. The **New Pivot** tool is displayed (see the following screenshot):

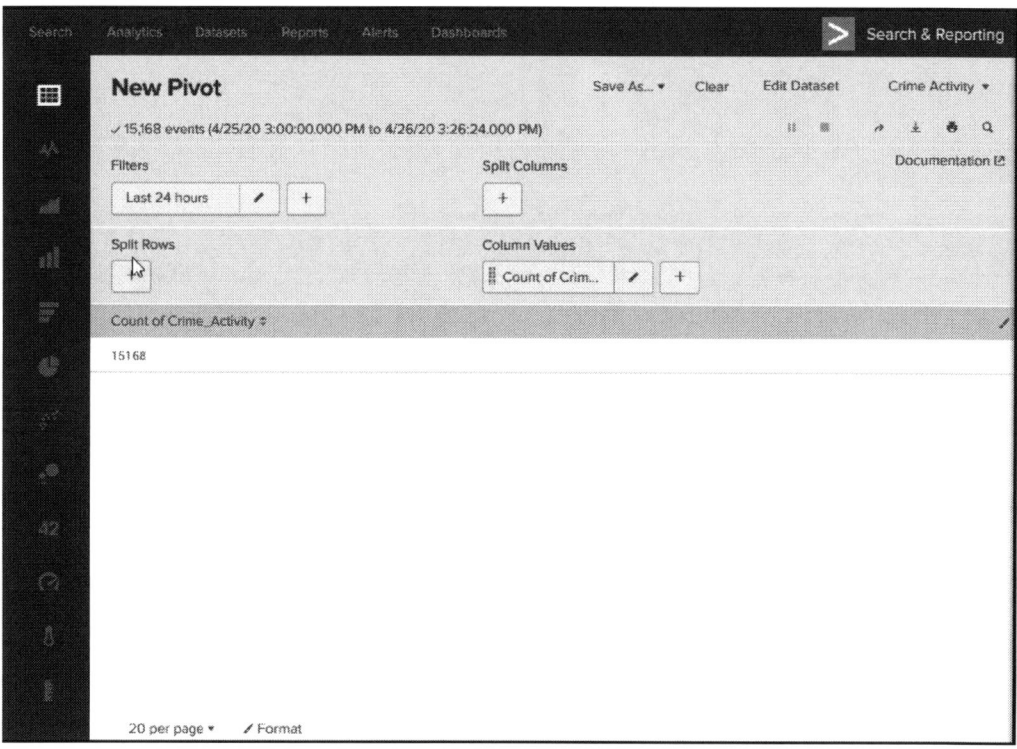

Figure 11.22 – Exploring the Visualize with Pivot option

On the **New Pivot** page, change **Filters** to **All Time**. Next, under **Split Rows**, click on the + button and select `crimedescr` and then **Add to Table**:

Figure 11.23 – Adding new pivot filters

Verify that under **Column Values** we have **Count of Crime_Activity**. The pivot should now refresh and look like this:

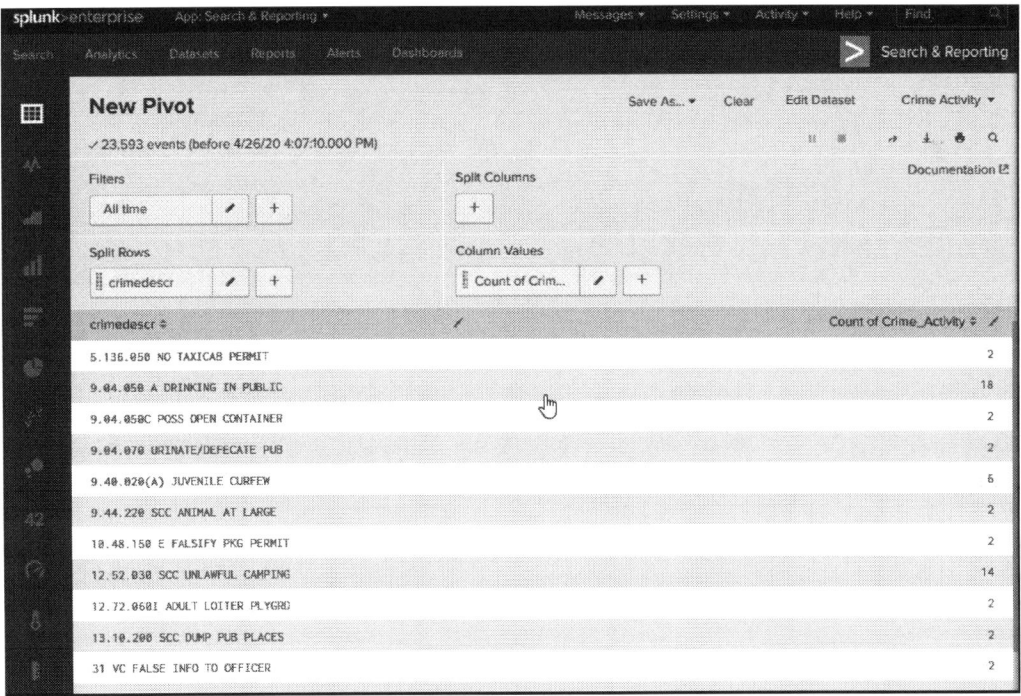

Figure 11.24 – Updated pivot view

260   Dashboards – Advanced Data Analytics

Now we have a table containing the number of each crime event within our time range. If we click on the pie chart icon, Splunk will automatically create a dynamic visualization of our data for us:

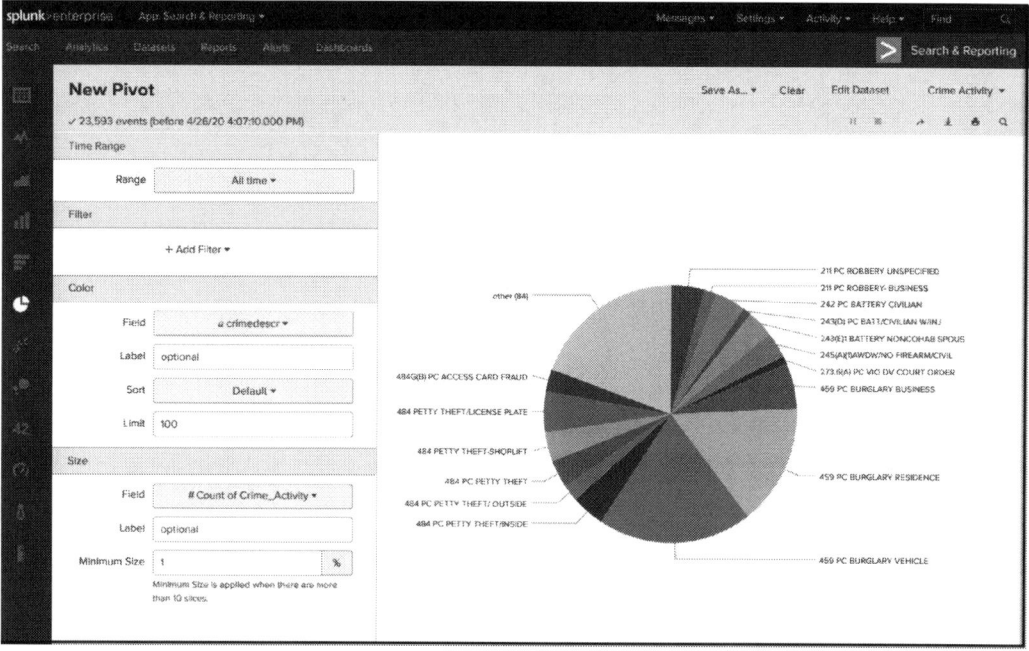

Figure 11.25 – Pie chart visualization of the pivot data

The pie chart visualization is dynamic in that you can change the time range, change the dataset field (from `crimedescr`), add a description (for the field), change the sort, and limit the results to a certain number. You can also click on the chart to see the selected value's details:

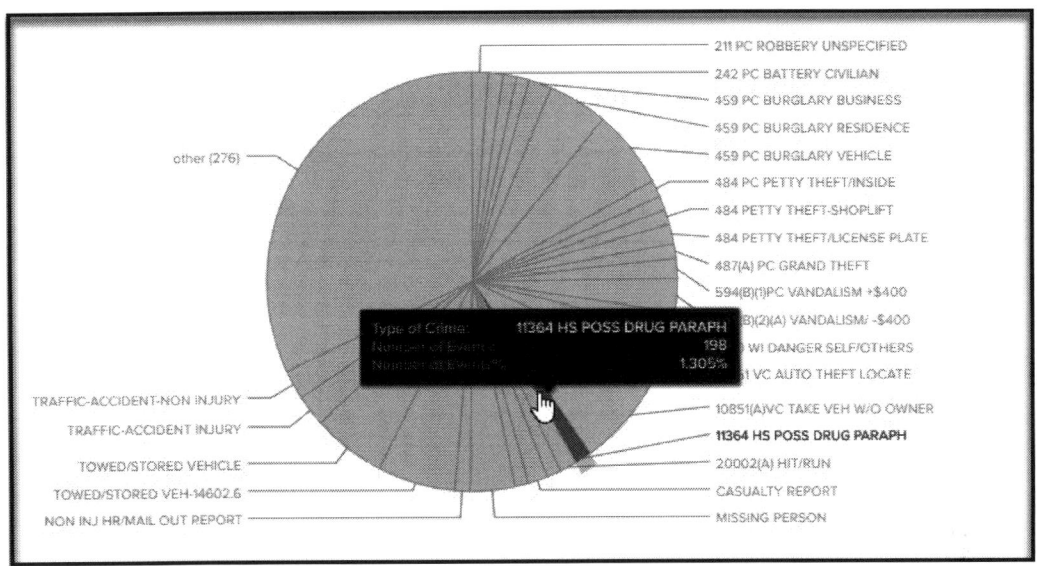

Figure 11.26 – Extended detail view

Next, let's click on **Save As...** then **Report**:

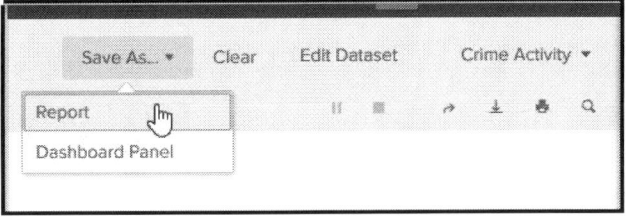

Figure 11.27 – Saving the pivot data as a report

On the **Save As Report** dialog, enter a **Title** and a **Description** and make sure **Time Range Picker** is set to **Yes**, then click **Save**:

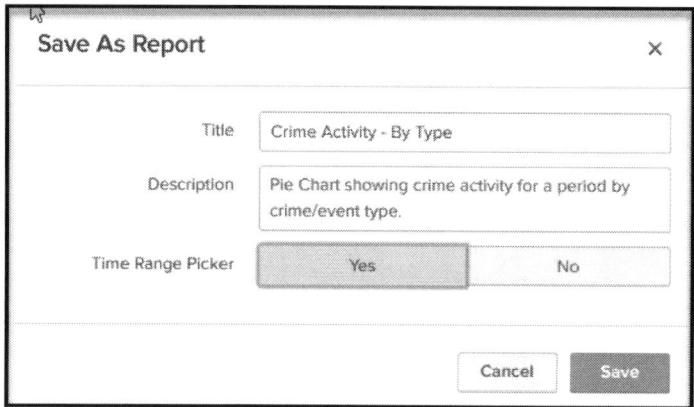

Figure 11.28 – Setting the properties of the report

Now that we have created the data model and saved it as a report, let's add the report to the dashboard.

Adding reports to the dashboard

Once Splunk saves our new report, you have the option to set **Permissions**, **Continue Editing**, **Add to Dashboard**, or **View**. We will choose **Add to Dashboard**, then on the **Save As Dashboard Panel** dialog, fill in the dashboard and panel details, and click on **Save**:

Exploratory data analysis—exploring data 263

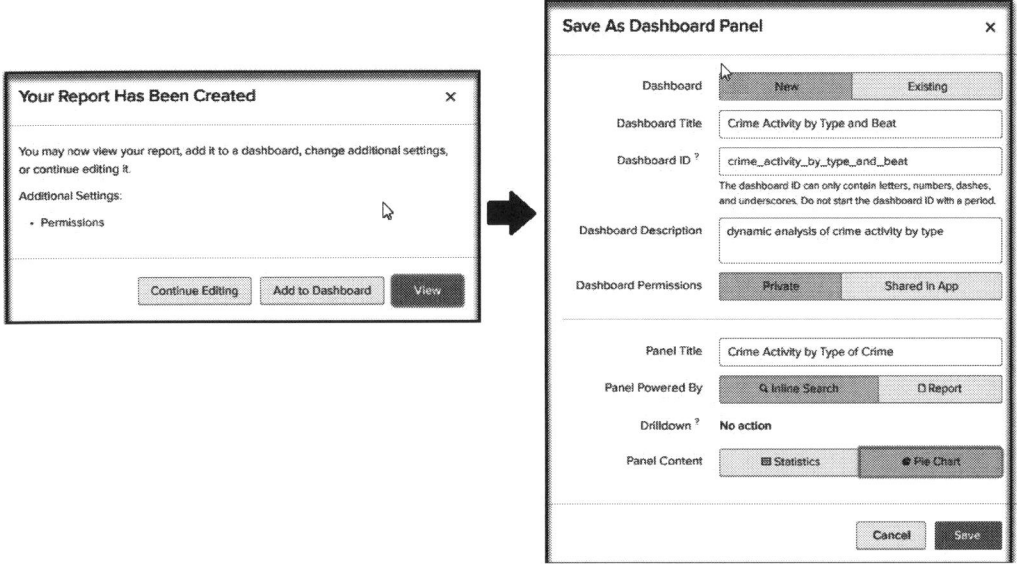

Figure 11.29 – Adding the report to the dashboard and setting the dashboard panel

Now we have a dashboard, based upon the dataset we created, which was based upon our CSV data input. As new crime data files are dropped into the folder we set up to be monitored, the dashboard will reflect the latest data insights. Before finishing up, let's evolve our dashboard by adding more panels. We can do this by clicking on **Edit**:

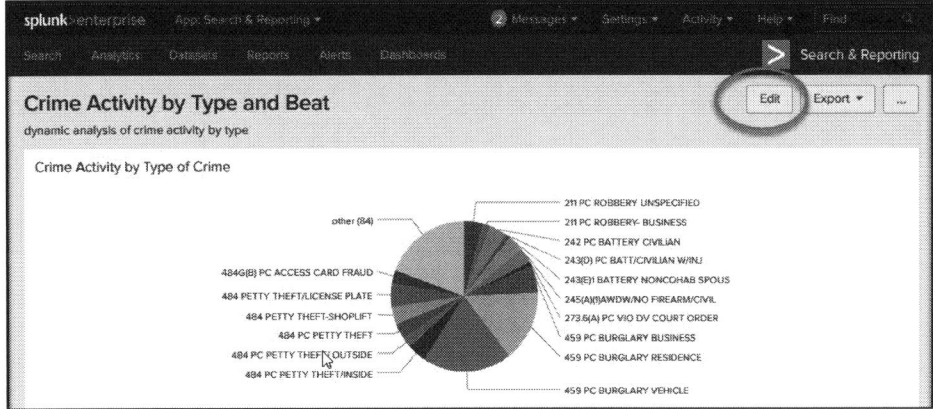

Figure 11.30 – Editing the dashboard

Now, in edit mode, click on **+ Add Panel**:

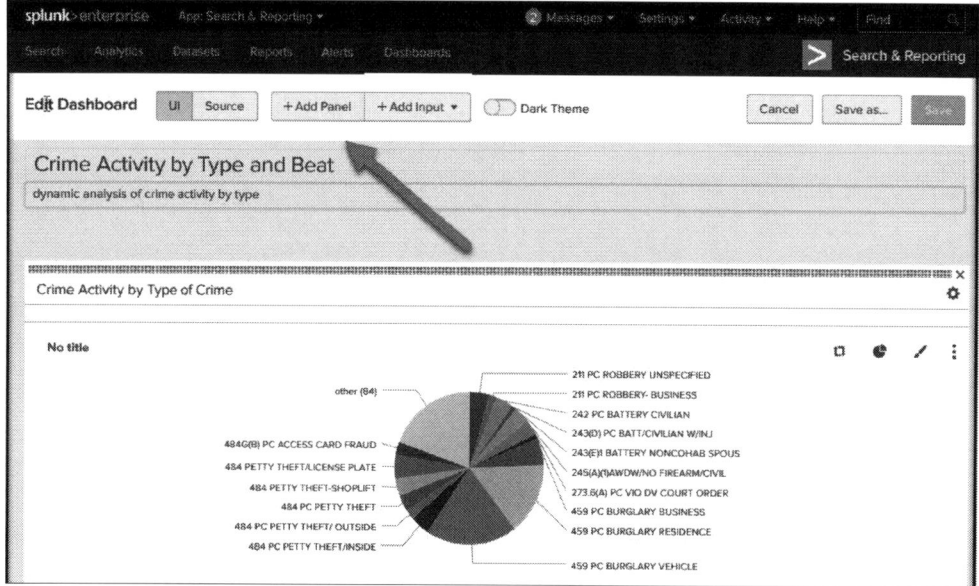

Figure 11.31 – Adding a new panel to the dashboard

Once you click on **+ Add Panel**, you can use the panel on the right to select the report we have already saved from the **New from Report** header. You'll see a **Preview** of the report summary (to make sure that you have selected the correct report), then click **Add to Dashboard**:

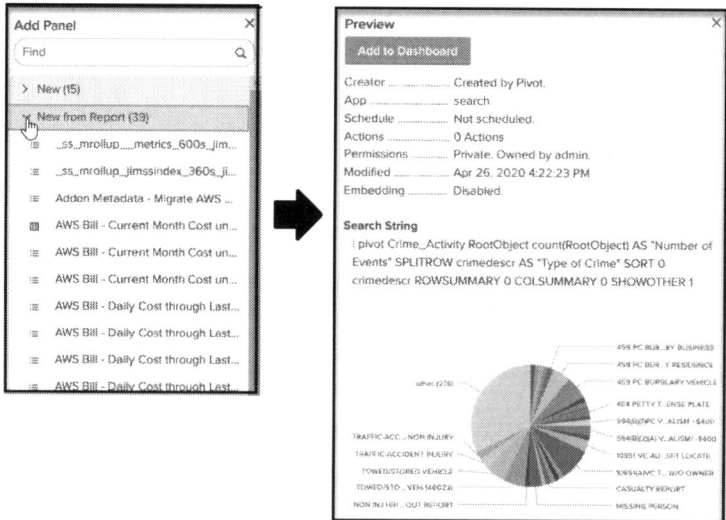

Figure 11.32 – Preview of the new panel

Now our dashboard has two panels (as shown in the following screenshot). Next, click on the title (**No title**) and enter the text `Crime Activity - By Beat` to describe this panel. After that, click on the edit search icon (highlighted on the right):

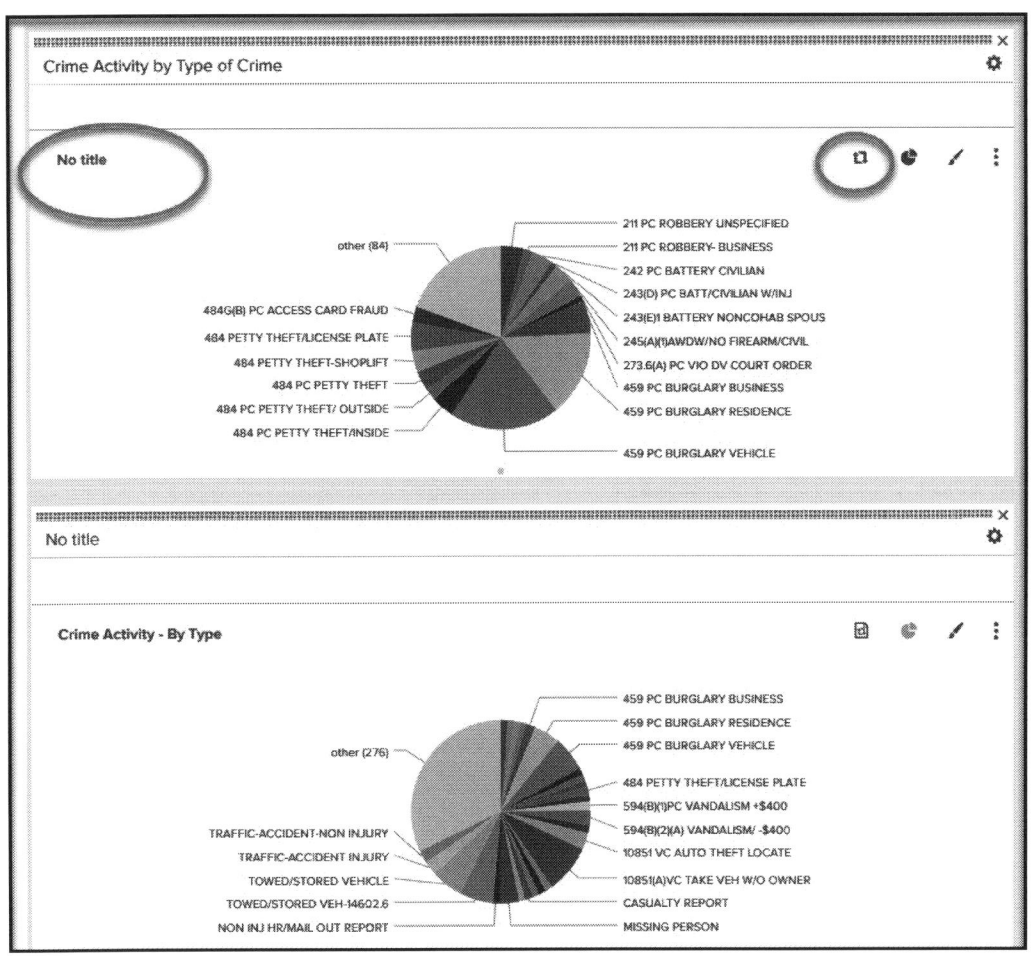

Figure 11.33 – Adding a title description to the new panel

On the **Edit Search** dialog, change the search as shown in the following screenshot, then click **Apply**:

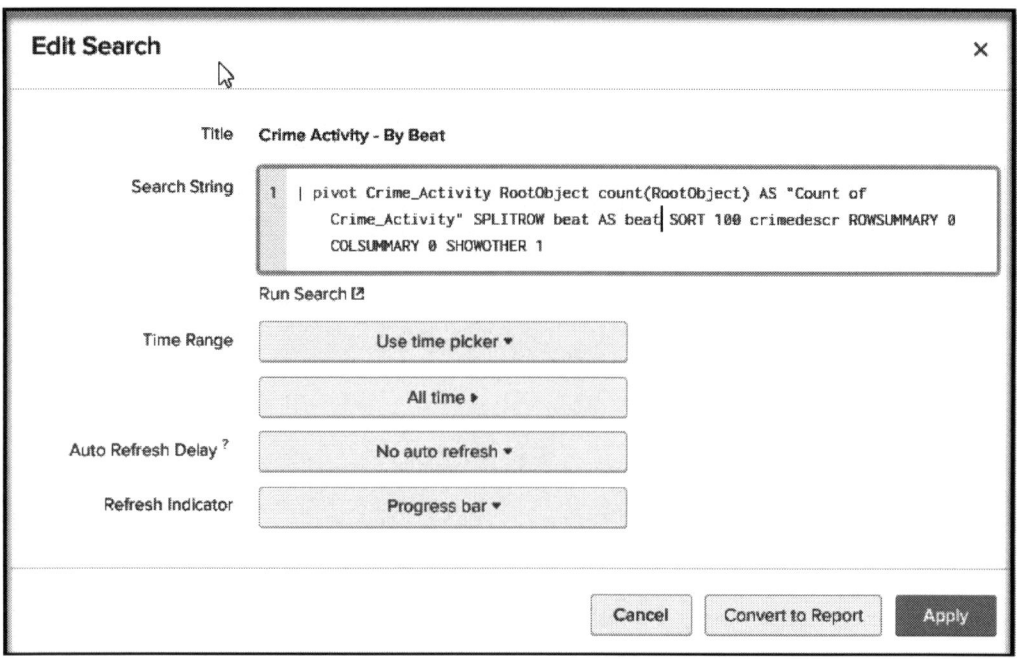

Figure 11.34 – Editing the search settings

Now we have a two-panel dashboard showing pie charts for crime activity by type and by beat:

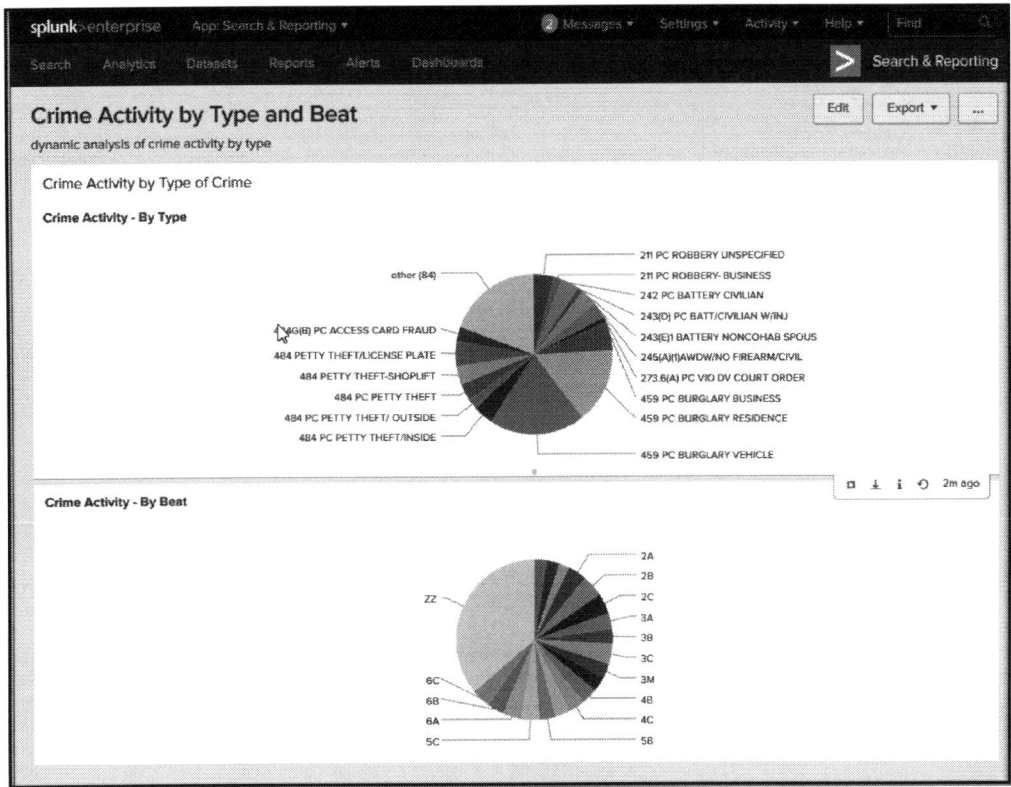

Figure 11.35 – Two-panel dashboard

In addition to visualizations, sometimes it is helpful to include within a dashboard a table-formatted report. For example, you can follow the preceding steps to add yet a third panel to the dashboard, this time reformatting and saving our report as a table/grid.

Finally, let's add a fun graphic as well by directly editing the HTML code of the dashboard. Let's finish the dashboard by clicking again on **Edit**, then **Source**. Splunk now shows the source code used to create the dashboard. Look for the `<panel>` and `</panel>` tags and add a new set between the existing panel tags.

268 Dashboards – Advanced Data Analytics

Within the new tags, add an HTML <img> tag. Next, edit the new HTML line to reference a saved image file:

```
<center><img src="/static/app/search/download.jpg" alt="Smiley face"></img></center>
```

After editing the code, click on **Save**:

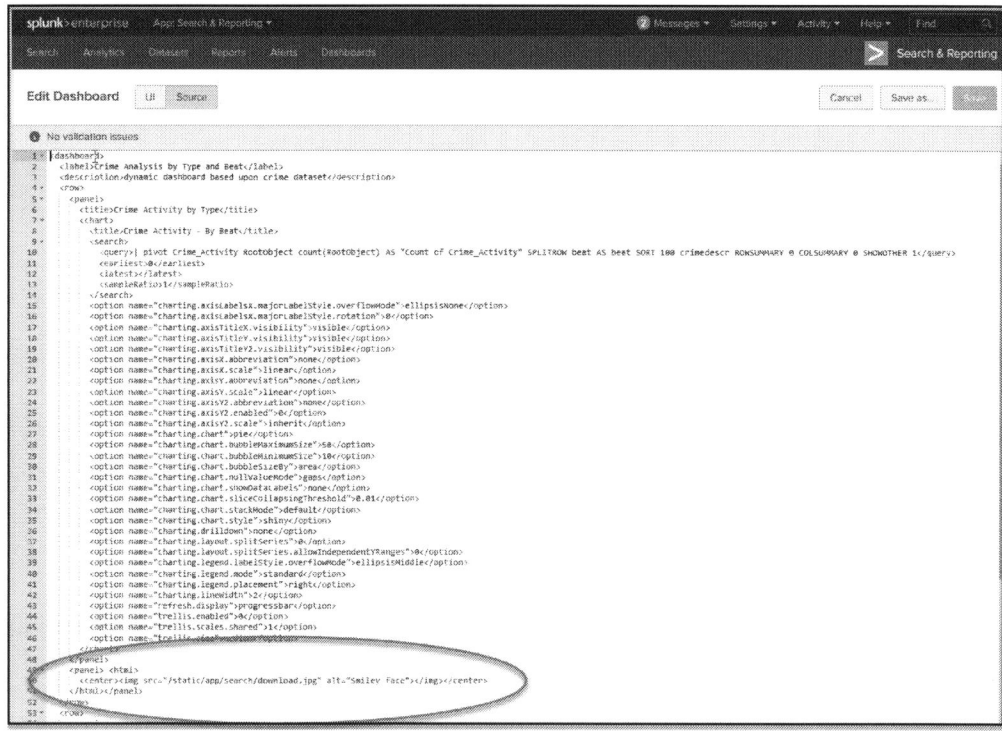

Figure 11.36 – Editing the dashboard HTML code

Now we can review our final product:

Figure 11.38 – Result of the edited dashboard

Now that we have learned how to add reports to the dashboard, let's begin with transaction analysis.

Transaction and transactional analysis

Splunk supports the concept of defining what are called (event) **transactions**. That is, you can associate certain related events so you can view them and perform analysis on them as a single event.

This **single view** (of multiple events that are related based upon certain criteria that you define) is referred to as a **single transaction**, or sometimes as a **session**. These transactions can include the following:

- Different events from the same source and the same host.
- Different events from different sources from the same host.
- Similar events from different hosts and different sources.

The `transaction` command is used to define transactions based on events that meet your constraints.

Transactions are made up of the raw text (the _raw field) of each member, the `time` and `date` fields of the earliest member, as well as the union of all other fields of each member. Additionally, the `transaction` command adds two fields to the raw `events`, `duration`, and `eventcount` fields. The values in the `duration` field show the difference between the timestamps for the first and last events in the transaction. The values in the `eventcount` field show the number of events in the transaction. These fields are important when performing most kinds of transactional analysis.

An example of transactional analysis

To illustrate the power of using transactions, let's go back to the crime data we used earlier in this chapter. Let's start with a simple search to visualize the number of *bad* or *fictitious checks* being passed within each beat. We know that the crime description (`crimedescr`) field in our data contains a numeric code and the crime we are interested in is #476. This means that we could create the following search command:

```
sourcetype="csv" crimedescr=476*   | chart count by beat
```

This generates the following visualization:

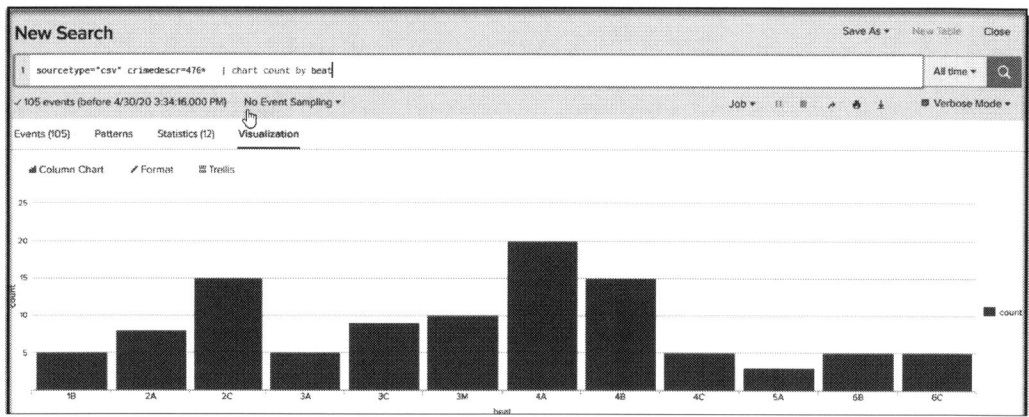

Figure 11.38 – Transactional analysis visualization

This provides us with the total number of fictitious checks passed for each beat for **All Time**. Nice! But what if we only care about when the total number of bad checks passed within the same beat is less than a certain number or threshold value?

Splunk transactions can make that easy. We can use the aforementioned transaction command to search only fictitious check crimes (`crimedescr=476*`) and (max) events of up to `9` (`maxevents=9`) within a beat, as follows:

```
sourcetype="csv" crimedescr=476*
| transaction beat  maxevents=9
```

The result is as follows:

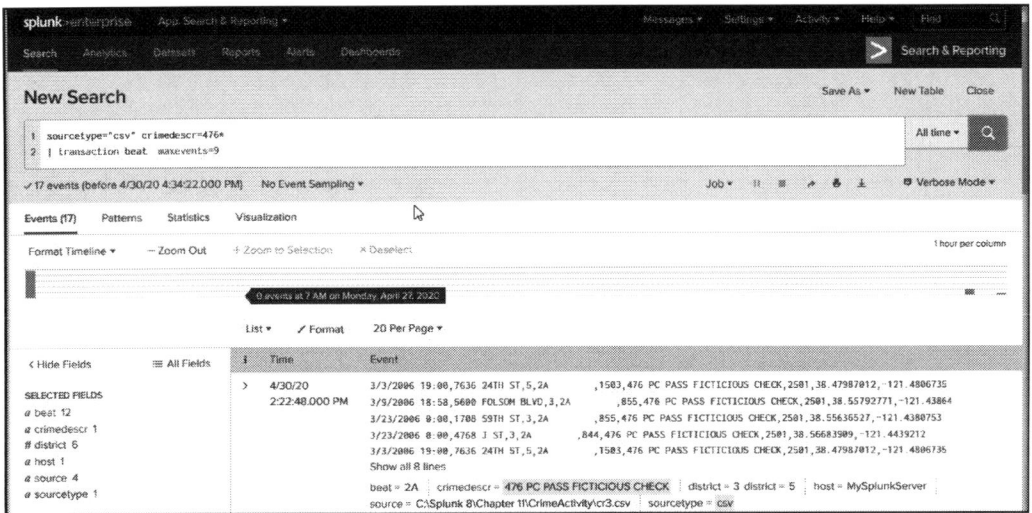

Figure 11.39 – maxevents search result

> **Hint**
> There are many ways to code Splunk searches. For example, using the `eval` command when you use the `transaction` command can be more efficient to convert transactions into more readable information.

If we add the `chart` command (as shown in the following command), the results are maybe a bit more interesting:

```
sourcetype="csv" crimedescr=476*
| transaction beat  maxevents=9
| chart  count by beat
```

Let's create another dashboard similar to the one we created earlier in this chapter! We can choose to save the preceding searches as dashboard panels and then use them (and a graphic) to create another Splunk dynamic dashboard:

Figure 11.40 – Adding a graphic panel to the dashboard

Now we have completed our transactional analysis example, as well as having reached the end of the chapter.

Summary

In this chapter, we reviewed the definition and objective of the analytics framework, used features and methods available within Splunk to explore data, and finished by exploring transactional analysis!

The next chapter covers the steps to detect suspicious events and patterns in data by constructing and using advanced event correlation searches.

12
Dashboards – Correlating Events

In the previous chapter, we covered the fundamentals of an analytics framework, and presented tips aimed at exploring data using Splunk datasets, the **table editor**, and the **pivot tool**, and finished the chapter with a transactional analysis example.

In this chapter, we will cover the difference between events and catalytic events, understand event correlation and techniques for correlating events, and then create a working event correlation dashboard.

The chapter will be broken down into the following main sections:

- Understanding catalytic events and correlations
- Event correlation
- Event correlation dashboards

Understanding catalytic events and correlations

Let's start this chapter with a review of events themselves. Events in Splunk are understood to be a **single data point**, similar to a record in a log file or another data element or data point.

When data is indexed, Splunk divides the incoming data into individual events. Each event is then assigned a timestamp, host, source, and source type.

Usually, a single event parallels with a single line of data, but some can have multiline events, and some inputs have multiple events on a single line.

Of course, when you run a search in Splunk, you get back results (events) that match your search criteria. Similar events are typically categorized together with event types.

> **Note**
> Events united by the fact that they can all be matched by the same search string are said to be of the same event type.

So, what is a catalytic event?

Events may be considered to be catalytic if they *act as a precedent or catalyst for some other event* and are typically defined as an event produced by a **correlation search**.

A correlation search is a type of search designed to detect suspicious or otherwise interesting events and patterns in data (that is, a catalytic event!). You can configure a correlation search to generate a catalytic event when search results meet conditions that meet objective criteria.

Correlation searches are usually set up to be run at regular intervals or continuously in real time to search for a particular pattern or type of activity. Usually, a catalytic event will include custom metadata fields to assist in the investigation of the defined conditions and to track event remediations.

Additionally, catalytic events are usually stored in a dedicated catalytic event index so they can be more easily reported on and analyzed. In fact, typically correlated event dashboards are developed to continuously monitor and report on catalytic events, as we'll see later in this chapter.

Understanding event correlation

Correlation is actually a statistical technique that can be used to show whether, and how strongly, pairs of variables are related. The standard example is always the height versus weight correlation, that is, taller people tend to be heavier than shorter people.

Event correlation is the process of finding relationships between (seemingly unrelated) events in data—perhaps from multiple sources—and understanding which events are the most relevant to a particular objective.

You can also automate the results of the correlation process to generate an alert each time the correlation criteria are met, and it is common to want to report on the frequency (as well as other aspects) of correlated events.

Splunk supports event correlation using various methods, such as **transactions**, **time/geographic location**, **sub-searches**, **field lookups**, and **joins**, that perform the following tasks:

- Identifying relationships based on the time proximity or geographic location (of events)
- Tracking a series of (related) events (even from separate data sources) together as a single event (or transaction)
- Using a sub-search to compare or test the results of one search against the results of another
- Correlating data across other sources (external sources) with lookups
- Using SQL-like inner and outer joins to link two completely different datasets together based on one or more common fields

Transaction-based correlations

Transaction-based event correlations are when a series of events are tracked as a single transaction *duration* or *event count*.

As an example, in the previous chapter, we used our crime activity data source and the `transaction` command to correlate the event of fictitious checks being passed within a beat and the number of checks passed (within the same beat) being under a specific numeric threshold:

```
sourcetype="csv" crimedescr=476*
| transaction beat  maxevents=9
```

Then we summarized the resulting grouping of events into a pie chart visualization, saved it as a panel, and built a dashboard with it (and other panels):

Figure 12.1 – Visual panel dashboard

Time/geolocation-based correlations

Time/geolocation-based event correlations are all, or any subset of, events that take place in a given time period and at a determined location.

For example, suppose the time range we choose is **All time** and our subset of events is sales occurring within a specific latitude and longitude, perhaps Italy (whose coordinates are 41.8719° N, 12.5674° E).

Using the following search command, we can correlate events using these two criteria and see the results represented on a dynamic, global cluster map visualization:

```
sourcetype=vendor_sales* | stats count by Code VendorID
 | lookup prices_lookup Code OUTPUTNEW product_name
 | table product_name VendorID
 | lookup vendors_lookup VendorID
 | where like(VendorLatitude,"41.8%") and like(VendorLongitude,"12.5%")
 | geostats latfield=VendorLatitude longfield=VendorLongitude count by product_name
```

This would give the following result:

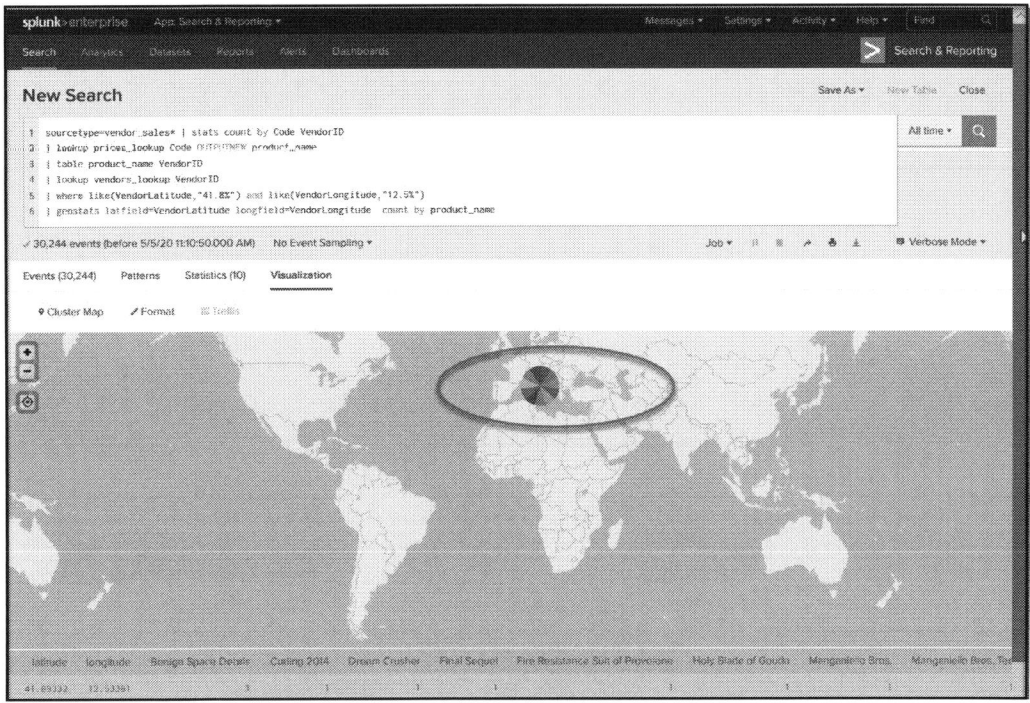

Figure 12.2 – Global cluster map visualization

> **Hint:**
> To generate a cluster map, use the `geostats` command. The `geostats` command generates events that include latitude and longitude coordinates for markers.

Subsearch-based correlations

In subsearch-based event correlations, the results of one search are used in another to create `if-then` conditions and return only the results if certain conditions are met in the second search. This enables what is called **sequential state-like** data analysis and allows you to evaluate events in the context of a *whole event set*.

Suppose we have two source types for different application logs. The event data from these logs shares at least one common field (in our example, we will use `EventType`). We can use the values of the `EventType` field to search for events in one source type based on a value that is not in the other source type.

A simple two-step example might be to first execute the following search—within the `WinEventLog:Application` source type, create a chart of the count of events by `EventType`:

```
sourcetype=WinEventLog:Application
| chart count by EventType
```

This would give the following result:

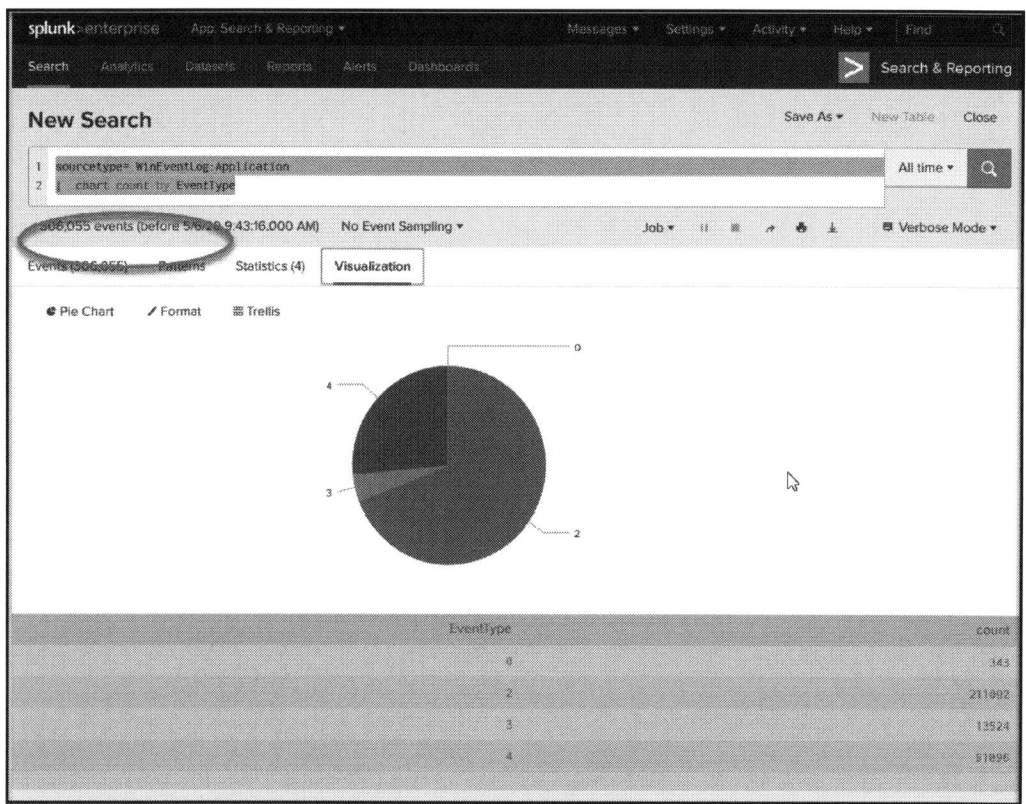

Figure 12.3 – Search result by EventType

We can notice that the search returns `306,055` events. As the next step in our example, we can add a `NOT` condition and a subsearch as follows:

```
sourcetype= WinEventLog:Application NOT [search sourcetype=
WinEventLog:System | fields EventType]
| chart count by EventType
```

This will give the following result:

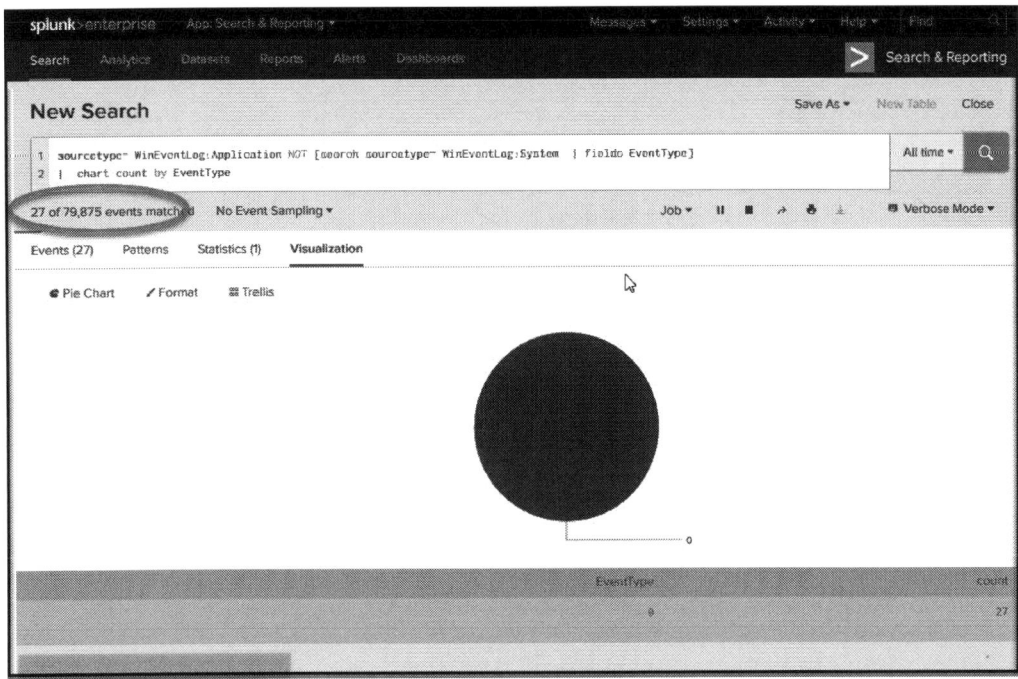

Figure 12.4 – Search result with a NOT condition

In this version of our search, the results will be events that occur in the `WinEventLog:Application` source type but that also do not appear within the event results of the `WinEventLog:System` source type while matching on the values in the `EventType` field.

Now we notice that the search only returns 343 events.

Lookup-based correlations

With lookup-based event correlations, data is correlated with external data sources to enhance, enrich, validate, or add context to the search results. The previous geolocation example used external files as lookups to enhance the results with vendor and product pricing information.

Join-based correlations

With join-based event correlations, you use SQL-like inner/outer joins (that is, the `join` command, or, to combine a search result set to itself, the `selfjoin` command) to link one dataset to another based on common fields (similar to the subsearch example shown earlier).

Event correlation dashboards

Event correlation dashboards are created in the same manner as any other Splunk dashboard, and if created in the context of a particular app (for example, if you are using the **Search & Reporting** app), will use that app context. After you create a correlation dashboard, you can, like any other dashboard, modify its permissions to share or manage access for other Splunk users. You can also modify the app context.

Ways to use event correlation in dashboards

There isn't really any difference between any dashboard you create in Splunk and a correlation dashboard.

That is, a correlation dashboard created in Splunk isn't created in a way that is different than the process of creating any other type of dashboard, such as we've used in previous chapters. You also use a correlation dashboard in much the same way as any other type of Splunk dashboard.

The real point is to determine the objective of a dashboard before beginning to develop it and then following a proven workflow as follows:

1. Identify the overall goal/objective (for the dashboard).
2. Identify the specific KPIs or catalytic events (that the dashboard needs to track).
3. Develop the individual SPL queries or correlation searches (that the dashboard will use).
4. Create the panels and construct the dashboard (using the SPL queries developed in *step 3*).
5. Review and confirm the context and permissions (of the dashboard).

In the next section of this chapter, we will follow the workflow stated here to create a working, dynamic event correlation dashboard.

Identifying an overall goal/objective

For our dashboard exercise, we are going to use the crime activity data we used in the previous chapter. The objective (or purpose) will be to have the ability to monitor the levels of criminal activity within beats that run active patrols versus those beats without active patrols.

For this exercise, we created a new Splunk source type (CSV_CD) from a loaded CSV file of crime data formatted with the following fields of data:

- Cdatetime (data of criminal event)
- Address (street address where the crime occurred)
- District (district where the crime occurred)
- Beat (beat where the crime occurred)
- Grid (grid where the crime occurred)
- Crimedescr (text description of the type of crime)
- ucr_ncic_code (National Crime Information Center code)
- latitude (latitude where the crime occurred)
- longitude (longitude where the crime occurred)
- active_patrol (Y or N indicating whether the beat is running active patrols)

Identifying the specific KPIs or catalytic events

The next step in creating our dashboard is to identify what it is we want to monitor. In this exercise, let's say that there are three areas or data points we want to report on and monitor.

These are as follows:

- The total count of beats that have criminal activity during the time range and do not have active patrols
- A comparison of the total number of crimes in all beats with no active patrol, and the total number of crimes in all beats that have active patrols
- A report of the crimes within the period for all beats without active patrols

In addition, we have decided how we want to lay out the areas or data points (from the preceding list) within three distinct dashboard panels, so we can create a kind of wireframe in the following way:

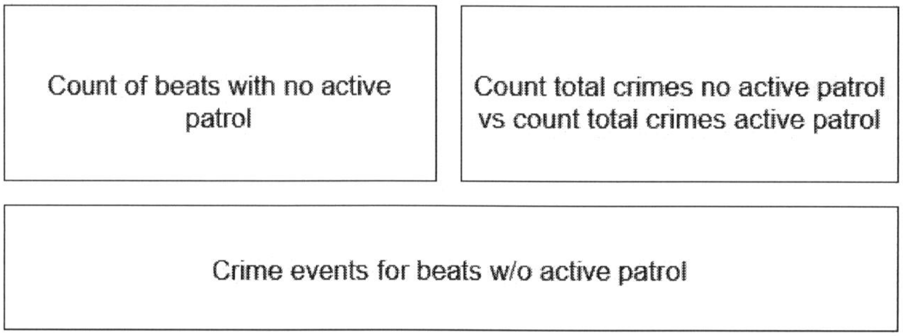

```
┌─────────────────────────────┐  ┌─────────────────────────────┐
│  Count of beats with no     │  │  Count total crimes no      │
│       active patrol         │  │  active patrol vs count     │
│                             │  │  total crimes active patrol │
└─────────────────────────────┘  └─────────────────────────────┘

┌───────────────────────────────────────────────────────────────┐
│          Crime events for beats w/o active patrol             │
└───────────────────────────────────────────────────────────────┘
```

Figure 12.5 – Wireframe layout for the new dashboard

Developing individual SPL queries/correlation searches

Now that we have our KPIs, as well as a layout for our new dashboard, it is time to develop our specific SPL queries. I prefer to develop the SPL code, test each query, and then save them until we are ready to save them as panels:

Query #1:

```
sourcetype=CSV_CD active_patrol="N"
| stats dc(beat)
```

In the preceding search command, we use both the `stats` command and the `dc` function to get a count of unique beats that do not have active patrols.

Query #2:

```
sourcetype=CSV_CD | stats count by active_patrol
```

In the preceding search command, we use the `stats` command to generate a count of beats that have criminal activity and no active patrol as well as a count of beats that have criminal activity and do have active patrols. The intention is to create a visualization with these statistics (rather than exposing the raw statistics returned by the search).

Query #3:

```
sourcetype=CSV_CD active_patrol="N" | table beat, crimedescr by beat
```

In the preceding search command, we use the `table` command to generate a table-formatted report of all the criminal activity for the period ordered by beat.

Now that we have the queries we plan to use, I've added the actual SPL commands to our wireframe layout:

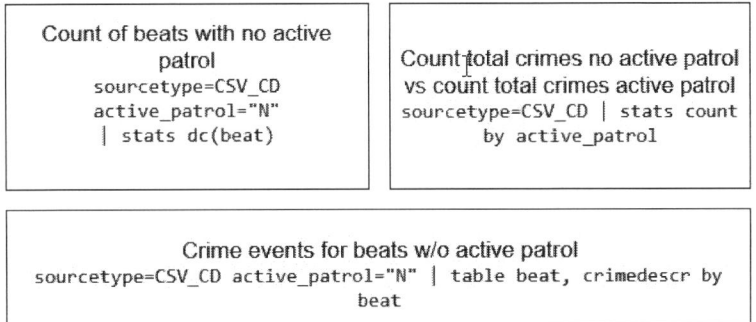

Figure 12.6 – Wireframe layout with the SPL command

Now that we have the wireframe of the dashboard laid out, we can start creating the panels and constructing the dashboard.

Creating the panels and constructing the dashboard

Now we can go back and save each of our three queries as individual dashboard panels, then use those panels to create our new dashboard.

The following are the steps involved:

1. From the **Search & Reporting** page, paste in our first query and rerun it. Next, verify the results and click on **Save As** then **Dashboard Panel** (as shown in the following screenshot):

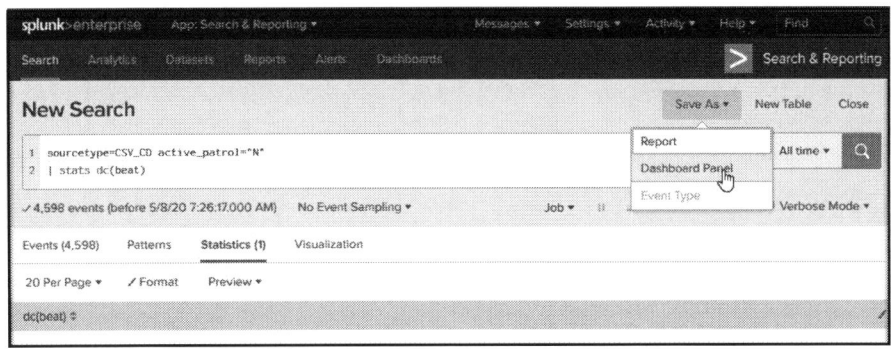

Figure 12.7 – Saving the first query as a dashboard panel

284　Dashboards – Correlating Events

2. From the **Save As Dashboard Panel** dialog (shown in the following screenshot), provide a **Dashboard ID**, **Dashboard Description**, and **Panel Title**:

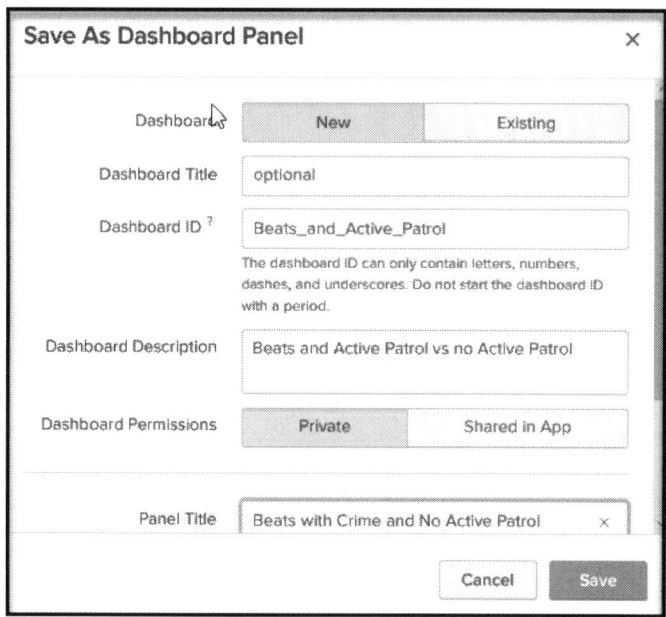

Figure 12.8 – Adding the dashboard panel details

3. Once you click **Save**, you will have the first panel for your dashboard. However, rather than displaying the raw statistics in the panel, we want to make our panel a little prettier. To do that, you can edit the dashboard panel and click on **Visualization** (shown in the following screenshot) then select **Single Value** as the **Visualization type**, then resave the panel:

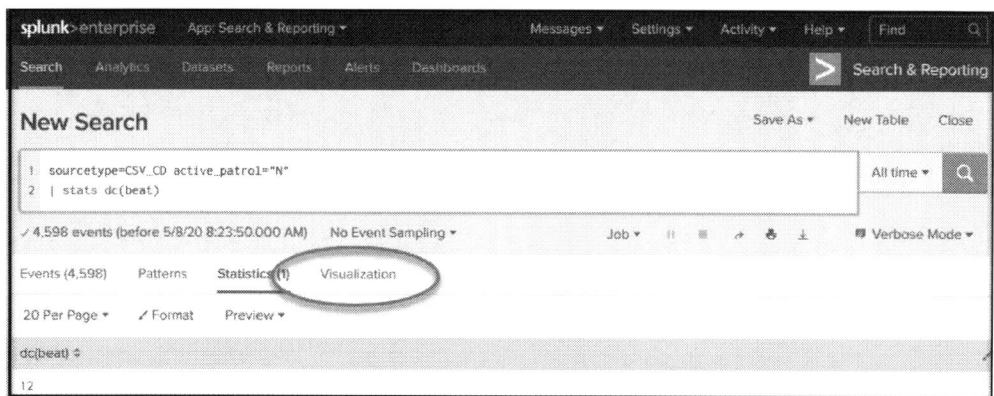

Figure 12.9 – Setting the visualization type

Now our panel looks a bit nicer:

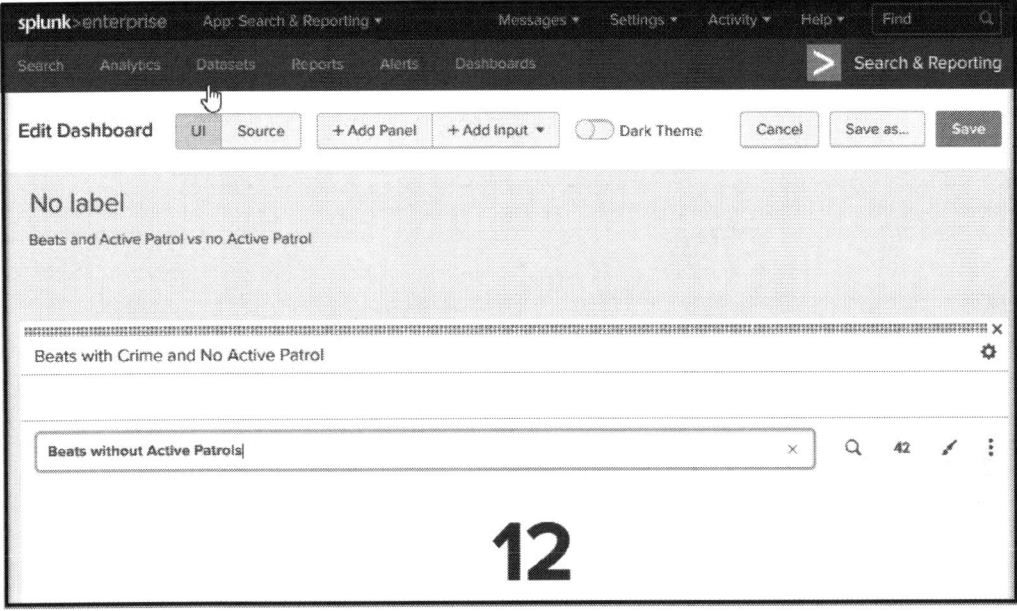

Figure 12.10 – View of the first query panel

Now let's move on to add the next query:

1. Go on to the next query and perform the same steps from *step 1* to *3* (run the query, verify the results, click on **Save As**, then **Dashboard Panel**):

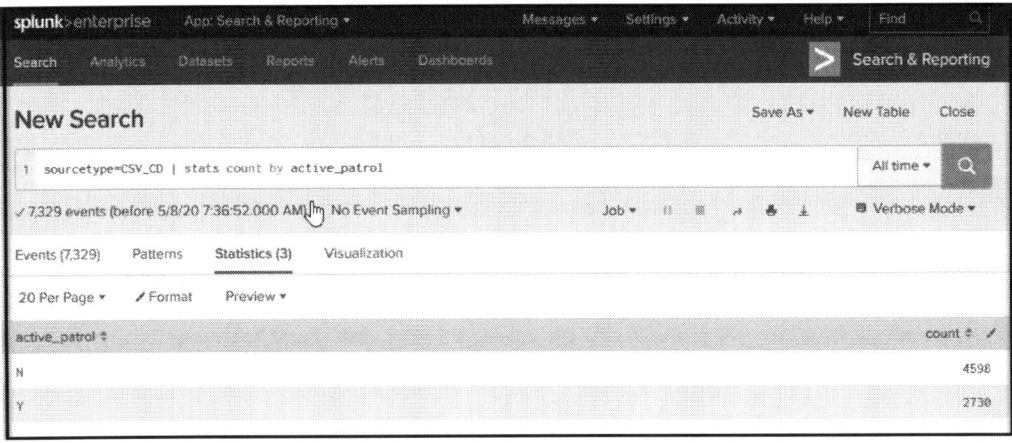

Figure 12.11 – Saving the second query as a dashboard panel

2. Similar to the previous panel, rather than exposing raw statistics, let's convert this query result to a **Column Chart** visualization before saving the panel:

Figure 12.12 – Converting the query result to a column chart

3. This time, on the **Save As Dashboard Panel** dialog (shown in the following screenshot), be sure to select **Existing** for **Dashboard** (rather than **New**) and then select the new dashboard name (I entered Beats_and_Active_Patrol as our new dashboard name when we saved the first query earlier):

Figure 12.13 – Setting up the second dashboard panel

Event correlation dashboards 287

4. Once you click **Save**, you can see that our new dashboard has been updated and it now includes both of our panels:

Figure 12.14 – View of the two added dashboard panels

5. Our dashboard has two panels but, by default, they appear one on top of the other. That's not what we indicated in our wireframe, so now click **Edit** (to edit the dashboard) and then drag and drop the panels to align them side by side (as shown in the following screenshot). Our dashboard layout is now changed to match our wireframe, so click on **Save**:

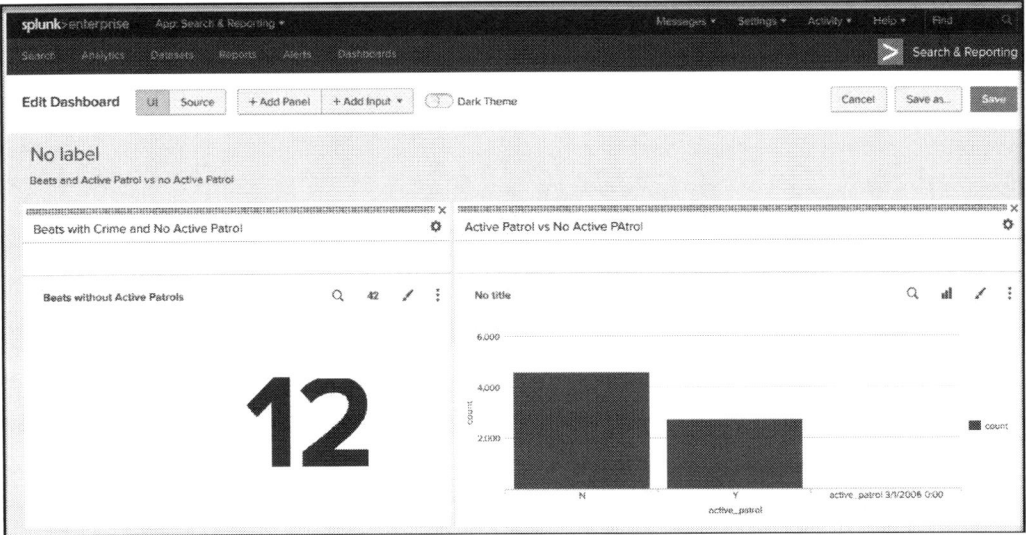

Figure 12.15 – Setting the layout of the panels

6. Finally, we can repeat the process (*steps 1 to 3*) to save our third query as the third dashboard panel. This one creates the table report:

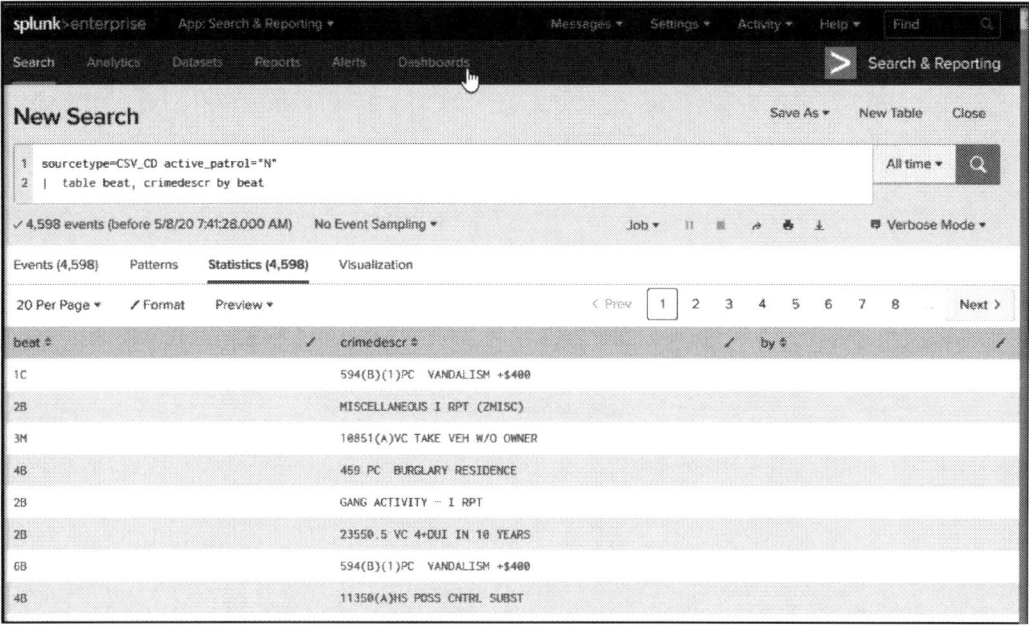

Figure 12.16 – Adding the third query as a dashboard panel

Once this panel is created and added to the dashboard, it really does look just like our wireframe:

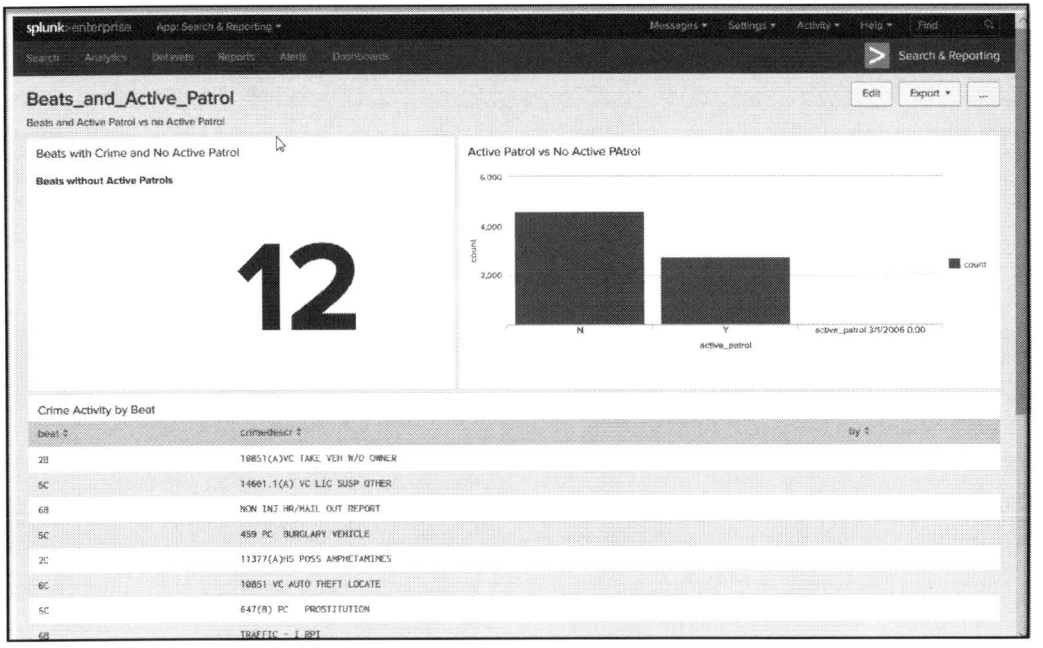

Figure 12.17 – Visualization of all three panels

7. Next, you can click on **Dashboards** to view the **Dashboards** page (shown in the following screenshot). From there, locate our new dashboard and click on **Edit** then **Edit Permissions**:

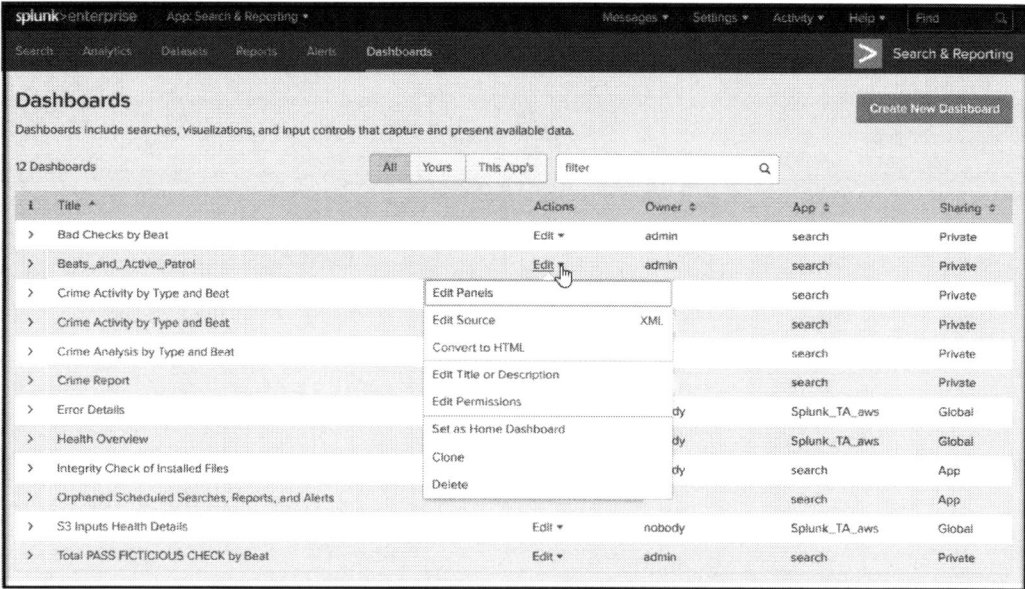

Figure 12.18 – Setting permissions for the dashboard

8. On the **Edit Permissions** dialog (shown in the following screenshot), set **Display For** to **All apps**, then click **Save**:

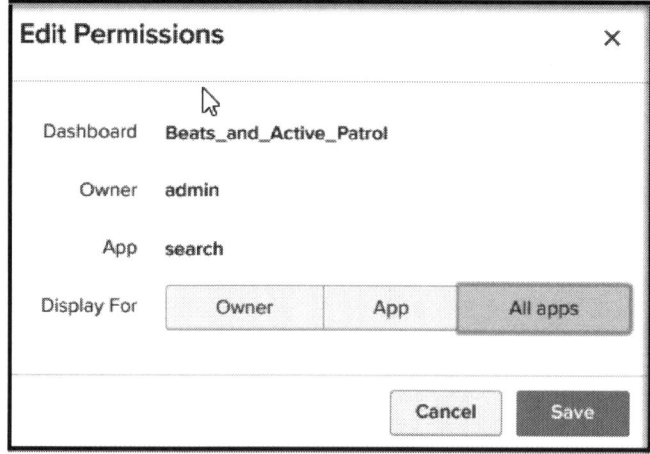

Figure 12.19 – Setting the display option to All apps

Now, back on the **Dashboards** page, notice **Sharing**:

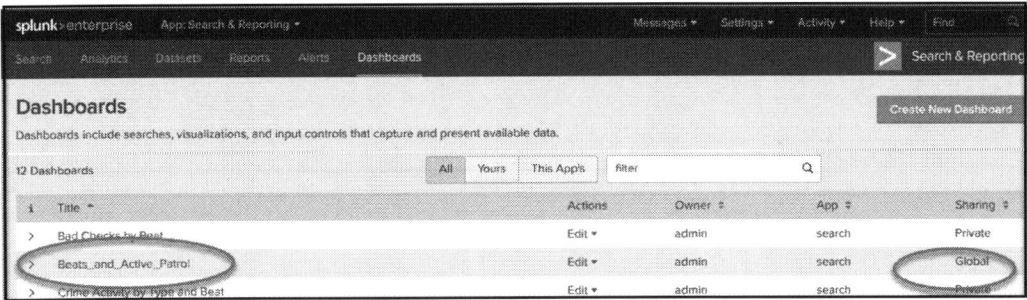

Figure 12.20 – Confirming the settings

When we created our crime data `Datainput`, we defined it as a **Files & Directories** type so that Splunk will monitor and index all new criminal activity data so our dashboard will always show the latest results.

Summary

In this chapter, we introduced the concept of catalytic events and how they differ from standard events, event correlation, and techniques to correlate events. Finally, we built a working, dynamic event correlation dashboard.

The next chapter will explain the value and practical use of the Splunk workflow.

13
Dashboards – Workflow Actions

In the previous chapter, we covered the difference between events and notable events, went over event correlation, looked at techniques for correlating events, and then created a working event correlation dashboard, which we designed to monitor and report on the theoretical correlation between crime activity levels and active patrols within a beat.

In this chapter, the focus will be on explaining the value and practical use of Splunk workflow actions.

The chapter will be broken down into the following main sections:

- Understanding knowledge objects
- Mastering workflows

Understanding knowledge objects

What is a Splunk knowledge object?

Knowledge objects are user defined, built, and shared with the intention of *enhancing the existing data* in Splunk, or to improve the usability of Splunk.

Knowledge objects are meant to be used to glean additional insights about the data you are working with. You can create knowledge objects for your own use and share them by assigning Splunk security. You will find that the more you use Splunk, the more categories of Splunk knowledge objects will be created and used. Knowledge objects are designed to leverage intimate knowledge that is developed about data or how it is used. Knowledge objects can save time and reduce the likelihood of errors.

Tags

A Splunk **tag** is a simple yet powerful and useful example of a Splunk knowledge object. For example, you can tag an event type or field/value and then search for it in the search bar by using the tag. Follow these steps:

1. Under **Settings**, then **Tags**, you can select **List by tag name** (shown in the following screenshot) to see the tags that may have already been set up:

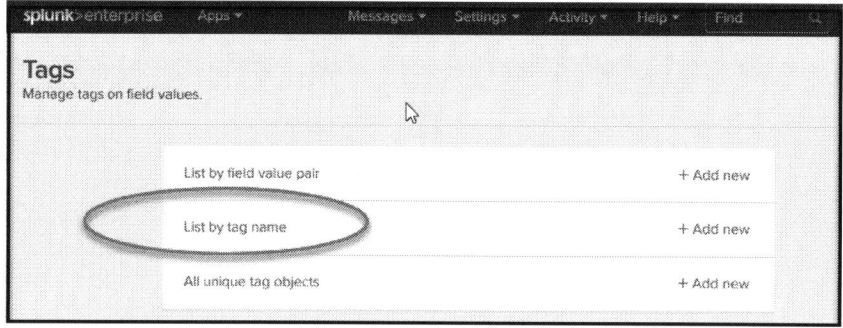

Figure 13.1 – Tagging an event

2. You can define a new tag by clicking on **Add New**, providing a name for the tag, filling in the field(s) and value(s), and then clicking on **Save**:

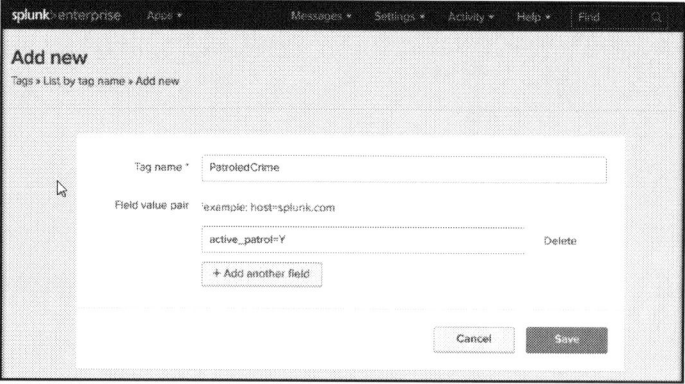

Figure 13.2 – Defining a new tag

As an example, we have created a new Splunk tag named `PatroledCrime`, which will be equal to the `active_patrol=Y` field. We have also created a reverse or opposite of this tag for `Active_patrol=N`. These tags are listed as follows:

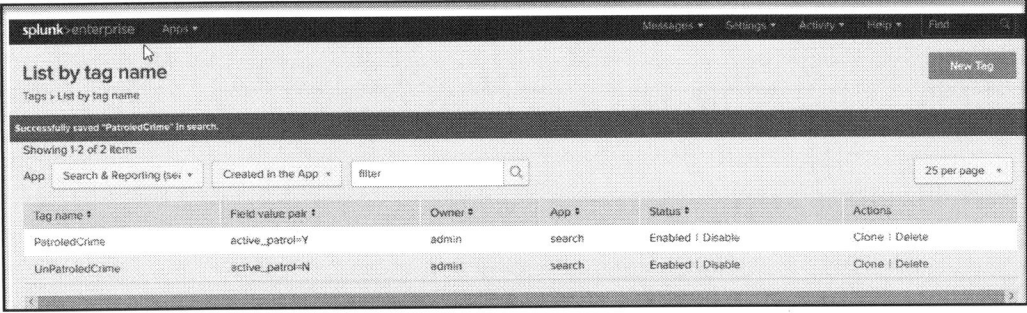

Figure 13.3 – List of the new tags

3. Once we have set up and saved our tags, we can then search our crime data using the tag by using the `tag::<field>=<tagname>` or `tag=<tagname>` syntax:

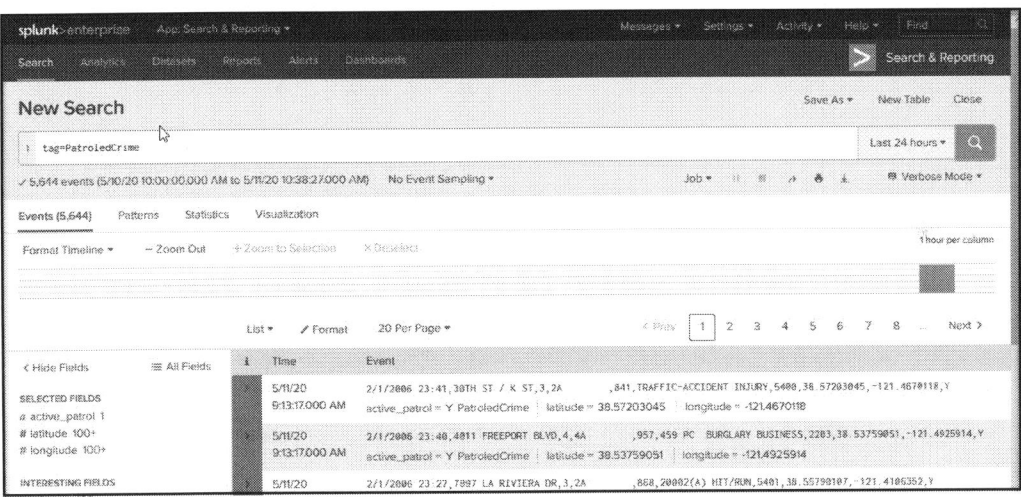

Figure 13.4 – Searching the crime data

In this example, we simply tagged a specific search as an **event type**. That is, the search lists specific source and host values as well as a field value:

- **Source**: `source="C:\\Splunk 8\\Chapter 13 - Dashboards - Workflow\\*"`
- **Host**: `host="MySplunkServer"`
- **Field**: `active_patrol=Y`

Any event type can have multiple tags. You can view all of the tagged fields by clicking on **Settings**, then **Tags**, then **List by field value pair**:

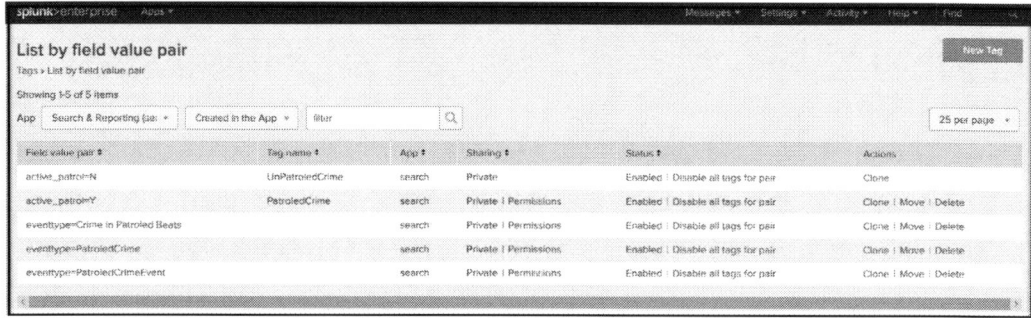

Figure 13.5 – Viewing all tagged fields

Now that we have learned about knowledge objects, let's see what knowledge object managers are.

Knowledge object managers

If you are a Splunk knowledge object manager, it will be your job to sort and manage the use of knowledge objects (searches, event types/tags, reports, field extractions, lookups, alerts, data models, transactions, workflow actions, and fields) across the Splunk deployment. It is valuable to have a knowledge object manager assigned to help organize and manage the creation and use of knowledge objects in large-scale Splunk environments.

We will now move on to a specific, extremely useful type of Splunk knowledge object—**workflow actions**. Keep the tag we just created in mind, since we'll use this tag example again a bit later in this chapter.

Mastering workflows

Splunk workflows provide the ability to create definable actions. They are highly configurable knowledge objects that you can use to permit an assortment of interactions or exchanges among fields in events and other web resources.

Workflow actions can be used for the following:

- To create HTML links that, for example, run searches in external search engines for field values (think Google!)

- To generate HTTP POST requests (to send data to a specified URI)
- To launch a secondary search using event field values

Splunk workflow actions have a wide variety of use cases, such as those that define activities that allow us to easily do the following:

- Use IP addresses to find domain information.
- Create entries in external systems based upon HTTP error values.
- Use event fields as parameters in secondary searches.
- Use event data to perform Google searches.

In the next section of this chapter, we will go over the steps required to create various working Splunk workflows action examples.

Creating a workflow action using Splunk web

Splunk allows us to easily set up workflow actions using Splunk web. All workflow actions are defined in the same way:

1. From the Splunk main page, click on **Settings** and then **Fields**:

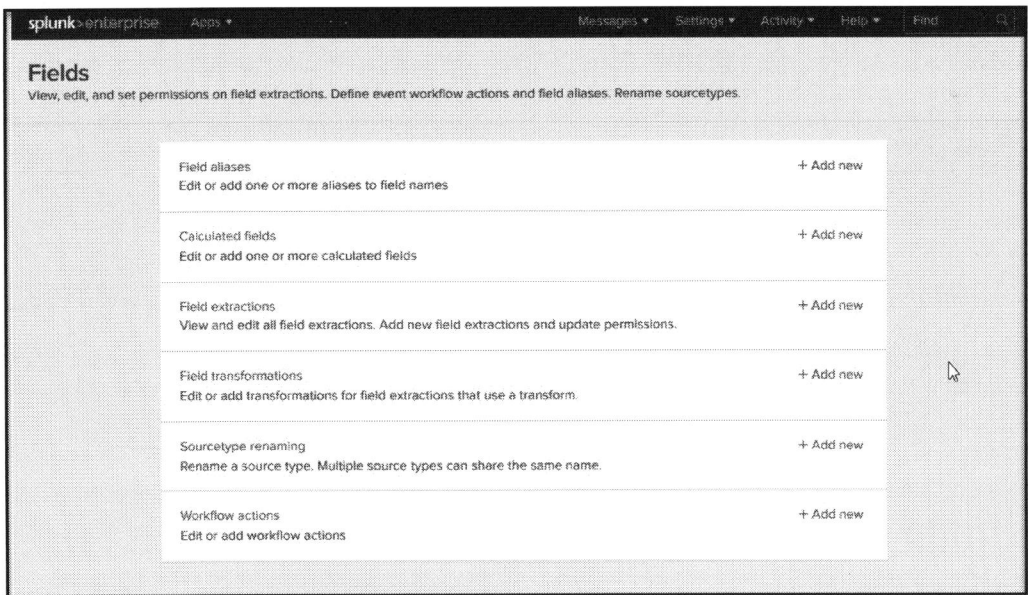

Figure 13.6 – Creating a workflow action

2. From the **Fields** page (shown in the preceding screenshot), click on **Workflow actions** (it's at the bottom of the list).

3. From the **Workflow actions** page, you can modify the workflow actions by clicking on their names, or you can create a new Splunk workflow action by clicking **Add New**. A GET workflow action can be used to create links to perform Google searches on specific values returned in a Splunk search.

In this example, we want to create a GET workflow to search Google for the crime description returned when using the tag we created earlier in this chapter. In other words, when you search with our tag (PatroledCrime), we want to be able to then easily perform a Google search on the description of the crime activity.

For example, if the search returned an event with the description 10853 VC MALIC MISCHIEF TO VEH, we want to obtain more details about that particular crime activity without having to leave Splunk.

To create this functionality, follow the upcoming steps to configure your workflow action.

The **Workflow actions** detail page is shown in the screenshot that follows. On that page, enter the following values:

1. First, we need to provide a name and set this workflow action as **Destination app**. Let's name the workflow action Google Crime Description and select **Search** as its app.

2. Next, enter Google $crimedescr$ for **Label**. This is the caption that appears for this action (this will be apparent when we test our workflow action).

3. For **Apply only to the following event types**, leave this field blank (so our action will apply to all event types).

4. For **Show action in**, select **Both** (so that our action will be part of the event and field menus).

5. For **Action Type**, select **link**.

6. Under **Link configuration** | **URI**, enter http://www.google.com/search?q=$crimedescr$.

7. For **Open link in**, select **New window**.

8. For **Link method**, select **get**.

Here is a screenshot of the entire page:

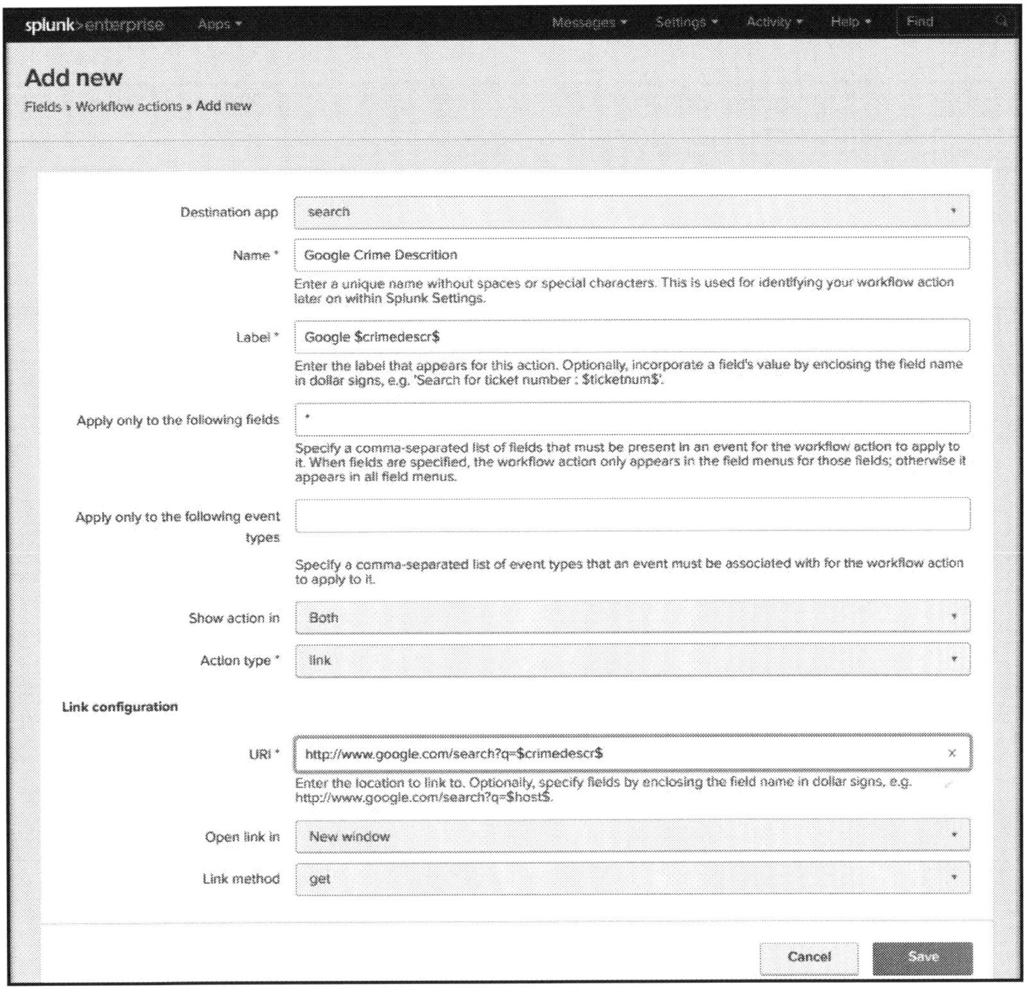

Figure 13.7 – Adding a new workflow action

Once you have entered the preceding values, click **Save**. Back on the **Workflow actions** page (shown in the following screenshot), we should now see our new Splunk workflow action:

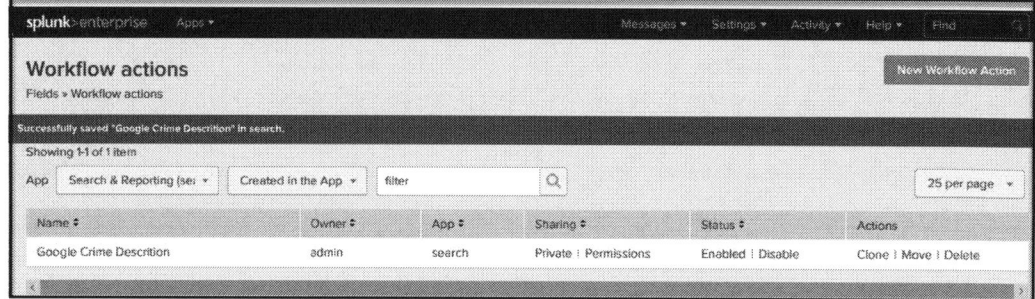

Figure 13.8 – New workflow action saved

We have created a new workflow action; now, let's test it.

Testing the workflow action

To see our Splunk workflow in action, go back to the **Search & Reporting** page and enter the tag search we created earlier, `tag="PatroledCrime"`:

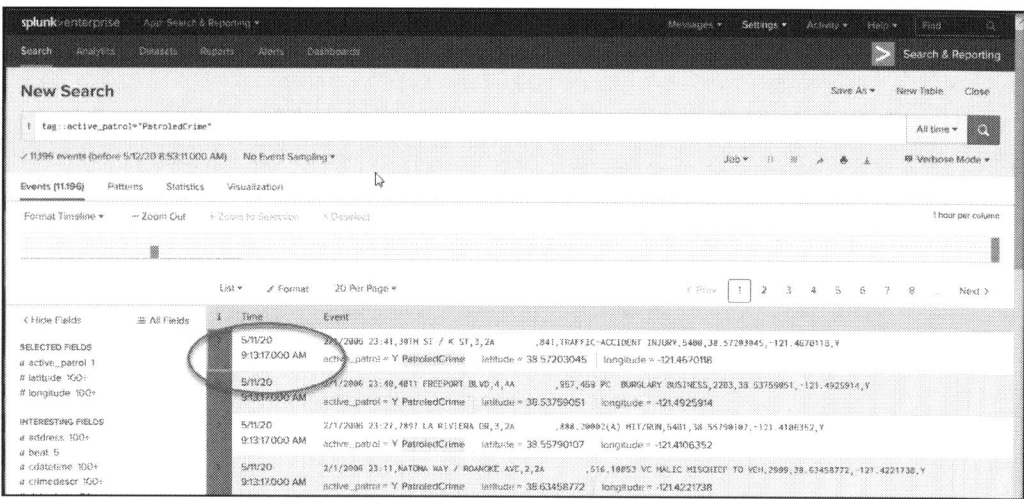

Figure 13.9 – Search the new tag

From the **New Search** results page (shown in the preceding screenshot), click on one of the > icons to expand an event:

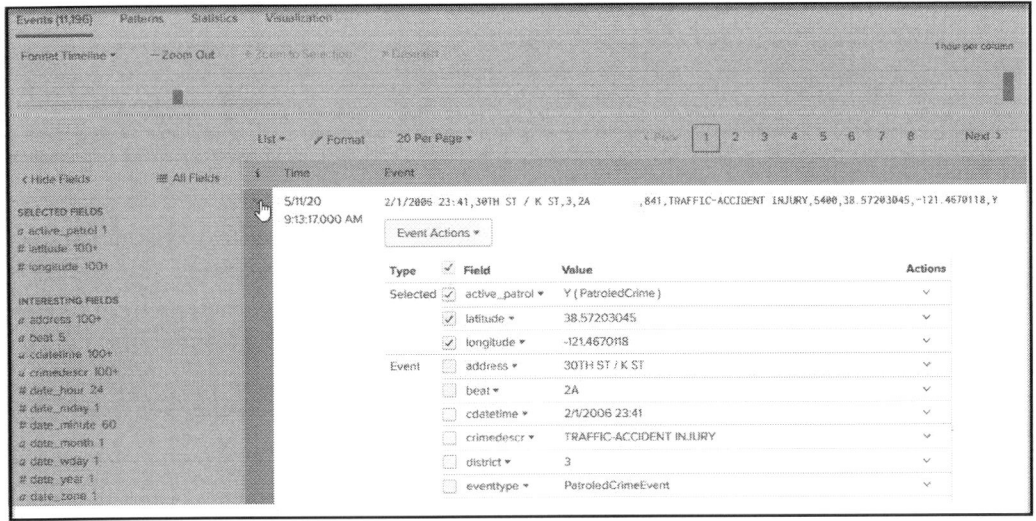

Figure 13.10 – Expanding a tag

Once the event is expanded, click on **Event Actions** and notice there is an action called **Google TRAFFIC-ACCIDENT INJURY** (or whatever the value for the `crimedescr` field is for the event you expanded):

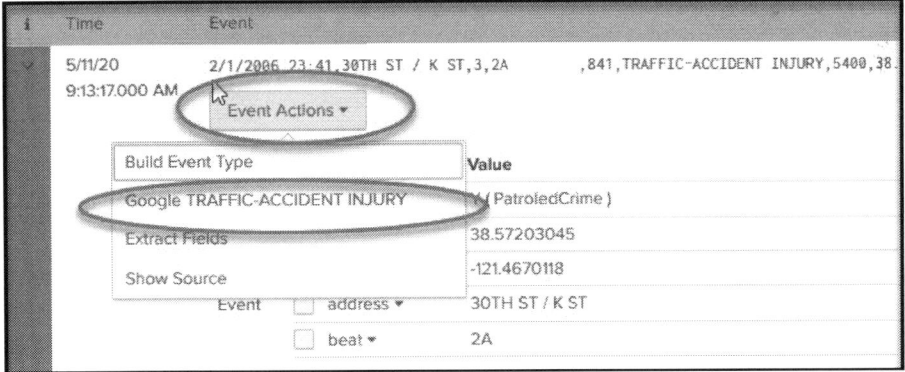

Figure 13.11 – The expanded event

If you click on this event, Google will open up in a new browser window (remember, we stated **Open link in** to be in **New window** when we set up the workflow action) and automatically search for the value of this field:

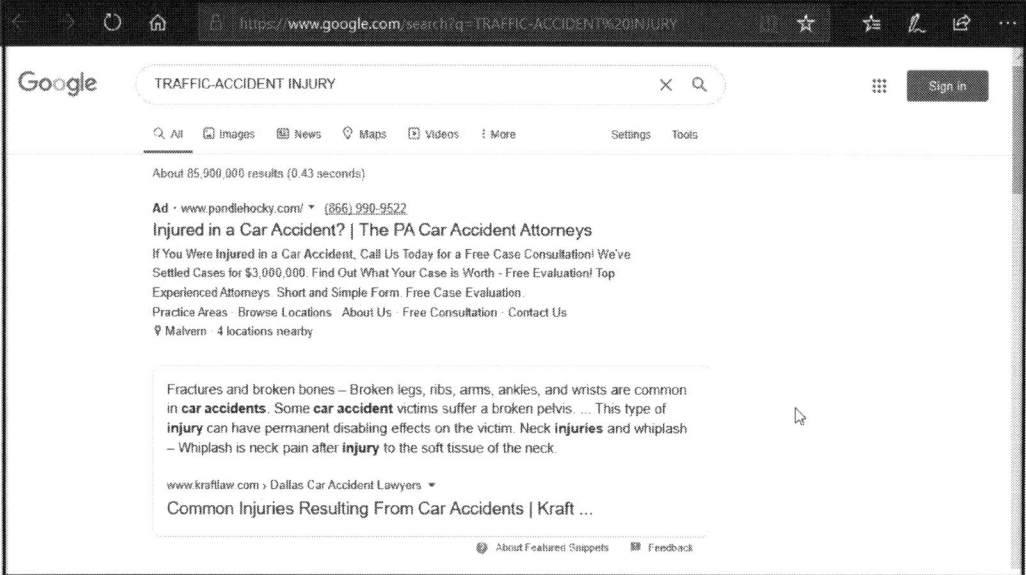

Figure 13.12 – The result of the event action

When we set up the new Splunk workflow action, when we set the **Show action in option**, we selected **Both**. Therefore, we can see that we also have the workflow action option available under the selected (field's) **Actions**:

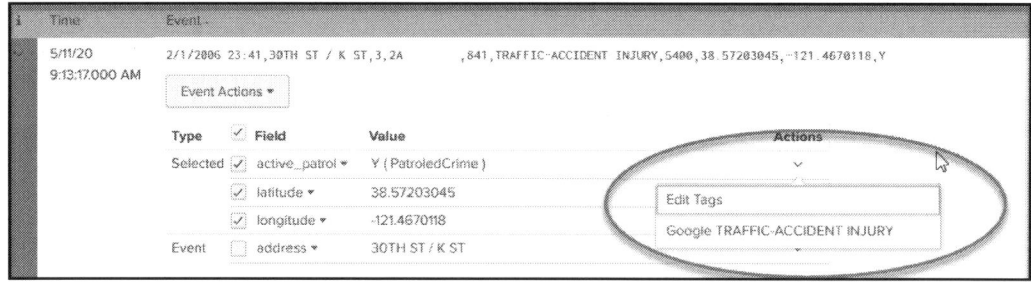

Figure 13.13 – Workflow action option

This is certainly a handy workflow action. I have another idea: suppose we wanted to allow the user to perform a Google search on any of the result fields. To do that, we can alter our Splunk workflow action (or create a new one) as follows:

- Change the **Label** value to be Google $@field_name$.
- Change the **Show action in value** to **Fields Menus**.
- And then change the **URI** value to http://www.google.com/search?q=$@field_name$+$@field_value$.

Now, when we run our search, the Splunk workflow action only appears under the field's **Actions** menu and is unique to the field we have clicked on (as shown in the following screenshot):

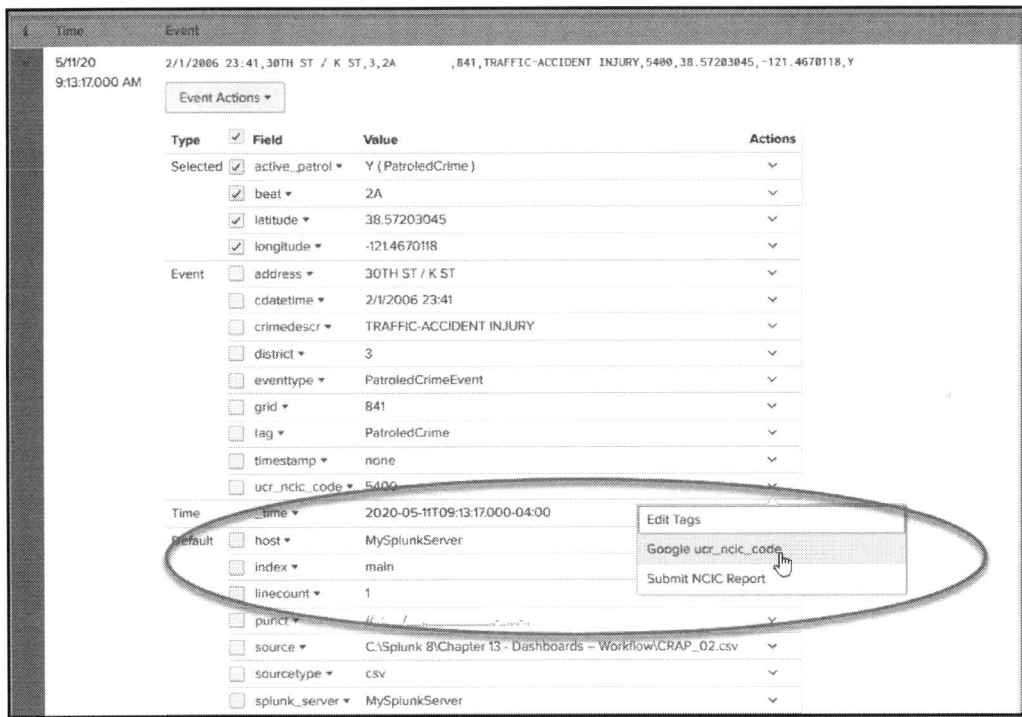

Figure 13.14 – New search results

Of course, clicking on the action will run the Google search for the field (in this example, the ucr_ncic_code field).

Another workflow action example

POST workflow actions produce an HTTP POST request to a URL that you specify when setting up the workflow action. This Splunk workflow action type supports the ability to insert entries into an external system by means of a set of applicable event field values.

You set up POST workflow actions in the same way as in the prior example.

From **Settings**, you can click on **Fields** and then **Workflow actions**. Then, again, you can use the **Workflow Actions** page to make modifications to existing workflow actions as well as add new workflow actions. Although this is similar to how the prior workflow action was created, a POST workflow action creates a POST request that is defined by an HTML form element, along with some inputs that are transformed into POST arguments. This requires that you identify each POST argument that will be sent to the URI that you also define, but we'll get to all this.

To create a POST workflow action, you need to provide the following information on the **+ Add New** (**Workflow actions**) page:

- Just like the prior example, the **Name** and the **Label** field enables you to name the workflow action and set the text that is shown in either the field or event workflow menus. The **Destination app** field also works in the same manner. For this example, I have selected/entered the following:

    a) **Destination app**: `Search`

    b) **Name**: `Submit NCIC Report`

    c) **Label**: `Submit NCIC Report`

- The following apply to fields/event types are also similar:

    a) **Apply only to the following fields**: `ucr_ncic_code`

    b) **Apply only to the following event types**: **Left blank**

- For **Show action in** (to indicate if you want the action to be visible in the **Event menu**, the **Fields menus**, or **Both**), select **Both**.
- Set **Action type** to **Link**.

- Under **URI**, indicate the web resource URL that responds to POST requests. Let's assume that in our example we are still working with crime activity data and certain `ucr_ncic_code` codes may appear that are new. In those cases, we want to easily be able to add them to our crime activity database. This database application is an online web application, and the URL is `http://NCICReporting.com`. The application has an **Incidents** page and allows you to add a new code. Therefore, the entire URL would be `http://NCICReporting.com/Incidents/new`:

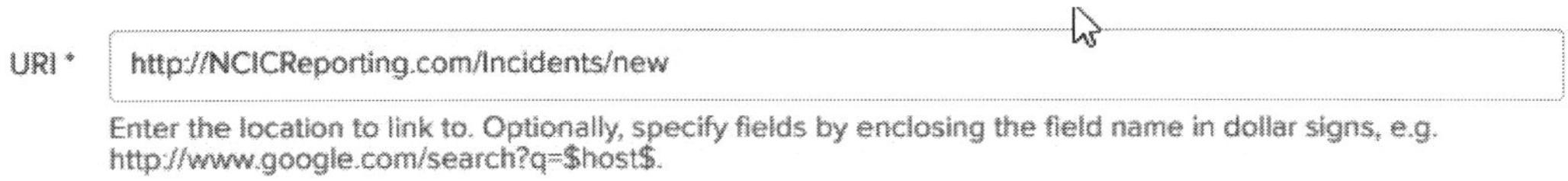

![URI field showing http://NCICReporting.com/Incidents/new](uri.png)

Figure 13.15 – URL for the new workflow action

Under **Open link in**, we want the new page to open in a new window, so select **New Window**.

Defining the POST arguments

This is where the POST workflow action setup differs from the prior example.

Set **Link method** to **post**. Under **Post arguments**, set the arguments that need to be sent to the web resource at the identified URL you indicated. The arguments are the IDs and values for what you want to be sent to the web application you are posting to. You can use field names wrapped in dollar signs to identify the field value from the Splunk event to be sent on both the key and value sides of the argument. In this simple example, we can enter the following:

Post arguments: `ncici_code = ncici_code $ucr_ncic_code$`

Here is a screenshot for reference:

Figure 13.16 – Defining post arguments

Once you have entered/selected the appropriate values, you can click **Save** to save the new POST workflow action definition.

306   Dashboards – Workflow Actions

The entire page is shown in the following screenshot:

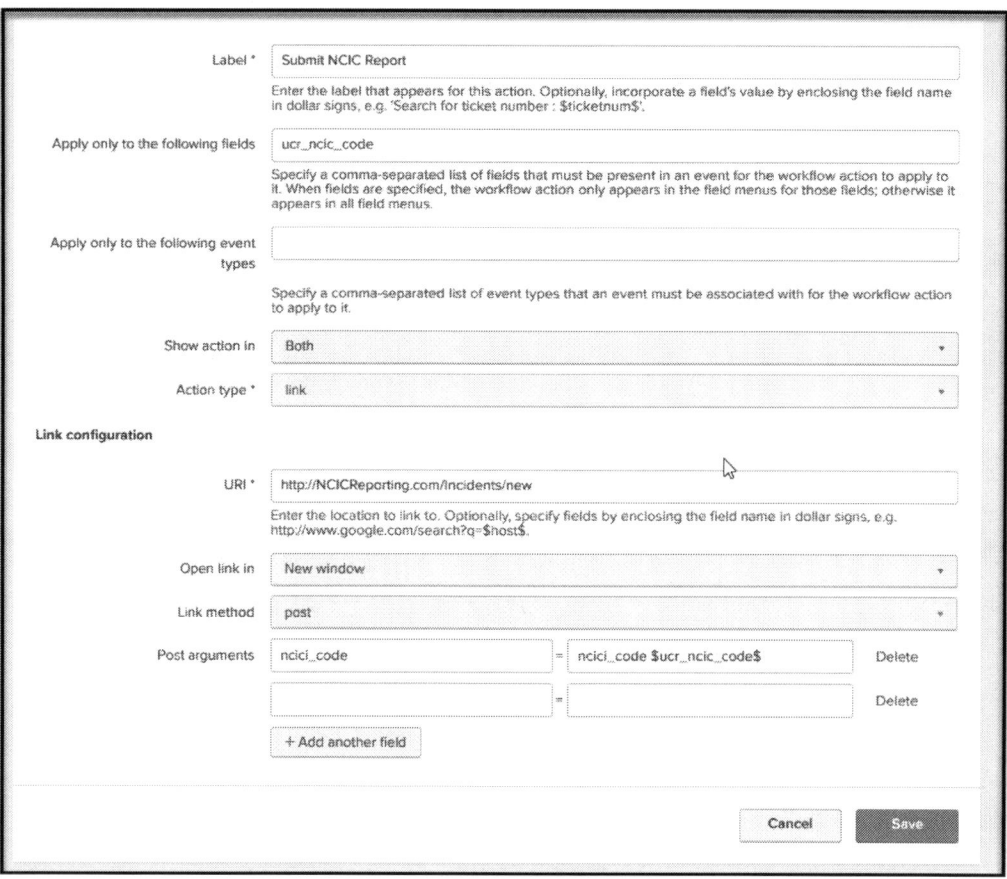

Figure 13.17 – POST workflow action definition

Once you have saved the POST workflow action, we can go back and run our familiar tag search, select and expand an event, and our POST event action is now available to us:

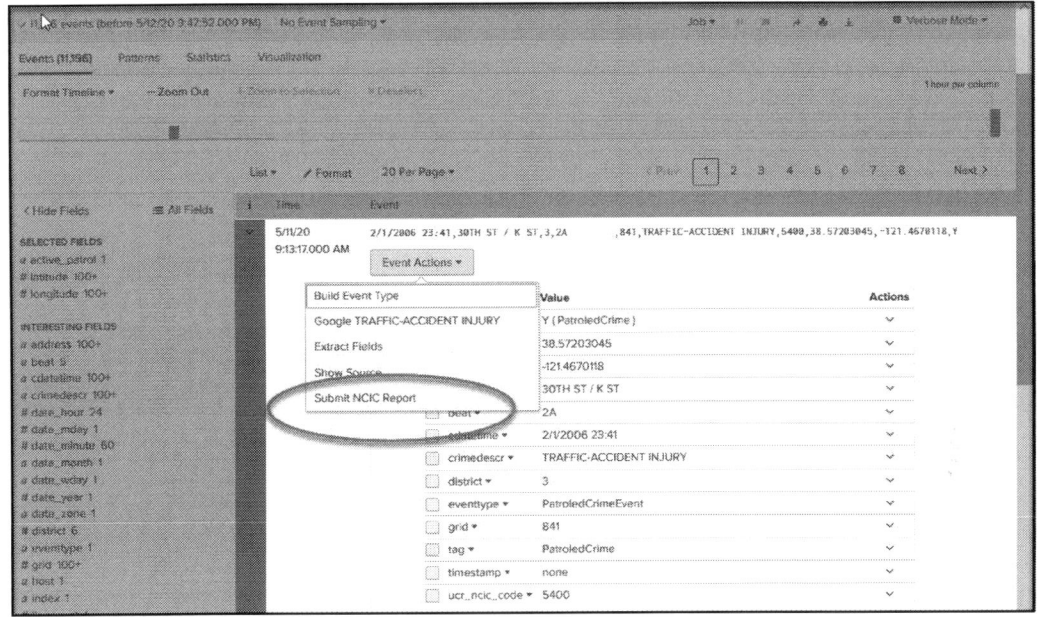

Figure 13.18 – POST workflow action added in the Event Actions

Clicking on the new event action (**Submit NCIC Report**) will post the value of the field (ucr_ncic_code) to the URL application we specified (http://NCICReporting.com/Incidents/new) in a new window:

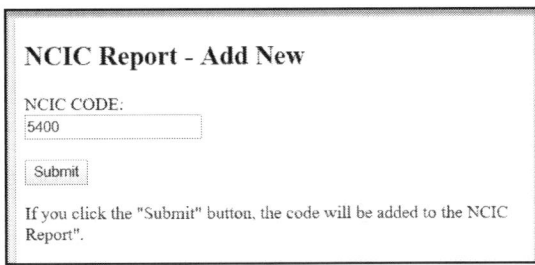

Figure 13.19 – Adding the code to the NCIC report

Secondary search workflow action example

Search workflow action types launch a secondary search using specific event field values from a search result event. This can be super handy.

Again, to set up a Splunk workflow action that launches a dynamically populated secondary search, you follow the same procedure we did for the preceding workflow action examples, but you set the **Action type** to **search** on the **Workflow actions** detail page. This will then permit you to configure the secondary search you want to launch as the workflow action. In this example, we want to again use our crime activity data and set up a workflow action that launches a secondary search on an event beat ID. In other words, if we execute a tag search by using `UnpatroledCrime` we will then want to launch a subsearch on a selected beat to yield all crime activity for that beat. Let's start by defining our new Splunk workflow action:

1. Assuming you are on the **Workflow actions** page (shown in the following screenshot), click on **New Workflow Action**:

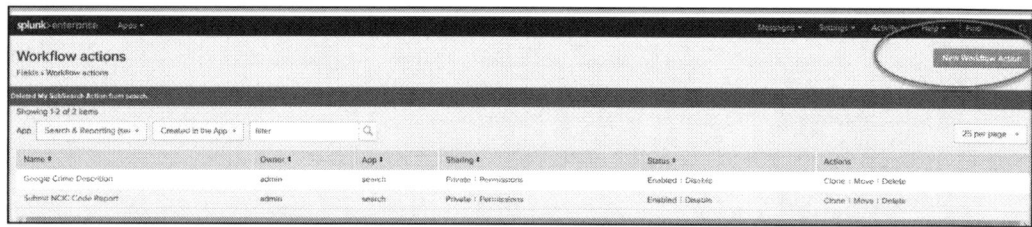

Figure 13.20 – Adding a new workflow action

2. Once again, like the prior examples, the **Name** and the **Label** fields enable you to name the workflow action and provide text to display. The **Destination app** also works in the same manner. For this example, I have selected/entered the following:

    a) **Destination app**: `Search`

    b) **Name**: `Subsearch Action on BEAT`

    c) **Label**: `Subsearch Action on BEAT`

3. The following apply to fields/event types are also similar:

    a) **Apply only to the following fields**: `beat`

    b) **Apply only to the following event types: Left blank**

4. For **Show action in** (to indicate whether you desire the action to be part of the **Event menu**, the **Fields menus**, or **Both**), select **Event menu**.

5. For **Action type**, we want the workflow action to run a (sub) search, so we set **Action type** to **Search**.

6. Under **Search Configuration**, for **Search string**, enter `beat=$beat$`.

7. For the **Search string** value, you use placeholders for values enclosed by dollar signs. Leave **Run in app** and **Open in view** blank.
8. Under **Run search in**, we want the new page to open in a new window, so select **New Window**. Leave **Time range** blank.

The entire page is shown in the following screenshot:

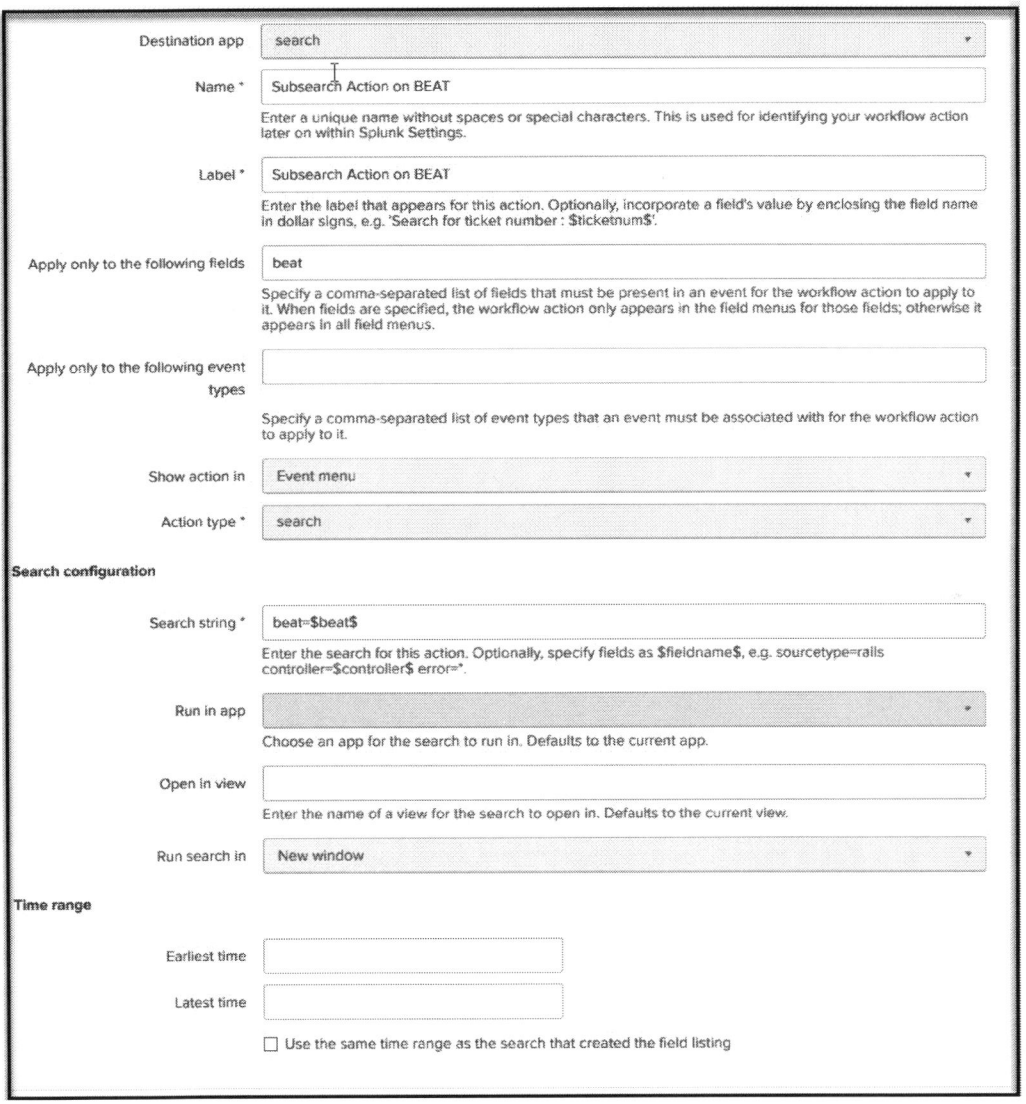

Figure 13.21 – New search workflow action definition

310   Dashboards – Workflow Actions

After you click **Save**, our new Splunk workflow action should be shown in the following screenshot:

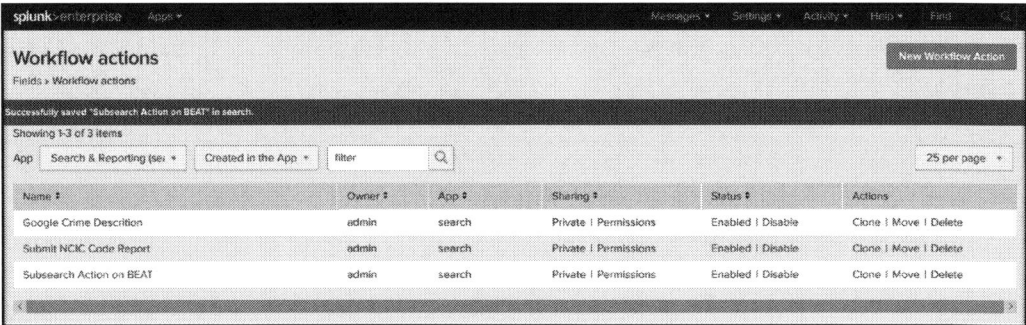

Figure 13.22 – New workflow action added

Now we are ready to try it out! Like we did in the prior examples, we can go back to the **Search** page and enter the tag search (this time, tag=UnPatroledCrime) and see the results.

Once again, we can select and expand any returned event, and we should be able to see our new Splunk workflow action (**Subsearch Action on BEAT**), as we can see in the following screenshot:

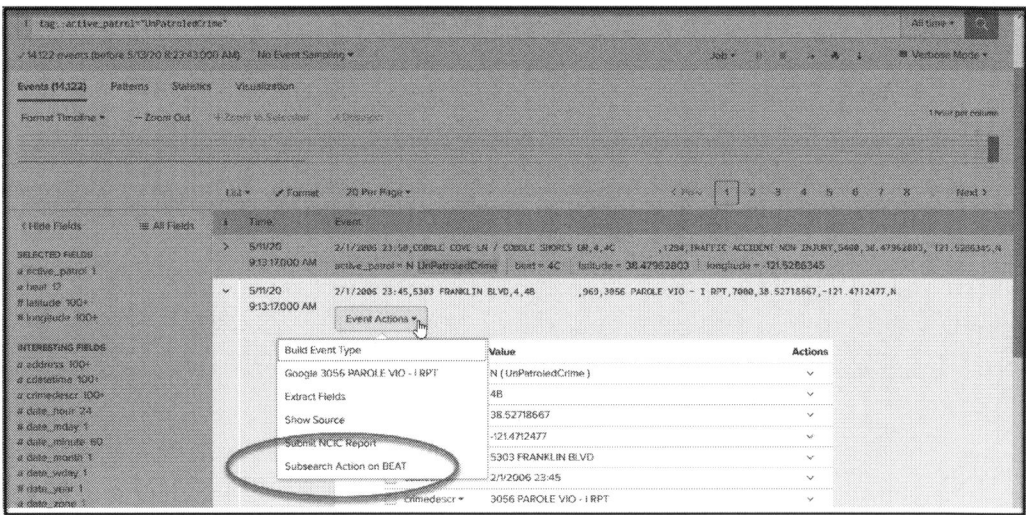

Figure 13.23 – Executing the search

Clicking on the action opens a new window and executes the subsearch that returns only those events for the selected event beat:

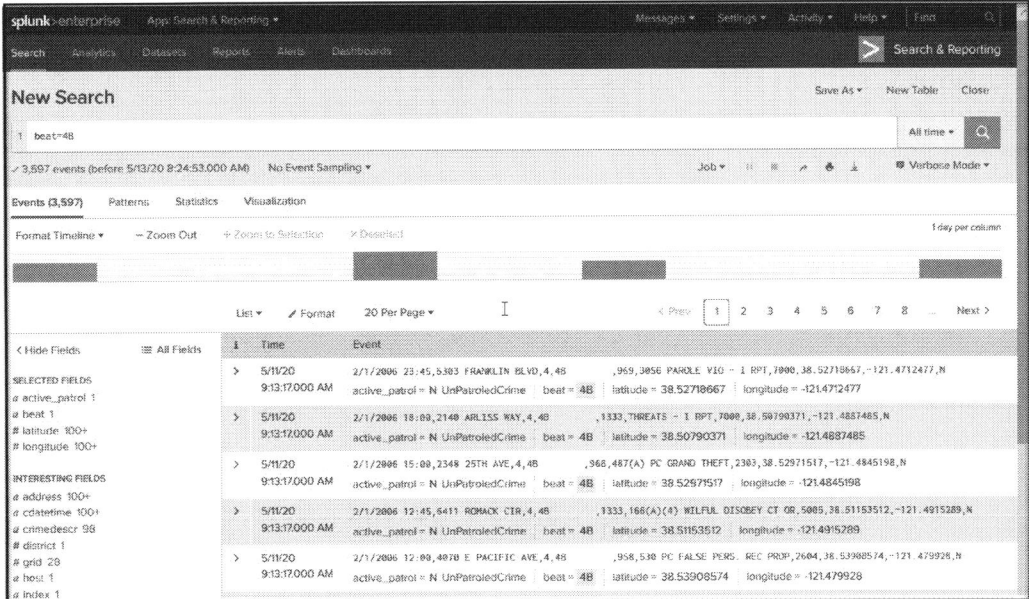

Figure 13.24 – Executing the subsearch

At this point, we have shown the practical use of Splunk workflows and demonstrated some working examples that you can experiment with and build on.

Summary

In this chapter, we used a tag example to illustrate the value of knowledge objects, then introduced workflow actions, which are very powerful knowledge objects. Finally, we created some simple workflows.

The next chapter will illustrate new methods and approaches for monitoring and maintaining Splunk environments using advanced dashboards.

14
Dashboards – Monitoring and Operability

In the previous chapter, we touched on knowledge objects and then focused on explaining the value and practical use of Splunk workflow actions. We finished by building three Splunk workflow actions.

In this chapter, we will illustrate some methods and approaches for monitoring and maintaining Splunk environments using advanced dashboards, such as the Splunk Monitoring Console, the Instrumentation app, and some miscellaneous resource search approaches.

The chapter will be broken down into the following main sections:

- Monitoring without searching
- Using the Splunk Add-on for Windows
- Creating single-page trending metrics

- Exploring Splunk platform instrumentation
- Exploring the Splunk Monitoring Console
- Performing triggered-based diagnostics

Monitoring without searching

Splunk is a tool with which you can monitor, search, analyze, and visualize all kinds of data in real time. Splunk is designed to easily and continuously monitor and read different types of log or other data, storing them as **indexed events**. Splunk users can then easily create spectacular visualizations of the data in various forms of dashboards. We should, by now, understand that using Splunk, you can create SPL search commands to monitor all types of data and metrics as well as setting up alerts to identify and report on particular events, such as when critical resources approach preset thresholds. We can even save these value-add searches to use on other occasions.

Simple search example

An example of a critical resource is available memory. Assuming a Microsoft Windows deployment, the **Microsoft Windows Performance Monitor** is a tool that administrators typically use to examine how programs running are affecting performance. The tool can be used in real time and can also be used to collect information in a log to analyze the data at a later time.

Splunk can easily access information generated by **Performance Monitor** (with some setup, which we will attempt in the next section), and you can create SPL commands to search it.

The following is a simple search of available memory trended over time:

```
index=main sourcetype="Perfmon:ProcessorInfo" counter="% 
Processor Performance"
 | eval {counter}=value | table host Value
```

The following screenshot is the generated visualization:

Figure 14.1 – Search visualization

Once we have access to the data generated by the **Performance Monitor** tool, we can carry on and create various Splunk knowledge objects to report, as well as monitoring and alerting when selected Windows resources approach or reach critical states—all without having to manually re-execute SPL commands.

Before we can explore any **search-less monitoring**, we need to set up access to **Performance Monitor** (**Perfmon**) data. As with most types of data, there's an app for (accessing) that.

In the next section, we will use the Splunk Add-on for Windows to easily access Microsoft Windows performance data.

Using the Splunk Add-on for Windows

This add-on is available for download and installation from Splunkbase. The objective of this add-on is to set up (for you) predefined inputs to collect Perfmon data from Windows systems and map it to normalize the data to the common information model, where you can easily query it.

316 Dashboards – Monitoring and Operability

We'll assume that you can find and install an app, so we won't go into those details here. You can find this add-on at `https://splunkbase.splunk.com/app/742/#/overview`:

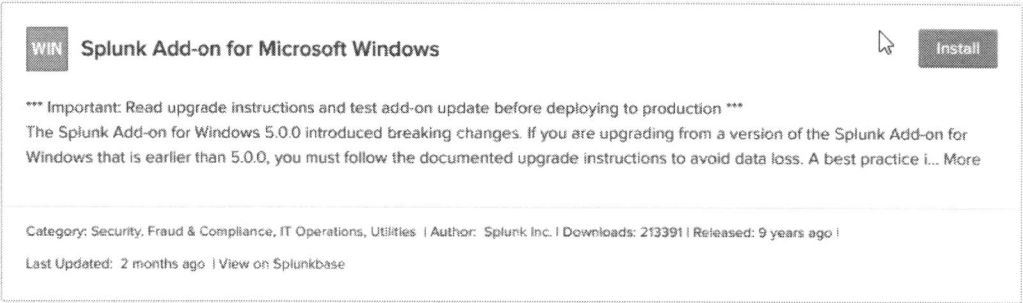

Figure 14.2 – Splunk Add-on for Windows

Once you have the add-on installed, if you go to **Settings**, then **Source Types**, you should be able to locate all of the `Perfmon` data source types that the add-on has set up for you:

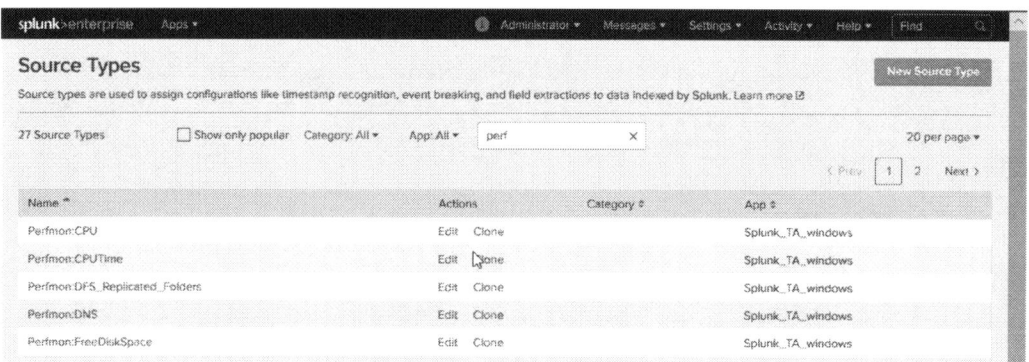

Figure 14.3 – Locating data by its source type

The next step is to configure some inputs to use these new source types. From **Settings**, select **Data Inputs** and locate and click on **Local Performance Monitoring**. From there, click on **New** to add a new input.

Monitoring disk activity

Suppose you want to monitor disk activity on your Windows server. To do that, on the **Add Data** page, do the following:

1. Add a unique collection name.
2. Click **Select Object** to get a list of the performance objects available on the Windows machine and select **FileSystem Disk Activity**.
3. In the **Select Counters** list box, click on **add all**.
4. In the **Select Instances** list box, click on **add all**.
5. In the **Polling interval** field, enter 125 (seconds).
6. Click the green **Next** button:

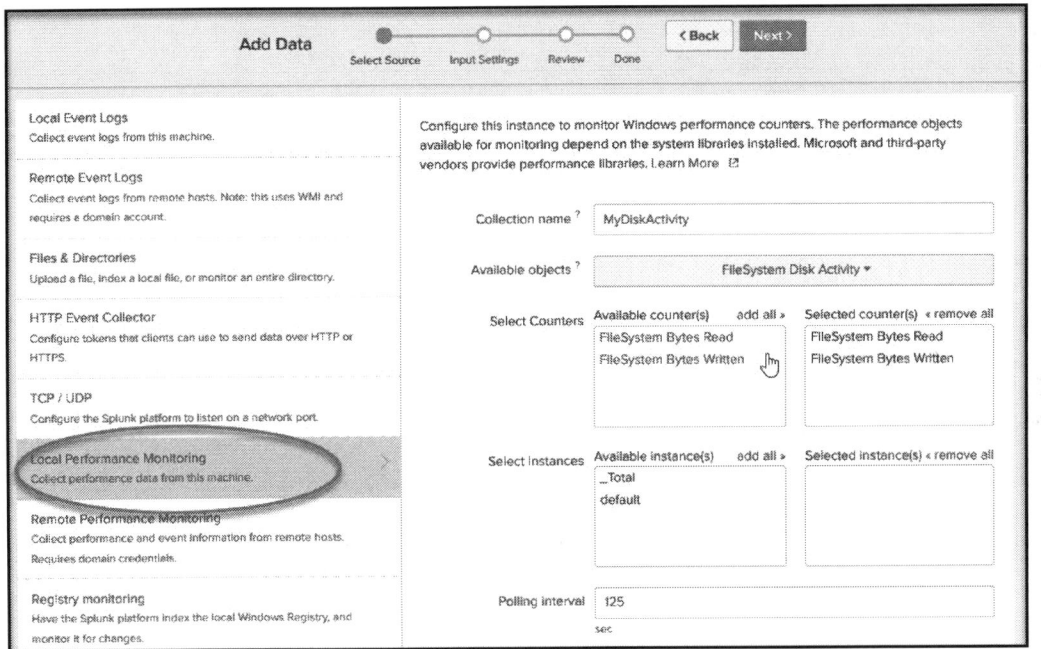

Figure 14.4 – Setting up disk activity monitoring

7. On the **Input Settings** page, the parameters are all optional; you can leave the defaults and just click on **Review**, then **Submit**.

318　Dashboards – Monitoring and Operability

You are ready to search this data (note that Splunk will start indexing the data after 125 seconds). Once indexing starts, it's easy to start monitoring the data points:

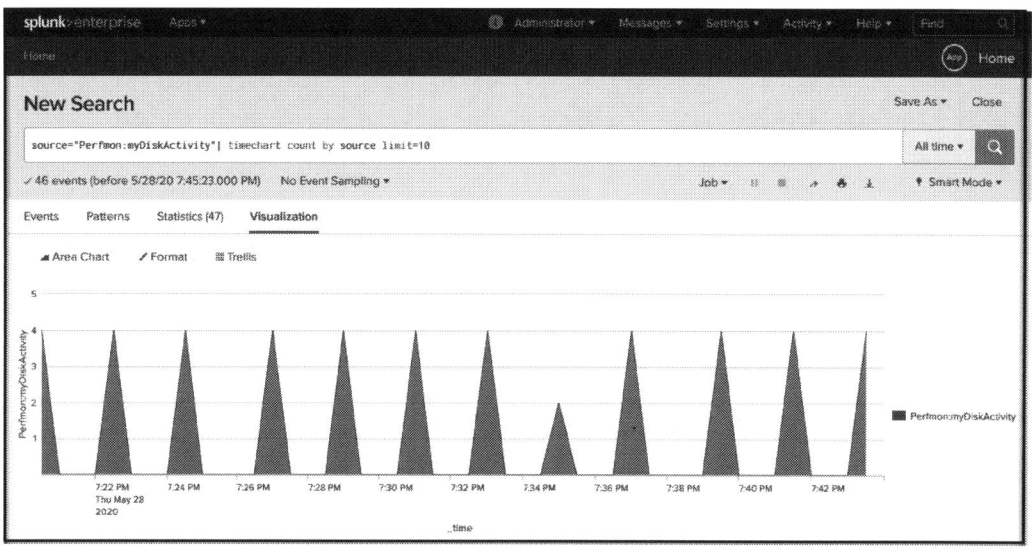

Figure 14.5 – Disk activity monitoring visualization

Creating single-page trending metrics

Once we have our Perfmon data metrics indexed and have built and saved some searches as reusable Splunk knowledge objects showing data points trending over time (for example, disk activity over time, which is shown in the previous screenshot), we can consider creating a **single-page trending metric**.

To do this, you need to convert the saved searches to create a single-value visualization and, to access sparklines and trend indicators, it is important that the search includes the `timechart` command. Using `timechart` means that time-series data becomes available to sparkline and trend indicator processing.

For example, we can take our earlier search command that visualized memory usage and modify it to this:

```
Sourcetype="Perfmon:ProcessorInfo" counter="% Processor Performance" | timechart count by source
```

The preceding search will create a single-value visualization (remember to change the visualization type) with a sparkline appearing below the single value generated with the `timechart` command, showing increases and decreases in the metric over the time range (specified in the search).

Next, we modify our disk activity search in the same fashion:

```
Sourcetype=Perfmon:* sourcetype="Perfmon:myDiskActivity" |
timechart count by source
```

Once the searches are modified, we can choose to save each as a dashboard panel and then combine the panels into a dashboard:

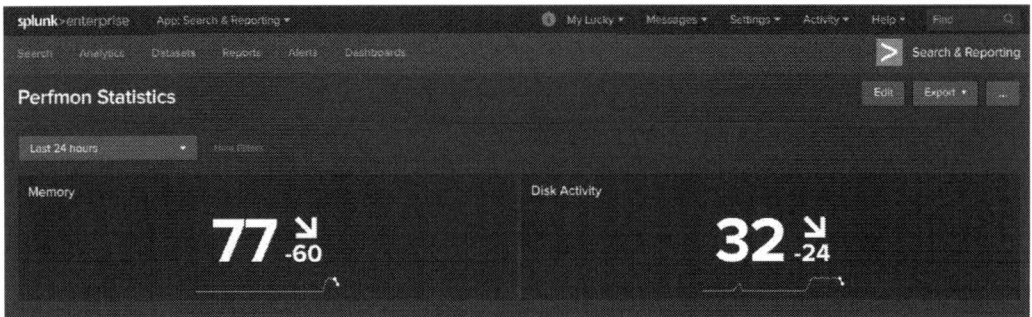

Figure 14.6 – Panels combined to form a dashboard

The visualizations we created used the time picker to set the date range. We can set the dashboard to include the time picker with a default value and allow the user to select a different time range. Another idea is to set the **Auto Refresh Delay** setting to **automatic refresh** and show the latest aggregated data.

In the next section, we will take a quick look at Splunk platform instrumentation.

Exploring Splunk platform instrumentation

Splunk platform instrumentation comes out of the box (if you are running the enterprise version) and refers to data that Splunk itself logs and populates within its `_introspection` index. Specifically, Splunk produces data about the Splunk instance and environment and *writes that data to log files* to aid in the reporting on and monitoring of system resource utilization that can affect Splunk performance.

In fact, similar data to what we looked at in the previous sections is accessible through Splunk platform instrumentation searches, such as `cpu_usage` (use the following search):

```
Index=_introspection component=PerProcess data.process=splunkd
(data.args="-p * start" or data.args="service") earliest=-1h |
timechart median(data.pct_cpu) as cpu_usage(%)
```

That would generate the following visualization:

Figure 14.7 – Instrumentation search results visualization

Splunk introspection data is valuable information to be used to monitor a Splunk environment and maintain operability. The information available is well documented, along with sample searches (such as cpu_usage in the preceding example), at https://docs.splunk.com/Documentation/Splunk/8.0.4/Troubleshooting/Abouttheplatforminstrumentationframework.

Similar to the aforementioned Perfmon data, introspection data includes the following:

- Operating system resource usage data for Splunk processes, by process
- Operating system resource usage data for the entire host (that is, all system and user processes)
- Disk object data
- **Key value** (**KV**) store performance data

It is well worth your time to read the online documentation and experiment with the sample introspection data queries.

In the next section, we will focus on another out-of-the-box Splunk tool that provides additional valuable information for monitoring a Splunk deployment, the Splunk Monitoring Console.

Exploring the Splunk Monitoring Console

The Splunk **Monitoring Console** is a search-based set of pre-built dashboards, a monitoring tool that lets you view detailed information about the performance of a Splunk environment. This provides visibility into many key areas of Splunk, including *search and indexing performance, resource usage, license usage*, and more.

The Monitoring Console will work with all types of deployment topologies, from standalone deployments to multi-site indexer clusters.

The **Monitoring Console** (previously known as the **Distributed Management Console**) is designed to be the Splunk Enterprise monitoring tool, providing dashboards that give insight into the following areas of a Splunk instance:

- Searching and indexing
- Resource and app key-value store usage
- Clustering
- Index and volume usage
- Forwarder connections and TCP
- HTTP event collector
- Licensing

The Monitoring Console leverages data from Splunk's internal log files (such as `metrics.log`), as well as data available from Splunk Enterprise platform instrumentation (which we touched on in the previous section).

Accessing the Monitoring Console

To access the console (assuming you have admin access), you click on **Settings** and then the **Monitoring Console** icon on the left:

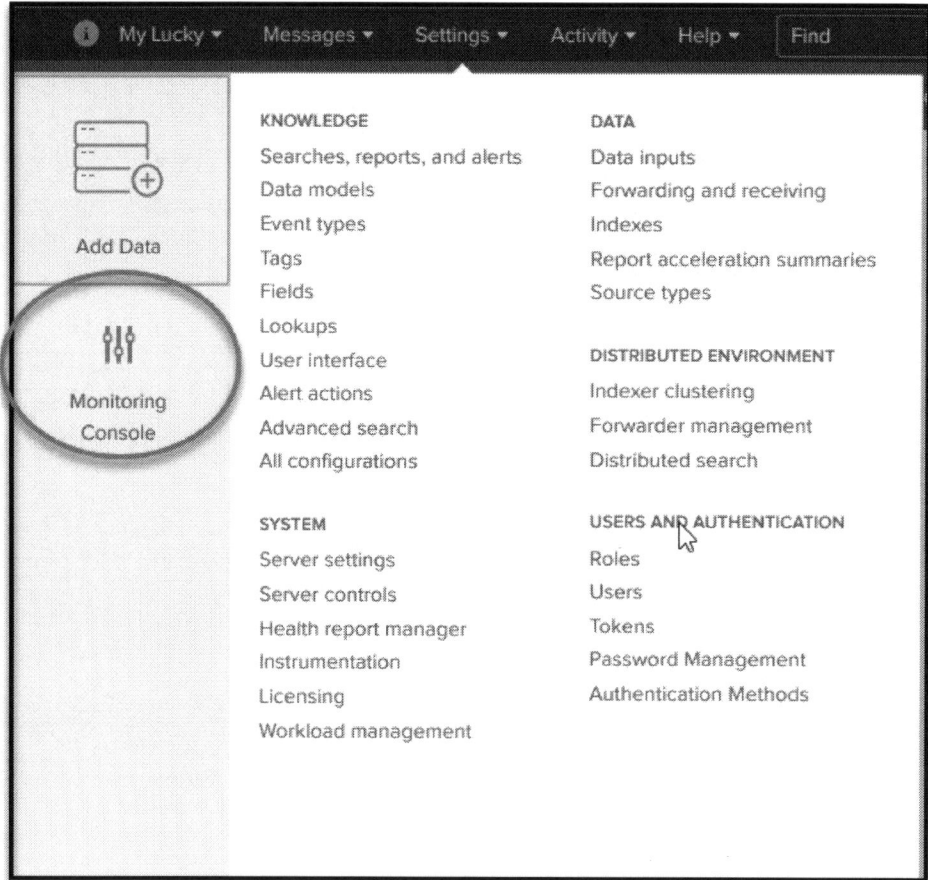

Figure 14.8 – Accessing the Monitoring Console

The home page of the Splunk Monitoring Console is the **Overview** page.

On this page, in the upper left, you will see the version of Splunk that is installed and running as well as the specifics of the operating machine, for instance, Windows, XX GB physical memory, and X CPU cores. In addition, the page is divided into clickable panels that provide helpful visualizations depicting the status of the Splunk environment. These include visualizations of the indexing rate, license and disk usage, concurrent searches, CPU usage, memory usage, and KV store status.

The bottom panel on the home page is the **Triggered Alerts** panel, which requires some configuration. We will cover this in the next section of this chapter.

Exploring the features of the console

There are many valuable features of the Splunk Monitoring Console, which should be investigated. For example, it comes with preconfigured health checks that you can modify, or you can even create or download custom ones.

Find the health check at **Monitoring Console | Health Check**. Start the health check by clicking **Start**:

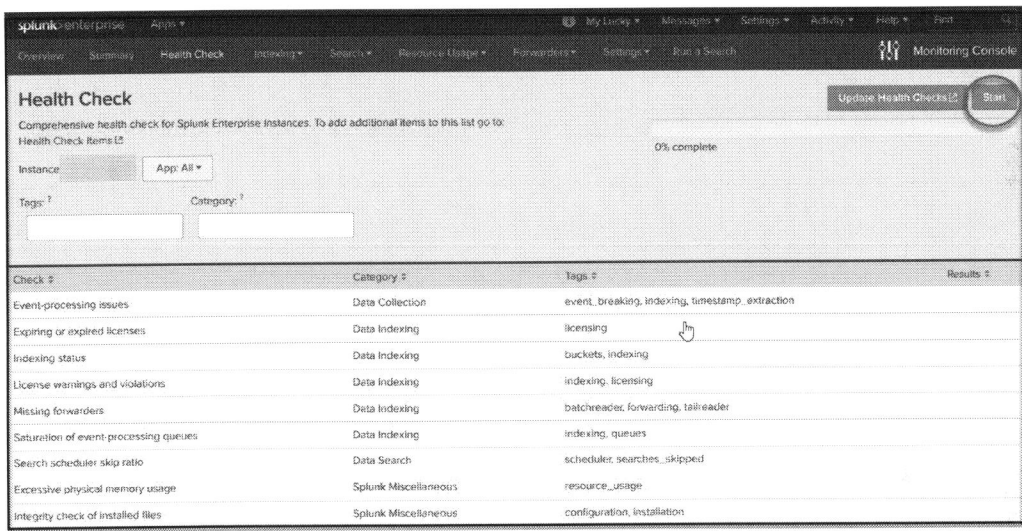

Figure 14.9 – Exploring Health Check

Health check items are really narrowly focused searches. Clicking on **Start** runs each of the searches sequentially. After all the searches are complete, the results are sorted by severity. The health check items can be sorted and filtered on the **Health Check** page (shown in the preceding screenshot) for clarity.

Before you run any health check items, you should click on **Update Health Checks**. This will prompt you for your Splunk credentials and then download and install the Splunk Health Assistant add-on (https://splunkbase.splunk.com/app/4603/).

The Splunk Health Assistant Add-on ensures that the Monitoring Console health check feature is up to date by assisting you in downloading and installing all new health check items as they become available:

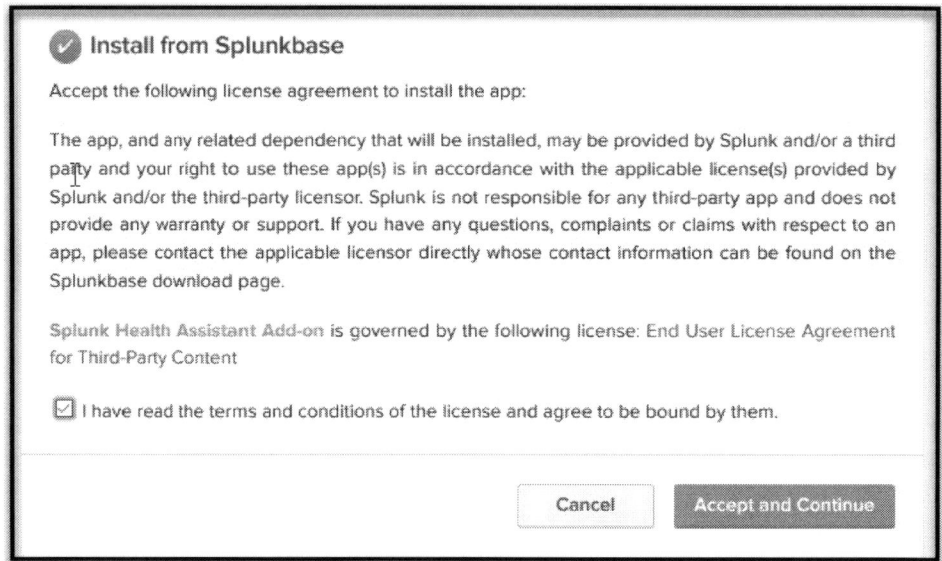

Figure 14.10 – Installing the Splunk Health Assistant Add-on

Once the add-on is installed, click on **Start** to run the health check items:

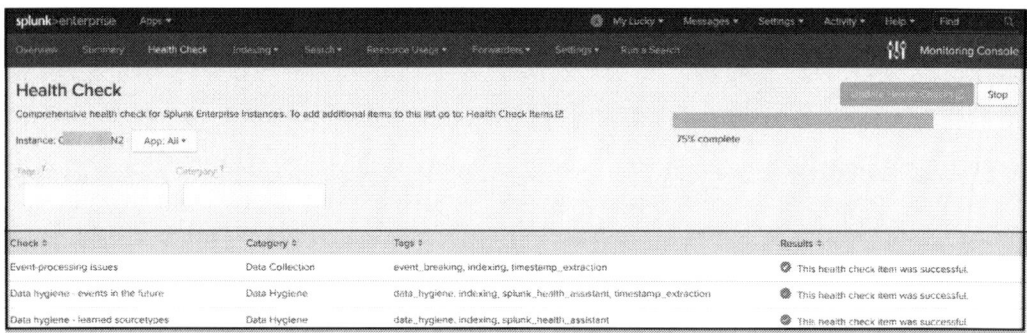

Figure 14.11 – Running the health check

Once the health check is complete, you can click on any of the health check items for details on that item, including suggested actions:

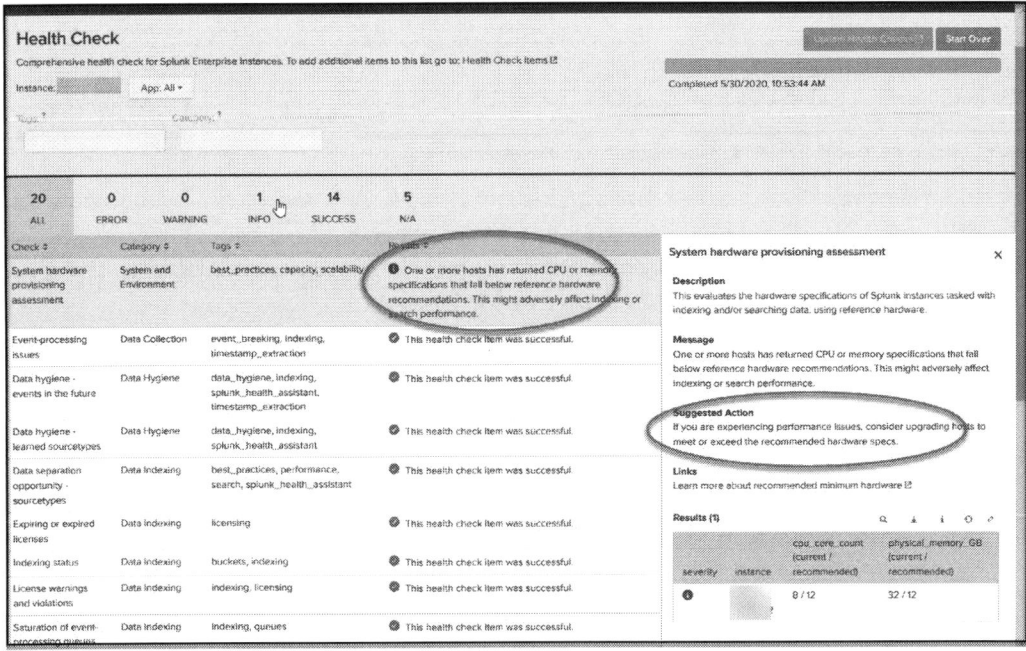

Figure 14.12 – Result and details of health check items

Now that we have learned how to perform health checks, let's explore trigger-based diagnostics.

Performing trigger-based diagnostics

On the bottom panel of the **Overview** page is the **Triggered Alerts** panel. Initially, the panel will display the message **Alerts require setup. Please set up your instance first**:

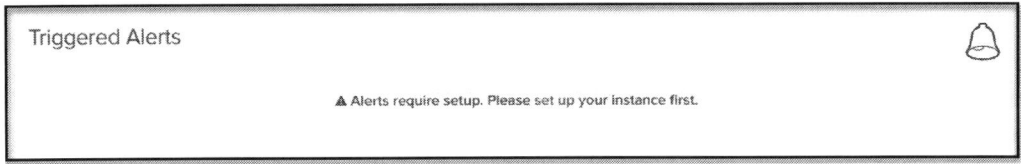

Figure 14.13 – Triggered Alerts

Once you click on **set up** (as shown in the preceding screenshot) and once you have followed the instructions, the **Triggered Alerts** panel will be ready for you to select, configure, and enable the platform alerts you are interested in. Platform alerts are saved searches included in the Monitoring Console and will trigger when conditions that might compromise the Splunk environment are met. When an alert is triggered, the **Triggered Alerts** panel will display a notification:

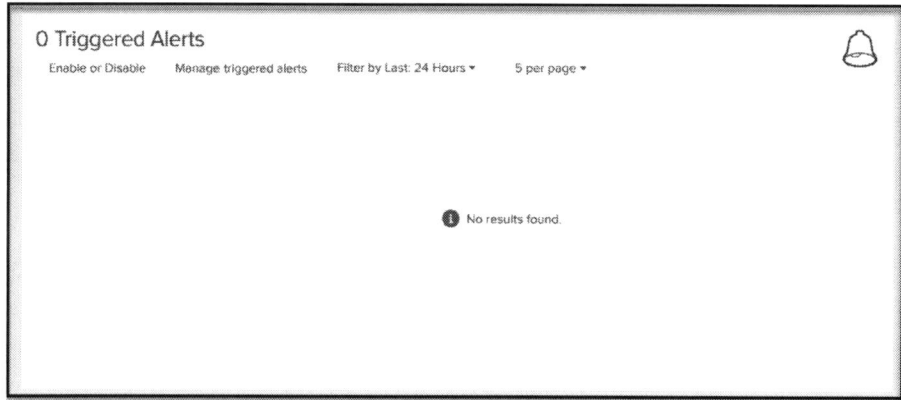

Figure 14.14 – Triggered Alerts panel

On the **Triggered Alerts** panel, you can click on **Enable** or **Disable** to view the platform alerts list (shown in the following screenshot). Notice that initially all alerts are disabled:

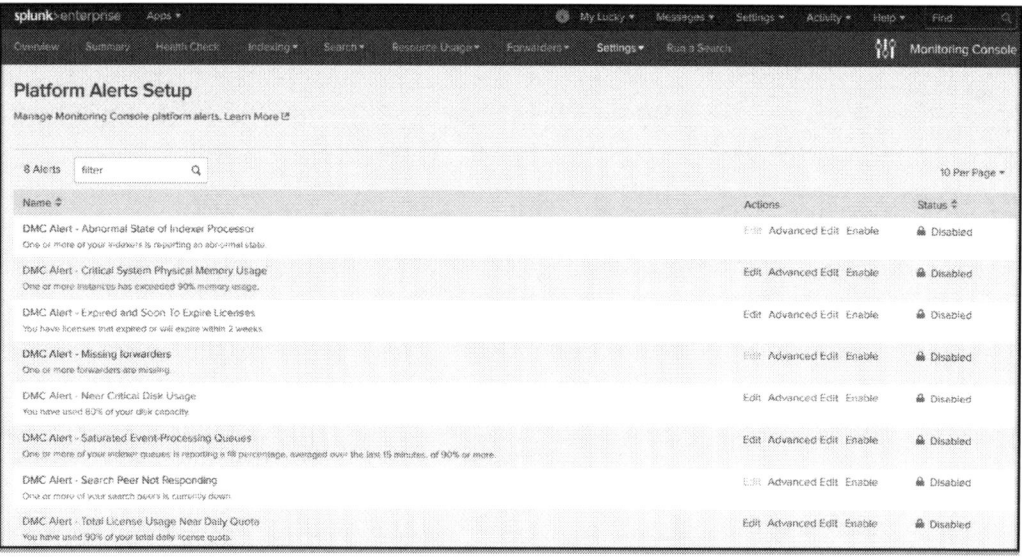

Figure 14.15 – Enabling and disabling alerts

Continuing the theme of this chapter, scroll down to **DMC Alert – Near Critical Disk Usage** and click on **Edit**. In the pop-up dialog, see that the default threshold is set to 80:

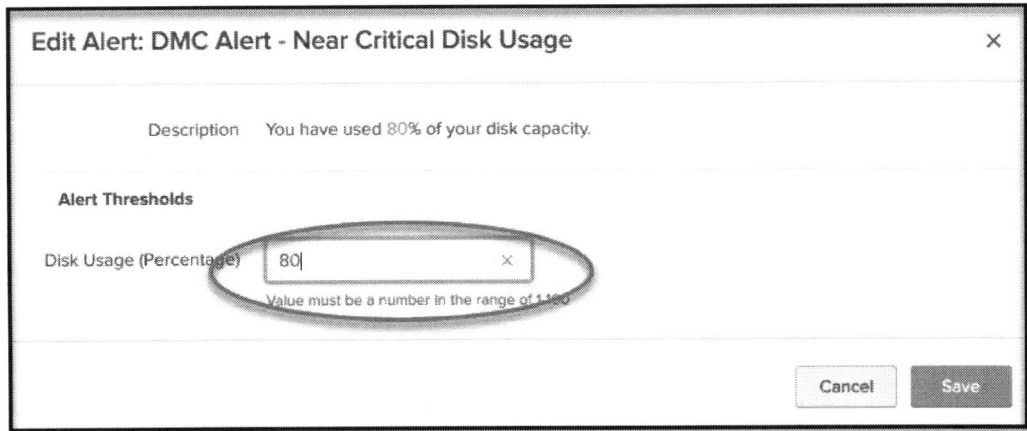

Figure 14.16 – Setting disk usage

Click **Save**. Next (for this same alert), click on **Advanced Edit**:

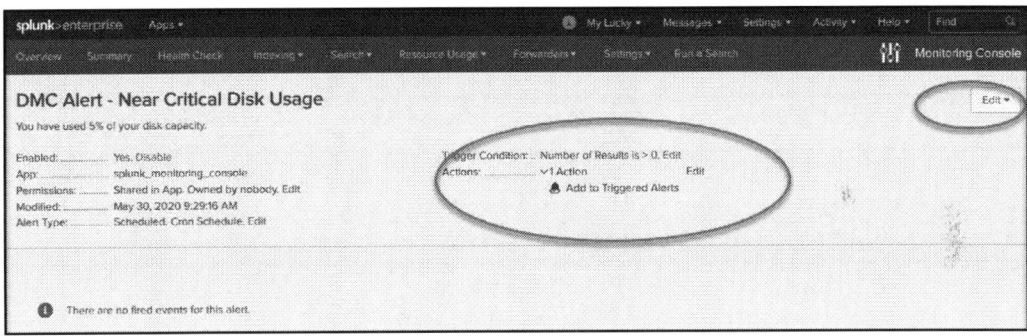

Figure 14.17 – Advanced edit

On this page (shown in the preceding screenshot), you have access to edit the trigger condition as well as the ability to set up actions for the alert. Furthermore, in the upper-right part of the page, you can click on **Edit** to edit the alert specifics, set permissions for the alert, and enable/disable or clone the alert. Finally, you can open the alert in search to test the alert:

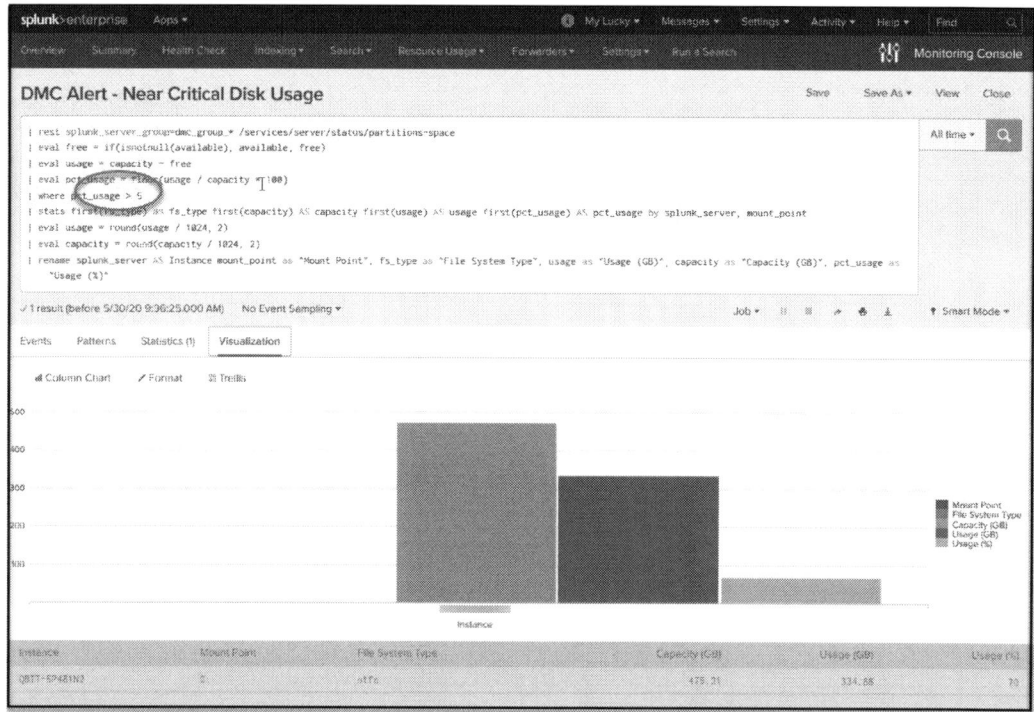

Figure 14.18 – The alert in the search visualization

To force this alert to trigger, I've modified the search by setting the threshold to 5% (rather than the more realistic 80%). If we go back to the **Triggered Alert** panel on the **Overview** page, now we can see the report:

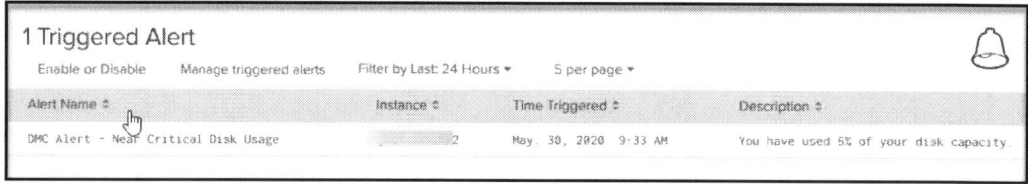

Figure 14.19 – Alert report added to the Triggered Alert panel

Clicking the alert in the **Triggered Alert** panel lets you drill into the details of the alert:

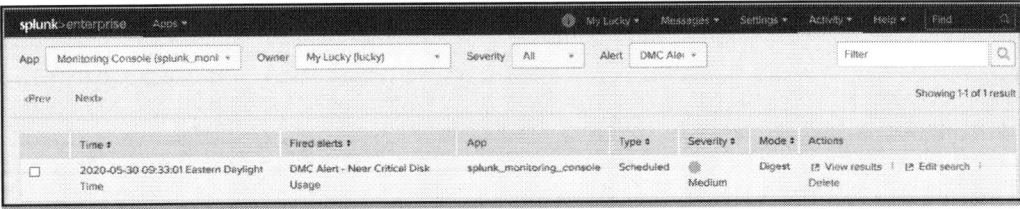

Figure 14.20 – Details of the alert

From here, you can see the date/time of when the alert was triggered, as well as the severity, and even view the results, delete, and/or modify/edit the alert search.

The Splunk documentation covers each of the default platform alerts at https://docs.splunk.com/Documentation/Splunk/8.0.4/DMC/Platformalerts?ref=hk. It is well worth the time to review the explanations of each of the alerts as well as experimenting with each. Congratulations! You have successfully learned how to monitor various reports on the dashboard.

Summary

In this chapter, we illustrated new methods and approaches for monitoring and maintaining Splunk environments using advanced dashboards, including platform instrumentation and the monitoring console.

The next chapter focuses on creating custom visualizations and updating dashboards using drag and drop with the UI-based dashboard editor.

15
Dashboards – Custom Visualizations

In the previous chapter, we covered some methods and approaches for monitoring and maintaining Splunk environments using advanced dashboards such as the Splunk **Monitoring Console**, the instrumentation app, and some miscellaneous resource search approaches.

In this chapter, we will focus on creating some custom visualizations and updating dashboards using features such as *drag and drop* and the Splunk UI-based dashboard editor.

The chapter will be broken down into the following main sections:

- Understanding dashboards and their look and feel
- Building a new Splunk dashboard
- Exploring the Beta app

Understanding dashboards and their look and feel

In software design, **look and feel** is a widely used term with respect to a **graphical user interface** or **GUI**, and includes the various characteristics or attributes of its design, including the following:

Look	Feel
Color	Buttons
Shape	Boxes
Layout	Menus
Font/Typefaces	
Images	

Fig 15.1 – Table of look and feel attributes

The look and feel of any dashboard are determined by the cumulative effect of the attributes used to build the dashboard. Some tools restrict how dashboards are developed, as well as the flexibility of the process controlling what, and how, attributes are used and blended together (with other attributes) to create not only an exciting, dynamic dashboard but also one that clearly adds value.

Splunk dashboards

Splunk dashboards and creative visualizations go hand in hand. In Splunk, you can lay out and format the panels within a Splunk dashboard in any manner that you want using a combination of actual HTML and **Cascading Style Sheets** (**CSS**).

In addition, you can also build dashboards with the same look as Splunk web apps, by utilizing the actual style sheet that Splunk uses by including a link to the `dashboard.css` file within dashboards you create. Using this stylesheet, not only will your dashboards have a similar look and feel, but some of the work required to format your dashboards will already be done for you.

By performing a **Save As** then selecting **Dashboard Panel**, a Splunk search can be easily saved as a simple XML formatted dashboard. Using this dashboard, although the user can (out of the box) *click to select* from a wide range of visualizations to view the data, it can still be challenging to find insights from the data being presented.

Since Splunk allows the addition of both **CustomJS** and **CSS**, using these approaches, you have additional opportunities to customize and extend dashboards.

To add JavaScript in a Splunk dashboard, you can create an `/appserver/static/` directory under `$SPLUNK_HOME/etc/apps/app_name/` and store any static CSS and JavaScript resource files you want to use. Once you create the folder and copy in your code, you'll need to restart Splunk to use it.

> **Note**
> Although it is easy to enhance a Splunk dashboard with CustomJS and CSS, keep in mind the potential maintenance cost when you upgrade Splunk. In other words, you'll need to regression test all custom code you develop outside of Splunk.

Thankfully, there is a Splunk dashboard editor that makes most dashboard customizations pretty straightforward. In the next section, we will use the current Splunk dashboard editor to create and customize a working Splunk dashboard example.

Using the dashboard editor

You can, for the most part, interactively use the Splunk dashboard editor to create, edit, and customize dashboards without writing a single line of XML code.

Using the dashboard editor, you can do the following:

- Create a dashboard
- Add panels to a dashboard
- Convert a dashboard to a form
- Use drag-and-drop to reorganize dashboard panels
- Edit dashboard searches
- Select and format visualizations used in a dashboard
- Edit the dashboard source code
- Convert a dashboard to HTML

Accessing the Splunk dashboard editor

You access the Splunk dashboard editor from an existing dashboard by clicking on the **Edit** button (see the following screenshot):

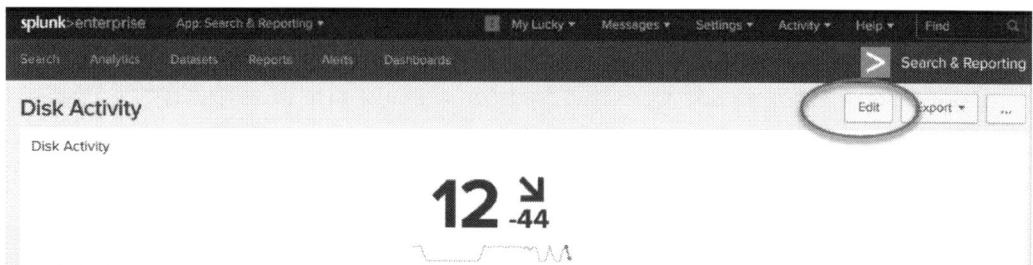

Fig 15.2 – Accessing the Splunk dashboard editor

From there, you can select **UI** or **Source** to change the editing mode. To save any changes you make to a dashboard, you can simply click **Save**, or just click **Cancel** at any time to exit without saving any changes you may have made to the dashboard.

In the next section, we will concentrate on building a new Splunk dashboard and then editing it to find just the right look and feel using some of the Splunk dashboard editor's various features. In the final section of this chapter, we will review the latest (still beta) version of the Splunk dashboard editor, but for now, we'll use the current features offered to build the next dashboard.

Building a new Splunk dashboard

A dashboard is simply an established or saved view that is made up of one or more panels. The panels can contain modules such as search boxes, fields, charts, tables, and lists. Most of the time, you create a dashboard by gluing together specific reports/panels you've already developed, tested, and saved.

An alternative method for creating a dashboard in Splunk is through the use of the dashboard editor.

Accessing the editor

To access the Splunk dashboard editor, you can click on **Create New Dashboard** (upper right) within the **Search & Reporting** app:

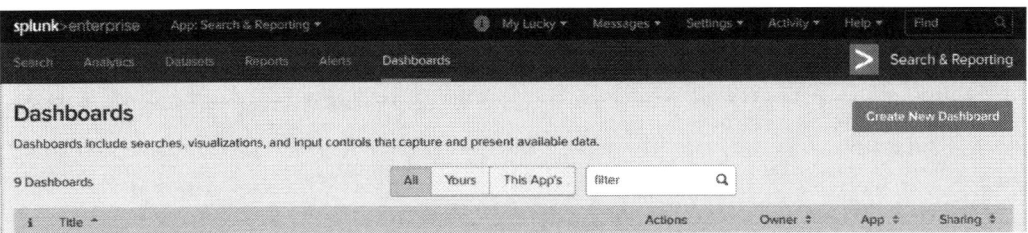

Fig 15.3 – Accessing the editor

From there, on the **Create New Dashboard** dialog (shown in the following screenshot) you can enter a **Title** and **Description**, set **Permissions**, and then click **Create Dashboard**:

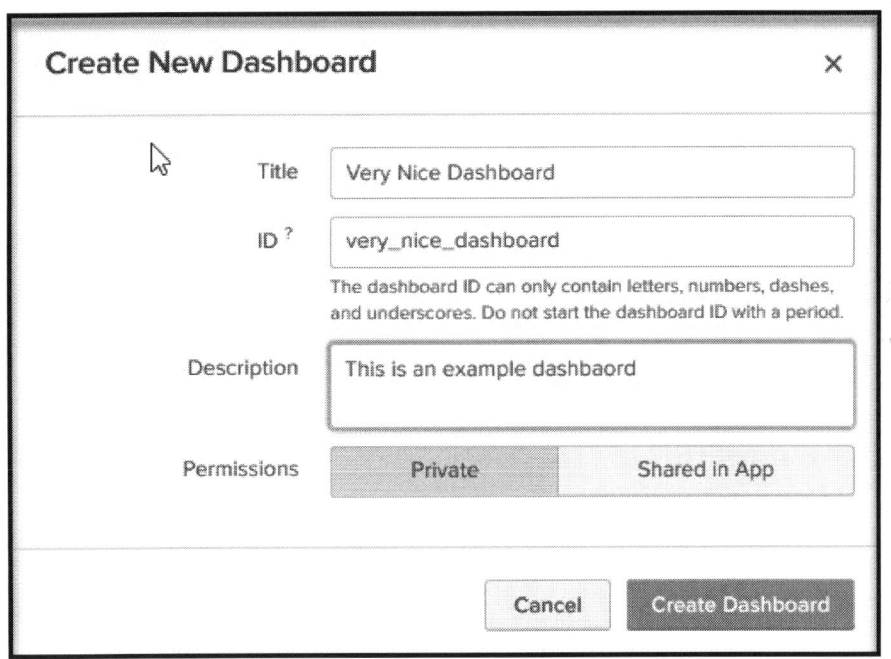

Fig 15.4 – Creating a new dashboard

Once Splunk creates the new dashboard, you'll see that you are in the dashboard editor, ready to edit your not very interesting but new dashboard:

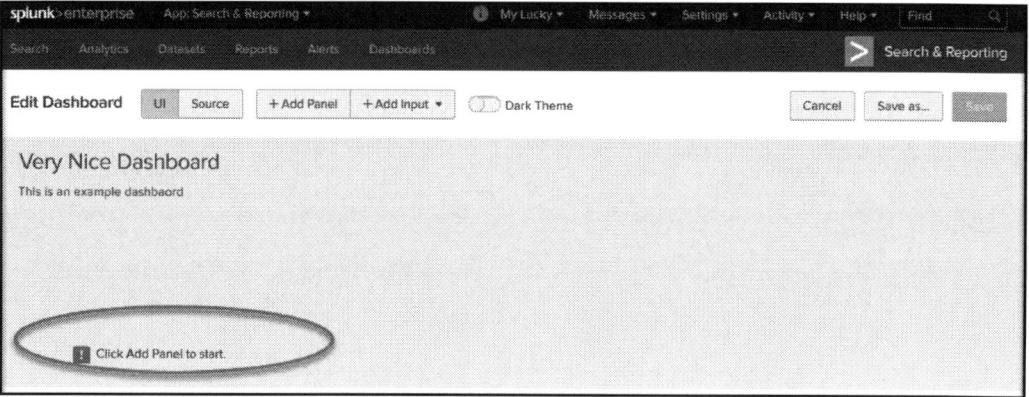

Fig 15.5 – Editing the dashboard

Starting with a search

More often than not, dashboard panels start with a search, which themselves start with a requirement or a data question. To illustrate, let's assume we start with a comma-separated vendors file (vendors.csv). Once it's uploaded to Splunk, we'll execute the following search command on the data:

```
Source="vendors.csv" | geostats latfield=VendorLatitude longfield=VendorLongitude count by VendorCity
```

The following is the result of the search:

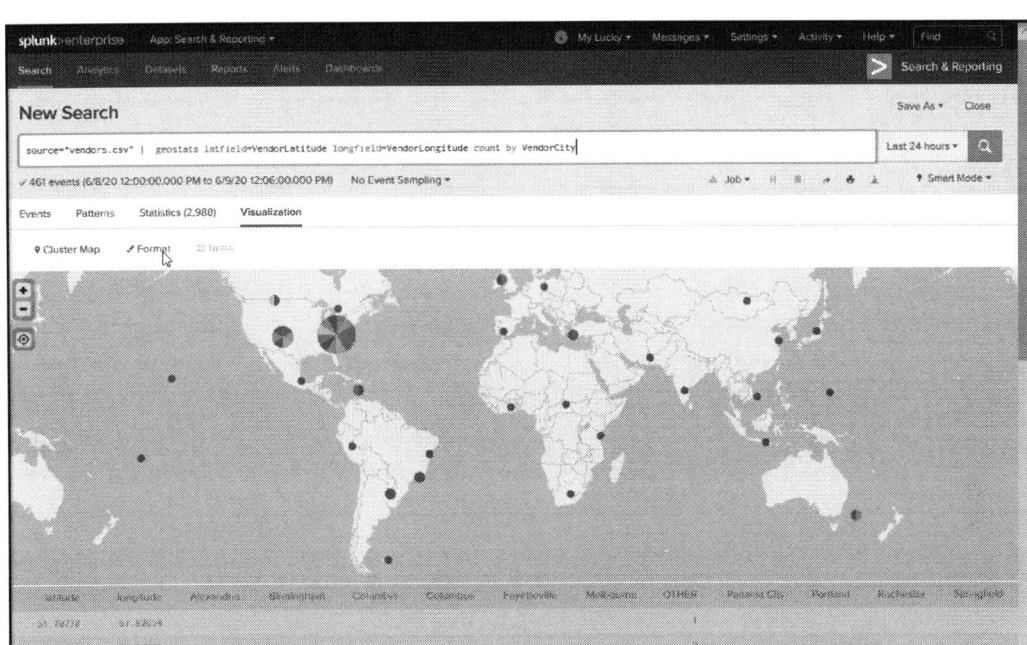

Fig 15.6 – Starting a new search

Within the search, the Splunk `geostats` command generates statistics and automatically summarizes the data (based on latitude and longitude fields in the events) and displays it on maps.

> **Note**
>
> The `vendors.csv` file includes both a `VendorLatitude` and a `VendorLongitude` field so the `geostats` command works nicely, here grouped by the `VendorCity` field. You can learn more about the command online at https://docs.splunk.com/Documentation/Splunk/8.0.4/SearchReference/Geostats#3._Count_each_product_sold_by_a_vendor_and_display_the_information_on_a_map.

Saving a panel

To accelerate things, let's perform a **Save As** and then select **Dashboard Panel**:

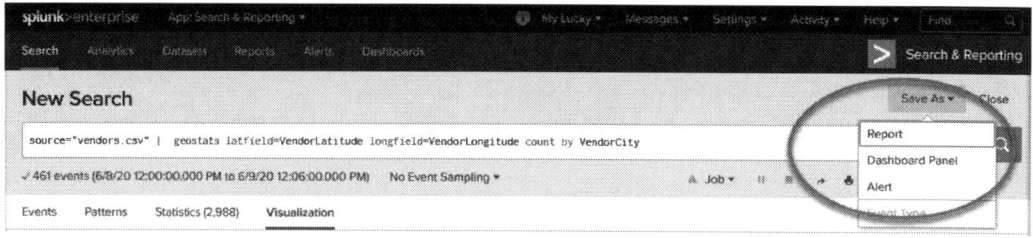

Fig 15.7 – Saving a panel

Next, fill out the **Save As Dashboard Panel** dialog (shown in the following screenshot) and then click on **Save**:

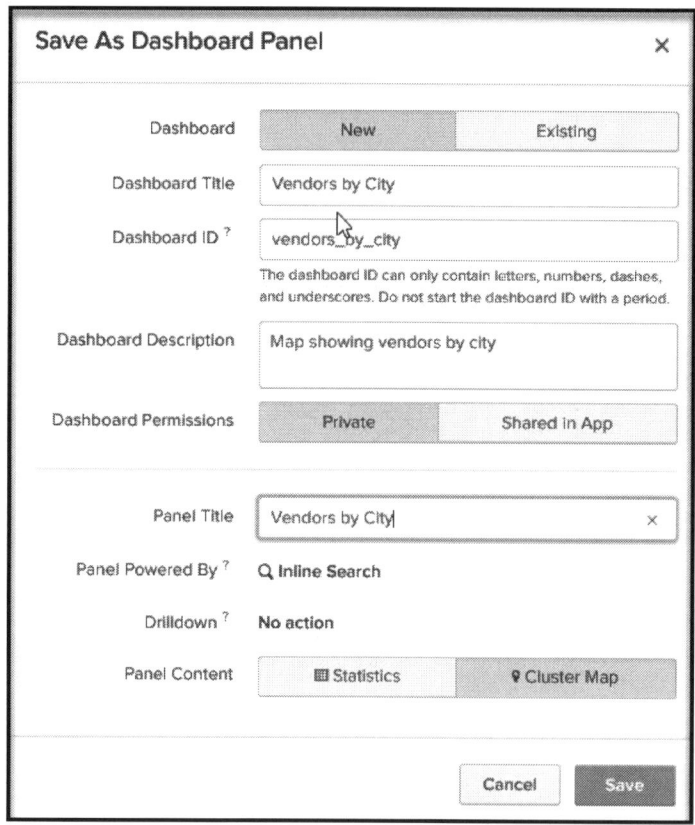

Fig 15.8 – Save As Dashboard Panel dialog

Splunk creates a dashboard panel from our search:

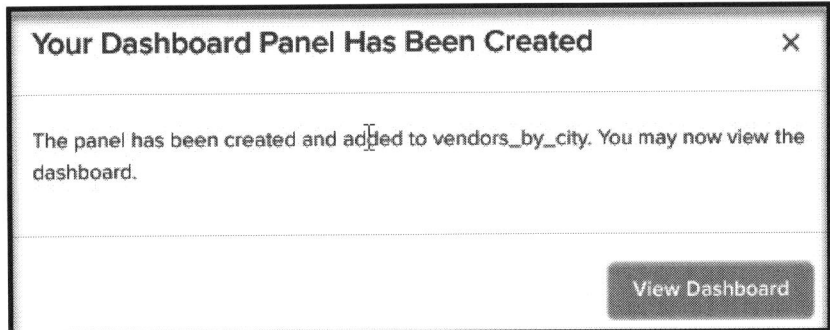

Fig 15.9 – New dashboard panel created

We now have a dashboard with just one report panel. To add more report panels, you can either run new searches and save them to this dashboard, or you can add saved reports to the following dashboard:

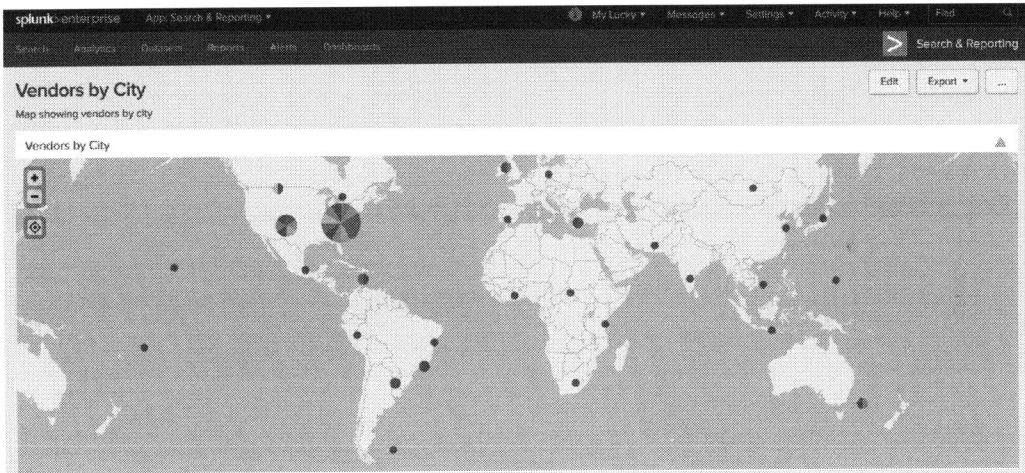

Fig 15.10 – Maps showing vendors by city

340   Dashboards – Custom Visualizations

For now, let's spend a little bit more time on this dashboard panel. First, notice the yellow warning icon at the upper right. If you click on it, Splunk displays an explanation (shown in the following screenshot). Evidently, there is a slight problem with our search:

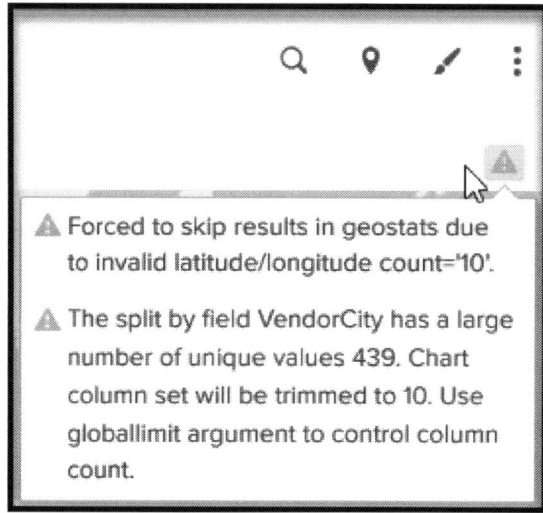

Fig 15.11 – Error details

From within the dashboard editor, you can click on **Edit**, then the edit search icon (shown in the following screenshot):

Fig 15.12 – Edit search icon

From here, you can edit and test the search command (using the **Edit Search** dialog shown in the following screenshot) until it is correct:

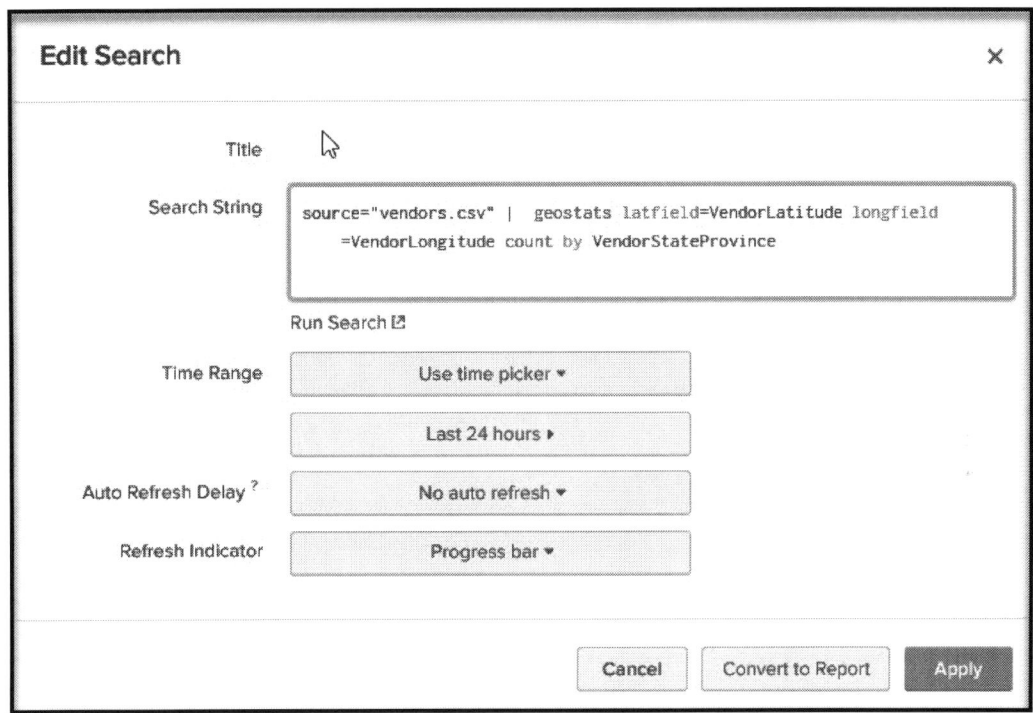

Fig 15.13 – Edit Search dialog

Once the search is ready, we can evolve our dashboard a bit more.

You can change the dashboard layout to prioritize specific panels or make room for additional content. To illustrate, let's click on **+ Add Panel**:

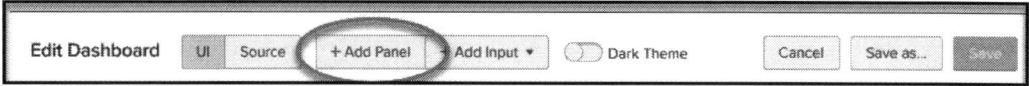

Fig 15.14 – Adding panels to the dashboard

Next, select **New** and then **Statistics Table**, fill in **Content Title** and **Search String**, and click **Add to Dashboard**:

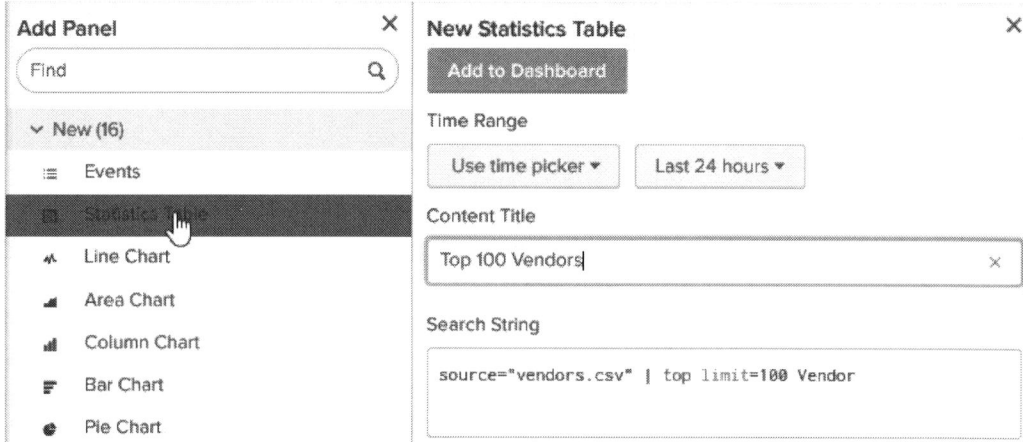

Fig 15.15 – New Statistics Table panel

Now that we have a second panel added to our dashboard, we can use the drag and drop feature of the dashboard editor to move the panels, repositioning them side by side.

Changing the theme

Now, go ahead and change the dashboard theme to dark from (the default) light. Dark seems to be the trending dashboard look, so within the dashboard editor, simply slide the theme slider and select dark (you'll need to save and refresh the dashboard to see its effect).

Adding a heat map overlay

To add another neat visualization to our dashboard, again from within the dashboard editor, you can click on the **Source** button to view the current dashboard source code:

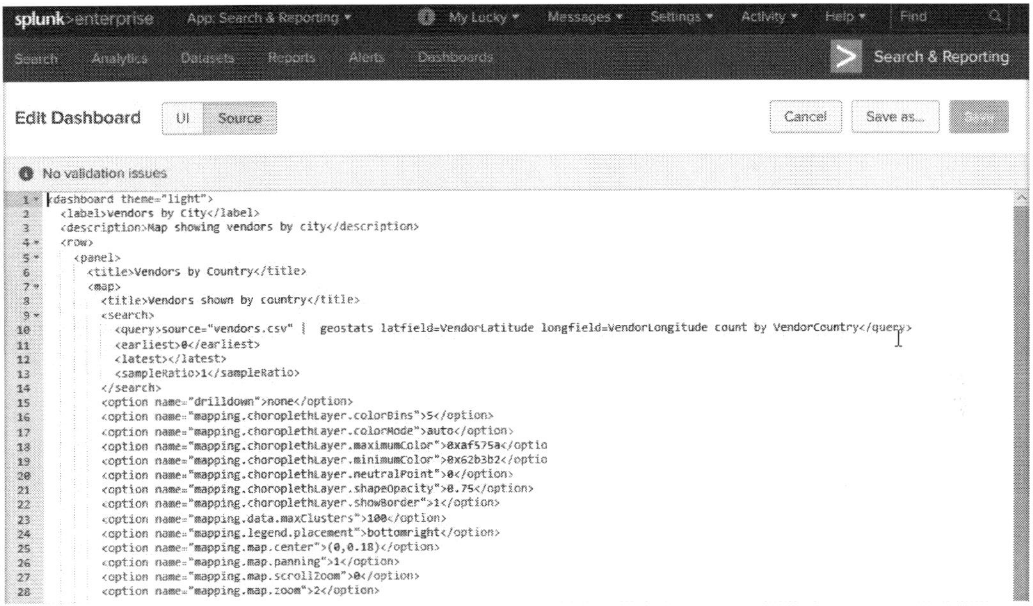

Fig 15.16 – Dashboard source code

In the edit source area, locate the second set of panel tags, `<panel></panel>`, where our new search/statistics table is defined and make sure the bold lines shown in the following snippet match:

```
<panel>
        <title>Top 100 Vendors</title>
        <table>
            <title>Our Vendors on a heatmap</title>
        <search>
            <query>source="vendors.csv" | top limit=100 Vendor</query>
            <earliest>0</earliest>
            <latest></latest>
        </search>
        <option name="dataOverlayMode">heatmap</option>
        <option name="drilldown">none</option>
```

344 Dashboards – Custom Visualizations

```
        <option name="refresh.display">progressbar</option>
        <option name="rowNumbers">true</option>
        <option name="wrap">true</option>
    </table>
</panel>
```

Once you have saved the code, click back on **UI**. We should now see our updated dashboard, exhibiting a cluster map visualization on the left and a statistics table with a heat map overlay visualization on the right:

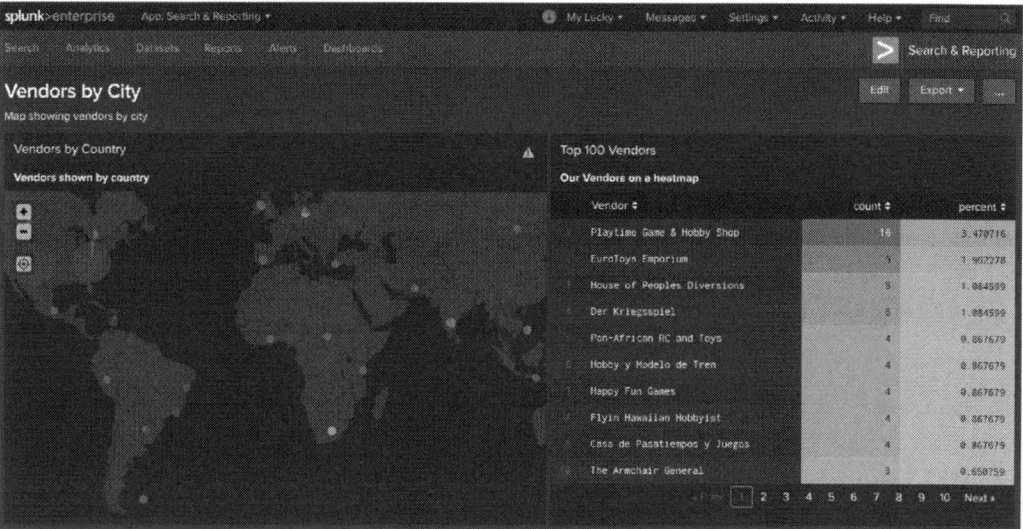

Fig 15.17 – Heat map visualization

Beautiful!

Adding images and icons

One more final edit before we move on to exploring the Beta app version of the Splunk dashboard editor. As we did in *Chapter 11, Advanced Data Analytics*, let's add an image to our dashboard.

Once again, click on **Edit** then **Source** and just after the first `<panel>` tag, insert the following lines of code:

```
<html>
<center>
<img src="/static/app/search/images1.png" alt="miner man"></img>
</center>
</html>
```

> **Note**
> Make sure you download the image (`images1.png`) and put the image file in the following path,
> `$SPLUNK_HOME/etc/apps/search/appserver/static`, then restart Splunk.

Next, click **Save** and sit back and admire our little interactive Splunk dashboard:

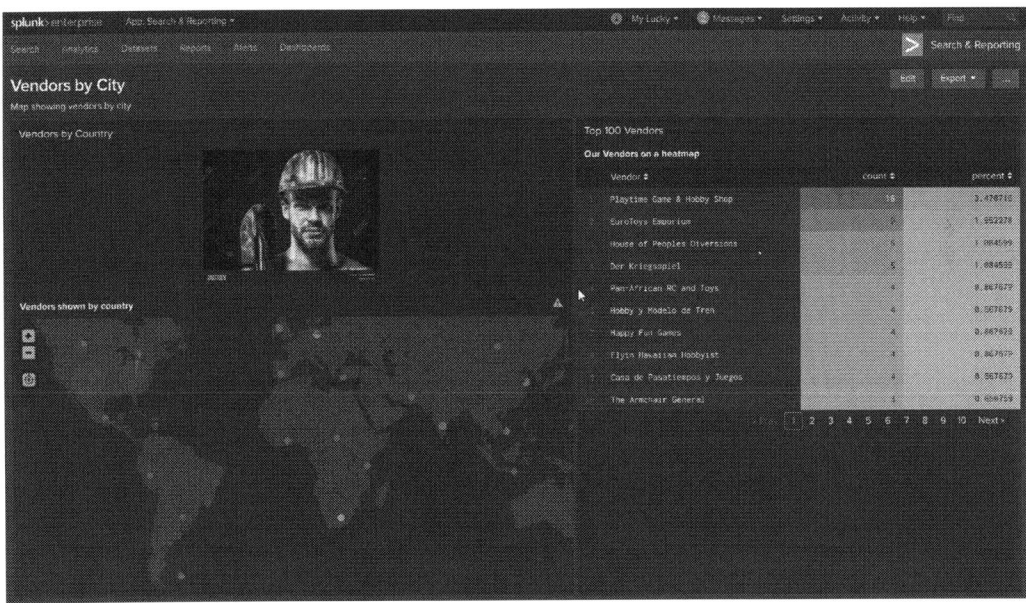

Fig 15.18 – Images added to the dashboard

Thus far in this chapter, we have used the existing Splunk dashboard editor to create and edit a pretty nice, yet simple, dynamic Splunk dashboard. In the next section, we will explore the latest version of the Splunk dashboard editor and try out some of its features to construct another working dashboard example.

Exploring the Beta app

The Splunk **Beta** app dashboard editor is available as of this writing online at `https://splunkbase.splunk.com/app/4710`.

The new Splunk dashboard app is an entirely new tool for developing dashboards and visualizations.

Constructed using an entirely different framework than classic dashboards, this (still in beta) app offers an entirely different visual editing experience, providing the ability to add and customize shapes, icons, text, and images (as well as supporting most classic visualizations), all on a drag-and-drop canvas editor. The new app also permits you to control the dashboard background (either via the use of color or by customizing it by adding background images). In addition, you can easily change visualization configurations in the side panel visual editor or in the new source editor.

This is all possible since the new beta dashboard app is built using JSON modules and not using XML (as the current Splunk dashboards are).

You install the app in the normal fashion, and once installed, it should appear under **Apps** from the main Splunk page (clearly marked **Beta**) as shown in the following screenshot:

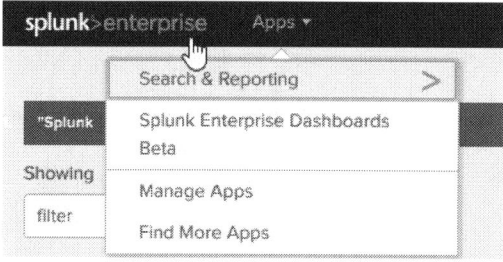

Fig 15.19 – Accessing the Beta dashboard

Exploring the Beta app 347

Clicking on **Splunk Enterprise Dashboards Beta** launches the startup or main page:

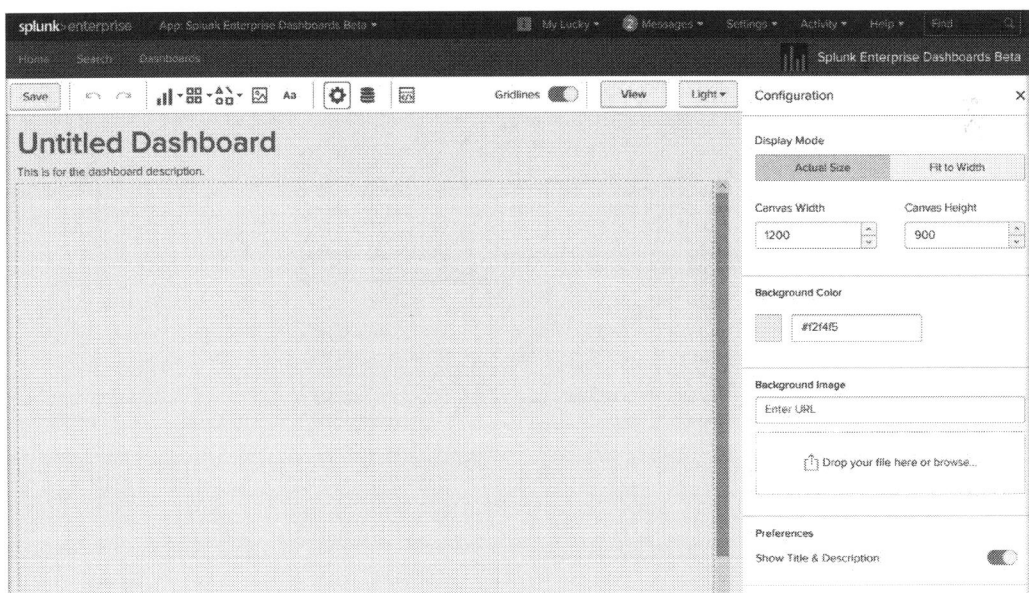

Fig 15.20 – The home page of the Beta dashboard

Let's jump right in by clicking on **+ Create a New Dashboard**. Right off, we see a very different workspace, known as the **visual editor**:

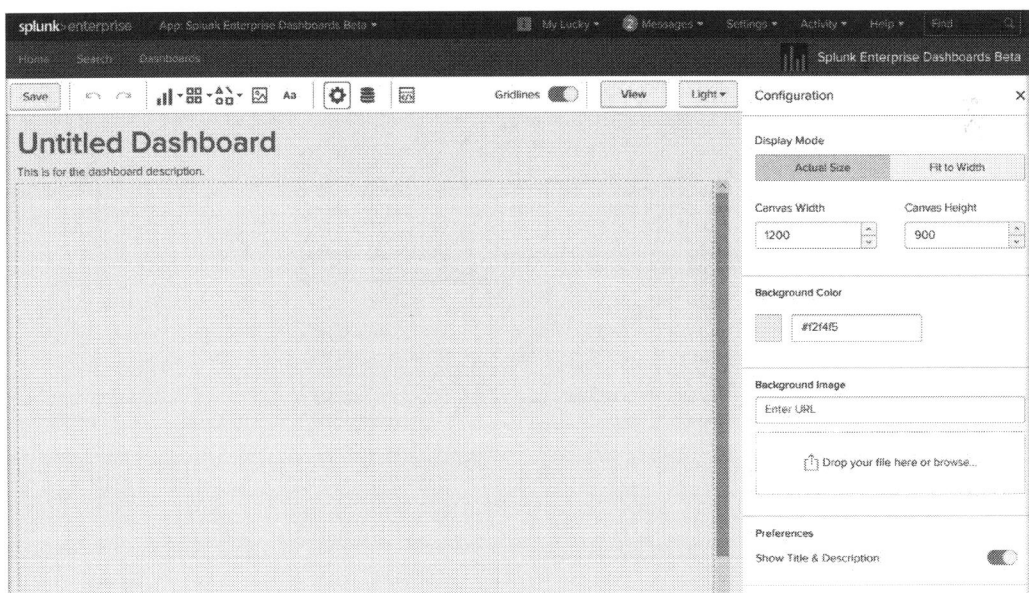

Fig 15.21 – The new dashboard editor workspace

The steps to finish creating a new dashboard in the new editor are pretty simple—give your dashboard a title, set its security (share/private), choose the theme (light/dark), and click **Save**. In the beta, to access and edit the dashboard source code, you can click on the source icon found on the editing toolbar.

Converting an existing dashboard

It is implied that, should the beta editor become part of the actual product, most of your existing dashboards would need to continue to work (within the Splunk environment) and be able to be converted so as to be able to edit and modify them with the new editor.

Let's try to convert the dashboard we created earlier in this chapter. To do this, you select the dashboard from the **Dashboards** page in the **Search & Reporting** app:

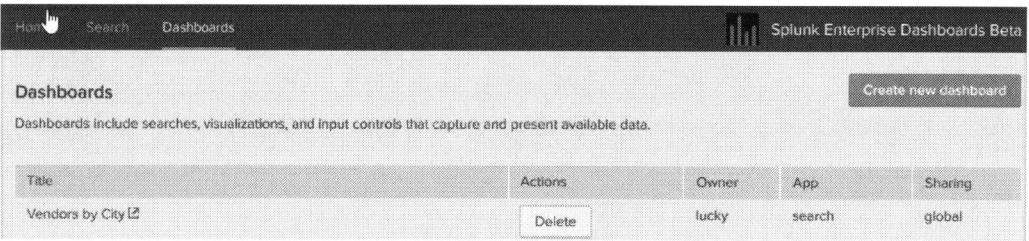

Fig 15.22 – Converting an existing dashboard

Click the ellipses (**...**) next to **Edit** and **Export** (shown in the following screenshot) and select **Open in Dashboard App (beta)** if the option is available. The dashboard will be cloned in the Splunk dashboards Beta app so that you will not lose the original dashboard:

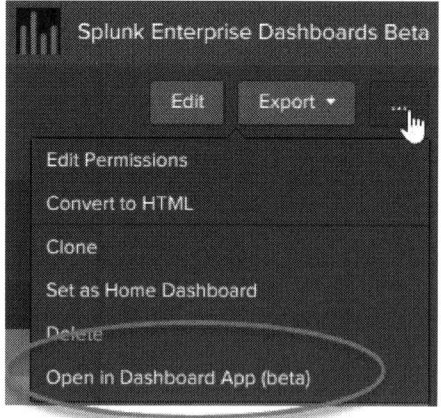

Fig 15.23 – Cloning the existing dashboard

The following screenshot shows our converted dashboard. Immediately, we see that one of our visualizations—the cluster map—didn't get converted because it is currently not supported in the beta dashboard editor:

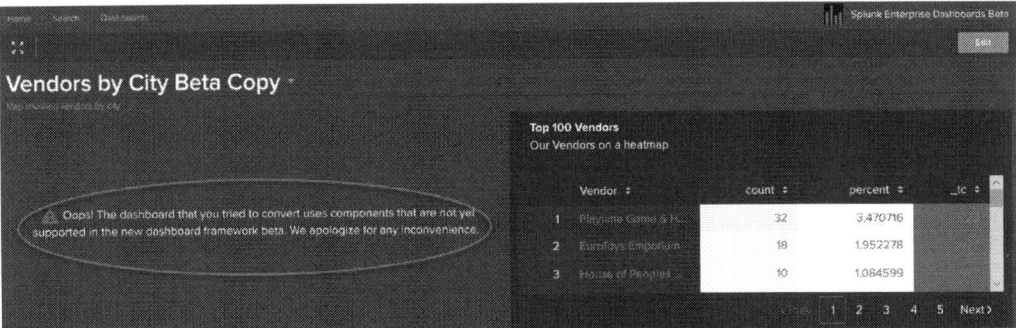

Fig 15.24 – New dashboard

Now, until we actually save it, we have a clone of our original dashboard. You can click on **Edit** to make modifications to it.

In the next sections, we will look at some of the features and functionalities of the new editor.

Resizing the canvas

The new dashboard editor canvas is reported to have default dimensions of 1920x1080 pixels, which is different than the *classic* Splunk dashboard editor. After conversion, you may need to refit or manually change the dimensions of the canvas in pixels. To do that, you can click anywhere on the canvas that does not contain a visualization and then change **Display Mode**:

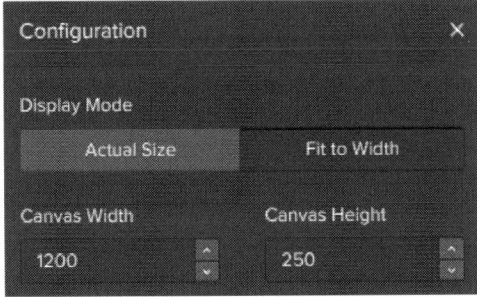

Fig 15.25 – Resizing the canvas

Actual Size displays the actual size in pixels and **Fit to Width** forces the canvas to take up the entire window. You can also change the dimensions of the canvas in pixels, using the **Canvas Width** and **Canvas Height** fields.

Setting a custom background

Believe it not, the background of a dashboard is important since it has a significant contribution to its overall look and feel. The background previously could be set by themes (dark or light). Using the new editor, you can choose both a color/custom color, as well as adding a custom image to the canvas background.

The default color is transparent. You can change it easily by clicking the dashboard canvas grid, then using the color palette:

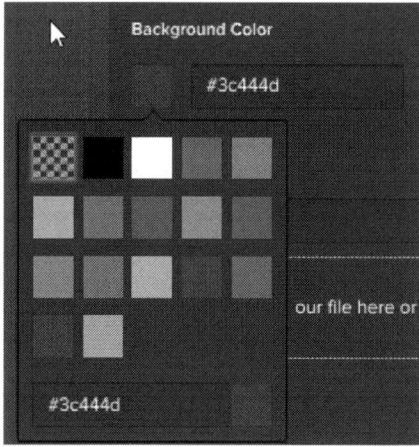

Fig 15.26 – Setting the background color

To add an image to a dashboard background, you can designate a `.JPG` and `.PNG` image file for the dashboard by using drag and drop, clicking **Browse...** (to navigate to a file), or even specifying a URL for web-based images:

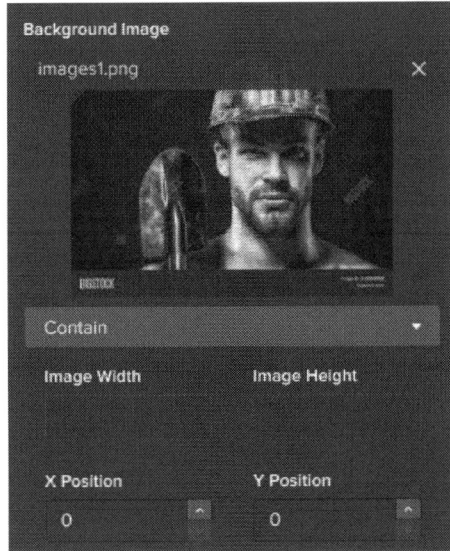

Fig 15.27 – Setting a custom image background

The drop-down selector under the image provides you with the ability to set some basic constraints on the image. For example, selecting **Contain** fits the image to the canvas width, **Cover** covers the entire canvas with the image, and **Custom** positions the image on the x axis and y axis and allows you to change the width and height in pixels.

Images are a bit tricky in that sizing and positioning may not always be optimal, but you can adjust and configure the sizing options to suit, click **View** to preview things, and then click **Save** when you have the dashboard looking like you want:

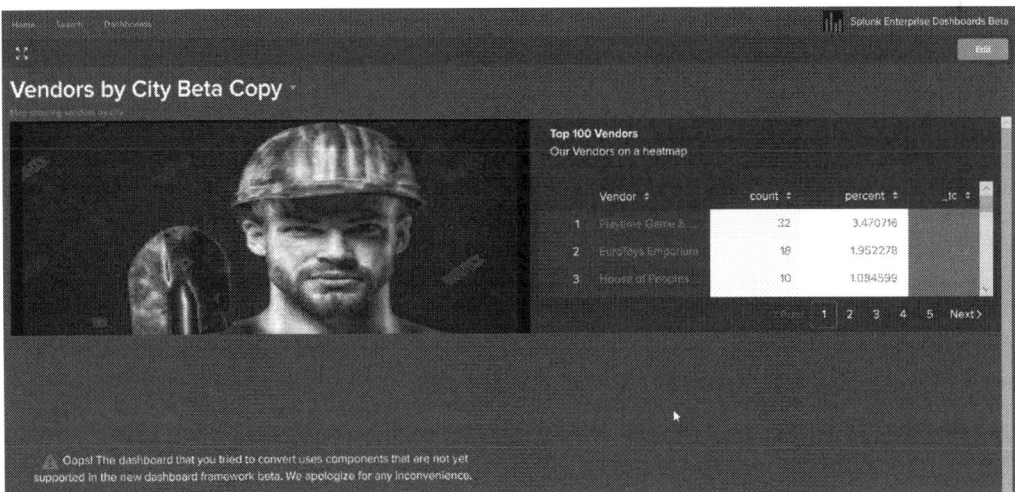

Fig 15.28 – New dashboard with the custom background

There we have our new dashboard with the custom image as the background.

The dashboard editing bar

You can use the dashboard editing bar (shown in the following screenshot) to add visualizations to the dashboard and then the **Configuration** panel to set most of the formatting options for those visualizations, similar to how we used the **Configuration** panel to set the background color and images in the preceding section:

Fig 15.29 – Dashboard editing bar

Some visualization options can only be set using the source code editor we mentioned when we first opened the beta dashboard editor. This is similar to the process we used earlier in this chapter when we added the heat map overlay visualization code to the dashboard example.

Editing the visualization source code

When we add a visualization to a Splunk dashboard, Splunk generates corresponding JSON code within the dashboard definition and gives it a unique ID (you'll see in the following code snippet, our heat map was assigned `"table_1"`). Most Splunk visualizations use the same general format. For example, the following code is what was generated from our converted dashboard's heatmap visualization. Hopefully, you will recognize some of the code values:

```
"table_1": {
        "type": "viz.table",
        "options": {
            "dataOverlayMode": "heatmap",
            "drilldown": "none",
            "refresh.display": "progressbar",
            "rowNumbers": true,
            "wrap": true
        },
        "dataSources": {
            "primary": "search_2"
        },
        "title": "Top 100 Vendors",
```

```
             "description": "Our Vendors on a heatmap"
        }
```

The interesting section in the preceding code is the `"options"` section. Some of these options can be set using the dashboard editor, but all options can be added and/or edited directly in the source code. Of course, these options vary, based upon the type of visualization.

Comparing the old and new editor

Take a minute and compare the underlying dashboard code within the existing Splunk dashboard editor (shown on the left) and the beta dashboard editor (on the right):

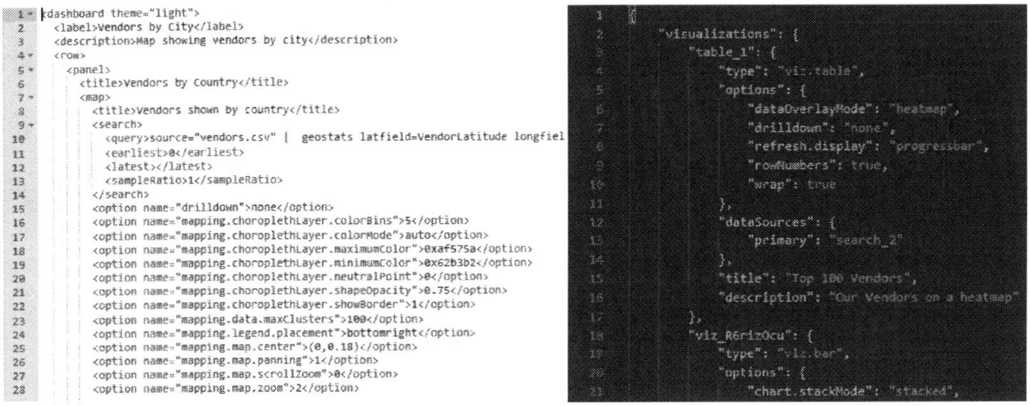

Fig 15.30 – Comparing the old and new editor

The concept is generally the same, in that code can be autogenerated by Splunk and then edited and/or enhanced directly in the dashboard editor.

Adding a visualization

Before we add a new visualization to our dashboard. Let's delete the map that didn't convert to our beta dashboard. To remove the broken visualization, simply click on it to select it and then hit the *delete* key. Gone!

354　Dashboards – Custom Visualizations

Now, to add a new visualization to our dashboard, we can click on the first graphical icon and select **Comparisons | Bar**:

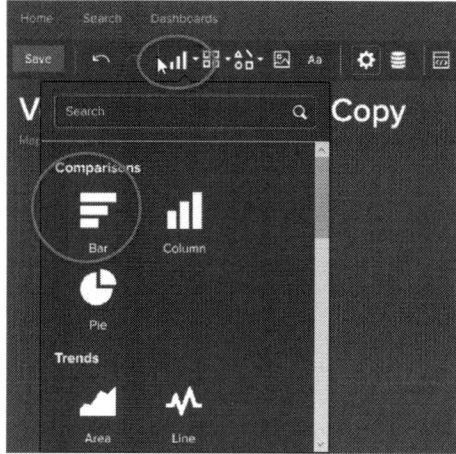

Fig 15.31 – Adding bar graphs

Next, in the configuration section, paste in a search command (you can leave the **Data Source Name** and **Time Range** default values):

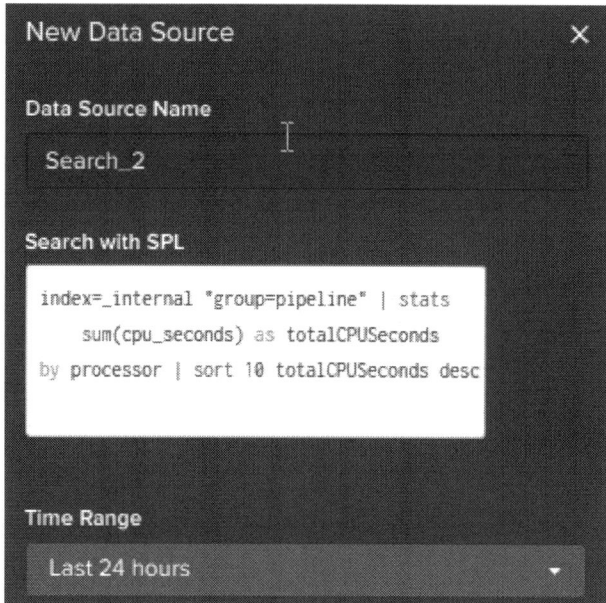

Fig 15.32 – Setting the visualization configuration

Once you've set up your data source (the search), you can review and change the visualization options of the **Configuration** panel to change the visualization type (from a bar) and view and/or set some other options, such as adding a title and description:

Fig 15.33 – Reviewing and changing the configuration

> **Note**
> When you make changes to options in the **Configuration** panel, those changes are reflected in real time on the dashboard.

After reviewing and updating the **Configuration** panel, you can use your mouse to position and resize the new visualization on the dashboard (we'll have to change our dashboard title and caption now, since it doesn't make much sense since we dropped the broken map visualization):

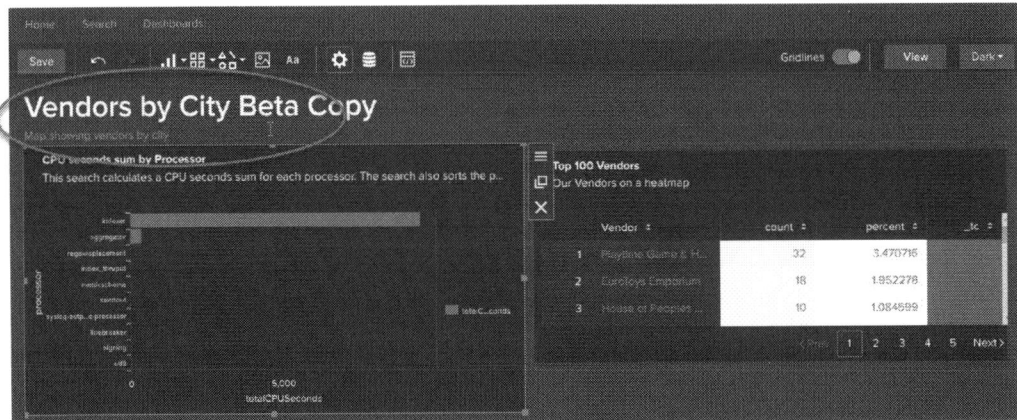

Fig 15.34 – Positioning and resizing the panels

Take a moment to click back into the dashboard source code editor, review the `"visualizations"` section, and find the new visualization section, `"viz_R6riz0cu"`:

```
"visualizations": {
    "table_1": {
        "type": "viz.table",
        "options": {
            "dataOverlayMode": "heatmap",
            "drilldown": "none",
            "refresh.display": "progressbar",
            "rowNumbers": true,
            "wrap": true
        },
        "dataSources": {
            "primary": "search_2"
        },
        "title": "Top 100 Vendors",
        "description": "Our Vendors on a heatmap"
    },
    "viz_R6riz0cu": {
        "type": "viz.bar",
        "options": {},
        "dataSources": {
            "primary": "ds_zJYlPgFc"
        },
        "title": "CPU seconds sum by Processor",
        "description": "This search calculates a CPU seconds sum for each processor. The search also sorts the processors with the ten highest sums in descending order."
    }
},
```

There are many more features within the new Splunk dashboard editor that you can (and should) explore.

Summary

In this chapter, we went over the idea of creating a dynamic look and feel for a Splunk dashboard, touched on using the current dashboard editor to create a dashboard, and spent some time editing the dashboard source code, trying drag and drop, (adding) images and icons, and finally, introduced the new, but still beta, Splunk dashboard app.

The next chapter introduces the Splunk **Machine Learning Toolkit (MLTK)** as an extension to the core Splunk platform; adding new SPL commands, macros, and visualizations.

Section 4: What Next?

This section covers the topic of machine learning with Splunk by introducing the Splunk **Machine Learning Toolkit** (**MLTK**) and providing instructions on accessing and installing, as well as the basic use of, the kit. Additionally, this section moves forward by providing an overview of the topic of Splunk Next, as well as a brief summary of each of its offerings. Finally, the section delves into adding the SplunkJS Stack libraries to a website, enabling the use of numerous web framework components, which can assist in interacting with and viewing Splunk data.

This section comprises the following chapters:

- *Chapter 16, Machine Learning Overview*
- *Chapter 17, Splunk Next*
- *Chapter 18, Dashboards – SplunkJS*

16 Machine Learning Overview

In the previous chapter, we covered creating various custom visualizations as well as updating existing dashboards using features such as *drag and drop* and performed a *test drive* of the Splunk beta UI-based dashboard editor.

In this chapter, we will focus on providing an overview of approaching the topic of machine learning with Splunk, introducing the Splunk **Machine Learning Toolkit** (**MLTK**), and provide instructions on accessing, installing, and the basic use of the kit using an illustrative use case.

The chapter will be broken down into the following main sections:

- Machine learning with Splunk
- Overview of the Splunk MLTK
- Implementing an MLTK use case

Machine learning with Splunk

The machine learning capabilities found in the latest version of the Splunk enterprise platform add to an already existing set of very useful data analysis features. They are not simply *black boxes* or difficult sophisticated algorithms, but easy to use tools that put deep data science and machine learning expertise to use.

Now, with the arrival of the Splunk MLTK, you have access to popular machine learning algorithms and can be productive almost immediately.

> **Note**
> Just to be clear, this chapter is not meant to teach machine learning or even explain how the various ML algorithms work but more to illustrate how powerful the Splunk MLTK is and how easy it is to install, configure, use, and understand.

Overview of the Splunk MLTK

The Splunk MLTK enables you to detect, predict, and prevent in areas that are important to your organization. Modeling **assistants** (maybe better understood as **wizards**), interactive practical examples, and tutorials (including videos) help you get going and create and operationalize your own predictive analytics, almost immediately, right out of the box.

What is the MLTK?

An **app** is an **application** that runs on the Splunk platform, and the MLTK is actually a Splunk-supported app available on Splunkbase for download, installation, and use.

Installation

The toolkit (available directly online at `https://splunkbase.splunk.com/app/2890`, or go to the Splunk main page, under **Apps**, and select **Find More Apps**) is a Splunk-supported app and is installed just like any other Splunk app (note that there will be a restart of Splunk required after downloading):

Overview of the Splunk MLTK   363

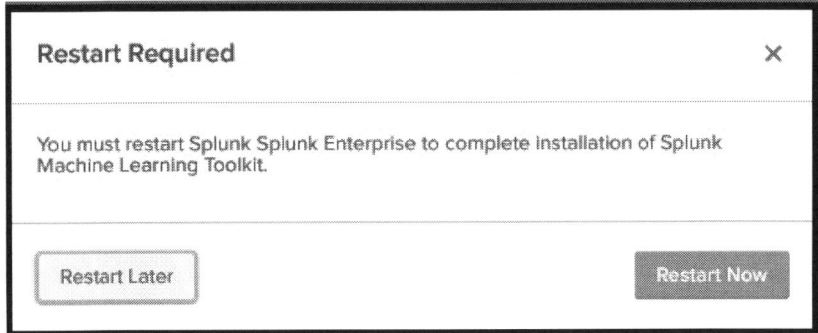

Figure 16.1 – Splunk restart after installing the Splunk MLTK

After the restart, the Splunk MLTK appears in the list as an available app:

Figure 16.2 – List of available apps

> **Note**
> To successfully run the Splunk MLTK, you need Splunk version 8.0 and you must install the **Python for Scientific Computing** add-on. You can download and install the Windows version from https://splunkbase.splunk.com/app/2883.

The Splunk MLTK is designed to enable users to create, validate, manage, and operationalize machine learning models – all through a guided user interface, without having to take the time and expense to implement a library of ML algorithms and infrastructure to run them against data. Throughout the rest of this chapter, we'll see how to install the kit, get it up and running, and create a few models.

> **Some interesting background**
>
> Machine learning is sometimes referred to as a process for generalizing using example or training data and these generalizations are also called **models** and are used to perform a variety of tasks, such as predicting the value of a field, forecasting future values, identifying patterns in data, and detecting anomalies from new data.

Opening the MLTK app

Once you open the MLTK app, you'll notice the convenient MLTK navigation bar (as shown in the following screenshot):

Figure 16.3 – MLTK navigation bar

The Splunk MLTK navigation bar includes eight tabs:

- **Showcase**
- **Experiments**
- **Search**
- **Models**
- **Classic**
- **Settings**
- **Docs**
- **Video Tutorials**

All of these tabs are worth investigating, particularly **Showcase**, which provides examples using the MLTK pre-populated with a sample dataset and then demonstrates the results.

The **Showcase** examples are organized by ML operation and industry:

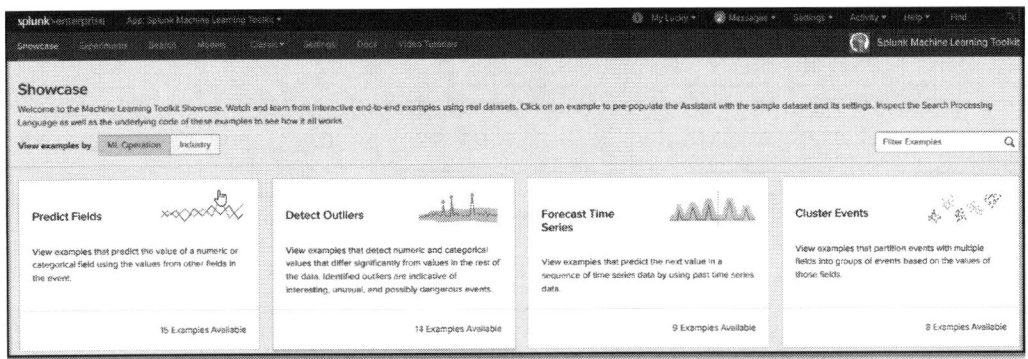

Figure 16.4 – Showcase examples

> **Tip**
> You can investigate MLTK features and the specifics of the navigation bar online at https://docs.splunk.com/Documentation/MLApp/5.2.0/User/AboutMLTK.

In the next sections of this chapter, we will use a practical use case to test drive the MLTK app and illustrate some of the features and functionalities the kit provides.

Implementing an MLTK use case

The scenario of our use case is that of an information technology services organization that makes its money by managing technology projects for customers. Obviously, there are a lot of factors that affect the profitability of a project and the executives of the firm are keen to identify which of those factors may have a positive effect on the net profit earned for upcoming projects.

The data we'll use for this exercise would have been extracted from a project-details database (as a **comma-separated value** (**CSV**) file) that includes one record per completed project (or one event), with each record containing various fields.

The following are the fields:

- Net Profit: This is the calculated net profit for a completed project.
- No Resources: As the number of technical resources assigned to the project changes during the life of the project, this number is the average number of resources working on the project at any given time.

- `Project Budget`: This is the total budgeted dollars in thousands to complete the project.
- `Amt on Travel`: This is the average amount spent on travel during the project.
- `Size of Organization`: This is the average number of full-time employees employed at the organization during the life of the project.
- `No of Competing Projects`: This is the number of other projects that were also active during the life of the project.

The following screenshot is a partial view of the file:

	A	B	C	D	E	F	G
1	Net Profit	No Resources	Project Budget	Amt on Travel	Size of Organization	No of Competing Projects	
2	231	3.0	294	8.2	8.2	11	
3	156	2.2	232	6.9	4.1	12	
4	10	0.5	149	3.0	4.3	15	
5	519	5.5	600	12.0	16.1	1	
6	437	4.4	567	10.6	14.1	5	
7	487	4.8	571	11.8	12.7	4	
8	299	3.1	512	8.1	10.1	10	
9	195	2.5	347	7.7	8.4	12	

Figure 16.5 – Partial view of the file

Now let's see what the MLTK can help us with.

What questions can the MLTK help with?

The executives of the organization are looking to understand the relationship between the calculated `Net Profit` value of each project and how it may be impacted by the `No Resources`, `Project Budget`, `Amt on Travel`, `Size of Organization`, and `No of Competing Projects` variables.

For example, would an increase in `Project Budget` or `Amt on Travel` increase or decrease `Net Profit` for a project? An assumption might be that perhaps projects with smaller budgets might cut out or reduce time spent on various project tasks, thus creating risk, or another assumption may be that spending less on travel – meaning less time directly interacting with the customer – may also cause difficulties.

In the next few sections, we will go through the steps required to use the Splunk MLTK app to help answer these questions. What is very exciting is that even if you have not been practicing data science for the past several years or aren't completely fluent in many machine learning algorithms, you can still be productive with the Splunk MLTK.

Uploading the data

So, first, our data (the CSV file) needs to be uploaded to Splunk so we can use it in our MLTK exercise. Since this file has been purposely extracted from another data source with the intention of being used as a sort of table of actual results, we will load it as a Splunk lookup table.

> **Note**
> Lookup tables are a matrix or mapping containing keys and corresponding values.

To load our data as a Splunk lookup table, from the Splunk main page, click on **Settings**, then **Lookups**, and then **Lookup table files**, and then finally, **Add new**. Be sure to save the file as projectSense.csv.

Once the file has been uploaded and saved, you can then navigate to the MLTK app (click on **Apps**, then **Splunk Machine Learning Toolkit**).

Once the app is loaded, click on the **Classic** menu, then **Assistants**, and finally, **Predict Numeric Fields**.

Since we have established that we want to predict what the net profit of a project may be – a numeric value – the **Predict Numeric Fields Experiment Assistant** option will come in handy. This selection is designed and built to use a selected machine learning regression algorithm to predict a numeric value from other fields in an event and determine how certain peripheral factors might contribute to a particular result.

In this use case, the technology project is the event, and fields such as Project Budget and Amt on Travel are some of the **peripheral factors** that will be considered as possible effectors of a project's net profit.

Populating model fields

On the MLTK **Predict Numeric Fields** page, under **Enter a search**, you can view the contents of the CSV file we uploaded by running the following Splunk search command in the search bar:

```
| inputlookup MyprojectSense.csv
```

The Splunk inputlookup command is used to search the contents of a lookup table. The lookup table can be a CSV lookup or a KV store lookup. In our case, it is the MyprojectSense.csv file we just uploaded.

The following screenshot is a view of the **Predict Numeric Fields** page showing our search command:

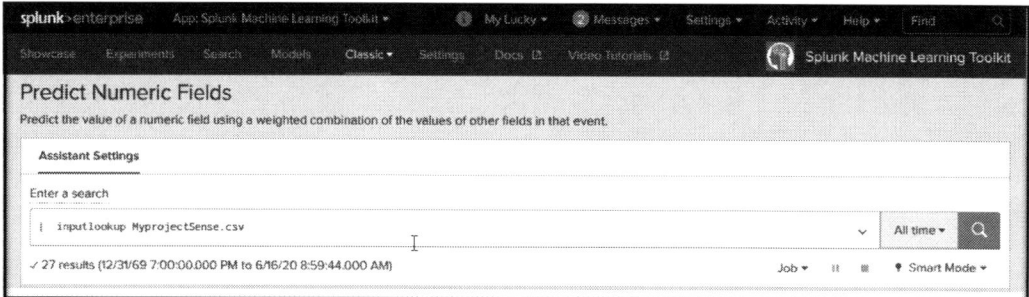

Figure 16.6 – Predict Numeric Fields page

Running the preceding search will populate the **Raw Data Preview** panel (as shown in the following screenshot) at the bottom of the page:

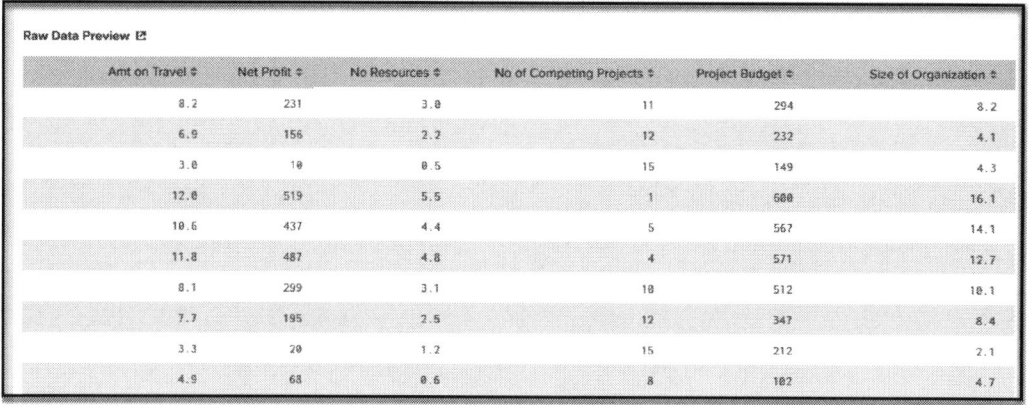

Figure 16.7 – Raw Data Preview panel

Below the **Preprocessing Steps** panel, we can see another panel where you can choose the type of algorithm to apply to this data, as well as the **Fields to predict** and **Fields to use for predicting** options (as well as other details):

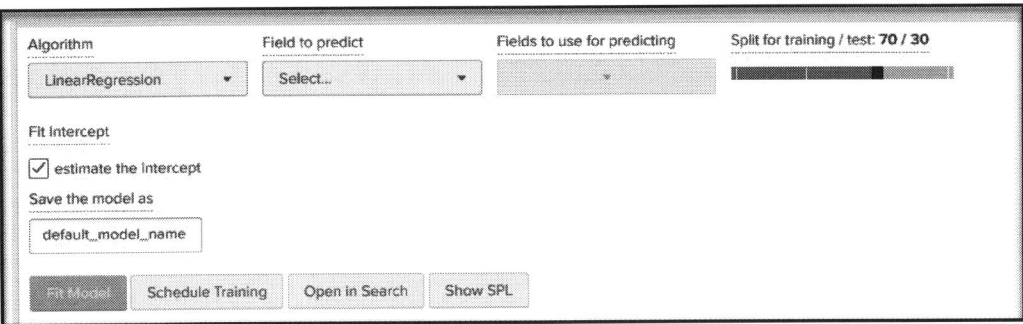

Figure 16.8 – Panel to select the algorithm

Now we have to select a machine learning algorithm for the MLTK to run on our data.

Selecting the algorithm

The **Predict Numeric Fields** experiment assistant supports the use of the following algorithms:

- LinearRegression
- RandomForestRegressor
- Lasso
- KernelRidge
- ElasticNet
- Ridge
- DecisionTreeRegressor

Some (algorithms) will fit better than others. The goal is to find and use the machine learning algorithm that is the most accurate at, or fits best for (in this use case), predicting a project's net profit.

An algorithm's performance will depend on the data and can be calculated and reviewed for each of the algorithms using the Splunk MLTK – which we will see soon.

In the panel where we select the algorithm (shown in the screenshot that follows), notice that the **Fields to predict** and **Fields to use for predicting** drop-down selectors are automatically populated from the data when we ran the search earlier.

Now we can go ahead and select **Net Profit** and all of the other fields respectively:

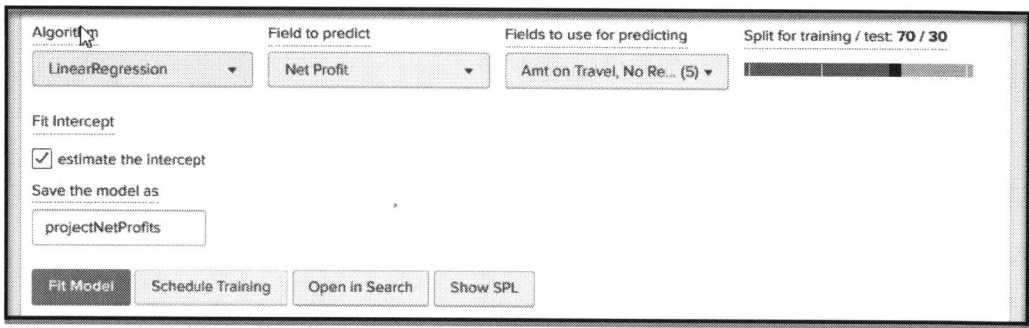

Figure 16.9 – Setting the other fields

For this use case, we can try the first-listed machine learning algorithm, the `LinearRegression` algorithm, and see how it fits for forecasting the net profit of potential projects. One more item: enter a name under **Save the model as**. I used `projectNetProfits` (more on model naming later in this chapter).

Fitting the model

Also, in the same panel, you need to set the **Split for Training** ratio. Let's just select **no split** for this use case. This indicates that the selected machine learning algorithm should use all of the data (in our `CSV` file) to create the model and generate the predictions.

To set the split, a horizontal slider is used (as shown in the following screenshot):

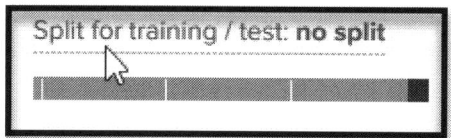

Figure 16.10 – Horizontal slider

Finally, to actually run the selected algorithm on the data, we can click on **Fit Model**. Splunk will then process the data and display visualizations that can be used to determine the performance of the selected algorithm as well as helping with any assumptions we've made about the data (in other words, would an increase in `Project Budget` or `Amt on Travel` increase or decrease `Net Profit` for a project?).

In the following screenshot, you can see **no split** selected and the highlighted **Fit Model** button:

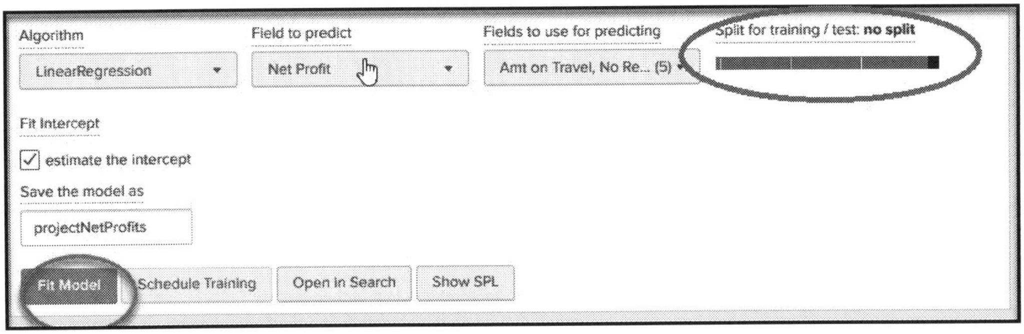

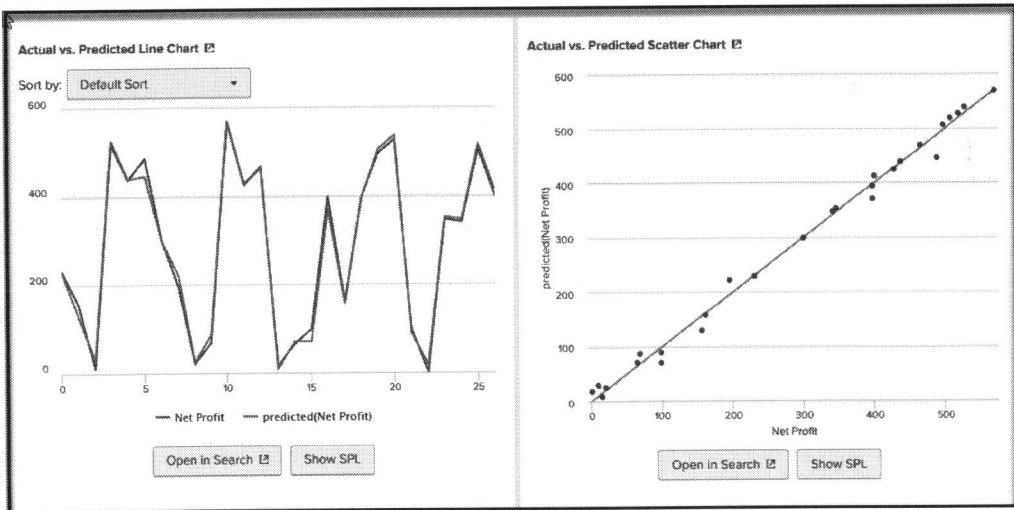

Figure 16.11 – Fitting the model

Now that we have fitted our model, let's look at the results.

Looking at the results

When the processing is completed, the first two resultant MLTK panels (shown in the following screenshot) show a side-by-side line chart and a scatter chart of actual project profit versus predicted project profit:

Figure 16.12 – MLTK result panels

372　Machine Learning Overview

Both of these panels present approaches to analyzing the performance of the linear regression model (that is, the results of running the linear regression algorithm against our data file).

An easier explanation of what we are looking for here is a close relationship between predictions and actual performance. The closer the prediction is to the actual result (the profit), the better (the performance).

The visualizations make it easier to identify whether the data fits or not (or, how well it fits). Since both charts show a close relationship (lines almost overlap each other and points are close to touching the line), it appears that the data fits well.

The second set of MLTK panels (shown in the following screenshot) show the differences between actual and predicted values (*Residual = Observed – Predicted*). These differences are known as **residuals** and are visualized using a **Residuals Line Chart** and a **Residuals Histogram** chart. The visualizations show a large deviation from the center and the residuals appear to be scattered on the charts. A random scattering of the data points typically means a good fit for the linear model:

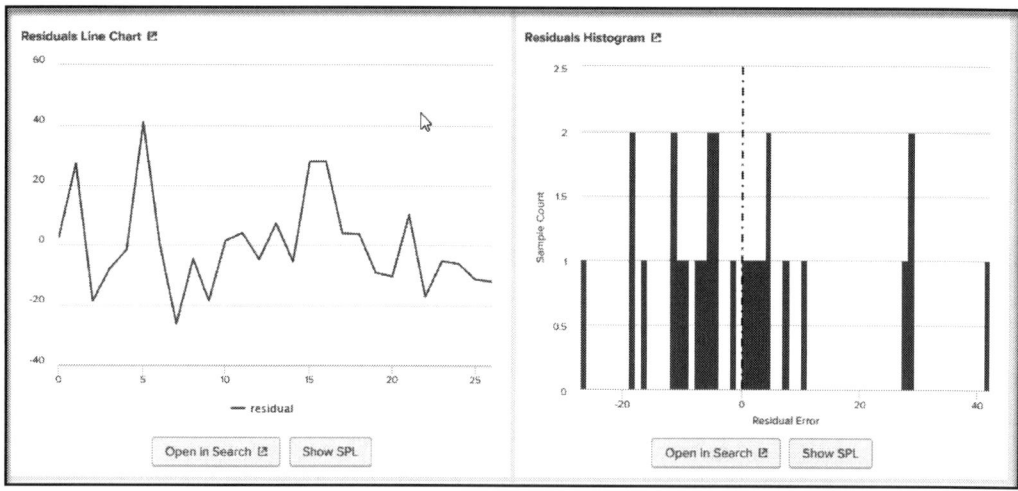

Figure 16.13 – Second set of MLTK result panels

The last set of MLTK panels displayed after the fit completes shows us the R-squared and the fit model parameters summary of the model.

This R-squared statistic shows how well the model explains the variability of the result. 100% (a value of 1) means the model fits perfectly. The closer the R-square value is to 1, the better the fit of the model.

The **Fit Model Parameters Summary** panel displays the coefficients associated with each variable in the regression model. A higher coefficient value shows a higher association of that variable with the result. A negative value shows a negative correlation:

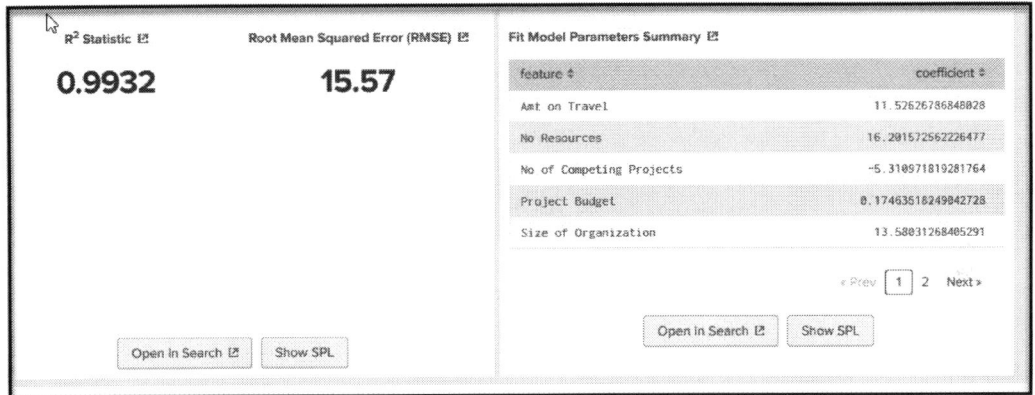

Figure 16.14 – Fit Model Parameters Summary panel

Let's now look at other algorithm options.

Other algorithm options

Circling back to what we mentioned earlier in this chapter about selecting the (best) algorithm to use, here is where we can, within the MLTK, easily go back and select a different algorithm, select the same field to predict (`Net Profit`), and all of the other fields for `Fields to use for predicting`, and simply run that algorithm against our data and compare the resulting visualizations and R-square of the model that is generated to see how it performed versus the previously selected algorithm (`LinearRegression`).

Naming the model

Remember to change the **Save the model as** name, perhaps using something to reflect the selected algorithm, to better identify your models and to prevent over-writing an already saved model. To view the existing models, you can click on **Models** in the Splunk MLTK navigation bar and view the **Models** page (as shown in the following screenshot):

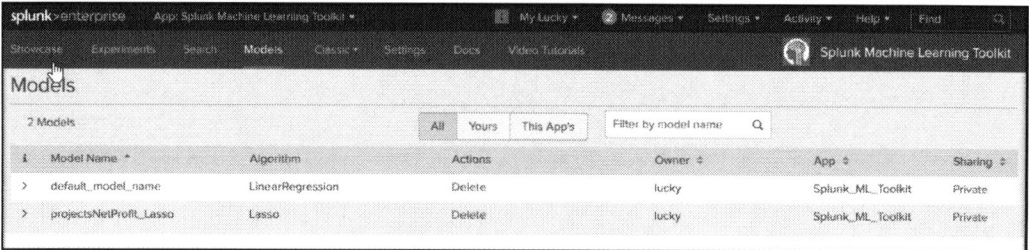

Figure 16.15 – Models page

For this test, we can select the `Lasso` algorithm:

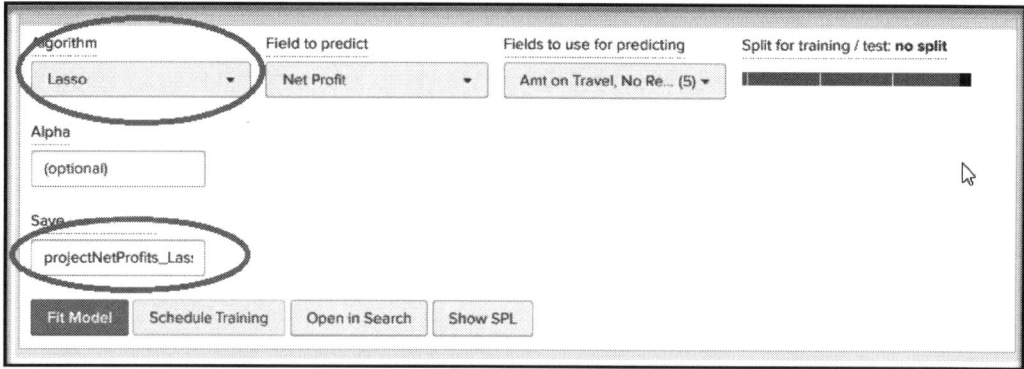

Figure 16.16 – Selecting the Lasso algorithm

Once we (again) fit the model (this time, using the `Lasso` algorithm), we see that the results are very similar to the prior run, and the R-square of the model is only slightly lower.

Here's the first panel set:

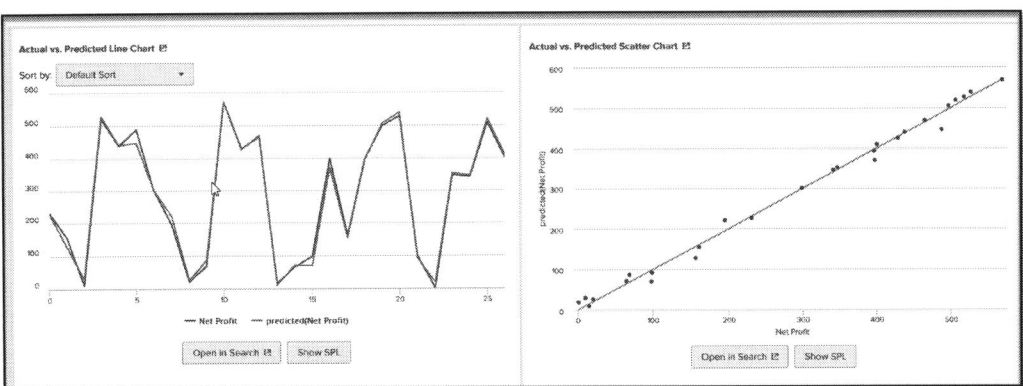

Figure 16.17 – First MLTK result panel

Here's the second panel set:

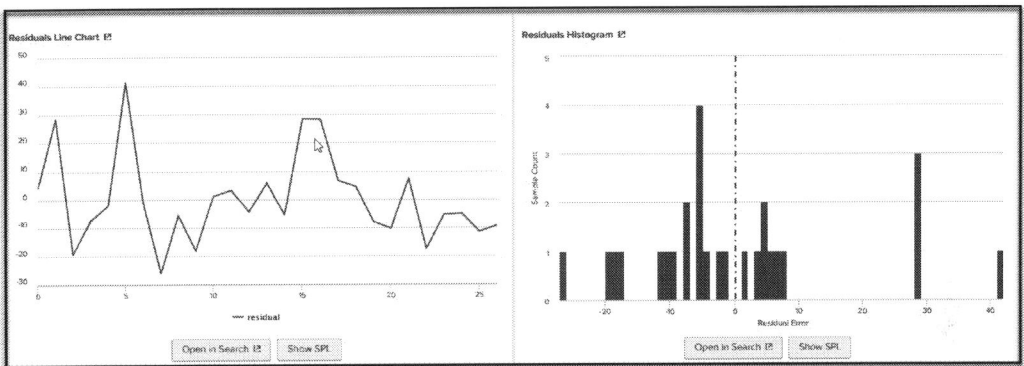

Figure 16.18 – Second MLTK result panel

Here's the third panel set:

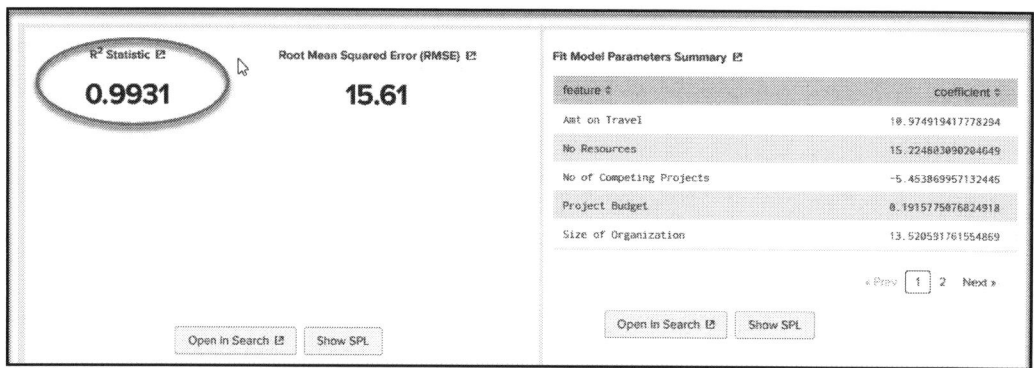

Figure 16.19 – Fit Model Parameters Summary panel

Now that we have named our model and tested the model with the `Lasso` algorithm, let's look at answering questions.

Answering questions

The Splunk MLTK comes with numerous custom search commands, referred to as **ML-SPL** commands. You can use these custom search commands on any Splunk platform instance on which the MLTK is installed.

For example, the `summary` command returns a summary of a machine learning model that was learned using the `fit` command:

```
summary default_model_name
```

The following screenshot is the results of the command on our initial `default_model_name` mode:

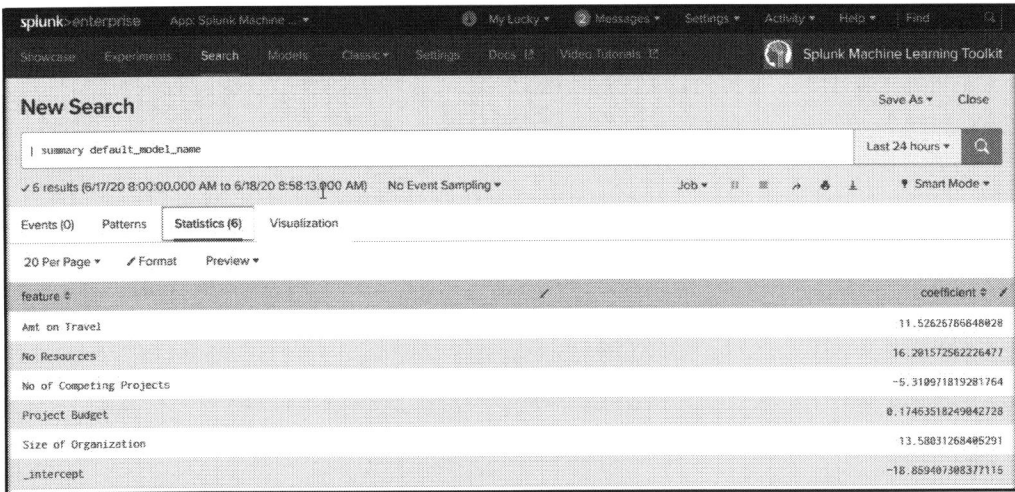

Figure 16.20 – Summary result

And the visualizations of the results are shown in the following screenshot:

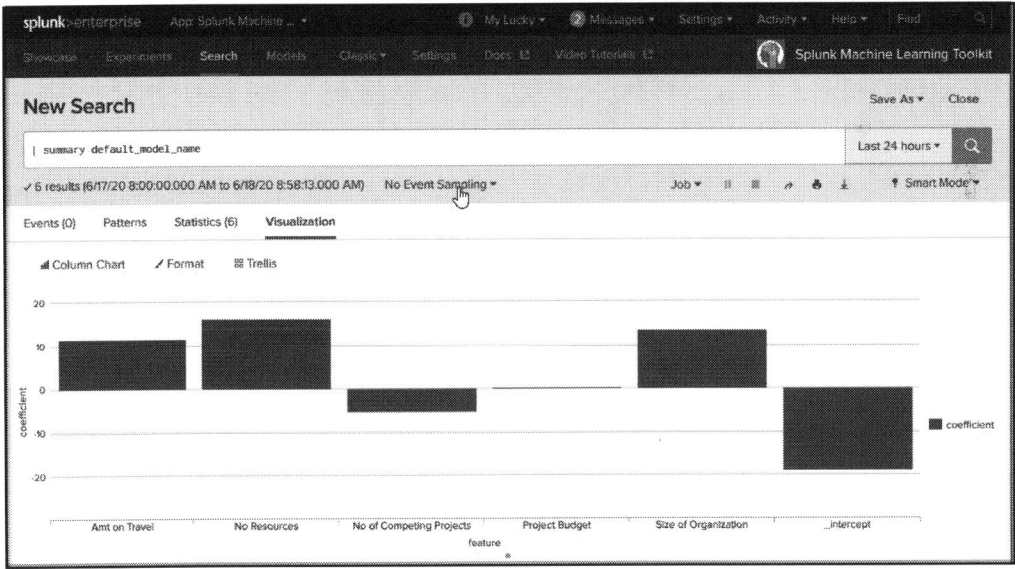

Figure 16.21 – Visualizations of the results

Other MLTK commands include `fit`, `apply`, `summary`, `listmodels`, `deletemodel`, `sample`, and `score`.

> **Info**
>
> You can read about and investigate these commands online at `https://docs.splunk.com/Documentation/MLApp/5.2.0/User/Customsearchcommands`.

In this chapter, we are not trying to teach machine learning or advise on interpreting the results of a machine learning model, rather we are providing a tutorial of sorts to introduce the Splunk MLTK.

With that in mind, we will not dig deeper here into the interpretation of the results of our MLTK generated model but move onto some additional features of the kit.

So, at this point, we have used the Splunk MLTK to do the following:

- Upload sample data as a lookup tablet
- Populate the model fields
- Select an algorithm
- Fit the model
- Analyze the results

Now that we have created a model or two and gained some understanding of how the MLTK works, we can click on the **Experiments** menu in the MLTK navigation bar.

Exploring the Experiments menu

Splunk MLTK experiments bring all aspects of a monitored machine learning pipeline into one interface with automated model versioning and lineage built in.

Once you save an experiment, Splunk creates a new **knowledge object** and keeps track of all the settings and modifications for that experiment.

This saved knowledge object enables you to do the following:

- Organize the experiment around a specific business problem (that is, predicting the net profit of a project)
- Keep all of the *modeling history* and refinements in a single spot

Implementing an MLTK use case 379

After clicking on **Experiments**, click on **Create New Experiment**. The **Create New Experiment** dialog (shown in the following screenshot) will be displayed:

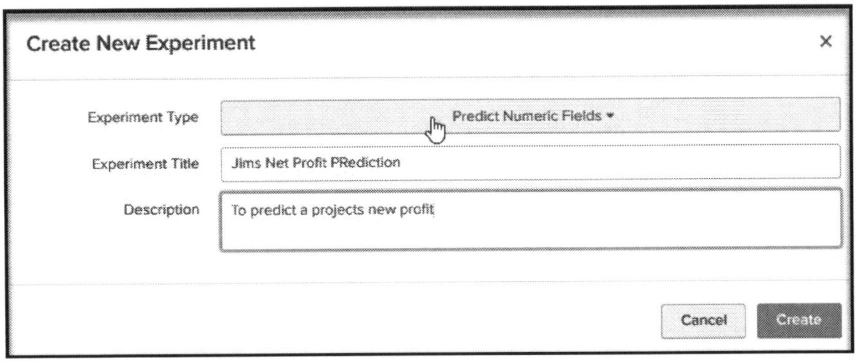

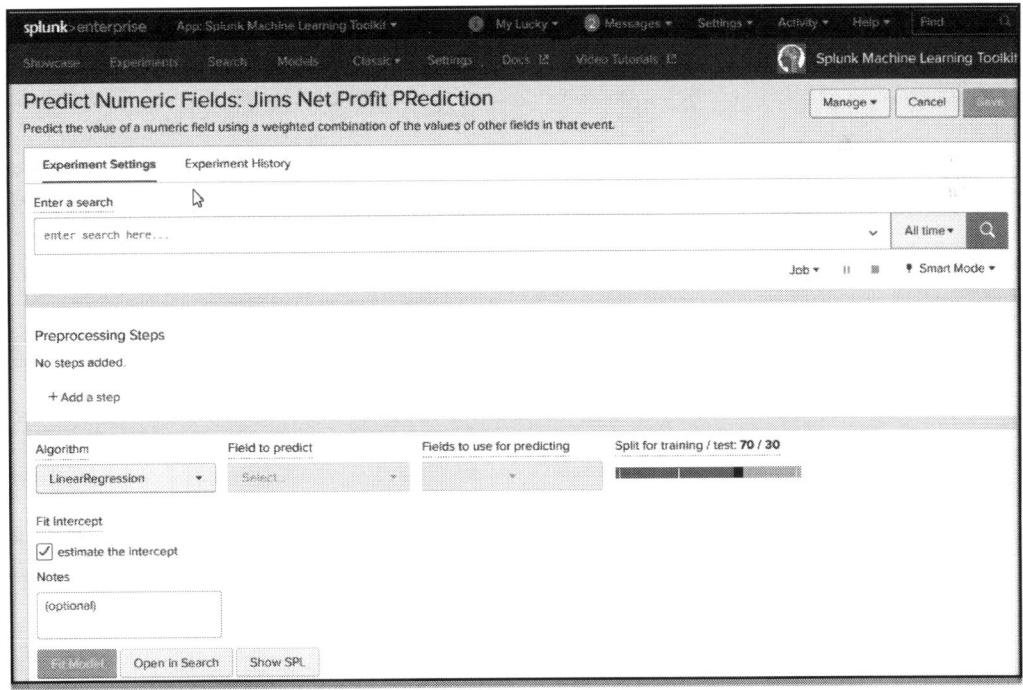

Figure 16.22 – Create New Experiment dialog

For **Experiment Type**, select (as we did earlier) **Predict Numeric Fields**, then add an **Experiment Title** name, a short description, and finally, click **Create**.

The experiment page (shown in the following screenshot) will be displayed. Notice that it is very similar to the model page we used in the preceding sections:

Figure 16.23 – Predict Numeric Fields: Jims Net Profit PRediction page

Notice that the **Save** button is disabled in the preceding screenshot and will be enabled only after a successful model fitting (shown in the following screenshot) is completed. Also note that the experiment is clearly marked as **Draft** (again, until the experiment is successfully saved):

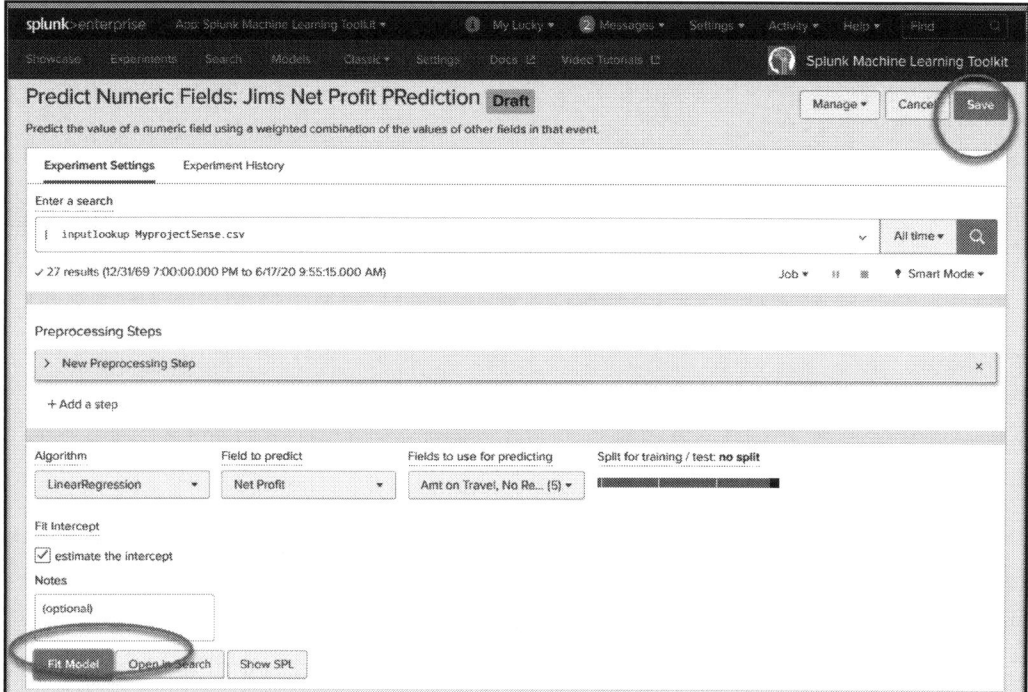

Figure 16.24 – Save enabled

Another feature to be aware of is the **Notes** box (as shown in the screenshot that follows).

With **Notes**, you have the ability to attach comments to your experiment (optionally) to track your changes as you refine and rerun your experiment:

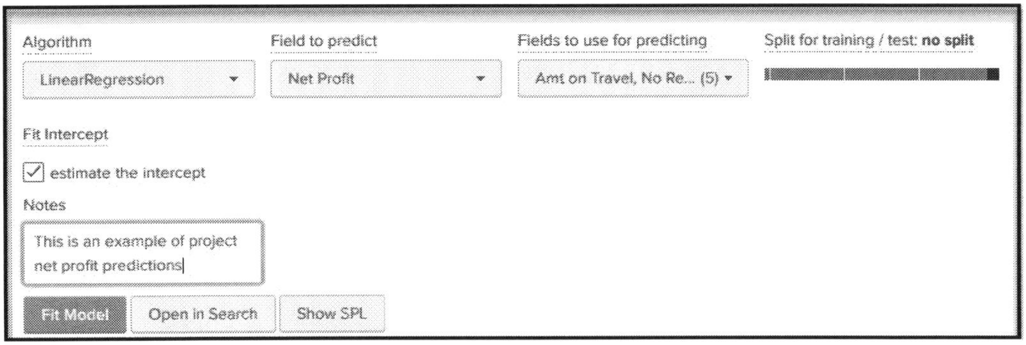

Figure 16.25 – Adding notes

When you click **Save**, you can add a formal **Experiment Title** name and a short description on the **Saving Experiment** dialog (shown in the following screenshot), then click **Save** again:

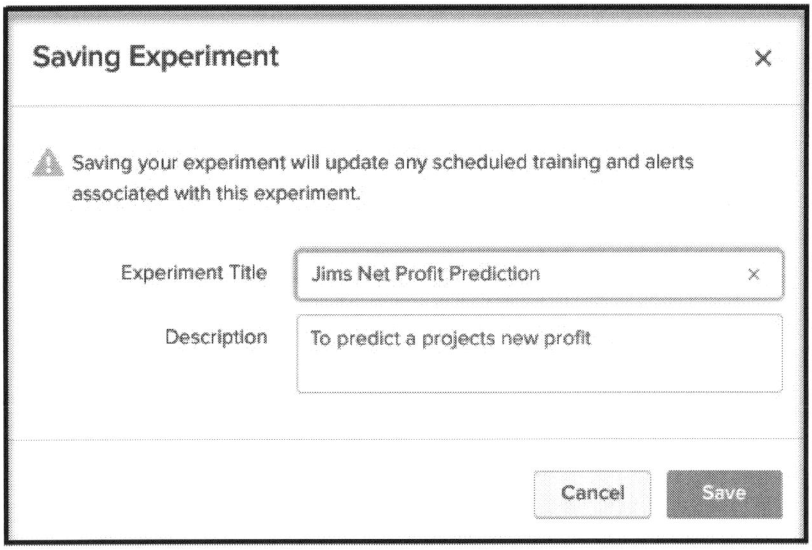

Figure 16.26 – Saving Experiment dialog

382   Machine Learning Overview

Once Splunk has finished saving your experiment, you can click **Continue Editing** or select **Go to Listings Page**:

Figure 16.27 – Experiment saved

If you select **Go to Listings Page**, the **Experiments** page will list your new experiment:

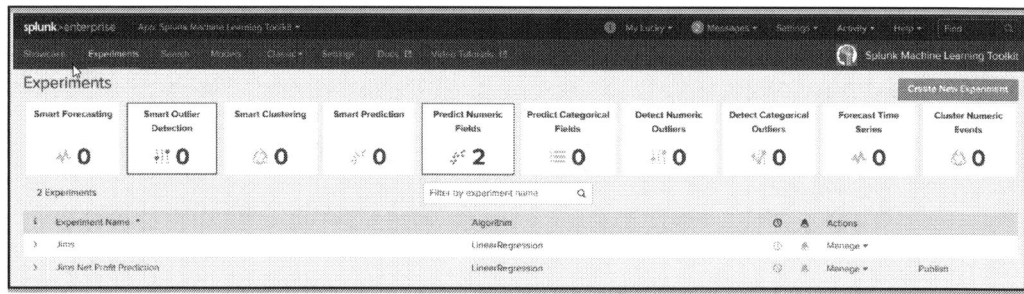

Figure 16.28 – Experiments page

From there, if you click on the experiment name, it will re-open for editing and refinement. Notice that, now, if you click on **Experiment History**, our experiment now has history:

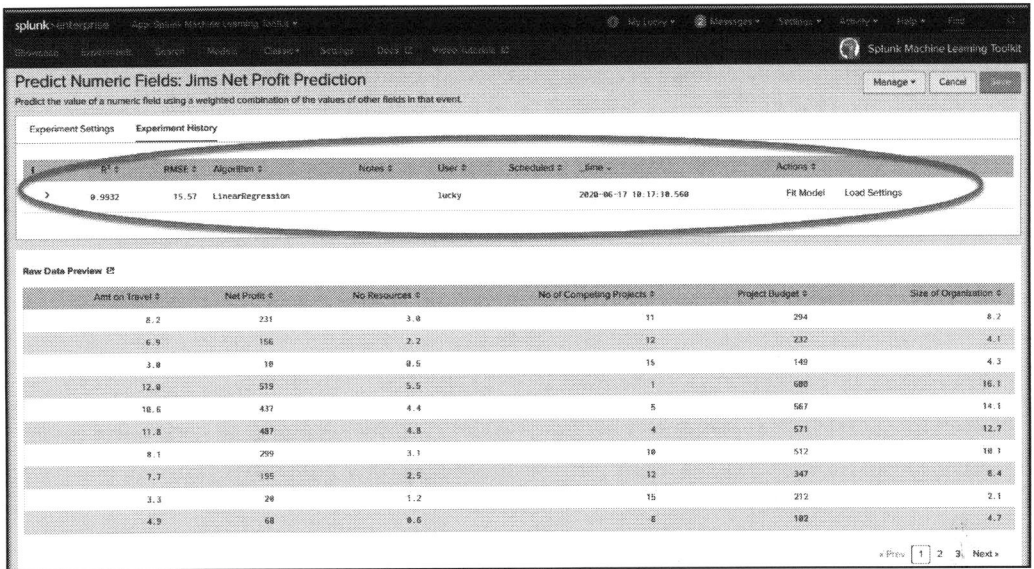

Figure 16.29 – Experiment History page

Now that we have fitted our model and explored experiments, let's refine our model.

Refining the model

After you *fit a model*, analyze, and validate the results, you typically make *refinements* and then run the fit again (optionally, but it's recommended, track your changes in the **Notes** text field as we mentioned earlier).

Some of the more typical refinements you can make include the following:

- Cut down on the number of fields selected in the **Fields to use for predicting** drop-down menu since too many fields can generate a distraction.
- Add data! Bring in new data to enrich the model.
- Build features on the raw data being used, modelling them on behaviors of the data instead of raw data points, using **SPL**, **streamstats**, or **eventstats**.
- Check the existing fields to ensure you are using categorical values correctly. For example, are you using `DayOfWeek` as a number (0 to 6) instead of as `Monday`, `Tuesday`, and so forth? Make sure you have the right type of value for categorical fields.

- Bring in context via lookups – **holidays**, **external anomalies**, and so on.
- Increase the number of fields (from additional data, feature building, and so on) selected in the **Fields to use for predicting** drop-down menu.

In this chapter, we have seen that the Splunk MLTK is really a Splunk-supported app that can be downloaded, configured, and ready for use in minutes. The app simplifies the steps for data preparation, reduces the steps needed to create a model, and saves the history of models executed and tested with. We also saw that one doesn't have to be a seasoned data scientist to use the app!

Summary

In this chapter, we introduced the Splunk MLTK as an extension to the core Splunk platform. The Splunk MLTK is an app that we downloaded, installed, configured, and then used to develop a simple linear machine learning model to indicate any relationship between various variables within data and how they could affect the net profit of an organization's implementation projects.

In the next chapter, we will discover the new Splunk Next functionalities.

17
Splunk Next

In the previous chapter, we covered the topic of using Splunk for machine learning by introducing the Splunk **Machine Learning Toolkit** (**MLTK**) and provided instructions on the access, installation, and basic use of the kit with an illustrative use case.

In this chapter, we will focus on providing an overview of the topic of Splunk Next as well as a brief summary of each of its offerings. The chapters in this book so far have been a mix of both theory and hands-on coding exercises and/or illustrative use cases.

In this chapter, we take a step back and provide a discussion of the offerings that are currently part of Splunk Next. This is because although all of them are important, some of the offerings originally part of Splunk Next are no longer available, currently not supported, or on a restricted beta testing program and not available to the general public.

The chapter will be broken down into the following main sections:

- What is Splunk Next?
- Splunk Developer Cloud
- Splunk Business Flow
- Splunk Data Fabric Search
- Splunk Data Stream Processor
- Splunk Cloud Gateway
- Splunk Augmented Reality

- Splunk Mobile
- Splunk Natural Language
- Splunk Insights for web and mobile apps
- Splunk TV

Let's get started!

What is Splunk Next?

Looking past the core platform and existing products, Splunk offers Splunk Next as a *set of beta tools* designed to complement and otherwise extend the existing Splunk platform's features and functionalities.

Various new tools or functionalities are regularly planned for, introduced, and beta tested, with some being discontinued, some *morphing* into new versions of their original design, and some finally making it into an actual production release or offering.

The fact is that there is no guarantee that anything specifically introduced within a Splunk Next timeframe will actually endure in the long term (and make it into the core or mainstream Splunk offerings). In addition, not all of these beta offerings are introduced in the public domain or available to everyone to review, test, and/or try out. Typically, you have to sign up for a beta test period and the offering will expire after the predetermined beta test period.

Finally, Splunk Next has been touted (by Splunk) as how the *new products of the world's beautiful and complex evolutionary process* are introduced.

For example, most recently, **Splunk Developer Cloud** (**SDC**) has morphed, so to speak, into part of DevOps, while **Splunk Business Flow** (**SBF**) has been discontinued, but the Splunk **Data Stream Processor** (**DSP**) has evidently made it as a legitimate offering.

The following table lists most of the original offerings in the recent Splunk Next:

Offering	Description
Splunk Developer Cloud	Intended to be a cloud portal where developers can build apps and access Splunk services.
Splunk Business Flow	Sort of an analytics-driven, Visio approach solution that allows users to explore and visualize business processes.
Splunk Data Fabric Search	You can use DFS to search across big data since it breaks up a search request and defines the sequence and location of how the various components of the search will be implemented so as to avoid typical bottlenecks.
Splunk Data Stream Processor	Used to collect unstructured or structured data from multiple sources and quickly turn large volumes of raw data into a single searchable source.
Splunk Cloud Gateway	A secure, cloud-based bridge for transferring data from a Splunk Enterprise or Splunk Cloud deployment to mobile devices.
Splunk Augmented Reality	Super cool! By simply scanning a QR code or NFC tag with, perhaps you phone, you can have direct access to the Splunk data and see Realtime augmented reality Splunk-powered gauges "over top" of real-world objects.
Splunk Mobile	Enables you to receive alerts and mobile-friendly dashboards on a mobile device.
Splunk Natural Language	Splunk Natural Language allows users to search and format Splunk data without knowing Search Processing Language (SPL).
Splunk Insights for Web and Mobile Apps	Address the needs of app developers to "build in" the ability to monitor activities and events within their apps.
Splunk TV	Provides the ability to view Splunk on any peripheral device instead of having to purchase a dedicated PC.

Figure 17.1 – Table of the recent Splunk Next offerings

In the following sections of this chapter, we'll try to add a little more detail, color, and perhaps insight into the functionalities as well as the current statuses of each of the aforementioned offerings.

Splunk Developer Cloud

The idea of the SDC was to provide developers with a place where they can *learn about and develop skills for* leveraging Splunk services, features, and functionalities without having to manage a local Splunk environment.

With the SDC, you have access to Splunk data services via REST APIs and SDKs from apps that you develop. You can send data to Splunk for ingesting and indexing, run searches against data, analyze data with functions, or even apply AI/machine learning algorithms to predict, cluster, or detect anomalies, and display the results in dashboards with a variety of UI elements and controls.

The SDC was a developer portal that provided access to online documentation, downloadable SDKs for Go and JavaScript, sample apps and code, and tooling to build apps that use SDC services.

Currently, the (public beta) SDC portal is now closed. A link to see the Splunk Enterprise Developer Portal (https://dev.splunk.com/enterprise) sends you to a **Sign up for a free developer license** page and basically encourages and allows you to download, set up, and run Splunk Enterprise *free* for 6 months, using a provided developer license.

It should be noted that other cloud portals (such as Microsoft Azure) offer (*pay for* or *pay as you go*) opportunities to deploy Splunk Enterprise as a single instance or a distributed cluster to quickly and easily get you started with Splunk (as shown in the following screenshot):

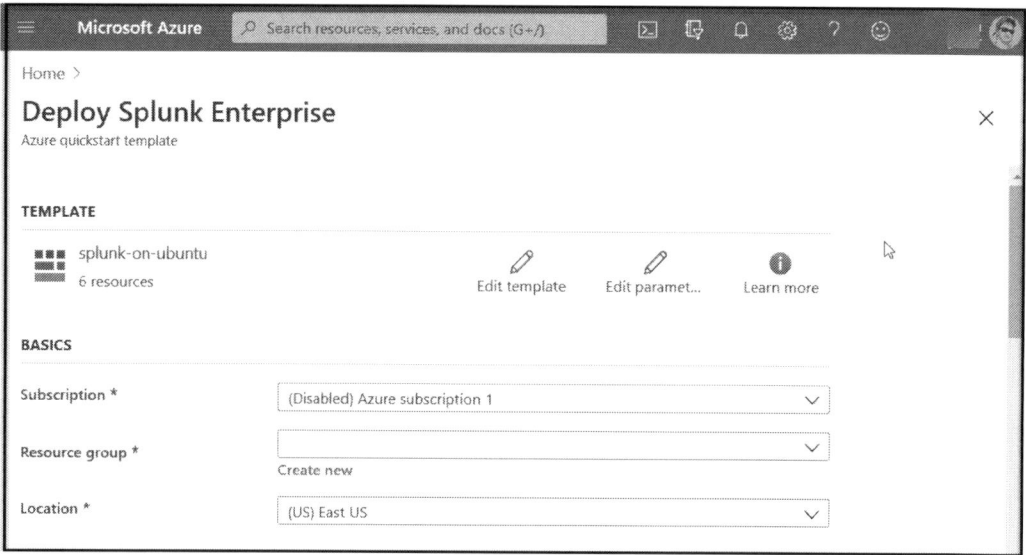

Figure 17.2 – Microsoft Azure offering to deploy Splunk Enterprise

You can read more about the Microsoft Azure offering at https://azure.microsoft.com/en-us/resources/templates/splunk-on-ubuntu.

Splunk Business Flow

To analyze data with SBF, you need to create what is referred to as a **flow model**. The term **flow model** refers to a grouping of discrete information that represents a transaction, session, or another business process that is configured within SBF. In a flow model, you define what field names you want to track and how you want to correlate events.

SBF is one of the Splunk Next offerings that, as of June 2020, is no longer available for purchase (although evidently the offering is still being supported if you are an existing customer).

Splunk Data Fabric Search

The **Data Fabric Search** (**DFS**) offering is called **an extended search platform** that uses distributed clusters designed to improve Splunk's searching performance.

At a high level, traditional Splunk searches run from a single search head. The search query comes in through the search head and the search results are returned back to the search head. DFS enhances search performance by distributing the processing of the search to the cluster, so that processing and memory requirements do not cause a holdup at the search head.

DFS basically connects massive datasets from different data sources, such as mainframe computers, databases, IoT devices, and multiple Splunk deployments, all of which may have different storage and retention policies, into a *single view* of the data. You can use DFS to search across multiple terabytes of data, literally billions of events with little or no performance bearing, to gather enterprise-wide insights into your data.

Sadly, again, as of May 2020, Splunk DFS is no longer available for purchase, although a *free version* is still available and usable in Splunk Enterprise version 8; however, the offering will not be supported after October 2021. It is unclear where this offering's functionalities will end up at this point.

Splunk Data Stream Processor

The Splunk **Data Stream Processor** (**DSP**) offering is a data stream processing service capable of processing data (from supported sources) in real time and sending that data to designated (supported) platforms.

You can use either **Search Processing Language 2** (**SPL2**) commands or the DSP Canvas Builder to create pipelines in DSP to process data. The canvas is a *visual* DSP UI for building pipelines.

> **Hint**
> A new version of SPL, called SPL2, makes the search language easier to use and more consistent, and it removes infrequently used commands. Read about it online at `https://docs.splunk.com/Documentation/SCS/current/SearchReference/Introduction`.

During the processing of a pipeline, Splunk DSP permits you to use special functions to perform transformations, which are validations (as well as other tasks) to be run on the data before that data is indexed.

The special tasks include the following:

- Aggregations based on specific conditions
- Formatting/categorizing based on specified conditions
- Masking sensitive or private information
- Decisional routing of high-volume/velocity data to multiple destinations
- Filtering/sub-setting by destination

> **Hint**
> The DSP function reference can be found online at `https://docs.splunk.com/Documentation/DSP/1.1.0/FunctionReference/Category`.

Splunk DSP is a cool, programmable tool that allows you to collect unstructured and/or structured data from multiple sources using a drag and drop interface. It even offers pre-built pipelines by creating templates for future use. It is not, however, part of or included in the Splunk Enterprise license (meaning it's available for an additional cost).

Splunk Cloud Gateway

Splunk Cloud Gateway is a required *companion app* for what are being called the **Connected Experiences** apps, such as Splunk Mobile, Splunk TV, and the Splunk AR or Augmented Reality offerings discussed in the next sections of this chapter.

Splunk Cloud Gateway is a secure, cloud-based *bridge* for transferring data from a Splunk Enterprise or Splunk Cloud environment or deployment to mobile devices.

With Splunk Cloud Gateway, (enabled) users can receive alerts, register and associate assets with Splunk data, and manage devices for Connected Experiences apps, just to name a few accessibilities.

In line with the typical Splunk strategy, Splunk Cloud Gateway is itself an app, and so to install it, you follow the same process as you would for most any other Splunk app:

1. Find it on Splunkbase (`https://splunkbase.splunk.com/`).
2. Download it.

3. Install it (a Splunk restart is required):

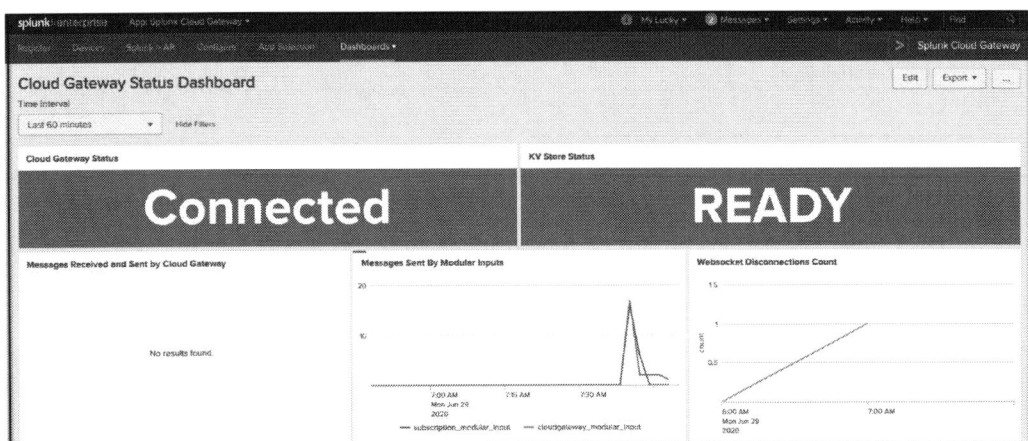

Figure 17.3 – Cloud Gateway Status Dashboard

Splunk Augmented Reality

I cannot say enough about this offering. With Splunk **Augmented Reality** (**AR**), Splunk leverages AR, a technology that *superimposes* a computer-generated image onto a user's view, creating a merged view or reality.

Consider a smartphone, camera, or other lens that has the ability to link real-time Splunk data to real-world objects and/or locations, so that users can consume, interact with, and take action with data where it actually exists.

This is sometimes referred to as creating a **connected experience**. Imagine seeing a Splunk-connected visualization through the lens or view of your camera, phone, watch, or other type of device.

You can use several techniques to access and interact with Splunk data in an augmented way, including **asset tags**, **beacons**, and something called **geofences**:

- Asset tags are barcodes or **Near-Field Communication** (**NFC**) devices that store data and wirelessly send information to devices. Asset tags allow Splunk AR to identify the data you're requesting.

- Beacons are **Bluetooth Low Energy** (**BLE**) devices that broadcast their location and associated data to nearby mobile devices. When you associate Splunk dashboards with beacons, Splunk AR presents the dashboards on your mobile device when you're in the beacon's region.

- Geofences are GPS-based boundaries that allow a device to trigger an action when the device enters or exits the area. You can create a virtual boundary on a GPS map, associate dashboards with the boundary, and have Splunk AR presents dashboards on a mobile device when it's within the virtual boundary.

Setting up AR with workspaces

Setting up Splunk AR involves installing and configuring the Splunk Cloud Gateway app (mentioned in the previous section), downloading and installing the Splunk AR offering, and then registering mobile devices.

A big part of making this work is through the use of what is known as **Augmented Reality workspaces**. An AR workspace is a *template* used to present Splunk data in an AR space.

What you do is associate or register an asset that produces or refers to data, link that asset with a Splunk AR workspace, and then fill the workspace with Splunk data (in other words, you build a special Splunk dashboard that is the AR workspace).

When you scan an asset, Splunk AR identifies the data you want to view, retrieves it from the Splunk instance, and displays the data on the AR workspace, through a registered mobile device. This allows you to see the dashboard visualizations you've built placed on top of real-world objects.

You can even interact with, resize and reposition, adjust, and add notes to those visualizations directly within the AR environment. There are plenty of videos online showing Splunk AR in action.

Splunk Natural Language (beta)

A **Natural Language** (**NL**) query consists only of *normal* or *human-typical* terms or words stated in the user's language, without any special syntax or format being required.

Splunk NL allows users to query a system and ask questions of Splunk without having to understand and know the **Splunk Processing Language** (**SPL**). Additionally, users can have the results of their queries instantly displayed in charts and text without having to format the results.

This is a process known as **Smart Data Discovery**, where the analytics system strives to provide insights to business users or citizen data scientists without requiring them to have traditional data scientist expertise.

Key objectives of the SPL offering include the following:

- Ability to use NL-type queries
- Ability to use both text and voice input to submit queries
- Queries to be SPL and/or SQL themed
- Support disambiguation (breakdown) and context correction
- Provide recommendations to the user, based upon history
- Learn from user activities
- Use smart data discovery

What does an NL query look like? How does it differ from an SPL or SQL query?

Taking a time/context question, such as *what is the total global sales by country in 2019?*, you might use an SPL command like this:

```
Source=global_sales | where year = 2019 | sort by country
```

Using SQL, the query might look like this:

```
Select global_sales where year = 2019 order by country
```

With an NL query, you'd be able to type this:

```
sales by country in 2019
```

You should be able to see the difference between the requests. The first isn't too bad (if you have some experience with Splunk SPL), but the third is clearly very easy to understand.

Some (maybe expected) documented examples of NL queries might be these:

- **Time** and **context** (`select` and `where`, as in our preceding example)
- **Aggregation** (`sum`) `average price Widget X is sold`
- **Ranked** (`order by`) `country with highest sales`
- **Exclusion** (`filtered by`) `sales by product excluding Widget X` and **range** (`countries where sales are > 10m`)
- **Compute** (`sum of units sold in Canada by store`)

Some more exciting NL queries include the following:

- **Identification** (`products with high sugar content`)
- **Comparison** (`number of service tickets in Q1 vs Q2`)

Giving back

Another exciting characteristic of an NL query is the way the offering is designed to *communicate back* to the user. With NL, the results will automatically produce relevant visualizations based upon the query executed. In addition, these visualizations are dynamic in that the user can interact with them to further analyze data and find additional insights.

Other unique communicative features include the narrative that is created via the use of the NL text (rather than perhaps cryptic programmatic syntax commands) as well its ability to automatically highlight points of importance and underscore relevant information.

This change in the way a user interacts with or queries their data provides for a much broader user appeal:

- Almost anyone can use it with minimal training being required.
- The *user experience* is simplified, allowing higher-level engagement and self-discovery.
- Almost immediately productive, so a faster time to value.

As of the time of writing, to test drive Splunk NL, you need to submit a request to be a candidate for the program (as long as you are a current Splunk customer).

> Hint
> If you are interested, to submit a request to try out the Splunk NL query offering, you can go online to `https://www.splunk.com/en_us/form/splunk-natural-language-search.html`.

Splunk Insights for web and mobile

The idea of Splunk Insights for web and mobile is to be able to leverage the power of various Splunk services to monitor an application with an app, an API key, and a **Software Development Kit** (**SDK**), and by passing data through a cloud service.

Tracking an application's level of quality and understanding and gauging user engagement is valuable and especially challenging when working with web or mobile applications.

Using the SDK, you can initialize sessions to automatically collect console logs, logged events, errors, environmental details, and page (or other) load times. Custom events can also be set up and tracked.

Once again, the Splunk Cloud Gateway offering is leveraged to link applications and pass data and other information.

Mobile apps

Splunk can be a powerful tool in cybersecurity, infrastructure monitoring, and forensic investigations. While it's great to use in the office, after-hours incidents require the ability to have data available immediately. Since most people carry a mobile device, such as a cell phone or a tablet, it's easy to see how dashboards and alerts on mobile devices can help bridge the information gap.

Splunk Mobile brings the power of Splunk dashboards to mobile devices, powered by (again) Splunk Cloud Gateway. Yes, you guessed it! While Splunk Mobile is installed on a mobile device, the Splunk Cloud Gateway links and feeds the mobile app from/with the Splunk Enterprise environment.

Between the two applications is Splunk's AWS-hosted CloudBridge. Traffic between Splunk Enterprise and the mobile device is protected by TLS 1.2 encryption.

Similar to how other connected experiences are configured, Splunk Mobile requires Connected Experiences apps in Splunk Cloud Gateway to be enabled and then the Splunk apps that should be allowed to show dashboards in the mobile app need to be selected.

> **Hint**
> As of the time of writing, you can find the download for Splunk Mobile in the Apple App Store at `https://apps.apple.com/us/app/splunk-mobile/id1420299852`.

Splunk TV

There are a number of pretty helpful/useful things you can do with this Splunk Next offering. That is, leveraging Apple TV, Splunk TV lets you browse and organize Splunk dashboards, focus on panels, create dashboard groups, and display impressive slideshows using the Splunk TV app.

To get started with Splunk TV, you'll need to install Splunk Cloud Gateway (as we described earlier in this chapter), the required companion app, on your Splunk Enterprise instance, as well as enabling Splunk TV using the **Configure** tab of the **Splunk Cloud Gateway** app:

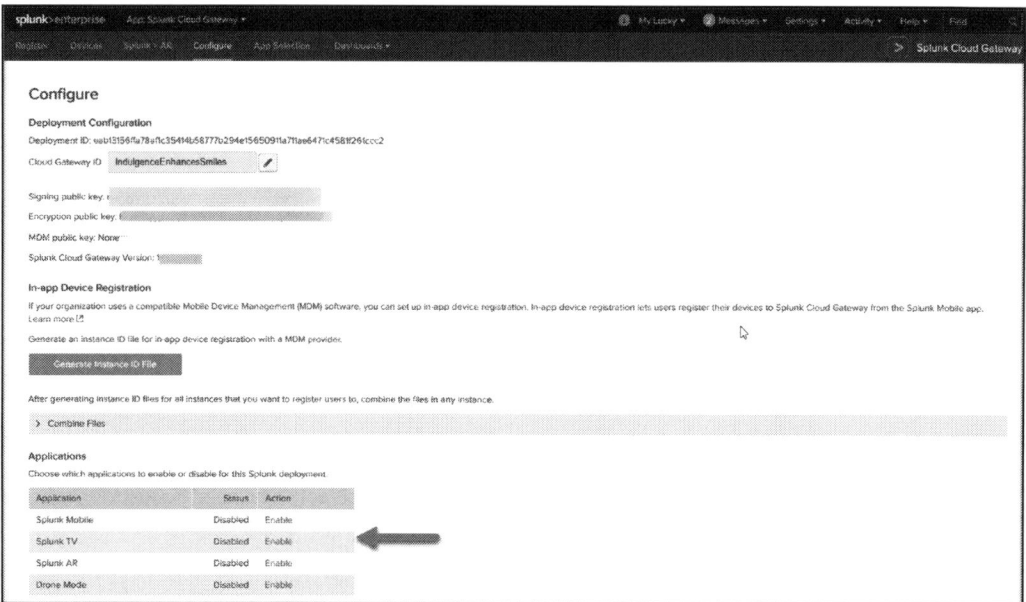

Figure 17.4 – Deployment Configuration page

Then, register your TV (again with the **Splunk Cloud Gateway** app, under **Devices**):

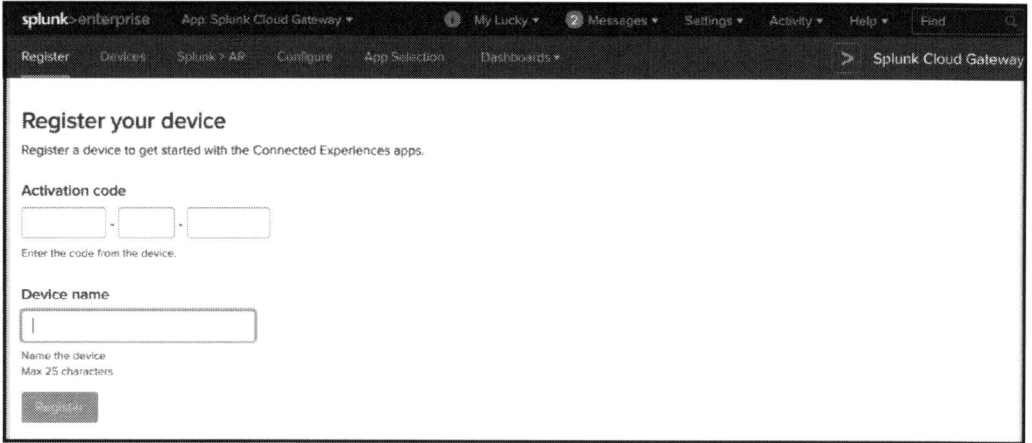

Figure 17.5 – Registering your device

Now let's look at some of my favorite dashboards.

My favorite dashboards

Not all Splunk dashboards and visualizations are supported by Splunk TV, but most can be modified for use. But once you download the Splunk TV app (on your TV), you can search for, browse, and *favorite* the Splunk dashboards you have access to.

One nice feature of Splunk TV is that you can create a dashboard slideshow of sorts by selecting a dashboard, then a panel, and then by clicking the **Play** button on your Apple TV remote. Each panel shows for (by default) 30 seconds. You can also swipe, play, and pause.

Summary

In this chapter, we introduced the Splunk Next program and listed and described each current or recent offering in the program. Although this chapter was based in theory, it is important to stay in the loop with the current and future tools and offerings Splunk is or may be planning.

In the next chapter, we will look at using the SplunkJS Stack libraries to further enhance web applications with Splunk functionality.

18
Dashboards – SplunkJS

In the previous chapter, we focused on providing an overview of the topic of Splunk Next as well as a brief summary of each of its offerings.

In the chapter, you will see how adding the SplunkJS Stack libraries to a website can enable the use of numerous **web framework** components that can assist in interacting and viewing Splunk data.

The chapter will be broken down into the following main sections:

- Understanding SplunkJS
- Getting started with SplunkJS
- SplunkJS and Splunk apps
- Adding SplunkJS to a web app

Understanding SplunkJS

To discuss SplunkJS, we have to start first by mentioning the Splunk Web Framework.

As you may (should) know, the Splunk Web Framework is a powerful application framework for enterprise-level developers to use to create custom dashboards and Splunk apps with tables, charts, forms searches, and other functionalities.

Included in the Splunk Web Framework is the SplunkJS Stack component, which is intended for developers who want to create Splunk apps using a familiar (that is, their own) JavaScript environment.

> **Note**
> Actually, the framework includes SDK support for Java, JavaScript, Python, Ruby, C#, and PHP.

Some of the key features of the Splunk Framework include the following:

- HTML5/CSS/JavaScript support
- Full-stack development
- Custom layout and visualizations
- Additional interactivity
- Templates
- SimpleXML-to-HTML conversion

As of Splunk version 6, there was a major overhaul to the Splunk Web Framework. The framework was then integrated directly into Splunk Enterprise, so you don't need to install anything else to start using the web framework.

In previous versions of Splunk, you needed to use a standalone version of the web framework; now, you are able to get going and work with the framework immediately by using a drag and drop interface, making it easy to get under the hood and interact with and customize the code directly.

Additionally, using the framework, developers don't even need to develop with Splunk to display Splunk indexed data. Developers can simply interface with Splunk API calls, search for data, and then display this returned data directly on their own websites and applications.

SplunkJS supports options to extend and integrate with Splunk functionalities, provides more flexibility with the look and feel (of an app), and also allows the integration and use of third-party visualization tools such as **Data-Driven Documents** (**D3**) and the KeyLines toolkit.

SplunkJS includes a number of tools to help you create and/or enhance Splunk apps, such as the following:

- Libraries for Splunk views and search managers for working with searches and interacting with Splunk data
- Backbone.js, to provide a **Model-View-Controller** (**MVC**) framework as a structure for your code
- RequireJS, to manage dependencies
- jQuery, to help manage the **document object model** (**DOM**)

So, using JavaScript (SplunkJS Stack) along with your favorite development tools, you can build rich interactive apps to access and manipulate Splunk data. You can also add third-party visualizations to your apps, as well as creating your own reusable views.

So, offered as part of the Splunk Web Framework, SplunkJS Stack is a practical set of libraries that can be used to add code to a web app or Splunk app using JavaScript.

The next section will outline the simple steps required to install the stack files.

Getting started with SplunkJS

To integrate Splunk into a web or Splunk app, you first need to install the stack files. To make the SplunkJS Stack libraries available for use, you need to follow these steps:

1. Download SplunkJS Stack from **splunk>dev Downloads** at `https://dev.splunk.com/enterprise/downloads`. Note that you'll have to scroll down to find it (see the following screenshot):

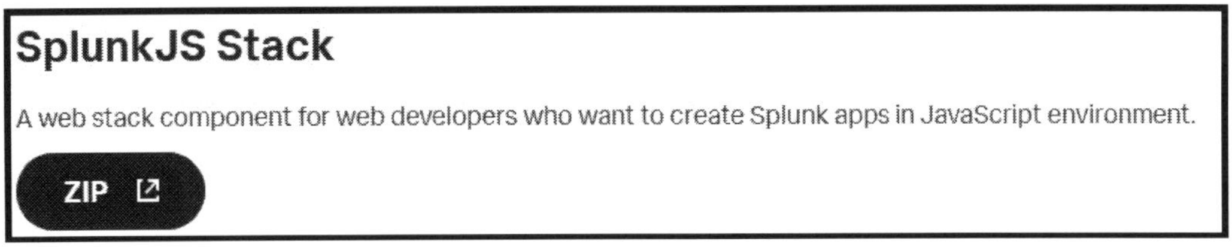

SplunkJS Stack

A web stack component for web developers who want to create Splunk apps in JavaScript environment.

ZIP

Figure 18.1 – Downloading SplunkJS Stack

2. Extract the files. The files will come in the form of a zipped file, which you'll need to extract to use.

3. Finally, once you have your files extracted, you need to copy those files (the contents of the `SplunkJS_Stack/static/` directory) to your website's static directory (more on this later in this chapter).

> **Note**
> There should be two sub-folders in the `SplunkJS_Stack/static/` directory, `splunkjs` and `splunkjs.min`.

Now, let's take a look at how we can use the power made available to us as with SplunkJS.

SplunkJS and Splunk apps

A reminder: a Splunk **app** is a *pocket of designated program code* that runs on the Splunk platform and is designed to analyze and display knowledge around a specific data source, dataset, and/or knowledge object(s). You can use SplunkJS Stack to develop and/or enhance the functionalities and offerings of the Splunk app.

Splunk apps run and appear within the Splunk web interface in Splunk Enterprise and rely on Splunk's app server to interact with `splunkd` to render data within or as HTML pages. Using SplunkJS, one of the selling points is to leverage the built-in navigation bars and headers of Splunk, to create the same look and feel as Splunk itself.

In this section, we'll walk through first creating a simple Splunk app and then enhancing it using features found in SplunkJS.

Creating a Splunk app

You can create a Splunk app using Splunk Web by following these steps:

1. On the Splunk Web home page, click the gear icon next to **Apps**, then click on **Manage Apps**.
2. Next, click on **Create app** (as shown in the following screenshot):

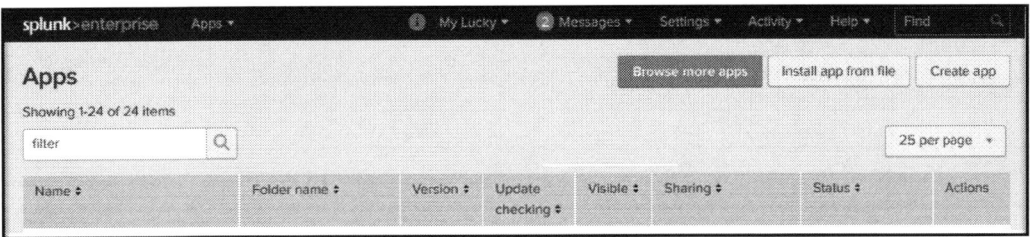

Figure 18.2 – Creating a Splunk app

3. On the **Add new** (app) page (shown in the screenshot that follows), you will need to provide the properties of the new app:

   a) **Name**: The name of your app, which appears in the Splunk Web list and menu of apps. The name maps to the label setting in the `app.conf` configuration file. If you plan to upload your app to Splunkbase, then you need to follow the naming conventions described in the **Naming conventions for apps and add-ons on Splunkbase** section in the **Working with Splunkbase** manual. Short app names are recommended to avoid issues with long file paths in Windows.

   b) **Folder name**: The name to use for the directory in `$SPLUNK_HOME/etc/apps/` (the name of the folder cannot contain the *dot* (.) character; you might want to use the name you assign to your app for clarity).

   c) **Version**: The app version string, which needs to be in the format of `#.#.#`, such as `1.0.0`.

   d) **Visible**: This indicates whether the app should be visible in Splunk Web. Apps that contain a user interface should be visible.

   e) **Description**: This is a description of the app. Previous versions of Splunk Enterprise displayed the description on the Splunk Home page; however, the current version of Splunk Enterprise does not use this description. If you plan to upload your app to Splunkbase, include a description, because Splunkbase uses it to validate the app package.

   f) **Author**: The author's name.

   g) **Template**: The *template* that will be used to create the app. The **barebones** template will create a *basic* app directory structure and minimal required supporting files. The `sample_app` template will create an app that includes sample dashboards, images, and CSS files for dashboard styling and behavior.

> **Tip**
>
> You can create and add custom app templates to `$SPLUNK_HOME/share/splunk/app_templates/`.

h) **Upload asset**: Click **Choose File** to upload a single image, HTML, JavaScript, CSS, or other asset file to your app:

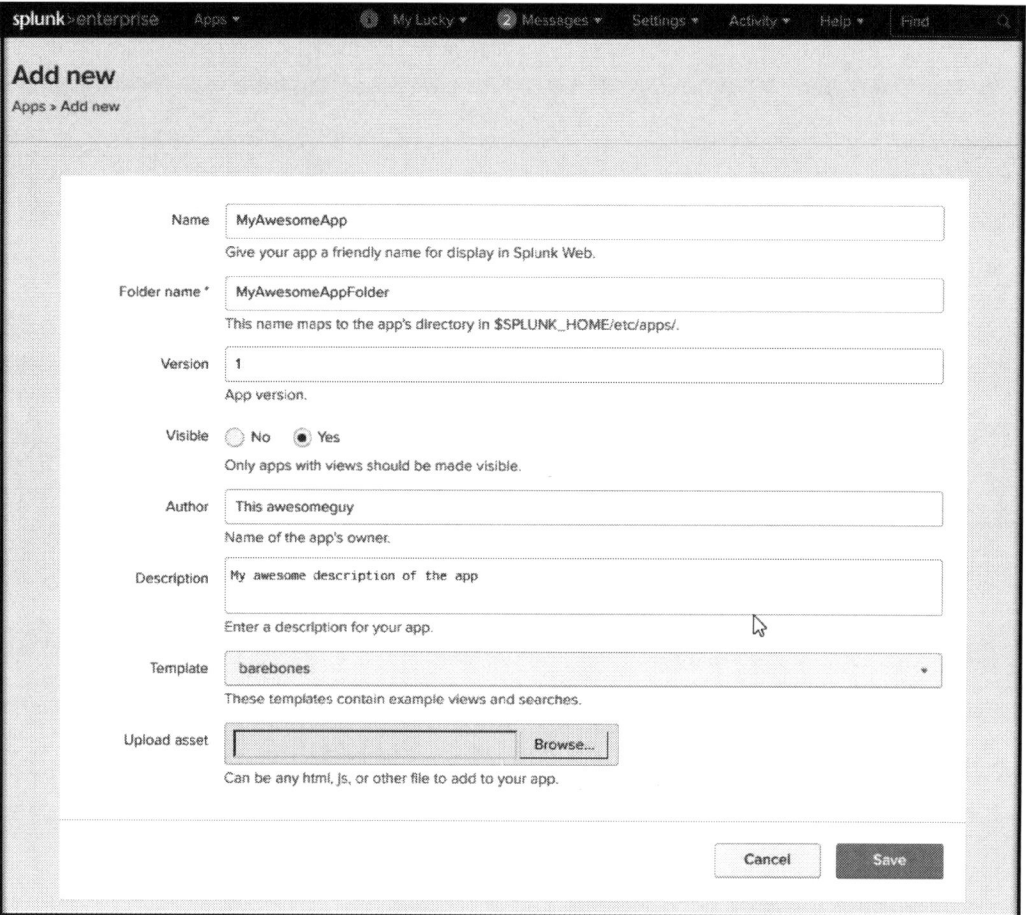

Figure 18.3 – Add new page

4. Now, click **Save** and you should now see your app listed on the **Apps** page (as shown in the following screenshot):

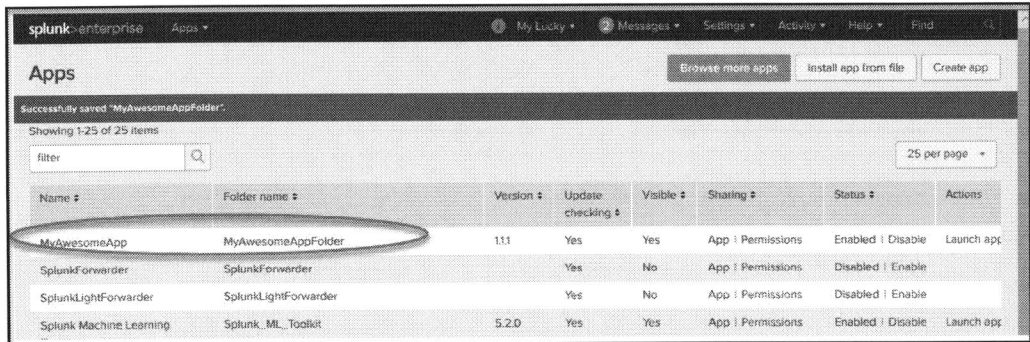

Figure 18.4 – Apps page

From there, you set the app's permissions and then launch it:

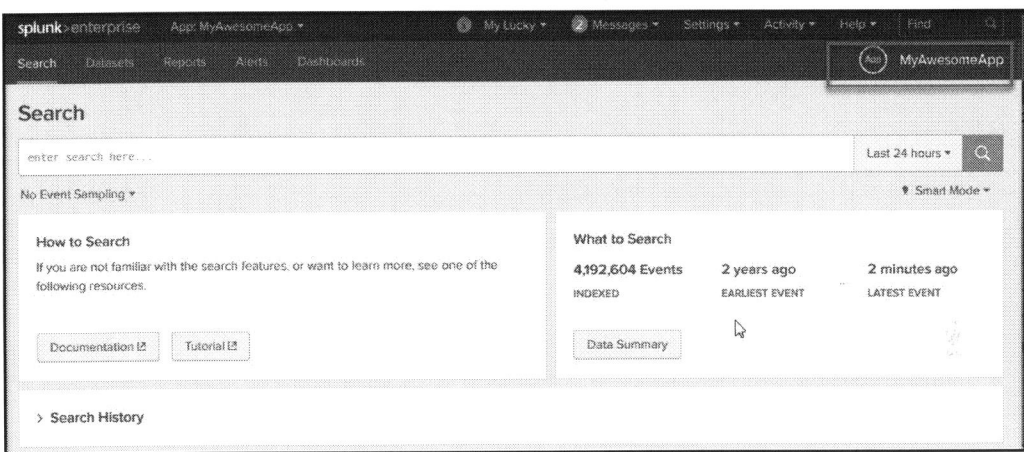

Figure 18.5 – Setting the app permissions

When you create a new app, a new directory for the app is created under the `$SPLUNK_HOME/etc/apps` directory; for instance, in this example, we should see `$SPLUNK_HOME/Splunk/etc/apps/MyAwesomeAppFolder`:

Name	Date modified	Type	Size
alert_logevent	5/28/2020 5:22 PM	File folder	
alert_webhook	5/28/2020 5:22 PM	File folder	
appsbrowser	5/28/2020 5:21 PM	File folder	
introspection_generator_addon	5/28/2020 5:21 PM	File folder	
launcher	5/28/2020 5:21 PM	File folder	
learned	5/28/2020 5:23 PM	File folder	
legacy	5/28/2020 5:21 PM	File folder	
MyAwesomeAppFolder	7/7/2020 3:23 PM	File folder	
sample_app	5/28/2020 5:22 PM	File folder	
search	5/28/2020 7:18 PM	File folder	
simple_xml_examples	6/9/2020 1:25 PM	File folder	
splunk_app_cloudgateway	6/29/2020 7:40 AM	File folder	
splunk_gdi	5/28/2020 5:22 PM	File folder	
splunk_health_assistant_addon	5/30/2020 10:52 A...	File folder	
splunk_httpinput	5/28/2020 5:22 PM	File folder	
splunk_instrumentation	5/28/2020 5:24 PM	File folder	
splunk_internal_metrics	5/28/2020 5:21 PM	File folder	
splunk_metrics_workspace	5/28/2020 5:21 PM	File folder	
Splunk_ML_Toolkit	6/17/2020 7:55 AM	File folder	
splunk_monitoring_console	5/30/2020 8:50 AM	File folder	
Splunk_SA_Scientific_Python_windows_x8...	6/15/2020 5:29 PM	File folder	
Splunk_TA_windows	5/28/2020 5:51 PM	File folder	
splunk-dashboard-app	6/10/2020 7:28 AM	File folder	

Figure 18.6 – The new app directory

So, now we have created a Splunk app, but it doesn't really do too much! Well, that is okay. The idea is to provide some basic examples of how we can use SplunkJS to enhance a Splunk app. To accomplish this, we will add a simple dashboard to our app.

Creating a dashboard in SimpleXML using the dashboard editor

First, launch our simple little app. Remember, it really doesn't do much or even look like anything much:

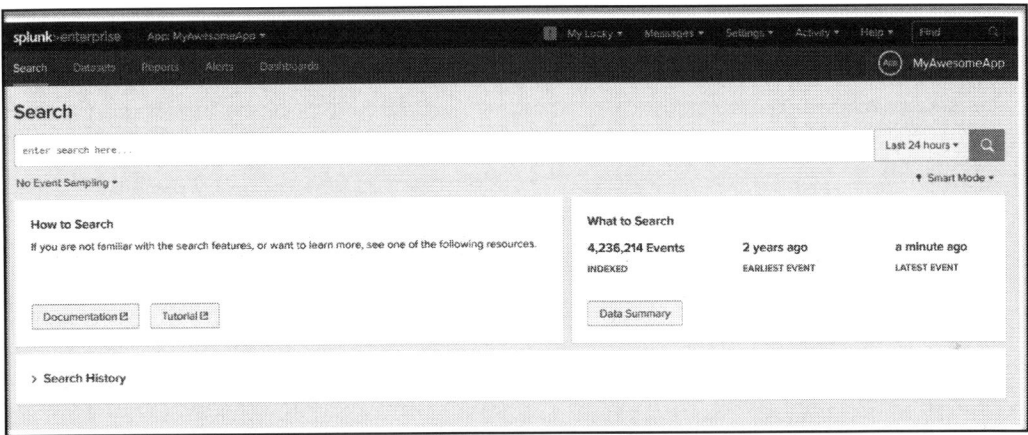

Figure 18.7 – Splunk Search page

From the app, click on **Dashboards**. From the **Dashboards** page, click on **Create New Dashboard**:

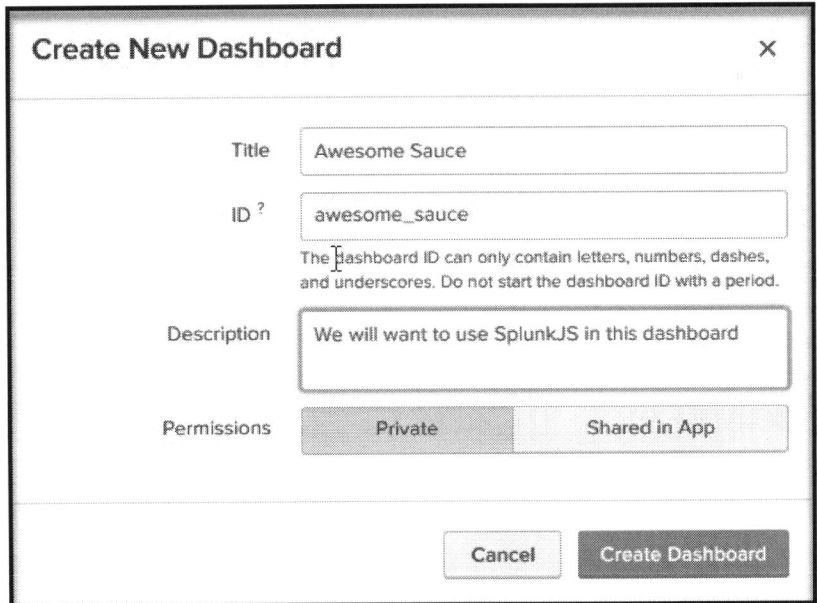

Figure 18.8 – Create New Dashboard dialog

Enter the details as shown in the preceding screenshot and click **Create Dashboard**; then you should see a new dashboard created as shown in the following screenshot:

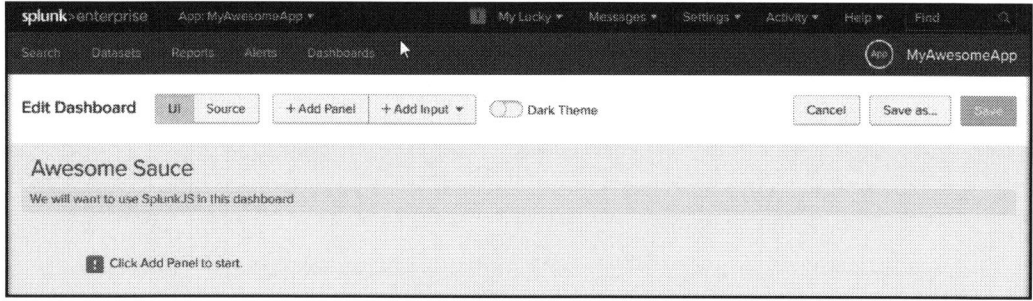

Figure 18.9 – New dashboard created

In *Chapter 15, Dashboards – Custom Visualizations*, we took a look at the beta dashboard editor; here we are back to the current editor. You can recall that you can use this interactive editor to create and edit dashboards without having to edit the underlying XML source code, but some advanced dashboard features are not available through this editor. The dashboard source code editor provides you with the ability to edit the XML code directly. To edit the XML code, you can do the following:

1. Select **Edit** to open the dashboard editor.
2. Click **Source** to open the source code editor.
3. Edit the source code.
4. If the **Save** button is disabled, correct any code with validation warnings or errors. Otherwise, click **Save** to save your edits.

Modifying the dashboard by adding a SimpleXML extension to it

Just to jump-start this exercise a bit, we can try out an extended XML dashboard that can be downloaded from the Splunk Developer site (https://dev.splunk.com/). It requires two files: an XML file (which defines the dashboard), example_chart.xml, and a JavaScript file (which uses SplunkJS Stack to interact with Splunkd and load the dashboard), example_chart.js.

SplunkJS and Splunk apps   409

Once you've downloaded the files, you need to drop them into our new apps folders:

1. Save the example_chart.xml file under our new apps folder, $SPLUNK_HOME/etc/apps/<app_name>/local/data/ui/views/.

2. Save the example_chart.js file in $SPLUNK_HOME/etc/apps/<app_name>/appserver/static/.

3. Once you have the files in place, you'll need to restart Splunk, log back in, open our app, and click on **Dashboards**. On the **Dashboards** page, you should now see the dashboard we created earlier in this chapter as well as the sample **Charts** dashboard that was created by the files we downloaded and added to Splunk:

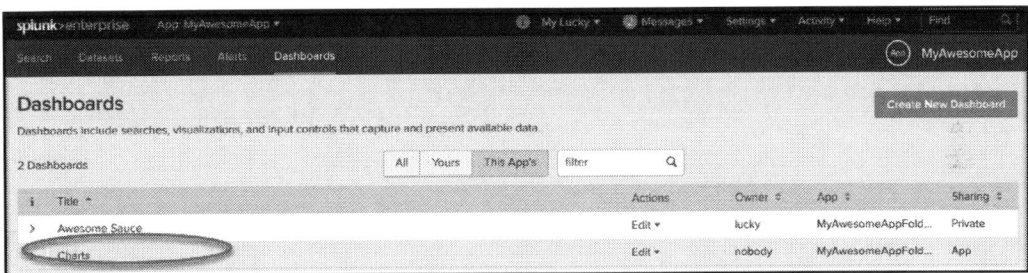

Figure 18.10 – The Dashboards page

4. If you click on **Charts**, we see the dashboard (a partial dashboard is shown in the following screenshot):

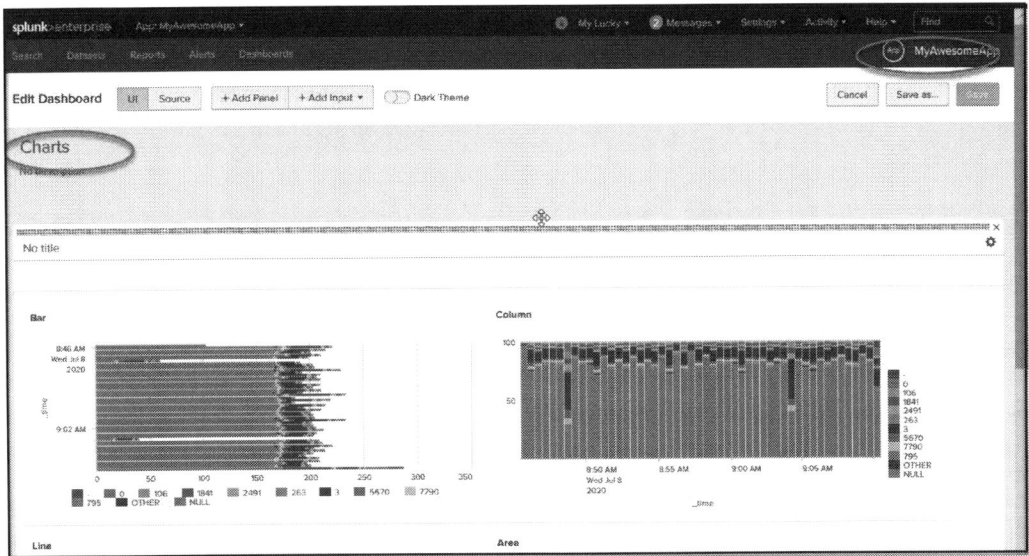

Figure 18.11 – The Charts dashboard

5. Take a moment in the dashboard editor and click on **Edit**, then **Source**, and you'll notice the extended XML code that creates the dashboard (shown in the following screenshot):

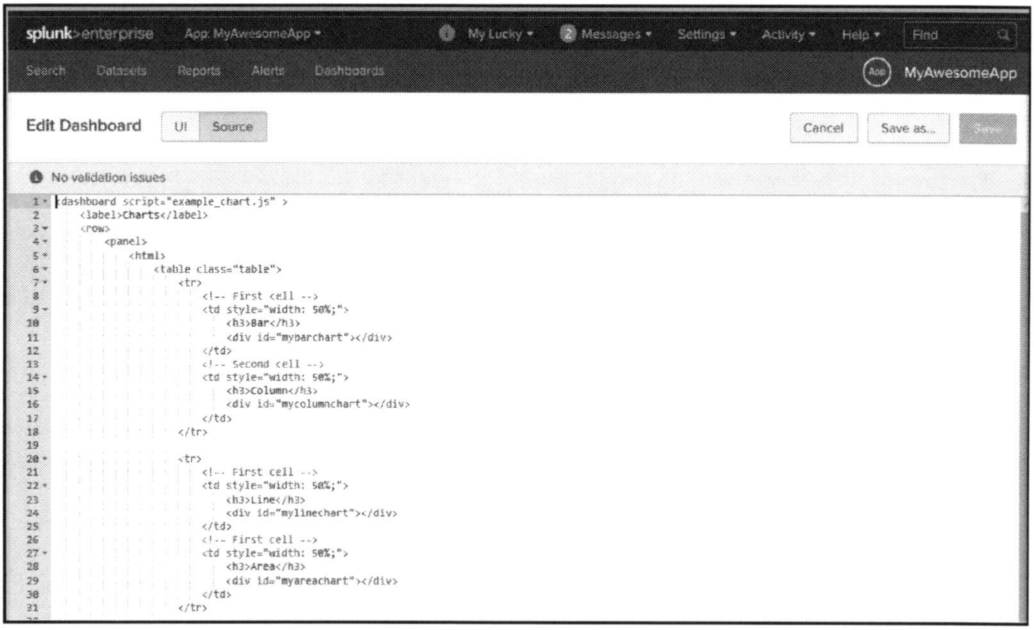

Figure 18.12 – The extended XML source code

Modifying the dashboard by converting it to HTML

There is a very simple process to convert Splunk SimpleXML dashboards into HTML. The objective for doing this is to let you start with autogenerated code that can then be modified and enhanced to suit.

By working in this generated HTML (and JavaScript), you can customize a dashboard beyond what you can do in SimpleXML, achieving things such as the following:

- Super-customized layouts
- Adding formatting/unique CSS/images (and whatever else you can do in HTML)
- Adding and customizing Splunk visualizations
- Customizing drilldown and other interactive behaviors
- Integrating with third-party visualizations

Sounds good, right? Well, before we try converting a dashboard, please note that *Splunk does not recommend converting SimpleXML dashboards to HTML; documentation is provided for legacy apps only* – and in my experience, this is because some functionalities within a Splunk SimpleXML dashboard seem to break during conversion.

> **Note**
> Just that general statement – that functionalities may break during conversion to HTML – does not mean that those items cannot be fixed without some work or additional coding. The recommended approach is to review, plan, and test each functionality within a dashboard as part of the conversion process.

Dashboard conversion example

Assuming you have permission to convert dashboards (specifically a role that has the `edit_view_html` capability), in Splunk Web, open the dashboard you want to convert, then click the ellipses (**...**) and select **Convert to HTML** (as shown in the following screenshot):

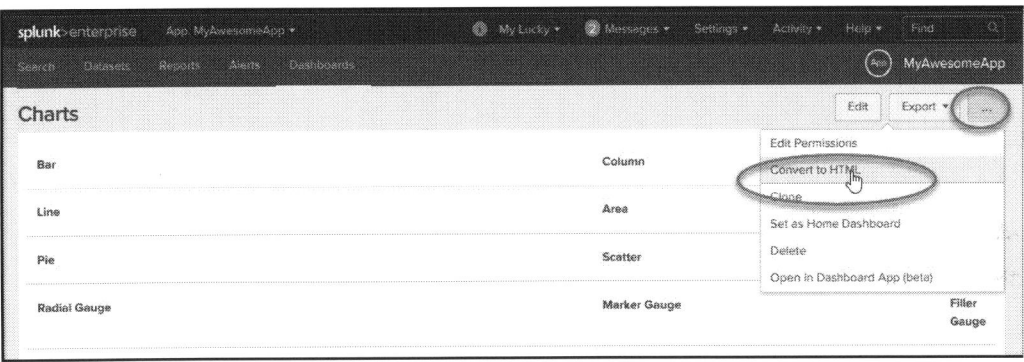

Figure 18.13 – Converting to HTML

Then, in the **Convert Dashboard to HTML** dialog (shown in the following screenshot), set the properties for the converted dashboard:

Figure 18.14 – Convert Dashboard to HTML dialog

Set the properties as shown in the preceding screenshot and click **Convert Dashboard**:

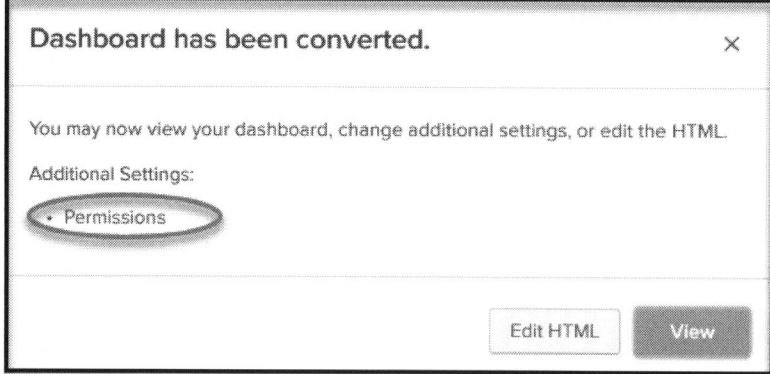

Figure 18.15 – Dashboard has been converted

You will see that the dashboard has been converted. You can also go to **Permissions** for additional settings or click on **View** to view the converted dashboard.

Getting back to our app

Earlier, we created a simple *do another* Splunk app and added a blank dashboard to it; then, we paused and explored an example of extending a SimpleXML dashboard using SplunkJS and two downloaded files. Let's go back and edit our dashboard and extend it.

Assuming we again have our app open, click on **Dashboards** and open our **Awesome Sauce** dashboard, then click on **Edit** and **Source**. Within the XML editor, you can make some minor changes.

On the dashboard tag, change it to `<dashboard script="Awesome_Sauce.js">`.

Next, let's add a dashboard panel as follows:

```
<row><panel>
    <html>
        <h3>A chart and an events viewer displaying results of a search</h3>
        <div id="mychart"></div>
        <div id="myeventsviewer"></div>
    </html>
</panel></row>
```

Once you have changed the code, click on **Save**.

Assuming there were no errors and your dashboard saved, we need to add the JavaScript file we added as a reference in the dashboard tag (`"Awesome_Sauce.js"`).

This file will look like this:

```
require([
    "splunkjs/mvc/searchmanager",
    "splunkjs/mvc/chartview",
    "splunkjs/mvc/eventsviewerview",
    "splunkjs/mvc/simplexml/ready!"
], function(
    SearchManager,
    ChartView,
    EventsViewerView
```

```javascript
) {
    // Instantiate the views and search manager
    var mysearch = new SearchManager({
        id: "search1",
        preview: true,
        cache: true,
        status_buckets: 300,
        search: "index=_internal | head 1000 | stats count by sourcetype"
    });
    var mychart = new ChartView ({
        id: "chart1",
        managerid: "search1",
        type: "bar",
        el: $("#mychart")
    }).render();
    var myeventsviewer = new EventsViewerView ({
        id: "eviewer1",
        managerid: "search1",
        el: $("#myeventsviewer")
    }).render();
});
```

The preceding .js file needs to be saved and dropped into our apps folder, $SPLUNK_HOME/etc/apps/<app_name>/appserver/static/.

Again, after you add this file you have to restart Splunk. Once we restart, open the app, click **Dashboards**, and then click on our dashboard (**Awesome Sauce**):

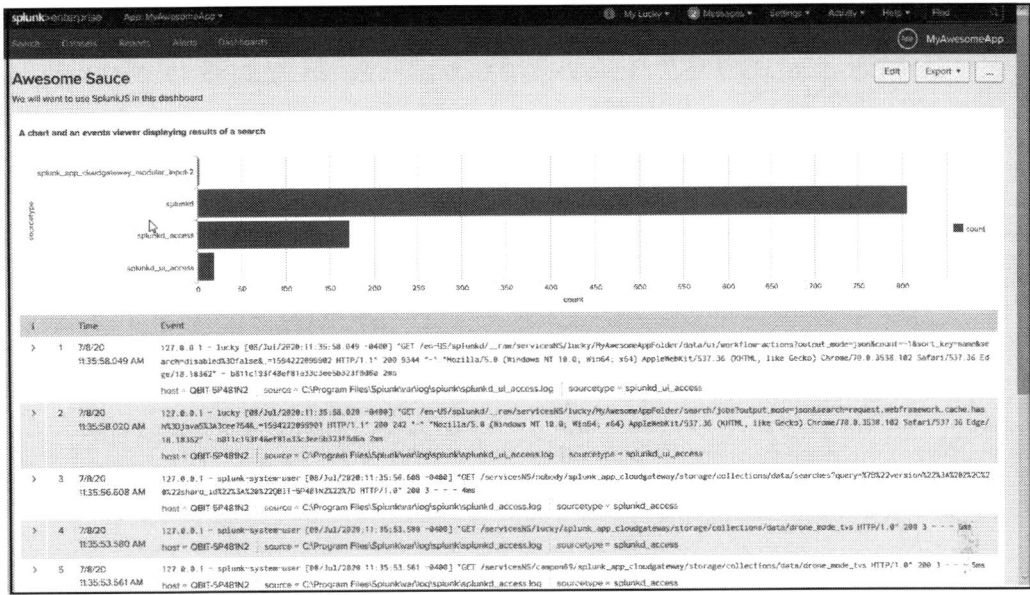

Figure 18.16 – The Awesome Sauce dashboard

Quite a difference! We've added a Splunk chart across the top of the dashboard and then we see Splunk events below.

Style sheets and custom tables

One more exercise. This one is a *three custom table-er* and uses the same sort of process as we used to enhance a SimpleXML dashboard. The dashboard displays the following:

- A table that includes a sparkline in the search results
- A table that shows how to format the sparkline and create a custom cell renderer
- A table that uses a custom row expansion renderer

Some of this code is available for download as well, and it's worth trying out, as I find starting with a straightforward example and modifying it to do what I want is the best and easiest way to learn how something works.

We will use our simple Splunk app again, so open it and click on **Dashboards**, then click **Create New Dashboard**. Once the dashboard is created for you, click on **Source** and paste in the following XML code:

```xml
<dashboard script="example_customtables.js" stylesheet="custom.css">
    <label>Custom table cell and row rendering</label>
    <row><panel>
        <html>
            <table>
                <tr>
                    <td style="width: 100%;">
                        <h3>Standard table cells</h3>
                        <div id="table-plain"></div>
                    </td>
                </tr>
                <tr>
                    <td style="width: 100%;">
                        <h3>Custom table cells</h3>
                        <div id="table-customcell"></div>
                    </td>
                </tr>
                <tr>
                    <td style="width: 100%;">
                        <h3>Custom expanding table rows</h3>
                        <div id="table-customrow"></div>
                    </td>
                </tr>
            </table>
        </html>
    </panel></row>
</dashboard>
```

Once you have pasted in the code, click **Save**.

Just like we did in the previous example, we need to add the .js file we referenced in the preceding dashboard tag (`<dashboard script="example_customtables.js" stylesheet="custom.css">`) as well as the custom style sheet .css file).

The .css file needs to go at `$SPLUNK_HOME/etc/apps/<app_name>/appserver/static/`.

And of course, now restart Splunk. After the restart, if we open our app, click **Dashboards**, and then select our newly added dashboard:

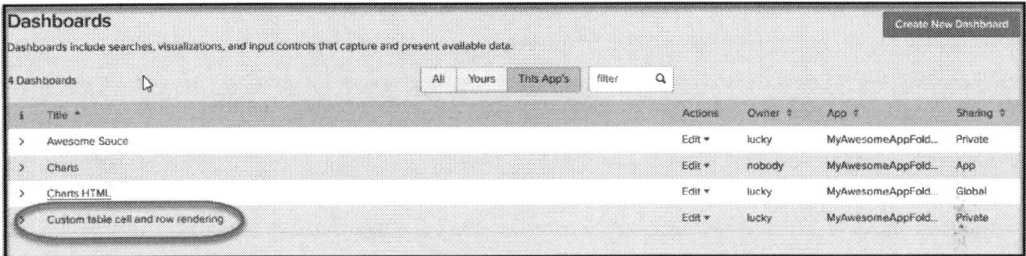

Figure 18.17 – The newly created dashboard

We can see (in the following screenshots) the three custom tables rendered in our dashboard:

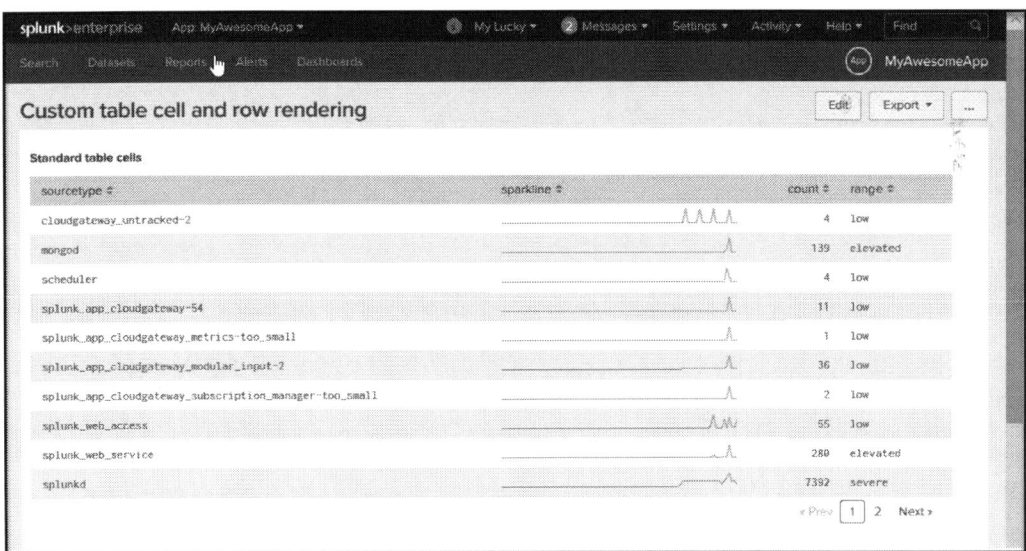

Figure 18.18 – Standard table cells

The following screenshot shows the custom table cells:

Figure 18.19 – Custom table cells

The following screenshot shows the custom expanding table rows:

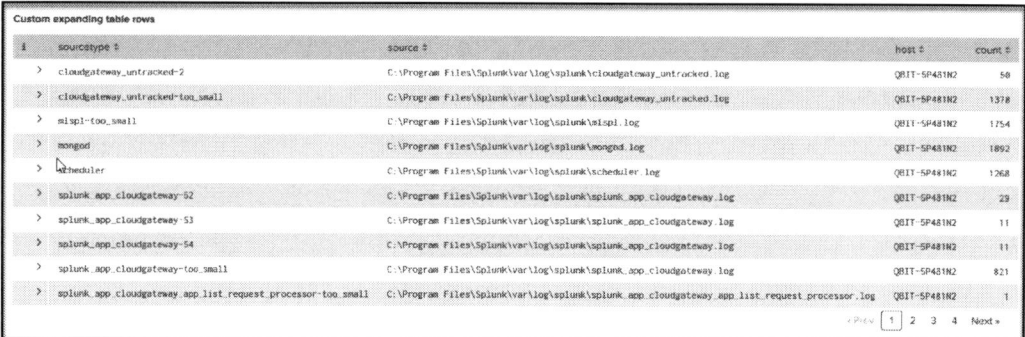

Figure 18.20 – Custom expanding table rows

The preceding examples are a mix of some downloaded code snippets (there are a bunch more that are ready for your enjoyment) and our own samples. All were served up using a very simple Splunk app we built.

In the next section, we will talk a bit about the use of SplunkJS in web apps.

Adding SplunkJS to a web app

For clarity, when we speak of a **web app** in this chapter's context, we really are referring to using JavaScript and SplunkJS Stack in an app running outside of Splunk Web.

Just as you can create and enhance powerful interactive *Splunk-enabled* apps hosted within Splunk Web; you can also use the same SplunkJS Stack to integrate Splunk and its functionalities into web apps running outside of Splunk Web.

Adding the SplunkJS Stack libraries to a website enables the use of all of Web Framework components (to interact and view your Splunk data) within that website.

Just like we did with our app running in Splunk Web, to use SplunkJS Stack within a web apps, you download SplunkJS Stack (which contains the necessary Web Framework libraries and styles) and drop them into the appropriate folders.

Because web apps that run outside of Splunk Web are running on a different server (other than the Splunk Web Server), there are a few important differences you'll need to deal with when implementing SplunkJS Stack in a non-Splunk Web app:

- **Communicating with Splunk**: Web apps that run outside of Splunk Web need to use a proxy server or **cross-origin resource sharing** (**CORS**) to communicate with the Splunk server.
- **Authentication**: Web apps that run outside of Splunk Web need to implement a custom authentication function to log users into Splunk.
- **Drilldown**: The default drilldown action for Splunk Web apps redirects users to the Splunk Search app. But for apps outside Splunk Web, a default drilldown action is not defined. To enable drilldown in those apps, you can create a default drilldown action by defining an `onDrilldown` function in the SplunkJS Stack configuration, or use click events to create drilldown actions for individual views.

The method to leverage SplunkJS Stack within non-Splunk Web apps is very similar to how it is done with a Splunk Web app. Since we've looked at several examples using Splunk apps, you can go online and review some of those same or very similar working examples.

> **Info**
>
> To add Splunk to your own web apps using SplunkJS Stack, refer to `https://dev.splunk.com/enterprise/docs/developapps/webframework/usesplunkjsstack/howtoaddsplunktowebapp`.

As a final note, out on Splunkbase there is SplunkJS demo app that can introduce and demonstrate to you how to use SplunkJS Stack. The app includes some great sample data and also contains JavaScript and CSS files that can be modified (just as I highly recommended earlier) to help you get up and running. The app can be found at `https://splunkbase.splunk.com/app/3735`.

Summary

In this chapter, we provided a description of what SplunkJS Stack is and how to locate, download, and install it into a Splunk environment, and we then presented some short examples of how to leverage some of its functionalities within a simple Splunk app.

This chapter brings us to the end of this book's journey. I sincerely hope you as the reader have enjoyed it and perhaps found it valuable.

Splunk on!

Other Books You May Enjoy

If you enjoyed this book, you may be interested in these other books by Packt:

Splunk 7 Essentials, Third Edition

J-P Contreras, Erickson Delgado, Betsy Page Sigman

ISBN: 978-1-78883-911-2

- Store event data in Splunk indexes, classify events into sources, and add
- data fields
- Learn essential Splunk Search Processing Language commands and best practices
- Create powerful real-time or user-input dashboards
- Be proactive by implementing alerts and scheduled reports
- Tips from the Fez: best practices using Splunk features and add-ons
- Understand security and deployment considerations for taking Splunk to an organizational level

Splunk Operational Intelligence Cookbook, Third Edition

Josh Diakun , Paul R. Johnson , Derek Mock

ISBN: 978-1-78883-523-7

- Learn how to use Splunk to gather, analyze, and report on data
- Create dashboards and visualizations that make data meaningful
- Build an intelligent application with extensive functionalities
- Enrich operational data with lookups and workflows
- Model and accelerate data and perform pivot-based reporting
- Apply ML algorithms for forecasting and anomaly detection
- Summarize data for long term trending, reporting, and analysis
- Integrate advanced JavaScript charts and leverage Splunk's API

Leave a review - let other readers know what you think

Please share your thoughts on this book with others by leaving a review on the site that you bought it from. If you purchased the book from Amazon, please leave us an honest review on this book's Amazon page. This is vital so that other potential readers can see and use your unbiased opinion to make purchasing decisions, we can understand what our customers think about our products, and our authors can see your feedback on the title that they have worked with Packt to create. It will only take a few minutes of your time, but is valuable to other potential customers, our authors, and Packt. Thank you!

Index

A

actions, Splunk workload management
  Abort search 50
  Display in Messages 50
  Move search to alternate Pool 50
alerts
  about 72
  editing 30-33
  management 171-173
  reviewing 30-33
  streaming 169-171
alert types
  real-time alerts 72
  scheduled alerts 72
algorithmic engine 9
analytical operations
  aggregation 162
  aggregation, selecting 162, 164
  data, filtering 166
  executing 162
  time range, comparing 164, 165
  time series, stacking 166
analytics 242
analytics frameworks
  fundamentals 242
analytics projects
  challenges, addressing 242
applying actions through direct
    table editing 255
arguments
  example 229-231
Augmented Reality workspaces 392
authentication configuration
  reloading, with Splunk CLI 88, 89
  reloading, with Splunk Web 88
automatic failover 101
automatic monitoring and
    remediation capability 49
AWS
  about 134
  configuring, in Splunk 135-138
  input, setting up 138, 139
  integrating, with Splunk
    environment 134, 135
AWS logs
  searching 140-145
Azure
  about 121, 122
  benefits, reference link 122
  integrating 122-124
  reference link 122
  solutions 121
Azure app account

426 Index

connecting to 124-134
Azure instance 121

B

base line 167
Bluetooth Low Energy (BLE) 391
bucket aging policy 57
bucket-boundary dimension 188
buckets 54, 57, 162
bundle actions
　configuring 108-110
Bundle Push Operation 109

C

Cascading Style Sheets (CSS) 332
catalytic events 274
categorical charts
　about 159
　multiple metrics 160-162
clustering
　disabling 112
　enabling 104-107
command-line interface (CLI) 19, 79
comma separated value (CSV) 152, 365
components 100
compression rate 204
compression ratio 204
Connected Experiences apps 390
correlations 274
correlation searches 274
counter 179
cross-origin resource sharing (CORS) 419
customized roles 87

D

dashboard
　editing 30-33
　reviewing 30-33
dashboard creation 118
data
　exploring, in Splunk 54
　monitoring, without searching 314
　search example 314, 315
data availability 102
data cleaning and/or parsing 118
Data-Driven Documents (D3) 401
data fidelity 102
data on-boarding 118
data pipeline
　about 54
　indexing 55
　input 55
　parsing 55
　searching 55
data rebalancing 110, 111
data recovery 102
data stack 180
default replication factor 103
disaster recovery planning 102
disaster recovery sites 113
disk activity
　monitoring 317
distributed deployment 211
Distributed Management Console 321
document object model (DOM) 401

E

event correlation
　about 275
　join-based correlations 280

lookup-based correlations 279
need, in dashboards 280
subsearch-based correlations 277-279
time/geolocation-based
  correlations 276, 277
transaction-based correlations 275
event correlation dashboards
  about 280
  catalytic events, identifying 281
  constructing 283-291
  goal/objective, identifying 281
  individual SPL queries/correlation
    searches, developing 282, 283
  panels, creating 283-291
  specific KPIs, identifying 281
events indexes 55
Exploratory Data Analysis (EDA)
  about 243
  data details, determining 243
  relevancy, establishing 243
Exploratory Data Analysis (EDA),
    performing with Splunk
  about 243
  data input, setting up 244-247
  data model, creating 247-261
  reports, adding to dashboard 262-269
extended search platform 389
external authentication 97

F

field aliasing 86
field encryptions 86
field obfuscation 86
file compression
  techniques 204
File/Directory Information Input app
  about 200

installing 200, 201
reference link 200
flow model 388
framework 242

G

generating command 226, 228
geofences 391, 392
granular access controls
  about 85
  sensitivity 86
  sensitivity, with legality 85
  sensitivity, with no legality 86
  super sensitivity 85
graphical user interface (GUI) 332

H

HEC status codes
  URL 186
Histogram data point (HDP) 187
histogram metrics
  about 179, 180
  after indexing 187-189
  Alerts 193
  before indexing 187-189
  count boundaries 189, 190
  counting 193
  event collector token, creating 183, 184
  example use cases 181
  histperc example 195
  ingesting 181-183
  percentiles, calculating 194, 195
  searching 192, 193
  summing 193
  validating 185, 186
HTTP Event Collector (HEC) 181

I

index cluster rolling restart
   performing 111, 112
indexer cluster 101
indexers
   about 101
   adding 211
   configuring 212-215
   installing 211
   used, for improving
      performance 215, 216
indexes 100
indexes, types
   events indexes 55
   metrics indexes 55
indexing 54, 55, 128
index replication 101
ingesting data 54
integration 118

J

join-based correlations 280

K

Key value (KV) 320
knowledge bundles 109
knowledge object managers 296
knowledge objects
   about 293
   tags 294-296

L

Logs2Metrics 69-71
lookup-based correlations 279

M

machine learning
   with Splunk 362
macro definitions
   about 232, 235
   reference link 232
macros
   about 223, 224, 226, 228
   creating 232-239
   previewing 224, 225
market-specific features 4
master node
   about 100, 101
   backing up 114
   configuring 108
   editing 108
memory usage patterns, monitoring
   reference link 42
memory usage patterns, troubleshooting
   reference link 42
Meta Woot!
   reference link 206
metrics
   searching 64-68
metrics indexes
   about 55
   creating 59-61
metrics indexers
   creating 61-63
Microsoft Azure offering
   reference link 388
ML-SPL commands 376
MLTK use case
   implementing 365, 366
models 364
Model-View-Controller (MVC)
   framework 401
multifactor authentication

about 97
reference link 98
multi-site configurations 114
multi-site configuration, versus
    single-site configuration
  reference link 116
multi-site index cluster
  about 113
  converting 115

N

Near-Field Communication (NFC) 391
NL queries
  documented examples 393
  offering 394

O

order of operation 50

P

password management 83
password policy 83, 84
peer nodes 100, 101
performance
  gauging 198
Performance Monitor (Perfmon) 315
permission granularity 87
pixel-level layout control 9
policies 49
POST arguments
  defining 305, 307
primary rebalancing 110
Prometheus
  about 181, 190
  documentation link 191, 192

reference link 188
push process 108
Python 3.7
  implementing 9, 10

R

real-time alerts 72
recovery
  practicing 114
reference line
  adding 167, 169
replicas 103
replication activity 102
replication factor 103
Representational State Transfer (REST) 79
residuals 372
resource allocation
  about 38
  in Splunk 38
resource pools 38, 48
role management 87
rules-based framework
  about 49
  order of operation 50
rules-based framework, workload rules
  objectives 49
rules-based framework,
    workload rules types
  monitoring rule 50
  search placement rules 50

S

scheduled alert illustration 72-74
scheduled alerts 72
schema on the fly 5
search affinity 102, 113

search exclusions 86
search expression 23
search head clustering 220, 221
search head node 101
search heads
  about 100
  adding 218-220
search-less monitoring 315
search macros arguments 228, 229
search performance
  addressing, through architecture 210
search performance, affecting factors
  about 198
  concurrent searches 207, 208
  custom data model definitions 206
  event sizes 205
  file sizes 199
  hardware 210
  number and type of apps 209, 210
  overall deployment architectures 209
Search Processing Language 2 (SPL2)
  about 389
  reference link 389
search processing language (SPL)
     5,150, 194, 223, 224
Search & Reporting app 17
secondary search workflow action
  example 307-311
sensitivity
  about 86
  with legality 86
  with no legality 86
sequential state-like 277
Service-Level Agreement (SLA) 193
session 269
single-page trending metrics
  creating 318, 319
single search head 216, 218

single sign-on (SSO)
  about 98
  reference link 98
single-site index clusters
  about 113
  converting 116
single transaction 269
site awareness 113
site replication factor 114
Smart Data Discovery 392
Software as a Service (SaaS)
  about 4
  horizontal technology platform 5
software development kit (SDK) 9, 394
specialized Splunk instances 100
SPL table command 202
Splunk
  EDA, performing with 243
  exploring 4
  horizontal technology platform 4
  resource allocation 38
  with machine learning 362
Splunk 8.0
  reference link 7, 9
Splunk 8.0, features
  about 6
  alert grouping 7
  analytics workspace 7
  enhanced workload
     management (WLM) 7
  exploring 6
  HEC timestamp extraction 8
  histogram metric datatype support 8
  migration, to Python 3.7 7
  monitoring and operability
     enrichments 8
  optimizations 8, 9
  Splunk dashboards (public beta) 9

Splunk, adding to web app
    with SplunkJS Stack
   reference link 419
Splunk Add-on
   installation link 316
   using, for Windows 315, 316
Splunk Add-on, for Windows
   disk activity, monitoring 317
Splunk analytics workspace
   alerts 169
   analyzing 157
   data, loading 152-157
   layout 151
   reviewing 150
   Split By, using 158
   using 151, 152
Splunk app
   about 402
   creating 402-406
   custom tables 415-418
   dashboard conversion, example 411-413
   dashboard, creating in SimpleXML
      with dashboard editor 407, 408
   dashboard, editing 413-415
   dashboard modification, by
      converting to HTML 410
   finding 120
   SimpleXML extension, adding for
      dashboard modification 408-410
   style sheets 415-418
   using 119
Splunk Augmented Reality (AR)
   about 391
   setting up, with workspaces 392
Splunk Authentication 83
Splunkbase
   about 119
   reference link 120

URL 390
Splunk Beta app
   canvas, resizing 349
   custom background, setting 350-352
   dashboard, converting 349
   dashboard editing bar 352
   existing dashboard, converting 348, 349
   exploring 346-348
   old editor, versus new editor 353
   visualization, adding 353-356
   visualization source code,
      editing 352, 353
Splunk bundle 108
Splunk Business Flow (SBF) 386, 388
Splunk CLI
   used, for reloading authentication
      configuration 88, 89
Splunk Cloud Gateway 390
Splunk components
   about 56, 100, 211
   forwarders 56
   indexers 56
   search head 56
Splunk dashboard editor
   accessing 334-336
   building 334
   heat map overlay, adding 343, 344
   icons, adding 344-346
   images, adding 344-346
   panel, saving 338-342
   theme, modifying 342
   using 333
Splunk dashboard editor, search
   working with 336, 337
Splunk dashboards
   about 332, 333, 397
   GUI 332
Splunk Data Fabric Search (DFS) 389

432   Index

Splunk Data Stream Processor
    (DSP) 386, 389, 390
Splunk deployment
  basics 99, 100
Splunk deployment, permissions
  reference link 257
Splunk Developer
  reference link 408
Splunk Developer Cloud (SDC) 386-388
Splunk Developer Program
  reference link 119
Splunk dispatch directory 203
Splunk Engine 9
Splunk Enterprise
  alert, adding 26-30
  alert, editing 30-33
  alert, reviewing 30-33
  dashboard, editing 30-33
  dashboard, reviewing 30-33
  data, adding 11-16
  data source, searching 17-24
  search, saving 24-26
Splunk Enterprise, capacity planning
  reference link 38
Splunk Enterprise Developer Portal
  URL 388
Splunk Enterprise SDK 10
Splunk, features
  about 5, 400
  alerting 6
  dashboarding 6
  data modeling 6
  indexing 5
  pivoting 6
  reporting 6
  searching 5
Splunk health report
  about 43, 44

  feature settings 44, 46
  status alerts 46
Splunk Insights
  for web 394
  for mobile apps 395
Splunk integration strategy
  about 118
  stakes 118, 119
Splunk internal authentication 97
Splunk internal authentication, methods
  about 97
  external authentication 97
  multifactor authentication 97
  single sign-on (SSO) 98
SplunkJS
  about 400-402
  stack files, installing 401, 402
SplunkJS Stack
  download link 401
SplunkJS Stack libraries
  adding, to web app 419
Splunk knowledge objects
  reference link 86
Splunk metric
  datatypes 178
  histograms 179
Splunk MLTK
  about 362
  installation link 362
  installing 362, 364
  overview 362
Splunk MLTK app
  algorithm options 373
  algorithm, selecting 369
  data, uploading 367
  experiments menu, exploring
    378, 379, 381, 382
  model fields, populating 367, 368

Index   433

model, fitting 370
model, naming 374, 376
model, refining 383, 384
opening 364, 365
questions, answering 376, 378
results, viewing 371, 372
usage 366
Splunk MLTK, features
  reference link 365
Splunk Mobile 395
Splunk Monitoring Console
  about 39
  accessing 322, 323
  CPU usage 41
  dashboard interpretation 40
  exploring 321
  features, exploring 323-325
  physical memory 41
  resources usage, deployment 40, 41
  resource usage dashboard 39, 40
  resource usage, instance 42
  resource usage, machine 42
Splunk Monitoring Console,
      Resource Usage
  about 43
  Workload Management
      Activity Instance 43
  Workload Management Overview 43
Splunk monitoring dashboard
  review hints 42
  reviewing 42
Splunk Natural Language (NL) 392
Splunk Next
  about 386
  offerings 387
Splunk password policies, configuring
  reference link 84
Splunk platform instrumentation

exploring 319, 320, 321
Splunk Platform Upgrade Readiness app
  about 11
  reference link 11
Splunk Processing Language (SPL) 392
Splunk replication factor 103
SPLUNK REST API User
  reference link 119
Splunk roles
  about 78
  admin 78
  power 78
  user 78
  can_delete 78
Splunk security
  about 78
  enhancements 78
  password management 83
  tokens 79, 80
Splunk-supported add-ons
  reference link 123
Splunk TV 395, 396
Splunk users 79
Splunk Validated Architectures
      (SVAs) 209
Splunk Web
  about 124
  used, for creating workflow
      action 297-300
  used, for reloading authentication
      configuration 88
Splunk workload categories
  ingest 49
  miscellaneous 49
  search 49
Splunk workload management
  advantages 47
  basics 48

feature 47
need for 47
rules-based framework 49
schedule based rules 51
techniques 42
Splunk workload management rules
  attributes 51
  policy-based tool 52
  use case 51
standalone deployment 210
steps, for custom role configuration
  inheritance 89, 90, 96, 97
  capabilities 91
  indexes 92, 93
  restrictions 94
  resources 95
storage 57, 58
storage metrics 58
storehouse 99
subsearch-based correlations 277-279
super sensitivity 85

T

Tape Archive (TAR) 109
time/geolocation-based
    correlations 276, 277
time range picker
  expanding 173, 174
  time range, zooming 174, 175
tokens
  about 79, 80
  creating 80-82
  using 82, 83
transactional analysis

about 269, 270
example 270-272
transaction analysis 269, 270
transaction-based correlations 275
transactions 269
trigger-based diagnostics
  performing 325-329

U

univariate dataset 179
user roles 61-63

V

virtual machine (VM) 38, 100, 121
Virtual Private Cloud (VPC)
  reference link 138
visual editor 347

W

web app
  SplunkJS Stack libraries, adding to 419
WebUI 83
Windows
  Splunk Add-on, using for 315, 316
workflow action
  creating, with Splunk web 297, 298, 300
  testing 300-303
workflow action, example
  about 304, 305
  POST arguments 305
workflows
  mastering 296, 297

workload management (WLM) 7
workload pools
  about 48
  default ingest category pool 48
  default search category pool 48
workspaces
  Splunk AR, setting up 392

Made in the USA
Columbia, SC
10 December 2020